Achievements in the Agri-Food Supply Chain Leading to Sustainable Foods IV

Achievements in the Agri-Food Supply Chain Leading to Sustainable Foods IV

Guest Editor

Dimitris Skalkos

MDPI

Basel • Beijing • Wuhan • Barcelona • Belgrade • Novi Sad • Cluj • Manchester

Guest Editor
Dimitris Skalkos
Chemistry Department
University of Ioannina
Ioannina
Greece

Editorial Office
MDPI AG
Grosspeteranlage 5
4052 Basel, Switzerland

This is a reprint of the Special Issue, published open access by the journal *Sustainability* (ISSN 2071-1050), freely accessible at: https://www.mdpi.com/journal/sustainability/special_issues/W674FDPA51.

For citation purposes, cite each article independently as indicated on the article page online and as indicated below:

Lastname, A.A.; Lastname, B.B. Article Title. *Journal Name* **Year**, *Volume Number*, Page Range.

ISBN 978-3-7258-7737-9 (Hbk)
ISBN 978-3-7258-7738-6 (PDF)
https://doi.org/10.3390/books978-3-7258-7738-6

Contents

About the Editor

Dimitris Skalkos

Dimitris Skalkos is currently a professor in food business management and innovation at the Laboratory of Food Chemistry, Department of Chemistry, University of Ioannina, Greece. He was previously an assistant and associate professor at The University of The Aegean, Greece (Department of Food Science & Nutrition) and a visiting assistant professor at The University of Toledo (Department of Chemistry), Ohio, USA. Dr. Skalkos's career expands far beyond academia and spans more than 30 years. He is: 1) the founder and first director of the Business Innovation Center (BIC) of Epirus, Greece; 2) the owner of Synthesis Consulting Ltd; 3) the co-owner of Paskal Herbal extracts S.A. He has worked as a business consultant for more than 20 years with 50 national and multi-national companies in various sectors, but mainly in the food sector. He has also worked as a project manager or scientific director on more than 20 EU funding programs involved in the promotion of innovation, innovative pilot actions, the establishment of academic spin-off companies, food product development, and food business management. His research interests currently focus on the development of all innovative aspects within agri-food supply chain businesses, including production, processing, organization, marketing, consumer motives and knowledge transfer. He has written 68 research papers and more than 20 conference proceedings, and he has authored around 40 oral communications at international scientific conferences.

sustainability

MDPI

Editorial

Achievements in the Agri-Food Supply Chain Leading to Sustainable Foods IV

Dimitris Skalkos

Laboratory of Food Chemistry, Department of Chemistry, University of Ioannina, 45110 Ioannina, Greece; dskalkos@uoi.gr; Tel.: +30-2651008345

In the previous three Special Issues, we researched the unprecedented rate and unforeseen consequences of global change over the last five years. The uncertainty caused by these rapid changes continues to grow today at an even faster rate. Food is the single strongest factor in optimizing human health and environmental sustainability worldwide [1]. As consumers play a key role in the transition to a more sustainable Agri Food Supply Chain (AFSC) system, it is essential to understand how consumers interpret "sustainability" in relation to the food supply chain. These insights are vital to improve quantitative consumer research on sustainability issues, while taking into account the consumer's point of view. Furthermore, these insights can be used to guide policymakers in suggesting informed guidelines and recommendations that align with consumers' understanding of food sustainability. Consumers have difficulty defining the concept "sustainability" and estimating the environmental impact of their food choices [2,3] and believe that sustainability does not (yet) influence their food choices. Currently, young consumers consider price, taste and individual health to be more influential than sustainability [4,5].

Sustainable agribusiness is needed to address food security challenges in the situation of increasingly limited production capacity. The role of consumer-based innovation and digitalization in supporting sustainable agribusiness and analyzing future directions is vital. Developments in consumer behavior that are beginning to focus on sustainable consumption must be supported by sustainable production in the context of a sustainable food system [6]. The key to maintaining consumer changes in relation to sustainable food production is the development of consumer-based innovation. Consumer nutrition environments are defined as places in which consumers interact with the food they eat; these food choices can impact human and planetary health. The development of comprehensive, reliable, and valid consumer nutrition environment measures that assess nutrient-dense food availability and food sustainability is important for research, planning, evaluation and advocacy, with the aim of improving consumer food environments for human and planetary health [7].

The food industry has significantly expanded and become globalized due to the growth of the economies of many countries and an increasing world population. The industry is consequently facing major sustainability challenges [8]. This industry, which feeds a world population of approximately 7.8 billion, will need to supply food to 9.7 billion individuals by 2050 [9]. Sustainability in food production means "that food is produced and consumed in a way that supports the well-being of generations" [10]. The definition of sustainable development has been given as "meeting the needs of the present without compromising the ability of future generations to meet their needs" [11]. The global food industry is at a turning point in its history. A growing body of academic research is focusing on sustainability at the intersection of social, environmental, and economic factors [12].

Discussions of sustainable practices in the food industry have become increasingly common in recent years [13]. Excluding the discussion of other sectors, the concept of sustainability in the food industry is highly controversial. According to [14], "sustainable food" is a very broad and vague concept for both consumers and policymakers. Future research should be multi-disciplinary and involve adjacent fields, including agriculture, agroecology, and climate science. There is also a need for research in the field of economic and social sustainability in the food industry. Studying research topics found in thematic map analysis, such as the effect of a sustainable diet on the food chain and the relationships between the agri-food system, sustainable agriculture, sustainable food systems, and sustainability of the food chain, is recommended for future research.

In this fourth Special Issue, three selected subjects on the achievements in the Agri-Food Supply Chain (AFSC) leading to sustainable foods are presented in 10 published papers. These include state-of-the-art approaches for sustainable AFSC (three papers), consumers' and stakeholders' perceptions of foods (four papers), and the use of innovative natural ingredients in the process of food production (three papers).

The three papers covering topics of sustainability in AFSC are as follows:

THE KEY ROLE OF COOPERATIVES IN SUSTAINABLE AGRICULTURE AND AGRIFOOD SECURITY: EVIDENCE FROM GREECE

Kalogiannidis et al. investigated the role of agricultural cooperatives (Acs) in promoting sustainable agriculture and agrifood security, employing a cross-sectional survey technique with data collected from 400 participants, with a particular emphasis on Greece. The model developed demonstrates how agricultural expansion may be achieved by collective bargaining, information sharing, resource sharing, and technological integration, improving agrifood security and sustainability.

IMPLEMENTING IRELAND's FOOD VISION 2030 WITHIN THE FRESH PRODUCE SECTOR: AN INVESTIGATION OF THE BARRIERS AND ENABLERS USING SYSTEMS THINKING PRINCIPLES

Kenny et al. investigated the effectiveness of the Ireland's food vision (FV) 2030 through thinking principles regarding the delivery of AFSC fresh produce. The results demonstrate that successful, long-term change will depend on the involvement and incentives of stakeholders within the supply chain approach to deliver long-term sustainability within the fresh produce sector, bringing benefits through transdisciplinary collaboration and fostering multiple stakeholder perspectives.

ENHANCING THE SUSTAINABILITY OF FOOD SUPPLY CHAINS: INSIGHTS FROM INSPECTORS AND OFFICIAL CONTROLS IN GREECE

Roukos et al. studied the perceptions, attitudes, and experiences of frontline inspectors in Greece to assess current challenges and opportunities for strengthening official food fraud controls. Overall, the findings highlight detection gaps, uneven resources across authorities, and the need for improved coordination and capacity building to support more efficient, transparent, and sustainability-oriented food fraud control in Greece.

The four papers covering the topics of consumers' and stakeholders' perceptions of foods are as follows:

YOUNG CONSUMERS' PRICE PERCEPTIONS IN PURCHASING FOODS: EVIDENCE FROM GREECE

Kalyva et al. investigated the price perceptions of young consumers (Gen Z) in purchasing foods in Greece to discover the determinants that ensure sustainable, future food consumption. The findings indicate that Gen Z pay more attention to the values of negative and positive parameters concerning price perceptions when purchasing food rather than quality, coupons and sales, low prices, and maverism, or even the prestige of the food's brand name.

https://doi.org/10.3390/su18042030

AUSTRALIAN CONSUMERS' DRIVERS AND BARRIERS TO PURCHASING LOCAL FOOD FROM ALTERNATIVE AGRI-FOOD NETWORKS

Lykins et al. aimed to identify Australian consumers' drivers and barriers in producing food growth locally from alternative grocery retailers. The results indicate that it is all too hard to account for a significant amount of unique variances. The findings from this study point to ways to encourage engagement with sustainable food systems, as well as critical barriers to overcoming disengagement.

THE NECESSARY TRANSITION TOWARDS HEALTHIER DIETS: AN ASSESSMENT OF REPLACING MEAT AND REFINED WHEAT FROUR WITH A MIXTURE OF DIFFERENT PLANT-BASED FOODS

Luna and Montes reviewed the idea of replacing meat and refined wheat flour with a mixture of different plant-based foods. The findings indicate that a rising share of consumers now pay close attention to the health and sustainability of their diets. As a result, reducing meat intake is becoming popular in certain groups, and plant-based products are proliferating the market. While many consumers are motivated primarily by the personal health benefits of reducing or eliminating meat, these dietary shifts also deliver environmental benefits.

EXPLORING HONEY CONSUMPTION AND SUSTAINABLE PRACTICES IN A SEGMENT OF ALGERIAN HOUSEHOLDS

Nakib et al. investigated honey consumption patterns among a specific segment of Algerian households, mainly young, educated, and digitally active individuals. The results indicate that consumer preferences are shaped by sensory attributes such as taste, type, and appearance while purchasing. Decisions are strongly influenced by trust-based relationships, with most respondents favoring direct acquisition from beekeepers or known individuals.

The three papers covering the use of innovative natural ingredients in the food production process are as follows:

EFFECT OF SILK FIBROIN AS A SUSTAINABLE SOLVENT ON THE EXTRACTION OF BIXIN FROM ANNATTO SEEDS (*BIXA ORELLANA* L.)

Borges et al. evaluated silk fibroin solution (SFS) for bixin extraction from annatto seeds, optimizing conditions using a Box–Behnken Design (BBD). The results demonstrate that SFS is an effective, sustainable alternative to traditional solvents, offering high extraction efficiency and minimal toxicity. This method aligns with green chemistry principles, providing a promising solution for bixin production.

IMPACT ON GRAPE JUICE QUALITY AND PHENOLIC COMPOSITION OF GREEK AUTOCHTHONOUS GRAPEVINE VARIETY MOUHTARO UNDER ABSCISIC ACID BIOSTIMULATION

Miliordos et al. examined the impact of the plant hormone abscisic acid on the phenolic compound accumulation in the autochthonous, red-colored Greek grapevine variety Mouhtaro. The results indicate that although no significant differences were observed in amino acids or anthocyanin and stilbene accumulation upon abscisic acid (ABA) treatment, the application of ABA at a higher dose resulted in increased concentrations of phenolic acids, flavan-3-ols, and flavonols, proving that the method for improving the grape quality characteristics of Mouhtaro was effective.

EXTRACTION METHODS, ENCAPSULATION TECHNIQUES, AND HEALTH BENEFITS OF ASTAXANTHIN

Panagiotakopoulos aand Nasopoulou reviewed the extraction methods, encapsulation techniques, and health benefits of astaxanthin. Their research sought to emphasize the significance of astaxanthin as a functional bioactive component with substantial poten-

https://doi.org/10.3390/su18042030

tial in nutraceutical and pharmaceutical applications by describing the extraction and encapsulation techniques and their health-promoting attributes.

Acknowledgments: As Guest Editor of the Special Issue "Achievements in the Agri-Food Supply Chain Leading to Sustainable Foods IV", I would like to express my deep appreciation to all authors whose valuable work was published in this Special Issue, thus contributing to its success.

Conflicts of Interest: The author declares no conflicts of interest.

List of Contributions:

1. Kalyva, Z.C.; Kosma, I.S.; Skalkos, D. Young Consumers' Price Perceptions in Purchasing Foods: Evidence from Greece. *Sustainability* **2024**, *16*, 5752. https://doi.org/10.3390/su16135752.
2. Kalogiannidis, S.; Karafolas, S.; Chatzitheodoridis, F. The Key Role of Cooperatives in Sustainable Agriculture and Agrifood Security: Evidence from Greece. *Sustainability* **2024**, *16*, 7202. https://doi.org/10.3390/su16167202.
3. Kenny, D.; Dermiki, M.; Britton, F. Implementing Ireland's Food Vision 2030 within the Fresh Produce Sector: An Investigation of the Barriers and Enablers Using Systems Thinking Principles. *Sustainability* **2024**, *16*, 7237. https://doi.org/10.3390/su16167237.
4. Panagiotakopoulos, I.; Nasopoulou, C. Extraction Methods, Encapsulation Techniques, and Health Benefits of Astaxanthin. *Sustainability* **2024**, *16*, 10859. https://doi.org/10.3390/su162410859.
5. Lykins, A.D.; Larder, N.; Sundaraja, C.; Newsome, L. Australian Consumers' Drivers and Barriers to Purchasing Local Food from Alternative Agri-Food Networks. *Sustainability* **2025**, *17*, 3093. https://doi.org/10.3390/su17073093.
6. Miliordos, D.-E.; Alatzas, A.; Kontoudakis, N.; Unlubayir, M.; Nikolakis, K.; Hatzopoulos, P.; Lanoue, A.; Kotseridis, Y. Impact on Grape Juice Quality and Phenolic Composition of Greek Autochthonous Grapevine Variety Mouhtaro Under Abscisic Acid Biostimulation. *Sustainability* **2025**, *17*, 4385. https://doi.org/10.3390/su17104385.
7. Borges, S.F.; Holanda, F.H.; De Maria, K.C.; Oliveira, S.S.C.; Jimenez, D.E.Q.; Leite, C.M.; Zucolotto, V.; Ferreira, I.M. Effect of Silk Fibroin as a Sustainable Solvent on the Extraction of Bixin from Annatto Seeds (*Bixa Orellana* L.). *Sustainability* **2025**, *17*, 7518. https://doi.org/10.3390/su17167518.
8. Luna, D.; Montes, V. The Necessary Transition Towards Healthier Diets: An Assessment of Replacing Meat and Refined Wheat Flour with a Mixture of Different Plant-Based Foods. *Sustainability* **2025**, *17*, 8357. https://doi.org/10.3390/su17188357.
9. Nakib, R.; Harbane, S.; Ghorab, A.; Saker, Y.; Escuredo, O.; Rodriguez-Flores, M.S.; Seijo-Coello, M.C. Exploring Honey Consumption and Sustainable Practices in an Segment of Algerian Households. *Sustainability* **2025**, *17*, 10669. https://doi.org/10.3390/su172310669
10. Roukos, C.; Kafetzopoulos, D.; Pavloudi, A.; Chatzitheodoridis, F.; Kontogeorgos, A. Enhancing the Sustainability of Food Supply Chains: Insights from Inspectrors and Official Controls in Greece. *Sustainability* **2026**, *18*, 1101. https://doi.org/10.3390/su18021101.

References

1. EAT-Lancet Commission. The Eat-Lancet Commission EAT-Lancet Commission Brief for Everyone. *Lancet* **2019**, *393*, 447–492.
2. van Bussel, L.M.; Kuijsten, A.; Mars, M.; van't Veer, P. Consumers' Perceptions on Food-Related Sustainability: A Systematic Review. *J. Clean. Prod.* **2022**, *341*, 130904. [CrossRef]
3. Skalkos, D.; Kalyva, Z.C. Exploring the Impact of COVID-19 Pandemic on Food Choice Motives: A Systematic Review. *Sustainability* **2023**, *15*, 1606. [CrossRef]
4. Kalyva, Z.C.; Kosma, I.S.; Skalkos, D. Young Consumers' Price Perceptions in Purchasing Foods: Evidence from Greece. *Sustainability* **2024**, *16*, 5752. [CrossRef]
5. Mastora, A.; Chatzitheodoridis, F.; Skalkos, D. Perceptions from Member-Consumers of a University Community for Sustainable and Healthy Eating: Evidence from Greece. *Sustainability* **2024**, *16*, 2213. [CrossRef]
6. Najib, M.; Sirajuddin, S.N.; Abror, A.; Fahma, F. Consumer-Based Innovation, Digitalization and Sustainable Agribusiness. *AIP Conf. Proc.* **2024**, *3098*, 040051.

7. Baker, K.; Burd, L.; Figueroa, R. Consumer Nutrition Environment Measurements for Nutrient-Dense Food Availability and Food Sustainability: A Scoping Review. *Arch. Public Health* **2024**, *82*, 7. [CrossRef] [PubMed]
8. Şimşek, E.K.; Kara, M.; Kalıpçı, M.B.; Eren, R. Sustainability and the Food Industry: A Bibliometric Analysis. *Sustainability* **2024**, *16*, 3070. [CrossRef]
9. UN DESA. United Nations Department of Economic and Social Affairs, Population Division (2022). In *World Population Prospects 2022: Summary of Results*; Department of Economic and Social Affairs Population Division: New York, NY, USA, 2022; Volume 3.
10. Baldwin, C. *Sustainability in the Food Industry*; WILEY: Hoboken, NJ, USA, 2012.
11. Niyommaneerat, W.; Suwanteep, K.; Chavalparit, O. Sustainability Indicators to Achieve a Circular Economy: A Case Study of Renewable Energy and Plastic Waste Recycling Corporate Social Responsibility (CSR) Projects in Thailand. *J. Clean. Prod.* **2023**, *391*, 136203. [CrossRef]
12. Wezel, A.; Herren, B.G.; Kerr, R.B.; Barrios, E.; Gonçalves, A.L.R.; Sinclair, F. Agroecological Principles and Elements and Their Implications for Transitioning to Sustainable Food Systems. A Review. *Agron. Sustain. Dev.* **2020**, *40*, 40. [CrossRef]
13. Zhou, X.; Pullman, M.; Xu, Z. The Impact of Food Supply Chain Traceability on Sustainability Performance. *Oper. Manag. Res.* **2022**, *15*, 93–115. [CrossRef]
14. Hindley, C. "Sustainable Food": Whose Responsibility Is It Anyway?: A Personal Commentary. In *The Routledge Handbook of Sustainable Food and Gastronomy*; Routledge: Abingdon, UK, 2015.

https://doi.org/10.3390/su18042030

sustainability

MDPI

Article

The Key Role of Cooperatives in Sustainable Agriculture and Agrifood Security: Evidence from Greece

Stavros Kalogiannidis [1,*], Simeon Karafolas [2] and Fotios Chatzitheodoridis [3]

1 Department of Business Administration, University of Western Macedonia, 51100 Grevena, Greece
2 Department of Accounting and Finance, University of Western Macedonia, 50100 Koila Kozanis, Greece; skarafolas@uowm.gr
3 Department of Management Science and Technology, University of Western Macedonia, 50100 Kozani, Greece; fxtheodoridis@uowm.gr
* Correspondence: skalogiannidis@uowm.gr

Abstract: This research investigated the role of agricultural cooperatives (ACs) in promoting sustainable agriculture and agrifood security, with a particular emphasis on Greece. A cross-sectional survey technique was employed, and data were collected from 400 farmers and professionals either employed by or associated with Greek agricultural cooperatives by administering an online questionnaire. A response rate of 96.5% was achieved. The study findings show that cooperative techniques bring about a positive shift in agrifood security and sustainable agriculture. Particularly, participants concurred that resource sharing among cooperative members increases farm productiveness and sustainability by 94.2% while improving access to credit and financial support by 91.5%. Moreover, 84.3% agreed that access to up-to-date information enhances the practice of sustainable agriculture, and 95.1% agreed that collective bargaining through cooperatives increases the prices of agricultural commodities. Regarding the application of advanced technologies in cooperative practices, 96.7% of the participants acknowledged that it improved farm efficiency. The cooperative model demonstrates how agricultural expansion may be achieved by collective bargaining, information sharing, resource sharing, and technological integration, while also considerably improving agrifood security and sustainability. These findings highlight the crucial importance of cooperatives in increasing the level of agricultural production, ensuring sustainability, and improving agrifood security in Greece.

Keywords: agriculture cooperatives; sustainable agriculture; resource sharing; information sharing; agrifood security

1. Introduction

Agricultural cooperatives (ACs) are crucial in helping vulnerable populations, including women and youth as well as small-scale farmers [1–3]. Through business models that are robust to shocks from the environment and the economy, they enable their members on an economic and social level and provide long-term rural employment [4–6]. Membership-based rural producer groups, including unions, cooperatives, and peasant associations, may assist with reducing rural poverty. Greece's government has acknowledged this fact and has made it a top priority to support cooperatives in rural and agricultural development as a means of fostering growth that benefits farmers [7–9]. Agricultural cooperatives have been the cornerstones of agricultural development and agrifood security, contributing significantly to the reduction in poverty, enhancement of food security, and creation of job opportunities [10,11]. Different kinds of cooperatives are formed and involved in various activities as a result of the government's initiatives; these include, but are not limited to, multipurpose primary agricultural co-ops, housing cooperatives, cooperatives for saving and credit, cooperatives for the arts, and cooperatives for livestock marketing and dairy, minerals, fisheries, sugar cane, and vegetable production [12,13].

Agricultural cooperatives are widely distributed across Europe and are ingrained in the agricultural landscape in nations like France, Italy, and Spain [13–15]. These cooperatives have expanded to cover a variety of tasks, including distribution, processing, and marketing, in addition to manufacturing. Through initiatives like the Common Agricultural Policy (CAP), the European Union acknowledges the value of cooperatives in accomplishing goals related to agricultural and rural development [16]. Greece's agricultural legacy has always been based on the use of agricultural cooperatives. High-quality products, fair trading, and sustainable agricultural methods have always been Greek cooperatives' major goals. Greek agricultural cooperatives have existed for many years but now face such contemporary problems as restricted credit facilities, competition from large-scale farmers, and compliance with regulatory requirements and the choice of new technologies to remain relevant [4,17]. To understand how Greek agricultural cooperatives will be able to overcome obstacles and carry on promoting sustainable agriculture and agrifood security, a broader European and global perspective is necessary [16]. In light of the current situation of agriculture, research on the role that cooperatives play in sustainable agriculture and food security is very pertinent [18–20]. This research attempts to provide a thorough picture of the potential and difficulties encountered by Greek cooperatives by examining the historical, global, European, and Greek viewpoints. This research employed a cross-sectional survey method based on an online self-completion questionnaire concerning Greek agricultural cooperatives. As such, the difference in methodology offers a quantitative evaluation of the extent of the contribution of cooperatives in Greece, which enriches the understanding of prior studies.

This study focused on examining the role of cooperatives in promoting sustainable agriculture and agrifood security, using Greece as a case study. The study was also guided by the following specific objectives:

1. To examine the effect of resource sharing in cooperatives on sustainable agriculture and agrifood security;
2. To establish the effect of agriculture information exchange in cooperatives on the sustainability of agriculture and agrifood security;
3. To examine the aspect of collective bargaining and market access in cooperatives and its influence on the sustainability of agriculture and agrifood security.

This study adds to a better understanding of how agricultural cooperatives could support sustainable farming practices, and it offers a comprehensive analysis of the many ways that cooperatives may impact agrifood security and sustainability, with a focus on information sharing, collective bargaining, resource sharing, and the integration of modern technologies. This study's findings have important implications for those in charge of making decisions, particularly regarding policies concerning the development of rural and agricultural areas.

2. Literature Review

2.1. Theoretical Review

The current study is informed by the New Institutional Economics (NIE) framework, specifically transaction cost economics (TCE) and collective action theory as they pertain to ACs. Transaction costs were first introduced by Coase [21] in his seminal paper on the nature of the firm, where he argued that there are always new ways of organizing transactions. He believes that transaction costs represent the core of all market imperfections. It seems that market failures are often due to the inefficient use of resources, which may be solved or at least reduced by applying cooperatives or other institutions for resource allocation [21]. This argument has laid the groundwork for the formation of the cooperative as an essential mechanism to address the problem of market failure [22]. As the theory's ground rules, it is assumed that transactions involve elements of risk in their outcomes, and that agents are self-serving with limited rationality [23,24]. Institutions are cost-minimizing structures, which may be modified and dynamic due to the sources and types of transaction costs (measurable and hidden) linked to the transfer of assets or the exchange of goods and services (from Williamson [23]). Firms can correct market inefficiencies and shortcomings through integration, which makes for efficient resource use in the long run. Companies integrate (cooperate) transactions to minimize the use of market intervention, minimize transaction costs, and correct market inefficiencies. Cooperatives are thus justified by economic theories based on their capacity and possibilities to either correct for or mitigate market failure. Similarly, people act collectively to solve social problems when they shift their focus from their self-interests to group interests, as the collective action theory by Olson [25] posits. In the context of cooperation, rewards and penalties which are incurred by each member of the group are assumed to affect the behavior of that member. Whereas the formation of a cooperative often demands common goals and transacting costs, this theory postulates that these components are not sufficient to accurately determine the effectiveness of collective action since individuals make self-interested cost–benefit calculations when participating in a group [26]. Therefore, based on the theory, the level of the success of an organization (such as a cooperative) depends on its ability to meet the concerns of the members and contain the issue of freeridership, which often arises when the number of members increases [27–30].

2.2. Resource Sharing in Cooperatives

Human interactions are frequently utilized for the dissemination of information concerning novel agricultural practices and technologies; in this context, the qualities of the informants and the structures of the networks are both critical [18]. This is of specific importance for small-scale and minority-owned rural farms, as they require access to innovative production and technological resources on the input side, in addition to market outlets, to remain competitive in comparison to larger farms. Informal networks (e.g., peer relationships) and interpersonal connections comprise the informal social networks (e.g., cooperative extension programs established by governments or institutions) to which farmers have access [3,31].

Social network theory is concerned with the interplay among nodes, which comprises organizations, businesses, and individuals [12]. Links are used to represent these exchanges [32]. On the basis of "social learning", analyses of social capital development and cultural evolution are included in the literature on information diffusion and innovation [32,33]. Diffusion of innovation often occurs as an unintended consequence of technology adoption; environments with robust social networks can enhance the efficacy of this process [17]. Moreover, cultural evolution occurs through social network-based interactions, in which community members adopt and replicate ideas or suggestions proposed by individuals considered to be authorities [4,34]. The trust that social capital embodies may be the most advantageous when utilized to address local concerns regarding the provision of public goods. Trust-based relationships are of the utmost importance for collaborative endeavors involving diverse groups, including farmer organizations representing minority and disadvantaged communities. The enhancement of their capacities with regard to regional agrifood systems and novel entrepreneurial prospects can be facilitated through collaborations between communities and farmers, as well as through interactions between institutions and individuals. It can also mitigate challenges such as food insecurity in the context of urban agriculture [35,36].

Thornton et al. [36] noted that, at this time, social network analysis (SNA) is widely utilized in numerous fields to comprehend the interrelationships between individuals and organizations, including those that are integrated into the supply chain. The nodes or foci, as well as the edges or links that delineate their connections, are descriptors for these interrelationships [34,37–39]. Although there exists a multitude of network metrics that can be calculated, the density and inter-node or intra-network distance are among the most commonly used. By employing these metrics, it is possible to assess networks against both the progression of time and against one another. SNA is utilized in the following domains: regional food system analysis; biodiversity; and forestry [6,40].

Diverse perspectives on knowledge and resource sharing among cooperative producers can be found in the existing literature. A subject that is frequently discussed concerns social processes and relationships that influence whether the exchange of knowledge among farmers is facilitated or hindered. Further building on this notion, the determinants that motivate farmers to impart agroforestry expertise obtained from extension services to their peers were examined in a study conducted by Pimbert [41]. Furthermore, the study provides evidence that informal social networks fail to facilitate the dissemination and interchange of information among agricultural practitioners. On the contrary, in terms of facilitating the exchange of seeds among producers, they exhibit superiority and greater efficiency [26].

Knowledge exchange is influenced by cooperative and competitive behaviors via the mechanisms identified by Candemir et al. [5]. Sabio et al. [42] found that cooperation between businesses positively impacts the knowledge transfer between suppliers and consumers. Furthermore, the researchers observed that as the degree of cooperation between organizations grew, so did the knowledge transfer between the two parties. Hence, an organization that cultivates a collaborative environment is presumed to attain a higher level of cooperation, thereby facilitating the dissemination of knowledge [43–46]. On the basis of the theoretical support and the supposition that knowledge sharing is influenced by cooperative behavior, it is hypothesized that knowledge sharing is positively influenced by cooperative behavior.

2.3. Agricultural Information Exchange in Cooperatives

Information is considered an essential commodity and a critical resource for development. It is an indispensable requirement that bestows success in endeavors of daily living, including agricultural pursuits. According to Kazungu and Kumburu [47], information is what every individual requires to make decisions. The exchange of information among stakeholders in the farming industry increases output and fosters agricultural progress. Identifying the information requirements is the initial step in gratifying these needs, according to Candemir et al. [5], and information-seeking processes consist of several stages preceding the identification of information sources and the acquisition of the required information. In addition, Oba and Ozsoy [12] state that information accessibility is critical to every facet of agricultural development. Consequently, they require pertinent information to effectively carry out these activities [14,38,48]. Numerous variables influence the choice of information source, such as educational attainment, income level, farm size, age, and geographic location. According to Kumar and Wankhede [38], rice farmers obtained their information from various sources, including personal experience, workshops and seminars, training, acquaintances and neighbors, the Ministry of Agriculture, agricultural magazines, extension officers, local government officials, non-governmental organizations, libraries specializing in agriculture, and posters [33,34]. In addition, the research conducted by Bognar and Gerald Schwarz [49] revealed that extension agents, friends, radio, and libraries were the primary information sources utilized by farmers to obtain agricultural data. In a similar vein, Mili and Arovuori [32] found that Turkish farmers relied heavily on information obtained from family members, neighboring farmers, extension services, input providers, and mass media. Hence, considering the individual preferences of farmers regarding specific information channels or sources, it is critical to conduct extensive research prior to selecting one that fulfils their information requirements [26].

A number of obstacles that hinder producers' access to agricultural information have been identified. For example, Pudak [50] identified several obstacles that hinder farmers' access to agricultural information. These barriers included obsolete information, a language barrier, a lack of awareness regarding the availability of various information sources, insufficient funds to purchase information, and a substandard format of the information carrier. Additionally, the research conducted by Gebremichael [6] identified several challenges that farmers face when attempting to obtain agricultural information. These encompass financial challenges, personnel or facility deficiencies, and information that is either insufficient or irrelevant. Furthermore, Aramendi et al. [33] identified two obstacles that farmers in Uganda face when attempting to obtain agricultural information: language barriers and a dearth of cooperation from other farmers regarding the sharing of agricultural information. According to Pimbert [41], several factors impede the dissemination of agricultural information to farmers. These factors comprise the scarcity of radios and televisions, the low literacy rate among farmers, and the insufficient number of personnel who have received training in agricultural information. A study was undertaken by Luo et al. [51] to examine the information requirements and search behaviors of farmers. The results obtained from this research indicated that the primary obstacles encountered by farmers in their pursuit of information were inadequate accessibility, unreliable information, a lack of cognizance regarding the sources of information available to them, and the delayed provision of information [51,52].

2.4. Collective Bargaining and Market Access in Agricultural Cooperatives

Collective bargaining possesses the capacity to augment economic influence within the agricultural industry [42]. An example of a negotiation that could occur is with a purchaser of agricultural products. A consensus may be reached between farmers and a particular company regarding the sale of maize to that company at a price set by the farmers. Farmers could also reach a consensus to not sell any produce to a company that is making investments in technologies that will benefit foreign competitors. Long-term success may result in increased prices. With influential input suppliers, collective bargaining could be utilized not necessarily to reduce the quantity of an expensive input but to negotiate a lower price. Engaging in negotiations with seed companies regarding "technology fees" offers an evident prospect. Additionally, farmers might negotiate with suppliers to alter their conduct. One potential consequence of a strong farmer group boycotting a company whose products are priced lower in another country than in the United States is that company's seed prices remain inadequate [51].

Inquiries pertaining to working conditions and benefits present supplementary prospects. A consensus could be reached by the members of a bargaining unit stipulating that no farmer would cultivate an excess of a particular number of acres [45,53]. An alternative approach would be for proprietors to contribute to the cost of health insurance for farmers and their families through collective bargaining. Farmers could negotiate collectively with suppliers to produce safer chemicals or with equipment manufacturers to produce safer machinery [41]. A powerful agricultural organization might be able to negotiate with the government for legislation that more closely matches their objectives. A bargaining unit might advocate for advantageous trade agreements as opposed to governmental payments. Ensuring the enforcement of robust legislation pertaining to corporate agribusiness would also be a legislative priority [18].

A review of the relevant literature has uncovered a number of obstacles and limitations that hinder the implementation of sustainable supply chain management, especially for SMEs. The inability of small farmers to attain economies of scale due to their high costs and the unequal bargaining power in the food chain have heightened obstacles to market entry and resulted in diminishing profit shares. As a result, small-scale producers face financial constraints that prevent them from allocating resources towards the enhancement of their operations, such as the production of competitive goods [54]. The critical role is that of "asymmetric information" control and flow, which prevents SMEs and large enterprises from having equal opportunities [18]. This inevitably results in high production costs, weak bargaining power, and so forth, ensnaring agrofood SMEs in a "vicious" cycle (Figure 1).

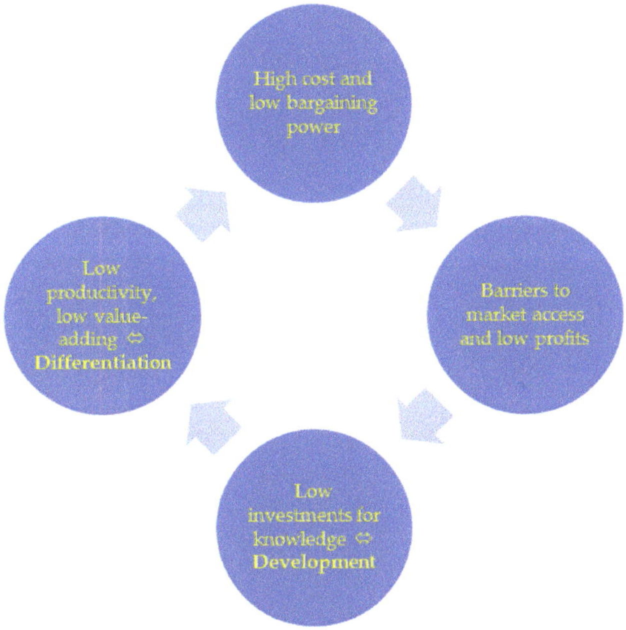

Figure 1. The "vicious" cycle of small farmers in agricultural cooperatives.

According to Pimbert [41], organization in cooperatives functions as a viable substitute for corporate mergers involving smaller farmers and larger farming conglomerates, which would not be prohibited under the majority of merger regimes. Pimbert [41] also distinguishes agricultural product supply by highlighting the inelasticity of demand, the unpredictability and unmanageability of supply, and seasonal variation. Nevertheless, farm consolidation has made only limited strides; substantial numbers of small family farms continue to operate, and numerous large farms that have consolidated a substantial amount of land remain family-owned [55,56]. Family farming has flourished in advanced economies despite the progressive expansion of agri-industrialization over the past century and government policies encouraging agribusiness enterprise [57–59].

2.5. Technological Integration into Cooperative Practices

Evaluating agricultural system technologies in terms of sustainability is a relatively new field of study [8,60]. Prior to recent times, the evaluation of agricultural technology impacts was based on a limited number of criteria that were generally unambiguous and quantifiable, including production, productivity, farm incomes, employment, and trade. It is more difficult to evaluate sustainability when environmental, social, and ethical factors are considered [18]. The interrelationships among different components of sustainability, the criteria for measuring and interpreting results, and the procedures for determining the efficacy of sustainable technologies, the most effective channels for their dissemination and adoption under varying conditions, and the associated costs and benefits, are frequently not crystal clear [2,18,61].

Technologies can facilitate the harmonization of profitable and sustainable food production requirements [42]. The primary objectives are to determine which technologies are the most effective under particular conditions and to establish and implement an appropriate incentive structure that promotes the attainment of sustainability goals while simultaneously improving worldwide welfare. This endeavor aligns with the policy principles that have been unanimously agreed upon by OECD ministers [26]. On occasion, environmental and food production objectives can be harmonized by implementing the proper technologies. Occasionally, achieving these objectives can be accomplished by merely modifying the scale, variety, and placement of agricultural output [10,62]. However, in order to achieve this balance, it is also necessary to establish and enforce the rights and obligations of farmers with regard to the implementation of technologies and practices. This requires consideration of the current property rights distribution and the circumstances under which they are entitled to compensation or are obligated to pay (polluter pays). Significant implications follow from the attribution of property rights with regard to the distribution of wealth, income, and equity [42].

Meemken and Qaim [63] noted that technological advancements have served as the foundation for agricultural development and productivity growth. Research influences the productivity of agricultural systems through the development of novel technologies that, if suitable for the conditions of the producers, will be swiftly embraced [64]. In the past, the onus has been on researchers and extension agents to identify and incorporate environmental and economic factors into the agricultural innovation development and introduction process. Generally, this is described as a top-down procedure, in which extension workers advocate for the use of the innovation that researchers develop, and farmers adopt or reject it according to the characteristics that are most significant to them [8].

Maican and Stępień [65] noted that production increases among those who adopt enhanced technologies, resulting in continuous socioeconomic progress. Higher earnings and reduced poverty have been linked to the adoption of improved agricultural technologies, improved nutritional status and decreased prices of staple foods, increased employment opportunities and earnings for landless laborers, and lower prices of staple foods [64]. The success of the Green Revolution in Asian countries is widely attributed to the adoption of advanced technologies. Conversely, those who have not adopted the status quo struggle to sustain a subsistence level of living due to socioeconomic stagnation, which ultimately results in deprivation. A new agricultural technology that improves the sustainability of food and fiber production is thus essential for economic growth and sustainable agrifood security [4,33,66]. Over time, an individual's evaluation of a technology may transition from being solely subjective to objective, as access to information diminishes the uncertainty surrounding its performance. Nevertheless, the availability of information regarding a technology does not guarantee that every cultivator will employ it [37,67]. Technology non-adoption may also ensue from information accessibility concerns. For example, in situations where the general public has limited knowledge about a particular technology, additional information tends to generate unfavorable attitudes towards its adoption. This is likely due to the fact that more information reveals an even greater information gap, which, in turn, raises the associated risk. Consequently, it is critical to guarantee that the information is accurate, consistent, and reliable. Farmers must be informed about the existence, benefits, and applications of technology in order to embrace it.

2.6. Research Hypotheses

Hypothesis 1 (H1). *Resource sharing in cooperatives positively affects sustainable agricultural practices and enhances agrifood security.*

Hypothesis 2 (H2). *Effective information exchange within cooperatives leads to improved sustainability in agriculture and better agrifood security.*

Hypothesis 3 (H3). *Collective bargaining and enhanced market access through cooperatives significantly contribute to the sustainability of agriculture and agrifood security.*

Hypothesis 4 (H4). *The integration of modern technologies in cooperative practices positively influences sustainable agricultural development and agrifood security.*

3. Materials and Methods

3.1. Research Design

In this study, the researcher adopted a cross-sectional survey design to assess the involvement of cooperatives in enhancing sustainable agriculture and agrifood security. An online questionnaire was developed, and email was used for distributing the study; it contained both multiple-choice questions and Likert-scale questions. The researchers employed this approach to integrate the various trends as identified in the data coherently. The survey was conducted among a random pool of experts in the agriculture sector in Greece.

3.2. Sample

The approximate number of 200,000 members and professionals in Greek agricultural cooperatives that formed the target population was estimated based on the records in national and regional cooperative associations in Greece. These sources availed rich data on the overall human traffic in the agricultural cooperatives nationwide. Considering this population, the sample comprising 400 respondents was selected, focusing on the farmers and employees of a cooperative. The sample size for the study was determined using the Yamane (1973) formula [68,69] to make sure that it was adequate to represent all the students in the study, as presented in Equation (1):

$$n = \frac{N}{1 + Ne^2} \tag{1}$$

where n is the sample size sought; N is the population; e is the level of significance; 1 is a constant.

Using a 5% (0.05) level of significance,

$$\text{Sample size}: \ n = \frac{200,000}{1 + 200,000\ (0.0025)^2} \Leftrightarrow n = 399.57 \cong 400$$

Simple random sampling was utilized to obtain the appropriate sample of this study.

3.3. Data Collection

The researcher used an online questionnaire to collect data from the selected sample. Using a five-point Likert scale, the questions were created with the study's aims in mind. In the previous agreement, the survey questionnaire was sent to the Greek farmer-members or professionals in agricultural cooperatives. The distribution was within the researchers' purview. Respondents received survey questions by email at the same time. After the survey was sent out, participants had one week (by email) to complete it. After the participation deadline, the researcher combined a raw data file from participants for data analysis. The numerous variables of this research were measured using a Likert scale consisting of agree and disagree ratings. Although a 100% response rate was not realized, an acceptable response rate of about 96.5% was realized, which gave a sound basis for analysis.

3.4. Data Analysis

The data collected using a questionnaire were coded and transferred to SPSS version 22 for analysis. SPSS (Statistical Package for the Social Sciences) is a comprehensive statistical software package used for data management, advanced analytics, and multivariate analysis, among others [70]. In this study, the data collected were analyzed and presented using descriptive statistics that provided frequencies and percentages through the use of SPSS. The data were interpreted and presented using descriptive statistics that yielded frequencies and percentages. The ANOVA (Analysis of Variance) method was used along with the R^2 (coefficient of determination) statistic and the regression coefficients (beta values) to determine the statistical significance of the regression coefficients in the model. Regression analysis was used to ascertain the general predictive power of the various independent variables on the dependent variable under investigation. In this case, a multiple regression model was essential for determining the different predictive values (Equation (2)) [71,72]:

$$Y = \beta_0 + \beta_1 X_1 + \beta_2 X_2 + \beta_3 X_3 + \beta_4 X_4 + \varepsilon \quad (2)$$

where Y is the sustainable agriculture and agrifood security; β_0 is a constant (coefficient of intercept); X_1 is the resource sharing in cooperatives; X_2 is the agriculture information exchange in cooperatives; X_3 is the collective bargaining and market access in cooperatives; X_4 is the integration of modern technologies into cooperative practices; ε is the error term in the multiple regression model; $\beta_1 \ldots \beta_4$ represent the four independent variables' regression coefficients.

The null hypothesis (H0) for each predictor states that there is no significant relationship between the predictor and sustainable agriculture and agrifood security. The null hypothesis was either rejected or failed to be rejected based on the decision rule, which stipulates that if $p < 0.05$, then H0 should be rejected; otherwise, H0 is not rejected. The study's hypotheses were tested at the 5% level of significance (0.05).

4. Results

This section interprets the various conclusions acquired after analyzing data gathered from the chosen research participants.

4.1. Demographic Characteristics

The majority of research participants (70.7%) were male, and the remaining portion (29.3%) were female. Most participants (59.7%) were between the ages of 31 and 40, with just 5.5% beyond the age of 50, and only 4.3 below 30 years. A slightly larger portion of participants (49.2%) had spent 5–10 years in the agriculture sector, and only 7% had less than 5 years of experience in agriculture.

4.2. Descriptive Results

The study established the effect of resource sharing in cooperatives on sustainable agriculture and agrifood security, and the results are presented in Table 1.

Table 1. Opinions on the effect of resource sharing in cooperatives on sustainable agriculture and agrifood security.

Statement	Agree	Disagree
Resource sharing among cooperative members enhances farm productivity and sustainability	94.2%	5.8%
Cooperative members are willing to share resources (e.g., equipment, seeds) with each other	71.4%	28.6%
Resource sharing within cooperatives leads to a reduction in production costs	56.4%	43.6%
Cooperative resource sharing contributes to better access to credit and financial support	91.5%	8.5%
Resource sharing in cooperatives positively impacts agrifood security in the region	56.2%	43.8%
Sustainable farming practices are more achievable through cooperative resource sharing	79.9%	20.1%

Source: authors' elaboration.

According to the findings in Table 1, the majority of survey participants (94.2%) agreed that resource sharing among cooperative members enhances farm productivity and sustainability. Among cooperative members, a significant portion (71.4%) were amenable to sharing resources, such as seeds and equipment. This need to participate is essential to cooperative success because it fosters a sense of community and shared accountability. It is crucial to remember, nevertheless, that around 28.6% of respondents disagreed with this statement, suggesting that there can be challenges or barriers to resource sharing in certain cooperatives. The majority of participants (56.4%) agreed that production costs are reduced when resources are pooled among cooperatives. Based on this finding, cooperative resource sharing might have a favorable economic impact by optimizing resource usage. Those 43.6% of respondents who disagreed may provide examples where resource sharing does not always result in cost reductions, perhaps due to inefficiencies or mismatches in resources. More than half (91.5%) believed that cooperative resource sharing has led to greater access to credit and financial aid. A total of 56.2% of respondents thought that resource sharing in cooperatives increases local agrifood security, while 43.8% of respondents disagreed. This discrepancy suggests that a variety of factors, including the particular conditions and traditions of each cooperative, can influence the relationship between agrifood security and cooperative resource sharing. Notably, a significant proportion of participants (79.9%) believed that collaborative resource sharing increases the accessibility of sustainable farming practices. This aligns with the broader notion that cooperatively exchanging resources and information facilitates the implementation of sustainable practices.

This study established the effect of agriculture information exchange in cooperatives on the sustainability of agriculture and agrifood security, and the results are presented in Table 2.

Table 2. Results on agriculture information exchange in cooperatives.

Statement	Agree	Disagree
Information exchange within cooperatives is an essential source of knowledge for sustainable farming	100%	0.0%
Cooperative members actively engage in sharing agricultural information and experiences	51.2%	48.8%
Access to up-to-date agricultural information improves the adoption of sustainable practices	84.3%	15.7%
Cooperative information exchange contributes to better pest and disease management.	70.3%	29.7%
The exchange of market-related information helps cooperative members make informed decisions	64.3%	35.7%
Information exchange leads to increased awareness of agrifood security issues among cooperative members	63.5%	36.5%
Cooperative information sharing enhances the resilience of agriculture in the region	79.3%	20.7%

Source: authors' elaboration.

As highlighted in Table 2, information exchange within cooperatives is considered an important source of knowledge in sustainable farming, since all the respondents agreed (100%) with the statement. On the aspect of cooperative members participating in the sharing of agricultural information and experience, 51.2% of them supported the statement while 48.8% of them opposed it. This means that although the exchange of information is acknowledged, its spate seems to vary within the cooperatives, maybe due to the level of communication technology or cultural differences within them. Most of the respondents (84.3%) strongly believed that up-to-date information increases the rate of the practice of sustainable farming skills and thus the need for the constant updating of information. But perhaps the 15.7% who disagreed operate in cooperatives where information is either stale or not sufficiently relevant to the members, suggesting that there is a lack in this area that has to be filled to ensure that all members gain equally. Information exchange also has its significance, where 70.3% of the respondents were of the view that cooperation leads to better pest and disease management. However, the 29.7% that disagreed may imply that, in some cooperatives, the information that is being provided is not well implemented because the quality of the information or the way it is disseminated is wanting. Also, 64.3% of respondents strongly agreed and 35.7% disagreed with the assertion that the "sharing of market-related information enables members to make informed decisions". This implies that there could be issues with regard to the access to and/or the effective use of market information. Finally, this study finds that most of the participants (79.3%) support the view that cooperative information sharing increases the stability of agriculture across their region, in support of cooperatives' overall role in agricultural sustainability in the region. But these discrepancies indicate that while information exchange is important, it is not uniformly beneficial and needs fine-tuning to enhance the cooperatives' experience.

This study assessed the aspect of collective bargaining and market access in cooperatives and its influence on the sustainability of agriculture and agrifood security, and the results are presented in Table 3.

Table 3. Opinions on collective bargaining and market access in cooperatives and their influence on the sustainability of agriculture and agrifood security.

Statement	Agree	Disagree
Cooperative collective bargaining raises agricultural commodity prices	95.1%	4.9%
Cooperative members' access to a variety of marketplaces had increased as a result of their combined efforts	71.5%	28.5%
Collective bargaining helps in negotiating favorable terms with suppliers and buyers	59.7%	40.3%
Increased market access through cooperatives positively impacts farm income	69.7%	30.3%
Market access through cooperatives contributes to agrifood security by ensuring a steady demand for produce	91.7%	8.3%
Cooperative bargaining and market access are essential for the sustainability of agriculture	35.6%	64.4%

Source: authors' elaboration.

The results in Table 3 show that the vast majority of the research participants (95.1%) agreed that cooperative collective bargaining raises agricultural commodity prices. This broad agreement implies that members understand the important role that cooperatives play in securing fair pricing for their farm products. This is encouraging for the cooperatives' capacity to use price negotiations to improve the financial security of its members. Second, 71.5% of participants agreed that cooperative members' access to a variety of marketplaces had increased as a result of their combined efforts. Collective bargaining is helpful in negotiating advantageous terms with suppliers and purchasers, according to 59.7% of participants. Even while this percentage is less than those for the first two claims, it still shows a significant degree of agreement. It implies that members think cooperatives help to enhance the conditions under which agricultural goods are sold and inputs are purchased, which helps to increase farmers' total profitability. Furthermore, 69.7% of participants agreed that cooperatives' expanded market access had a favorable effect on agricultural revenue. The fact that 91.7% of participants thought that market access via cooperatives ensures a consistent demand for products, which helps with agrifood security, is one of the most noteworthy results. Furthermore, 64.4% of participants disagreed with the notion that cooperative bargaining and market access are necessary for agriculture to be sustainable, whereas just 35.6% of participants agreed.

The study examined the effect of integrating modern technologies into cooperative practices, and the results are presented in Table 4.

Table 4. Opinions on integrating modern technologies into cooperative practices and its influence on sustainable agricultural development and agrifood security.

Statement	Agree	Disagree
The integration of modern technologies in cooperative practices enhances farm efficiency	96.7%	3.3%
Cooperatives that invest in technology experience improved crop yields.	74.5%	25.5%
Modern technologies reduce the environmental impact of farming within cooperatives	40.5%	59.5%
Technology adoption leads to cost savings for cooperative members.	51.7%	48.3%
Technology-integrated cooperatives have better access to online markets.	83.5%	16.5%
The use of technology in cooperatives is essential for ensuring agrifood security.	35.6%	64.4%

Source: authors' elaboration.

Table 4 shows that the majority of research participants (96.7%) agreed that incorporating contemporary technology into cooperative operations improves agricultural efficiency. The high degree of agreement indicates that members are aware of how technology might improve agricultural practices inside cooperatives. Significantly, 74.5% of respondents said that investing in technology increases agricultural production for cooperatives. This suggests that a sizable proportion of participants thought that increased agricultural output may result from the use of technology. A significant 59.5% of respondents disagreed with the 40.5% who felt that farming in cooperatives had less of an environmental effect due to contemporary technology. This disagreement emphasizes the need for further research on the particular environmental advantages and difficulties of technology adoption in cooperatives. A total of 51.7% of respondents, or somewhat more, believed that using technology in cooperatives saves members money. Remarkably, 83.5% of participants agreed that cooperatives with technological integration have superior access to online marketplaces. This high degree of agreement is indicative of the perception that technology makes it easier to access markets, which may be essential for cooperatives looking to expand their consumer bases. Merely 35.6% of participants concurred that using technology in cooperatives is crucial to guaranteeing agrifood security. This finding suggests that a sizeable percentage of participants may be skeptical regarding the clear connection between technology and agrifood security, which may point to the need for more research and awareness in this area.

This study also identified the different outcomes resulting from sustainable agriculture and agrifood security.

Figure 2 shows that a majority of respondents (48.4%) said that higher food production is the most important result of sustainable agriculture and agrifood security. This implies that a considerable rise in food production has resulted from the policies and procedures implemented in Greece, perhaps including enhanced farming methods, better resource management, and cooperative farming arrangements. A total of 24.2% of respondents then mentioned increased food availability and affordability as a major result of agrifood security and sustainable agriculture. This suggests that cooperative initiatives in conjunction with sustainable agriculture methods have increased food accessibility for the general public, perhaps via lower costs or improved routes of distribution. Moreover, according to 14.7% of participants, climate change resistance has been significantly improved by sustainable agriculture. In light of global climate change, this includes the capacity to tolerate and adjust to climatic changes and environmental problems. Additionally, 6.7% of respondents pointed to a decrease in the use of chemicals in agriculture. The enhancement of crop diversity, as noted by 4.3% of respondents, is another positive outcome. Diverse crops contribute to a more resilient and sustainable agricultural system, reducing the dependency on single-crop varieties and enhancing biodiversity. A small percentage (1.7%) noted other benefits, such as reduced food waste, the preservation of crop varieties, and the provision of safe and healthy food.

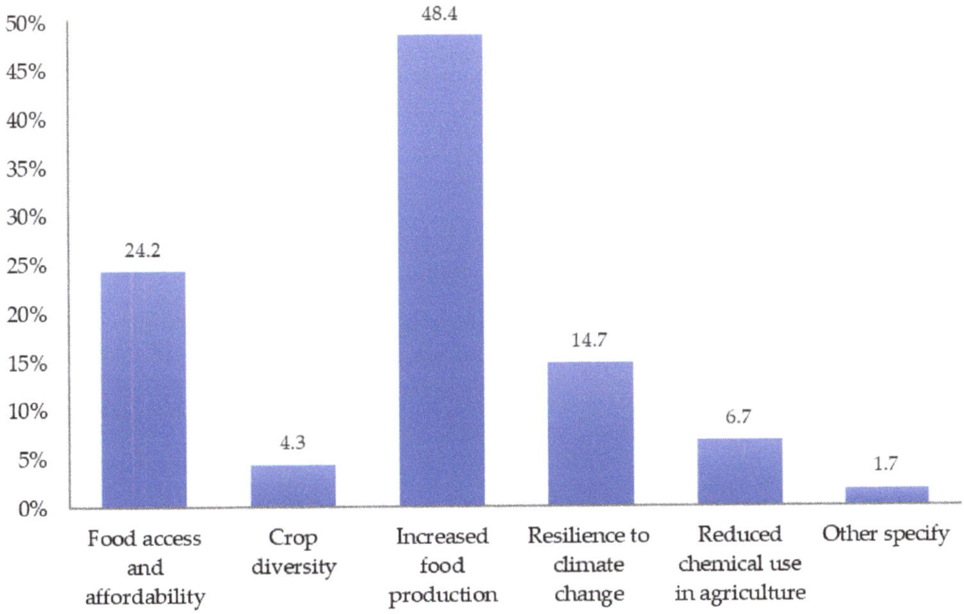

Figure 2. Outcomes of sustainable agriculture and agrifood security.

4.3. Results of Regression Analysis

Regression analysis helped to ascertain the extent to which sustainable agriculture and agrifood security is predicted by the different aspects of agriculture cooperatives, and the results are presented in Table 5. The positive multiple correlation coefficient (R) of 0.814 indicated that the four independent factors were favorably associated with sustainable agriculture and agrifood security. Furthermore, the R-Square value reveals that the four independent factors result in a 69.1% change in the general sustainability of agriculture and agrifood security.

Table 5. Summary of regression analysis model.

Model	R	R-Square	Adjusted R-Square	Std. Error of the Estimate
	0.814 [a]	0.691	0.679	0.1372

[a] Predictors: (constant): resource sharing in cooperatives, agriculture information exchange in cooperatives, collective bargaining and market access in cooperatives, the integration of modern technologies into cooperative practices.

A one-way ANOVA was conducted to determine whether the linear regression model matched the data well, or whether the four independent variables of this study were excellent predictors of the dependent variable. Since F (4386) = 52.413, $p < 0.05$, the model was deemed a satisfactory match for the data (Table 6).

Table 6. Analysis of Variance (ANOVA) for predicting sustainable agriculture and agrifood security.

Model	Sum of Squares	Df.	Mean Square	F	Sig.
Regression	36.040	4	18.361	52.413	0.016
Residual	30.108	382	0.027		
Total	66.148	386			

Dependent variable: sustainable agriculture and agrifood security. Predictors (constant): resource sharing in cooperatives, agriculture information exchange in cooperatives, collective bargaining and market access in cooperatives, the integration of modern technologies into cooperative practices.

The model's unstandardized coefficients were investigated to determine the role of cooperatives on sustainable agriculture and agrifood security.

The standardized coefficient shows in Table 7 the proportionate contribution of each independent variable to the dependent variable in terms of the standard deviation of the model. However, it is not an exact measure of the extent to which each individual predictor accounts for the dependent-variable variability. However, the R^2 of 0.691 is more appropriate to assess the proportion of the total variance in sustainable agriculture and agrifood security explained by the whole model. For instance, the estimated coefficient for resource sharing in cooperatives is 0.281, meaning that for every increase in resource sharing by one unit, there would be a corresponding increase of 0.281 units in sustainable agriculture and agrifood security. This predictor is statistically significant with a T value of 3.736 ($p < 0.01$). The standardized coefficient (beta = 0.397) reveals the resource sharing importance comparatively to the other predictors, but it provides no information on how much variability in sustainable agriculture and agrifood security results from resource sharing only. Likewise, the coefficient for agriculture information exchange in cooperatives is 0.186, which indicates that for each unit change in information exchange, there would be a change of 0.186 units in sustainable agriculture and agrifood security. This predictor is also a statistically significant $t = 9.195$, $p < 0.01$, while the beta of 0.213 indicates the relative influence and not the proportion of variance accounted for. The coefficient for collective bargaining and market access in cooperatives is 0.192, which means that the model predicts a 0.192 unit increase in sustainable agriculture and agrifood security. This predictor is statistically significant with $T = 11.411$, $p < 0.01$, but the beta of 0.142 shows the relative size of the predictor in the context of the model. Finally, the integration of modern technologies into cooperative practices has an estimate of 0.342, which implies a positive and substantial influence on the promotion of sustainable agriculture and the security of agrifoods. This predictor has a very high level of statistical significance, with T = 13.511, $p < 0.01$. The relative impact is again measured by the standardized coefficient (beta = 0.282) and not the coefficient of determination.

Table 7. Regression coefficients and significance levels for predicting sustainable agriculture and agrifood security.

Model	Unstandardized Coefficients		Standardized Coefficients	t	Sig.
	B	Std. Error	Beta		
(Constant)	0.318	0.136		2.438	0.016
Resource sharing in cooperatives	0.281	0.057	0.397	3.736	0.003
Agriculture information exchange in cooperatives	0.186	0.067	0.213	9.195	0.021
Collective bargaining and market access in cooperatives	0.192	0.049	0.142	11.411	0.002
Integration of modern technologies into cooperative practices	0.342	0.049	0.282	13.511	0.000

Dependent variable: sustainable agriculture and agrifood security.

The first hypothesis (H1) suggests that resource sharing in cooperatives positively affects sustainable agricultural practices and enhances agrifood security. This is supported by the regression coefficient (B = 0.281, $p = 0.003$), which indicates a significant positive effect. Resource sharing likely leads to the more efficient use of inputs, reduced costs, and the ability to implement more sustainable farming practices due to pooled resources. The second hypothesis (H2) posits that effective information exchange within cooperatives leads to improved sustainability in agriculture and better agrifood security. The coefficient (B = 0.186, $p = 0.021$) confirms this positive relationship. Information exchange can include sharing best practices, innovative farming techniques, and market information, all of which contribute to more sustainable and productive agricultural practices. Hypothesis three states that collective bargaining and enhanced market access through cooperatives significantly contribute to the sustainability of agriculture and agrifood security. The model shows a strong positive effect (B = 0.192, $p = 0.002$), suggesting that cooperatives' ability to negotiate better terms with suppliers and buyers and access larger markets is crucial for sustainable agriculture and ensuring agrifood security. Hypothesis four posits that the integration of modern technologies into cooperative practices positively influences sustainable agricultural development and agrifood security. The highest coefficient in the model (B = 0.342, $p = 0.000$) strongly supports this hypothesis. Modern technologies can include advanced irrigation methods, sustainable energy sources, and precision farming techniques, all of which significantly boost agricultural sustainability and agrifood security.

5. Discussion

This study aimed at evaluating the contribution of cooperatives towards sustainable agriculture and agrifood security in Greece. There are several branches of specialized knowledge that farmers' production activities within a cooperative project require; the cooperative is the institution that defines and integrates all the specialized knowledge. In this case, each of these specialized groupings is a practice; thus, the producers in addition to the co-op divisions are also a practice [53]. The boundaries of the agricultural cooperative include related fields of knowledge, which are relevant to a specific practice in agriculture. From this point of view, the agricultural cooperative can be viewed as a community of communities (of practices), a sense-making organization that facilitates the exchange between different communities by providing the rules of engagement. The principles and values of the cooperative are used by agricultural cooperatives as a basis on which the community is built. Another suggestion is that an identity is required for the formation of an innovative production system [33].

Acquisition of knowledge and information is crucial in the advancement of the agriculture industry [51,52]. To be able to plan what they are to do, which technology to use and, lastly, when and where to market their crops and livestock, farmers require vital information. Therefore, it can be concluded that there is a positive correlation between agriculture progress and knowledge. To obtain agricultural security and self-sufficiency and to attain their full production capacity, farmers require quality information [7]. This is one of the important roles that cooperatives have in the disbursement of loans for agriculture. To improve agricultural production and advance social and economic development, the aforesaid cooperatives have been assigned the responsibilities of procuring materials for industries, extending technical advice, supplying agricultural inputs, organizing the procurement, marketing, and processing of agricultural produce, and providing credit facilities to agricultural workers, craftsmen, and producers. For the purpose of giving long-term loans to farmers in an effort to finance capital improvements and land development, cooperative land development organizations have been established. However, there is also a certain degree of conflict towards the disclosure of information between people and institutions, since information is regarded as a valuable asset. Since collaboration is crucial for information exchange, cooperative conduct may be helpful in this context [34]. Pimbert [41] states that knowledge can only be acquired through collaboration. In a study by Kalfas et al. [45], cooperation and knowledge sharing in a credit union were examined and showed that cooperation does depend on cooperation in a competitive organizational environment, and that cooperation is a necessity to bring about knowledge sharing. Economic sustainability is vital for any community to achieve long-term growth and development. This is achieved through the provision of employment opportunities, access to credit facilities, and market opportunities for small-scale producers by cooperatives. By availing affordable products and services, increasing members' incomes, and decreasing poverty, cooperatives assist in combating poverty [10,37,73]. As for the issue of agrifood security, it can be stated that sustainability is one of the most critical components of sustainable development. Cooperatives embrace such programs as a way of promoting sustainability in agriculture among its members. They advocate for the adoption of clean energy sources, the minimal generation of waste, and organic farming practices. Moreover, cooperatives ensure ethical production and consumption, since they ensure that their products are made sustainably for the environment [41,74–77].

This study provided findings showing that resource sharing among cooperative members improve farm output and sustainability considerably. This goes in tandem with the findings of earlier research that resource pooling in cooperatives was attributed to optimum resource utilization and low costs of production [24,45]. The tendency of the participants to overemphasize the positive effects of resource sharing is in line with Gebremichael [6], who also noted such effects on the cooperatives in Ethiopia. However, it is noteworthy that a relative number of respondents did not share this opinion, which may point to the existence of certain barriers or inefficiencies in some of the cooperatives, as described by Candemir et al. [5]. This may be arising from a lack of trust, poor management, or the unfair distribution of gains within the cooperatives. Subsequent studies should explore these barriers in depth and suggest strategies to combat them in order to enable every member to gain the maximum possible advantage from the sharing of resources.

This study established that communication in cooperatives plays a vital role in effective agricultural practice and food security in the sector. This confirms the literature by Kumar and Verma [38] and Bognar and Gerald Schwarz [49] that stipulates that the timely acquisition of appropriate information is central to success in agriculture. This study also supports Mili and Arovuori's work [32], which states that proper information sharing improves pest and disease control and market decisions. The overwhelming emphasis on the significance of the information exchange makes it imperative for cooperatives to establish sound communication channels. These platforms can help in spreading the word on best practices, new technologies in farming, and market information in a bid to enhance the production and sustainability of agriculture. Collective bargaining and market access through cooperatives were revealed to affect farm income and agrifood security. The positive impact of collective bargaining in achieving better prices and other terms is also consistent with the findings of Pimbert [41], who also reported the same in other studies. The high percentage of participants who appreciated the role of market access through cooperatives is in line with the study conducted by Dhillon and Moncur [29] on the participation of cooperatives in extending market opportunities for smallholder farmers. However, some participants disagreed about the effectiveness of collective bargaining and market access for the sustainability of agriculture, and one participant mentioned that the effectiveness of these strategies requires further research to understand under which conditions they are most helpful. Subsequent studies should establish variables that affect the effectiveness of collective bargaining in various sectors of agriculture and come up with ways of increasing its effectiveness.

Cooperative practices were noted to have received a boost through the integration of modern technologies into agricultural practices. This finding agrees with the conclusions of Branca et al. [18] and Kashiwagi and Kamiyama [78] that point at technological development in agriculture as a determinant of overall productivity. The subjects of the study recognized that technology helped them to increase their yields and access online markets for their products, which accords with the literature on the positive effects of technology on agriculture [64,65]. Nonetheless, participants were divided on the effects that modern technologies had on the environment. Some of the participants were aware of the positive impact of technology on the negative impacts on the environment, while others had negative perceptions of technology. This indicates that there is a need to continue conducting studies to identify the effects of technology on the environment and to encourage the use of technologies that are helpful to the economy and have a positive impact on the environment as well.

The multiple correlation coefficient is 0.814 and is positive, which confirms these findings and shows a close relationship between the independent variables and sustainable agriculture and agrifood security. The R-Square value is equal to 0.691, which indicates that the model has high explanatory characteristics. These outcomes highlight the importance of resource sharing, information exchange, collaboration in purchasing, and technology application in improving agrifood security and the sustainability of agriculture. More so, the regression analysis showed that resource sharing within the cooperatives is positively related to sustainable agriculture and agrifood security ($B = 0.281$, $p < 0.01$). This aligns with the conclusion made by Ahmed and Mesfin [30] that states that cooperatives help to improve members' welfare by providing resources and minimizing transaction costs. Likewise, the flow of agricultural information within cooperatives also enhances sustainability and agrifood security ($B = 0.186$, $p < 0.01$), and other researchers have also opined that information is crucial for agriculture [46]. To sum up, the current research not only supports the findings of previous studies but also enriches the body of knowledge by presenting concrete findings regarding the Greek context. Thus, the results point to the significance of cooperation arrangements in enhancing long-term agriculture practices and agrifood availability. It will be useful for future works to continue to investigate the issues pointed out in Section 2.2. Resource Sharing in Cooperatives, and to determine the actual impacts of the technology implementation on the cooperative environment. Finally, these findings should inform policymakers in designing policies for financing agricultural cooperatives so that they are capable of contributing to sustainable development and food security.

6. Conclusions

This study assessed how Greek cooperatives promote agrifood security and sustainable agriculture. In this light, this study provides evidence that cooperatives positively impact agricultural production, resilience, and food security by promoting pooled access to resources, information, markets, and technology. Cooperative membership also implies the sharing of resources in a way that boosts farm productivity and sustainability, and it implies access to credit and other forms of support. This kind of approach not only increases the yields of agricultural produce but also promotes sustainable methods of farming. Accessible and timely information in cooperatives enhances the adoption of sustainable practices and the management of pests and diseases and increases the awareness of agrifood security. Open communication increases the flow of information on best practices and effective solutions within cooperatives, thereby improving the sustainability of agricultural practices. Cooperatives through bargaining and better market access greatly affect farm income, the prices of commodities, and agrifood security through guaranteed markets for the produce. In general, cooperatives' bargaining power with suppliers and buyers improves market conditions and provides farmers with better capital security. The incorporation of advanced technologies in cooperative practices enhances the productivity and output of agriculture. Hence, the advancement in technology, if embraced by cooperatives, will lead to increased productivity and improved market access, which, in turn, will promote agriculture and food security. The research objectives were well responded to. The practice of cooperation in resource sharing, information exchange, bargaining power, and technology transfer has revealed the effectiveness of sustainable agriculture and agrifood security, including the role of cooperatives in agricultural advancement and food security improvement.

6.1. Implications and Recommendations

Theoretical Implications: This study contributes to the New Institutional Economics (NIE) paradigm, including transaction cost economics (TCE) and collective action theory. It reaffirms the fact that cooperatives are capable of averting market failures, minimizing transactions costs, and facilitating collective action, thus providing an empirical backing to the theoretical view that defines cooperatives as institutions that correct market imperfections and improve resource mobilization.

Practical Implications: Subsidies, tax incentives, and other support measures should be provided to the formation and functioning of agricultural cooperatives by policymakers. Efficient and more reliable information dissemination mechanisms in cooperatives can improve market intelligence and the uptake of best practices. Increasing the use of contemporary technologies in cooperative activities increases the efficiency and sustainability of agricultural purposes.

Political Implications: At the political level, this study implies that governments should appreciate and encourage the involvement of cooperatives in the attainment of national and regional policies in agriculture. Optimizing policies, funding, and legislations for cooperatives will improve the ability of these institutions to boost sustainable agriculture and food security. Cooperatives can be used as an instrument by political leaders to fight rural poverty, enhance food security, and stimulate community development.

Managerial Implications: From a managerial point of view, the leaders within the cooperative should ensure that everyone within the organization is a sharer. Communication should be enhanced in order to ensure the provision of information and information on best practices. Cooperative managers should consider incorporating modern technologies to enhance the productivity and sustainability of the cooperatives. Education and training help cooperative members to become knowledgeable and skilled in order to exploit new technologies and practices.

6.2. Areas for Further Research

Further research is required to examine the challenges and obstacles cooperatives face when attempting to share resources, and to propose workable solutions to these problems, as the results indicate that, despite the research emphasizing the benefits of resource sharing, there is still some resistance to it.

Author Contributions: Conceptualization, S.K. (Stavros Kalogiannidis) and F.C.; methodology, S.K. (Simeon Karafolas) and S.K. (Stavros Kalogiannidis); software, S.K. (Stavros Kalogiannidis); validation, S.K. (Simeon Karafolas) and F.C.; formal analysis, S.K. (Stavros Kalogiannidis) and F.C.; investigation, S.K. (Stavros Kalogiannidis) and S.K. (Simeon Karafolas); resources, F.C.; data curation, F.C. and S.K. (Simeon Karafolas); writing—original draft preparation, S.K. (Stavros Kalogiannidis); writing—review and editing, S.K. (Stavros Kalogiannidis); visualization, S.K. (Simeon Karafolas) and S.K. (Stavros Kalogiannidis); supervision, F.C. and S.K. (Simeon Karafolas); project administration, S.K. (Stavros Kalogiannidis) and F.C.; funding acquisition, S.K. (Simeon Karafolas). All authors have read and agreed to the published version of the manuscript.

Funding: This research received no external funding.

Institutional Review Board Statement: 216/30-5-2024.

Informed Consent Statement: Informed consent was obtained from all subjects involved in the study.

Data Availability Statement: Data are available upon request.

Acknowledgments: The authors thank the editor and the anonymous reviewers for the feedback and their insightful comments on the original submission. All errors and omissions remain the responsibility of the authors.

Conflicts of Interest: The authors declare no conflicts of interest.

References

1. Zlati, M.L.; Florea, A.M.; Antohi, V.M.; Dinca, M.S.; Bercu, F.; Fortea, C.; Silvius, S. Financing Romanian Agricultural Cooperatives' Investments for the 2023–2027 Horizon. *Sustainability* **2023**, *15*, 2306. [CrossRef]
2. Heyl, K.; Ekardt, F.; Roos, P.; Garske, B. Achieving the nutrient reduction objective of the Farm to Fork Strategy. An assessment of CAP subsidies for precision fertilization and sustainable agricultural practices in Germany. *Front. Sustain. Food Syst.* **2023**, *7*, 1088640. [CrossRef]
3. Santos-Larrazabal, J.; Basterretxea, I. Intercooperation, flexicurity and their impact on workers: The case of Fagor Electrodomésticos. *Ann. Public Coop. Econ.* **2022**, *93*, 607–635. [CrossRef]
4. Semou, V.; Sergaki, P.; Tremma, O. Measuring the Economic Contribution of Agricultural Cooperatives to the National Economy: The Case of Greece. *Open Agric. J.* **2022**, *16*. [CrossRef]
5. Candemir, A.; Duvaleix, S.; Latruffe, L. Agricultural cooperatives and farm sustainability—A literature review. *J. Econ. Surv.* **2021**, *35*, 1118–1144. [CrossRef]
6. Gebremichael, B.A. The Role of Agricultural Cooperatives in Promoting Food Security and Rural Women's Empowerment in Eastern Tigray Region, Ethiopia. *Dev. Ctry. Stud.* **2014**, *4*, 96–109.
7. Ma, W.; Marini, M.A.; Rahut, D.B. Farmers' organizations and sustainable development: An introduction. *Ann. Public Coop. Econ.* **2023**, *94*, 683–700. [CrossRef]
8. Grillotti Di Giacomo, M.G.; De Felice, P. COVID-19 pandemic: Warning for the sustainability of European agri-food systems. *Belgeo* **2022**, *4*, 1–25. [CrossRef]
9. Gkatsikos, A.; Natos, D.; Staboulis, C.; Mattas, K.; Tsagris, M.; Polymeros, A. An Impact Assessment of the Young Farmers Scheme Policy on Regional Growth in Greece. *Sustainability* **2022**, *14*, 2882. [CrossRef]
10. Trivellas, P.; Mavrommati, S.; Anastasopoulou, A.; Grapas, C.; Kallikantzarou, E. Agro living Labs: Creating innovative, sustainable, resilient and social inclusive food systems. *IOP Conf. Ser. Earth Environ. Sci.* **2023**, *1185*, 012036. [CrossRef]
11. Beaudoin, C.; Joncoux, S.; Jasmin, J.-F.; Berberi, A.; McPhee, C.; Schillo, R.S.; Nguyen, V.M. A research agenda for evaluating living labs as an open innovation model for environmental and agricultural sustainability. *Environ. Chall.* **2022**, *7*, 100505. [CrossRef]
12. Oba, B.; Ozsoy, Z. Unifying nature of food: Consumer-initiated cooperatives in Istanbul. *Soc. Bus. Rev.* **2020**, *15*, 349–372. [CrossRef]
13. Gervasi, O.; Murgante, B.; Maria, A.; Chiara, A.C.R.; Scorza, F.; Karaca, Y.; Torre, C.M. Computational Science and Its Applications—ICCSA 2023 Workshops. In *Proceedings of the 23rd International Conference on Computational Science and Its Applications, ICCSA 2023*; Gervasi, O., Murgante, B., Taniar, D., Apduhan, B.O., Braga, A.C., Garau, C., Stratigea, A., Eds.; Springer Cham: Lesvos Island, Greece, 2023.
14. Namanya, B. Farmer Mobilization through Agricultural Cooperatives and Farmers Welfare in Western Uganda: A Case of ACPCU Ltd. *Int. J. Curr. Sci. Res. Rev.* **2022**, *5*, 248355932. [CrossRef]
15. OECD. Promoting Investment Climate Reforms in Morocco's Agri-Food Sector; Rabat, Morocco, 2021. Available online: https://policycommons.net/artifacts/3838187/promoting-investment-climate-reforms-in-moroccos-agri-food-sector/4644079/ (accessed on 28 April 2024).
16. European Parliament. *Ensuring Food Security and the Long-Term Resilience of EU Agriculture*; European Parliament: Strasbourg, France, 2019.
17. Marcis, J.; Bortoluzzi, S.C.; de Lima, E.P.; da Costa, S.E.G. Sustainability performance evaluation of agricultural cooperatives' operations: A systemic review of the literature. *Environ. Dev. Sustain.* **2019**, *21*, 1111–1126. [CrossRef]
18. Branca, G.; Cacchiarelli, L.; Haug, R.; Sorrentino, A. Promoting sustainable change of smallholders' agriculture in Africa: Policy and institutional implications from a socio-economic cross-country comparative analysis. *J. Clean. Prod.* **2022**, *358*, 131949. [CrossRef]
19. Kalogiannidis, S.; Syndoukas, D. The Impact of Agricultural Extension Services on Farm Output: A Worldwide Viewpoint. *Res. World Agric. Econ.* **2024**, *5*, 96–114. [CrossRef]
20. Lu, Y.; Zhang, Y.; Hong, Y.; He, L.; Chen, Y. Experiences and Lessons from Agri-Food System Transformation for Sustainable Food Security: A Review of China's Practices. *Foods* **2022**, *11*, 137. [CrossRef]
21. Coase, R.H. The Nature of the Firm. *Economica* **1937**, *4*, 386–405. [CrossRef]

22. Pereira, J.R. Producer Cooperatives: A Transaction Cost Economic Approach. *SSRN Electron. J.* **2014**, 1–22. [CrossRef]
23. Ouchi, W.; Williamson, O.E. Markets and Hierarchies: Analysis and Antitrust Implications. *Adm. Sci. Q.* **1977**, *22*, 540. [CrossRef]
24. Kalogiannidis, S.; Chatzitheodoridis, F. Strategic communication and sustainable agricultural competitiveness: A Greek case study. *Int. J. Sustain. Agric. Manag. Inform.* **2023**, *5*, 96–114. [CrossRef]
25. Olson, M. *The Logic of Collective Action: Public Goods and the Theory of Groups*; Harvard University Press: Cambridge, MA, USA, 1965; ISBN 0674537513.
26. FAO; IFAD; UNICEF; WFP; WHO. *The State of Food Security and Nutrition in the World 2023: Urbanization, Agrifood Systems Transformation and Healthy Diets across the Rural–Urban Continuum*; FAO: Rome, Italy, 2023; ISBN 978-92-5-137226-5.
27. Bokoumbo, K.; Berge, S.; Johnson, K.A.; Yabi, A.J.; Yegbemey, R.N. Cooperatives and sustainability: The case of maize producers in the plateaux region of Togo. *Heliyon* **2023**, *9*, e17345. [CrossRef] [PubMed]
28. Sikwela, M.M.; Mushunje, A.; Fuyane, N. The role of cooperatives in empowering smallholder farmers to access markets: A case study of Eastern Cape and KwaZulu Natal cooperatives in South Africa. *Int. J. Dev. Sustain.* **2016**, *5*, 536–552.
29. Dhillon, R.; Moncur, Q. Small-Scale Farming: A Review of Challenges and Potential Opportunities Offered by Technological Advancements. *Sustainability* **2023**, *15*, 15478. [CrossRef]
30. Ahmed, M.H.; Mesfin, H.M. The impact of agricultural cooperatives membership on the wellbeing of smallholder farmers: Empirical evidence from eastern Ethiopia. *Agric. Food Econ.* **2017**, *5*, 6. [CrossRef]
31. Joseph, L.; Stephenson, M.O.; Zanotti, L.; Ricot, S. Sustainable agriculture and food sovereignty in Haiti: Sharing knowledge and shaping understanding of food systems at the University of Fondwa. *Front. Sustain. Food Syst.* **2023**, *7*, 1230763. [CrossRef]
32. Mili, S.; Arovuori, K. The Struggle to Sustain Agriculture in EU Southern Neighbourhood Partners: Improving Data and Policies. *EuroChoices* **2023**, *22*, 50–57. [CrossRef]
33. Oñederra-Aramendi, A.; Begiristain-Zubillaga, M.; Cuellar-Padilla, M. Characterisation of food governance for alternative and sustainable food systems: A systematic review. *Agric. Food Econ.* **2023**, *11*, 18. [CrossRef]
34. Mindlin, Y.; Novikov, M.; Ignatyeva, O. Clusters and cooperatives as a tool of sustainable food security: A comparative analysis. *IOP Conf. Ser. Earth Environ. Sci.* **2022**, *1043*, 012038. [CrossRef]
35. Spielman, D.J. *Innovation Systems Perspectives on Developing-Country Agriculture: A Critical Review Innovation Systems Perspectives on Developing-Country Agriculture: A Critical Review*; Division Discussion Papers; International Food Policy Research Institute: Washington, DC, USA, 2005.
36. Thornton, P.K.; Loboguerrero Rodriguez, A.M.; Campbell, B.M.; Kavikumar, K.S.; Mercado, L.; Shackleton, S. *Rural Livelihoods, Food Security and Rural Transformation under Climate Change*; Global Commission on Adaptation: Rotterdam, The Netherlands; Washington, DC, USA, 2019.
37. Bose, S.; Al-Jabri, O.S.; Osman, N.M.; Al Habsi, S.H.; Al Shidi, R. Role of small and medium enterprises and agricultural cooperatives in promoting sustainable agriculture for rural development and food security. *Amity J. Agribus.* **2017**, *2*, 1–21.
38. Kumar, V.; Wankhede, K.G.; Gena, H.C. Role of Cooperatives in Improving Livelihood of Farmers on Sustainable Basis. *Am. J. Educ. Res.* **2015**, *3*, 1258–1266. [CrossRef]
39. Sridhar, A.; Balakrishnan, A.; Jacob, M.M.; Sillanpää, M.; Dayanandan, N. Global impact of COVID-19 on agriculture: Role of sustainable agriculture and digital farming. *Environ. Sci. Pollut. Res.* **2022**, *30*, 42509–42525. [CrossRef]
40. Nyawo, P.H.; Olorunfemi, O.D. Perceived Effectiveness of Agricultural Cooperatives by Smallholder Farmers: Evidence from a Micro-Level Survey in North-Eastern South Africa. *Sustainability* **2023**, *15*, 10354. [CrossRef]
41. Pimbert, M. Transforming food and agriculture: Competing visions and major controversies. *Mondes Dev.* **2023**, *199–200*, 361–384. [CrossRef]
42. Sabio, R.P.; Lehoux, P.; Rastoin, J.L. Characterizing food systems to better understand their vulnerabilities: A case study in Québec and São Paulo. *Renew. Agric. Food Syst.* **2023**, *38*, e25. [CrossRef]
43. Malindretos, G.; Sardianou, E.; Briana, M. Farmers' Perception on Contract Farming in the Post-COVID Era: Empirical Study in Greece. *Sustainability* **2023**, *15*, 14696. [CrossRef]
44. López-Felices, B.; Velasco-Muñoz, J.F.; Román-Sánchez, I.M.; Ángel Aznar-Sánchez, J. Socioeconomic and technical factors determining the adoption of hedgerows around greenhouses in southeast Spain. *Agric. Econ.* **2023**, *69*, 212–222. [CrossRef]
45. Kalfas, D.; Kalogiannidis, S.; Papaevangelou, O.; Chatzitheodoridis, F. Assessing the Connection between Land Use Planning, Water Resources, and Global Climate Change. *Water* **2024**, *16*, 333. [CrossRef]
46. Bochtis, D.; Benos, L.; Lampridi, M.; Marinoudi, V.; Pearson, S.; Sørensen, C.G. Agricultural Workforce Crisis in Light of the COVID-19 Pandemic. *Sustainability* **2020**, *12*, 8212. [CrossRef]
47. Kazungu, I.; Kumburu, N.P. Agripreneurship as a panacea for food security in Tanzania: A systematic review. *Heliyon* **2023**, *9*, e13305. [CrossRef]
48. Richards, T.J.; Klein, K.K.; Walburger, A.M. Principal-Agent Relationships in Agricultural Cooperatives: An Empirical Analysis from Rural Alberta. *J. Coop.* **1998**, *13*, 21–34. [CrossRef]
49. Bognar, J.; Schwarz, G. *Sustainable & Resilient Value Chains*; SHERPA Position Paper; SHERPA Rural Science–Society-Policy Interfaces: Brussels, Belgium, 2023; Available online: https://rural-interfaces.eu/wp-content/uploads/2023/05/SHERPA-Position-Paper-Resilient-Sustainable-Value-Chains.pdf (accessed on 12 May 2024).
50. Pućak, J.; Šimleša, D. Is Social Entrepreneurship Better for Workers? The Influence of Work Experience in Croatian Social Cooperatives on Perceived Well-Being. *Rev. Sociol.* **2020**, *50*, 7–30. [CrossRef]

51. Luo, J.; Han, H.; Jia, F.; Dong, H. Agricultural Co-operatives in the western world: A bibliometric analysis. *J. Clean. Prod.* **2020**, *273*, 122945. [CrossRef]
52. Barbu, M.; Delabre, I. *Report on Sustainability in Agri-Food Value Chains: Case Studies from the Mediterranean Regions and the Middle East*; Agricultural Voices Syria; Falmer: Brighton, UK, 2021; Available online: https://agricultural-voices.sussex.ac.uk/wp-content/uploads/2021/07/Report-on-Sustainability-in-Agri-food-Value-Chains_-Barbu-Delabre-2021.pdf (accessed on 14 April 2024).
53. Sundram, P. Food security in ASEAN: Progress, challenges and future. *Front. Sustain. Food Syst.* **2023**, *7*, 1324368. [CrossRef]
54. Izuchukwu, A.; Erezi, E.; David Emeka, E. Assessing the Impact of Farmer-to-Farmer Communication Networks on Knowledge Sharing and Adoption of Sustainable Agricultural Practices in Africa. *Int. J. Agric. Earth Sci.* **2023**, *9*, 58–76. [CrossRef]
55. Llewellyn, R.S.; Brown, B. Predicting Adoption of Innovations by Farmers: What is Different in Smallholder Agriculture? *Appl. Econ. Perspect. Policy* **2020**, *42*, 100–112. [CrossRef]
56. Nera, E.; Paas, W.; Reidsma, P.; Paolini, G.; Antonioli, F.; Severini, S. Assessing the Resilience and Sustainability of a Hazelnut Farming System in Central Italy with a Participatory Approach. *Sustainability* **2020**, *12*, 343. [CrossRef]
57. Kalogiannidis, S.; Kalfas, D.; Patitsa, C.; Chalaris, M. Relationship between Climate Change and Business Risk: Strategies for Adaptation and Mitigation: Evidence from a Mediterranean Country. *Wseas Trans. Environ. Dev.* **2024**, *20*, 276–294. [CrossRef]
58. Tuyen, M.C.; Sirisupluxana, P.; Bunyasiri, I.; Hung, P.X. Perceptions, Problems and Prospects of Contract Farming: Insights from Rice Production in Vietnam. *Sustainability* **2022**, *14*, 12472. [CrossRef]
59. Wollni, M.; Zeller, M. Do farmers benefit from participating in specialty markets and cooperatives? The case of coffee marketing in Costa Rica 1. *Agric. Econ.* **2007**, *37*, 243–248. [CrossRef]
60. Gai, M.; Yang, Q. Synergistic study of the green efficiency and economic resilience of agriculture from a sustainable development perspective: Evidence from Northeast China. *Environ. Sci. Pollut. Res.* **2023**, *30*, 77568–77592. [CrossRef] [PubMed]
61. Reinhardt, T. The farm to fork strategy and the digital transformation of the agrifood sector—An assessment from the perspective of innovation systems. *Appl. Econ. Perspect. Policy* **2023**, *45*, 819–838. [CrossRef]
62. UNIDO. UNIDO Directorate of SDG Innovation and Economic Transformation; United Nations 2023. Available online: https://www.unido.org/news/unido-global-town-hall (accessed on 10 April 2024).
63. Meemken, E.-M.; Qaim, M. Organic Agriculture, Food Security, and the Environment. *Annu. Rev. Resour. Econ.* **2018**, *10*, 39–63. [CrossRef]
64. Tabe-Ojong, M.P.J.; Aihounton, G.B.; Lokossou, J.C. Climate-smart agriculture and food security: Cross-country evidence from West Africa. *Glob. Environ. Chang.* **2023**, *81*, 102697. [CrossRef]
65. Stępień, S.; Maican, S. *Small Farms in the Paradigm of Sustainable Development*; Michalska, M., Ed.; Wydawnictwo Adam Marszałek: Toruń, Poland, 2020; ISBN 9788381802505.
66. Daum, T. Mechanization and sustainable agri-food system transformation in the Global South. A review. *Agron. Sustain. Dev.* **2023**, *43*, 16. [CrossRef]
67. Lepe, M. The Role of Agriculture Cooperatives and Farmer Organizations on the Sustainable Agricultural Practices Adoption in Uganda. Master's Thesis, Ghent University, Ghent, Belgium, 2021.
68. Yamane, T. *Statistics, An Introductory Analysis*, 2nd ed.; Harper and Row: New York, NY, USA, 1967.
69. Singh, A.S.; Masuku, M.B. Sampling techniques & determination of sample size in applied statistics research: An overview. *Int. J. Econ. Commer. Manag.* **2014**, *2*, 1–22.
70. McCormick, K.; Salcedo, J. *SPSS Statistics for Data Analysis and Visualization*; John Wiley & Sons: Hoboken, NJ, USA, 2017.
71. Kalogiannidis, S.; Kalfas, D.; Papaevangelou, O.; Chatzitheodoridis, F.; Katsetsiadou, K.-N.; Lekkas, E. Integration of Climate Change Strategies into Policy and Planning for Regional Development: A Case Study of Greece. *Land* **2024**, *13*, 268. [CrossRef]
72. Kalogiannidis, S.; Kalfas, D.; Chatzitheodoridis, F.; Lekkas, E. Role of Governance in Developing Disaster Resiliency and Its Impact on Economic Sustainability. *J. Risk Financ. Manag.* **2023**, *16*, 151. [CrossRef]
73. Li, S.; Huo, X. Estimating the effects of joining cooperatives on farmers' recycling behaviors of pesticide packaging waste: Insights from apple farmers of China. *Ciência Rural* **2023**, *53*, e20220229. [CrossRef]
74. Tsoulfas, G.T.; Trivellas, P.; Reklitis, P.; Anastasopoulou, A. A Bibliometric Analysis of Short Supply Chains in the Agri-Food Sector. *Sustainability* **2023**, *15*, 1089. [CrossRef]
75. Ahmadpour, A. Effective Factors on Application of Sustainable Agricultural Practices by Paddy Farmers (Case of Rural Production Cooperatives Members). *Int. J. Agric. Manag. Dev.* **2016**, *6*, 81–91.
76. Park, J.L.; Friend, D.B.; Manley, M.T.; Boyd, B.L. Leadership in agricultural cooperatives. In *Handbook of Research on Cooperatives and Mutuals*; Edward Elgar Publishing: Cheltenham, UK, 2023; pp. 135–147. ISBN 9781802202618.
77. Sdrolias, L.; Semos, A.; Mattas, K.; Tsakiridou, E.; Michailides, A.; Partalidou, M.; Tsiotas, D. Assessing the Agricultural Sector's Resilience to the 2008 Economic Crisis: The Case of Greece. *Agriculture* **2022**, *12*, 174. [CrossRef]
78. Kashiwagi, K.; Kamiyama, H. Effect of adoption of organic farming on technical efficiency of olive-growing farms: Empirical evidence from West Bank of Palestine. *Agric. Food Econ.* **2023**, *11*, 26. [CrossRef]

sustainability

MDPI

Article

Implementing Ireland's Food Vision 2030 within the Fresh Produce Sector: An Investigation of the Barriers and Enablers Using Systems Thinking Principles

Denis Kenny [1], Maria Dermiki [2] and Fiona Britton [3,*]

1 Keelings, FoodCentral, St. Margarets, Co., K67 NN28 Dublin, Ireland; denis_kenny@keelings.com
2 Department of Health and Nutritional Sciences, Atlantic Technological University, F91 YW50 Sligo, Ireland; maria.dermiki@atu.ie
3 Department of Environmental Science, Atlantic Technological University, F91 YW50 Sligo, Ireland
* Correspondence: fiona.britton@atu.ie

Abstract: The Irish Food Vision 2030 (IFV 2030) seeks to restructure Ireland's agricultural food system to deliver long-term social, economic, and environmental sustainability in keeping with its commitment to the European Green Deal and the 2030 Sustainable Development Goals. This study investigates the effectiveness of the IFV 2030 in delivering on this commitment across the fresh produce supply chain in Ireland using a combination of data collected from stakeholders through a survey and systems thinking principles. A review of the literature and Foucault's genealogical methods guided the development of the survey. Systems thinking principles were used to review the IFV 2030 and assess its capacity to deliver large-scale change for a sustainable Irish food system. Barriers to change were identified, including historical patterns of behaviour between EU and Irish policymakers that have repeatedly hindered progress towards large-scale change events. The results demonstrate that successful, long-term change will depend on the involvement and incentives of stakeholders within the supply chain. Continuous stakeholder engagement is required through a bottom-up organisational and supply chain approach to deliver long-term sustainability within the fresh produce sector. Using a systems thinking lens brings benefits through transdisciplinary collaboration and fosters the multiple stakeholder perspectives needed to deliver new ideas and solutions.

Keywords: systems thinking; food systems; food security; trade-offs; climate change; ripple effects; large scale change

1. Introduction

The food supply chain is not only significant to global food security, but it is also important to the anthropological functioning of human existence [1–3]. Hence, the way food is produced needs to be planned for posterity. Critical actors and organisations within the food system supply chains contribute to the "well-being of society" by ensuring societal stability through food security, employment, trade, and social development [4]. Meeting food demands for a growing global population while achieving sustainability goals presents a complex and significant challenge for food producers globally [4,5].

The Food and Agriculture Organization (FAO) estimates that 38% of global land is under agricultural management [6]. Current agricultural practices are having significant impacts on biodiversity, global water security, and degradation of land and ecosystem services [7–9]. Pravalie [8] demonstrated 17 land degradation pathways occurring globally and that current agricultural practices are economically unsustainable as a result. As such, the current food system poses a threat to long-term food, trade, and environmental security, with potentially irreversible consequences [4,5,10–14]. Pravalie [8] predicts an increase of 60–70% in current annual food production will be needed to feed an estimated 9 billion people by 2050. The enormity of this challenge will be compounded by estimates that annual yield will fall by 50% in certain parts of the world in the next 20 years [9,15].

Europe, along with other nations, are actively taking steps to encourage food producers to adopt more sustainable practices [4,5]. Europe has introduced a roadmap through the European Green Deal (EGD) Farm to Fork (F2F) strategy that is specifically aimed at restructuring the food system [5]. The F2F strategy centres on the Sustainable Development Goals (SDGs) and requires all member states to demonstrate economic, social, and environmental sustainability through responsible food supply chains.

In 2021, Ireland introduced the Irish Food Vision 2030 (IFV 2030) to implement the goals of the EGD-F2F strategy [16–18]. This requires Agri-organisations to restructure their current business strategies to achieve sustainability goals for long-term viability across the entire supply chain.

However, a report for the European Union by Science Advice for Policy by European Academies (SAPEAs) concluded that the implementation strategy is failing to deliver the goals of the F2F [19]. SAPEAs determined that the EGD proposals for implementation across all member states are full of complex information and conflicting messages. SAPEA suggested that green targets are missed due to the limited workable policy of current implementation strategies [19].

As an EU member state, Ireland is obligated to implement the directions of the EGD F2F. In Ireland, national large-scale change (LSC) is coordinated and driven by the Department of Agriculture, Food and Marine (DAFM). The DAFM affirms, through the IFV 2030, the importance of achieving all the 17 SDGs for a secure and sustainable food system. Historically, Ireland has struggled to reach its green targets [20–22]. This is further supported by a recent review conducted by the Environmental Protection Agency (EPA) and Climate Change Advisory Council (CCAC) that demonstrated that Ireland is not on track to reach its National Climate Action Plan targets set by the EGD F2F and IFV 2030 [20,22,23]. Moreover, SAPEA analysis of the EGD and a report by Clark [21] showed that Ireland is ranked 8th among the fourteen EU nations in the "Sustainable Progression Index".

The horticultural fresh produce industry in Ireland is the fourth largest sector after dairy, beef, and pigs [24]. The fresh produce sector in this study refers to the commercial horticulture fresh produce supply chain from primary production (farm) to the customer (retailer) for the production of fresh food for public consumption. The current study considers six sub-sectors related to societal dietary health [25]. The sub-sectors include field crops, protected crops, soft fruit, top fruit, potatoes, and mushrooms; this study excludes produce for amenity horticulture.

A report by Teagasc [26] (Irelands semi-state owned agricultural and food development authority) described the importance of the fresh produce sector, considering the role it plays on societal health, since healthy food contributes to mental and physical well-being, while unhealthy diets low in consumption of fruit and vegetables are one of the major risks related to non-communicable disease [21]. Clark [21] also demonstrated how Ireland's food production ranks poorly against the UN's SDGs. Sustainable transformation within the fresh produce supply chain was selected as the focus of this paper owing to the critical role fresh produce plays in societal well-being.

1.1. Theoretical Framework

Research by Redman [27] demonstrated that for a system to incorporate sustainable change, it needs to include the resilience capacity to maintain its function in spite of unforeseen shocks or pressures. It is imperative that sustainable transformation is both robust and flexible to avoid failure or regression [13,27–29].

The literature unanimously identifies resource depletion, biodiversity loss, land use issues and GHG (Greenhouse Gas) emissions as major global concerns that can only be addressed by Large Scale Change (LSC) [5,13,30–32]. Hornsey et al. [33] characterised this as a "wicked system" or "wicked problem" [34]. Arnold [16] and Thomas [18] corroborate this, depicting land, biodiversity and GHG emissions as significant issues or "wicked problems" associated with an unsustainable food system.

Wicked systems associated with food systems not only affect humankind but have a major consequence on the natural world's food supply, habitats, and ecosystem functionality [7,35]. The committee and strategists behind the development of IFV 2030 describe the food system as a multi-dimensional and complex agri-system associated with issues that could be considered wicked problems [16–18]. Hornsey et al. [33] warned of the complexity of intervening in a wicked system, where small changes in a system can lead to larger and unintended changes, or trade-offs, between connected systems, known as a "ripple effect".

1.1.1. Foucault's Genealogical

Foucault's concept is a qualitative research method that delves into human and social science behaviour and identifies patterns of historical and current political discourse [36]. The methodology outcome uses text and content for a clear understanding of patterns involved in social and political transformational relationships for LSC events. Foucault's genealogy, as a predicate on behavioural change, can be useful in establishing important baseline information on the knowledge and skills already functioning within the IFV 2030. Foucault's genealogical method analyses historical policy behaviours and interactions, allowing critique of the present based on three criteria:

1. Formation—based on a set of rules that forms objects, concepts, and theoretical options.
2. Transformation—with emphasis on the "point in time" at which changes in policy or the implementation of new policy were decided.
3. Correlation—Isolating the discourse in the context of social, political, and economic relationships to find a repeated path of dependence, also known as Foucault's order of discourse [36].

Table 1 uses Foucault's genealogical method to identify and compare progressions of the IFV 2030 for LSC against historical LSC events within Irish agriculture. Table 1 was generated by reviewing the scientific literature to outline patterns of similarity through Foucauldian critical discourse analysis that inhibit the successful implementation of the IFV 2030.

Table 1. Analysis of Historical Large Scale Change (LSC) and the Ireland Food Vision (IFV) 2030 using Foucault's genealogical method.

Large Scale Change: Historical Patterns Vs IFV 2030			
Year	**Ireland's Inception into the EU**	**Year**	**Implementing The IFV 2030**
1972	Ireland casts a vote and strongly agrees to join the EU (EEC) among the other member states, however, there is variable multi-governance issues and poor understanding of structure [37].	2019	The EGD F2F is introduced to all member states; Shows variable multi-governance issues and poor understanding [19].
1973	Ireland joins the EU. Use of directives and policy introduction accompanied by heavy funding [37].	2019	IFV 2030 use of directives and policy introduction accompanied by heavy funding [17].
1973	Economic, behavioural and cultural change required to support new directives and policies [37].	2019	Economic, behavioural and cultural change required to support new directives and policies [19]
1973	Agriculture to comply with EU standards, CAP reformation [37].	2020	Agriculture to comply with Europe and CAP and standards [38,39].
1977	EU timelines not met and hindered by limited capacity to review structures and processes [37].	2021	EPA shows the Irish GHG emissions increased by 4.7 per cent in 2021 compared to 2020 [40].
1977	Reactive and adhoc period in relation to policy implementation [37].	2022	Reactive and ad-hoc implementation for transformative policy for sustainability [19,39,41].
1977	Systematic approach introduced, but with little collaborative communication and cohesion to achieve a smoother transition to EU structures and policies [37].	2022	An attempt at a systematic approach with lack of cohesion between departments. Ireland seems to be lacking a systems approach to transition the EGD through the IFV 2030 for a sustainable food system [38,39].
1992	Limited workable policy through implementation strategies/MacSharry CAP reform [37].	2023	Limited Workable policy through current implementation strategies [20,22].
1999	Ireland struggles to implement EU directives.	2023	Ireland struggles to implement EU directives.

Table 1 demonstrates how EU policy and directives are received and disseminated by Ireland through a certain type of political discourse. Foucault's genealogical method discerned any outcomes of the IFV 2030 based on historical EU and Irish convergence for LSC using discourse analysis. As seen in Table 1, academic literature and government papers indicate that historical Irish behavioural change, through LSC methods (EU Directives and policy), follows a reactive and wasteful chain of events [37]. Two reports on separate LSC events demonstrated that historical and current political discourse hinder implementation strategies.

A review of papers analysing historical interactions between EU policy direction and Irish enactment into national policy shows similar transitioning trajectories. Jackson et al. [19] concluded that the EGD-F2F political discourse for implementation strategy is restricting information on workable policy. Table 1 shows a repeated path of dependence between historical EU and Irish political channels and the modern political processes for the implementation of the IFV 2030. The research papers viewing both historical and current implementation described the same issues for the successful execution of LSC. Repeated political neglect towards knowledge and understanding of co-creation are causing barriers and delays in the integration of EU F2F initiatives for a sustainable food system through the IFV 2030.

Overall, the literature implies that the current implementation of the F2F and IFV 2030 roadmap (Table 2) for sustainability is being disseminated through regulatory bodies. The research so far showed the targets of the EGD F2F and IFV 2030 are not delivering on goals to protect degrading ecosystems and biodiversity, enhance land use practices, and reduce GHG emissions.

Table 2. A summary of the IFV 2030 main priorities for GHG emissions, Biodiversity, and Land Use [42].

IFV 2030 GOALS		
Goals	**Activity**	**Mission#Goal**
GHG	There are seven goals in this mission that aim to deliver a climate-neutral food system by 2050, with verifiable progress achieved by 2030 (i.e., emissions reductions, carbon sequestration, improvements in air quality, restoration, and enhancement of biodiversity).	Mission 1—Goal 1
Biodiversity	It is envisaged that by 2030, 10% of farmed area will be prioritised for biodiversity, spread across all farms throughout the country [42]	Mission 1—Goal 1; 2; 3; 4
Land Use	The IFV 2030 missions directs primary producers towards care and use of multiple ecosystem services (i.e., supporting biodiversity and land use) [42]	Mission 1—Goal 1; 2; 3; 4

Table 2 shows critical environmental issues (land use, biodiversity loss, and GHG emissions) that are incorporated into the IFV 2030 for LSC in the fresh produce supply chain, each important to the IFV 2030 objectives for a sustainable food system and the stakeholders' sustainability goals.

1.1.2. The 3 Pillars of Sustainability Framework

Figure 1 shows the three pillars of sustainability for the fresh food sector, which worked as a concept map for this study, using insights from the literature review and the IFV 2030 missions (Table 2). Each pillar shows a suite of activities pertaining to the stakeholder's transdisciplinary inputs and responsibilities for a sustainable food system model. Figure 1 uses a multidisciplinary approach, using the empirical evidence gathered from the literature review as a sustainability framework. The social and economic pillars represent well-being, growth, and prosperity [43]. The environmental pillar represents the critical elements of the ecosystem's well-being [43].

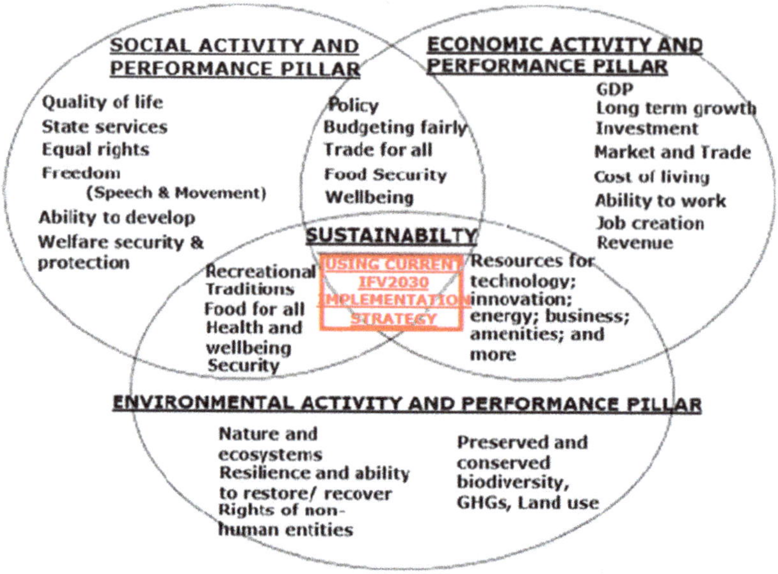

Figure 1. The three pillars of sustainability for the fresh produce sector.

The principles of Figure 1 are fundamental in achieving a resilient food system, one with a harmonised system of social, environmental, and economic activity [12]. The red text box, central to Figure 1, illustrates how sustainability is currently being directed by the IFV 2030 (Table 2) regulatory bodies within the fresh food supply chain. It identifies how the implementation of the EGD-F2F and IFV 2030 roadmap is being disseminated for a sustainable socio-economy, with climate neutrality at the core [5].

1.1.3. Organisational Harmonisation

According to Ademi et al. [44] and Fortis et al. [45], standards and frameworks are explorations for learning among organisations that guide the activities and performance of their objectives. In terms of the commercial horticultural fresh produce supply chain stakeholders and respective organisations, Ademi et al. [44] demonstrated that knowledge transfer overcomes the barriers to implementing sustainable measures through LSC. Ademi et al. [44] described this as "knowing about one's own as well as others' expertise enables team members to retrieve needed knowledge efficiently and effectively from the 'experts' within the group". The complexity and difficulty are in the altering of the core functioning of the stakeholder organisations with the impregnation of sustainability into organisational embedded structures [44,45]. According to Siddh et al. [32] and Ademi et al. [44], the nexus approach is key to achieving sustainable change, warranting accountability and ensuring sustainability initiatives are equal across multiple organisations, as outlined in Figure 1.

1.2. Aims and Objectives

The overall aim of this study was to employ a sustainability assessment by investigating the potential of the EGD F2F and IFV 2030 as a roadmap for the transition to a sustainable fresh produce supply chain in Ireland. Sustainable performance is determined by the behavioural and collaborative engagement of all the supply chain stakeholders [32,46]. The fresh produce sector is no exception to that, and as demonstrated by Siddh et al. [32], to be viably sustainable within the fresh produce sector, multiple organisations must be involved in several partnerships that interact together. This includes the entire supply chain from factor markets, primary production (Farm), storage, distribution, consumption, and waste [12].

This study aims to explore the views of key stakeholders across the fresh produce supply chain towards the implementation of Ireland's Food Vision 2030. Moreover, this paper looks bilaterally at the Irish fresh produce sector among the commercial supply chains through the analysis of historical and current pathways for LSC. Through a design framework, this study aims to provide actionable recommendations regarding missed environmental and climate targets for a sustainable Irish food system. Systems dynamics was used to define a successful strategy for the implementation of the F2F and IFV 2030.

2. Methodology

2.1. Data Collection

A mixed methods approach was used to collect data from key stakeholders/actors within the fresh produce supply chain. The term stakeholders in this study refers to organisations within the fresh produce supply chain. Insights were sought on stakeholders' current interconnectedness, knowledge and understanding of sustainability, and engagement in policy implementation for sustainable change within the supply chain. All data related to LSC focused on the EGD F2F and IFV 2030. The data was collected by means of an online survey and analysed using systems thinking methods.

This study reviewed academic literature and government white papers to guide the systems thinking methodology for a design framework. Foucault's genealogical approach, based on the literature, focused on historical and current EU Directives for policy change knowledge sharing and behaviours and interactions associated with political challenges. This included key policy documents and data relating to the EGD-F2F strategy, Common Agricultural Policy (CAP) and Ireland's Climate Action Plans for 2030. The focus is on current practices within the fresh produce supply chains, particularly those relating to environmental sustainability.

Emphasis was placed on current stakeholder engagement, knowledge, and understanding from a bottom-up–top-down structure of policy and LSC strategies as directed by the IFV 2030. The three pillars of sustainability [47] using transdisciplinary collaboration and the UN Sustainable Development Goals (SDGs) were reviewed as part of this study as a model for long-term sustainability for posterity. The iceberg model framework structure was used to present the findings

2.2. Iceberg Model Framework Structure

The framework was based on the principles of systems thinking (the layout structure of the entire article follows the iceberg model (Table 3 demonstrates the mixed methods using a design framework used for this paper).

Table 3. The Iceberg Model Mixed Methods and Design Framework.

Systems	Tools	Diagnostics	Description/Use
React	Literature Reviewed	Event	Observable Behaviour: analyse the literture and white papers.
Anticipate	Foucault's Methodology/System Archetypes	Patterns	Foucault's historical analysis Methodology/System Archetypes documenting patterns of Behaviour based on the literature reviewed
Design	Survey	Structures	Identify underlying systemic structures through a survey
Transform	Systems Dynamics and Concept Maps	Mental Model	Potential to transform the system using system dynamics and concept maps: potential for LSC through the 3 pillars of sustainability

2.3. Survey

The aim of the survey was to enhance understanding of the current state of play across the sector in relation to the IFV 2030, particularly the level of awareness and knowledge of the policy, existing collaboration and interconnectedness across the supply chain, and the willingness amongst individual stakeholders to engage with and deliver on the IFV 2030 policy objective.

Based on the literature reviewed for this study, the survey was created based on an investigative model for knowledge transfer, policy understanding and willingness for change.

The survey was developed in Qualtrics XM (first release 2005, copyright year 2021, US, available online at https://www.qualtrics.com) and approved by the research ethics committee of Atlantic Technological University, Sligo (FSS202310 and 21 March 2023). The survey was piloted before going live with target participants from 6 May to 10 June 2023. The question grid of the survey can be seen in the Supplementary Materials.

2.3.1. Participants Selection

The participants selection for this study was based on detailing the current functioning and organisational learning of the fresh produce supply chain and were selected based on 3 main stakeholder organisations: government (policy writing and regulation), primary producer (farming), and retailer (buyer). This was to elicit 3 main facets important to systems thinking and true long-term LSC events.

Four main points were examined when considering stakeholder insights into LSC for the Fresh Produce Sector through the IFV2030:

(1) Participant's current knowledge of the IFV2030 implementation and interconnectedness using a bottom-up, top-down knowledge base (i.e., level of collaboration between key stakeholders of the fresh produce supply chain).
(2) Participants' current involvement is both internally within their sector (i.e., level of collaboration between actors within sector organisations) and holistically within the supply chain management for sustainable change.
(3) Participants Knowledge and understanding for the implementation of the IFV2030
(4) Level of buy-in and willingness to be involved in the implementation of the IFV2030

2.3.2. Participant Recruitment

The participants for the survey were recruited via gatekeepers via different media (i.e., email and social media apps). Participant information was provided to inform them about the anonymity of the participant's participation and the rules for information use.

Participants representing a bottom-up-top-down structure and providing data relating to the three key stakeholders for the fresh produce supply chain captured 25% responses from a senior management level, 44% of responses representing junior to middle management roles, and 31% identifying as either general operatives or an undefined/undisclosed ranking.

2.4. Systems Thinking Methodology

This study used system thinking methodologies to understand the complexity of the food system and associated supply chains. The addition of systems dynamics was guided by insights from the literature reviewed, which informed a design framework for actionable recommendations. System archetypes were used to identify common patterns of behaviour that characterise the barriers to the successful implementation of the IFV 2030. Through understanding the system archetypes, effective levers for mitigating such barriers can be identified [13].

2.5. Data Analysis

Data analysis via the online survey focused on three key stakeholders (Government, Primary Producer and Retailer) in the fresh produce supply chain. A total of 46 participants represented the respective stakeholder groups, distributed as follows: Government (26%), Primary Producers (48%), and Retailers (26%). Most respondents were recruited from major retailers, with the exception of one respondent who worked as a distributor for the retailer and a second who was involved in a Co-op store. IBM SPSS was used to generate uni-variate statistics (percentages, means, standard deviation, and range). Excel was used to generate tables and graphs.

Table 4 summarises how systems thinking tools were used in this study to explore complex problems and diagnose root cause issues and anomalies pertaining to LSC events [14,29].

Table 4. Systems thinking tools were used for this study.

System Thinking Tools for Analysis and Design		
Tools	**Description**	**Source**
Iceberg Method	A framework to interrogate relationships within the system, seeking patterns and root cause identification.	[13]
System Dynamics	Use of diagrams to display system elements and identify system flows and cascading events	[14]
System Archetypes	Systems archetypes are used to identify and analyse patterns of behaviour in a system and produce solutions to reoccurring problems.	[13]
Concept maps	A tool to illustrate and use critical thinking to identify and map system components and connections	[48]
Foucault's Genealogical Method	A pattern identification tool based on historical behavioural that can help predict a future outcome.	[36]

3. Results and Discussion

3.1. Survey Results

The survey provided critical insights into the involvement of stakeholders in critical policy change for sustainability across the fresh produce supply chain. Participant selection focused on providing insights from bottom-up/top-down perspectives relating to decision-making within respective organisations and across the supply chain. The data collected from the survey responses was aggregated according to the three stakeholder groups. Participants provided data relating to their position of responsibility within their organisations, with 25% of respondents holding senior management positions, 44% representing junior to middle management roles and 31% identifying as either general operatives or an undefined/undisclosed ranking. All respondents within their sectors showed an average of over 9 years of service for their respective organisations. This experience implies an important level of disciplinary knowledge when assessing the participant's responses in the context of their organisations. Furthermore, Goyal [49] showed that experienced employees are more inclined to achieve the SDGs, and studies also suggest that longer-serving employees are better equipped with the skillsets needed to envision and facilitate sustainable change [44,45,50,51].

Figure 2 provides insights into the level of awareness respondents have in relation to climate change and its impact on the food sector. All respondents have some awareness of climate change, and the majority of respondents across all stakeholder groups recognised climate change as a threat to the food sector (government, 84%; food producers, 82%; and retailers, 75%). Awareness levels are important to establish as a foundation for engagement and sustainable transition.

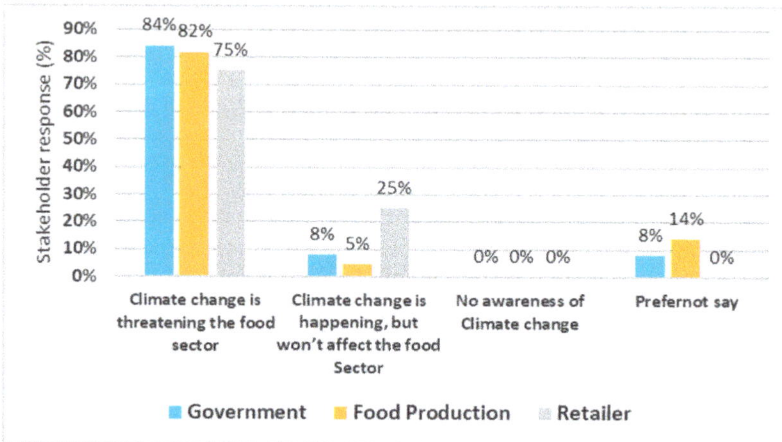

Figure 2. Respondents' opinion regarding the impact of climate change on the food sector.

Whole System Interaction for LSC

To analyse the level of collaboration and connectedness within the fresh produce supply chain, each respondent was asked a series of questions to identify their level of involvement, buy-in and willingness to participate in policy implementation. The survey investigated the respondent's perception of the policy development process from the bottom-up (i.e., ideas in relation to company goals involving all levels of employees within an organisation) supported by top-down management (i.e., Leadership) within their respective organisations in the fresh produce supply chain.

The majority of government respondents (policy writers) perceive the process of policy development to be consultative (67%), but less than 10% consider it to be collaborative. Respondents from the retail sector believe the process of policy writing is mostly consultative (42%), with some believing it to be collaborative (17%). This contrasts with responses from Primary Producers, where just 18% believe the process to be consultative and 0% view it as collaborative.

Respondents who believed there was no engagement also differed across each stakeholder group. Just 8% of government employees surveyed believe there is no engagement in policy development, whereas this stands at 17% and 27% amongst retail and primary producer stakeholders, respectively.

This data indicates that stakeholder actors differ in their perception of how policy is developed and implemented with respect to stakeholder engagement and collaboration.

Skippari et al. [52] demonstrated how perceptual barriers can be as damaging as actual barriers in preventing collaborative innovation and achieving intended outcomes. As demonstrated in the survey, a key group of actors within their respective sectors perceive the process to be non-collaborative. Skippari et al. [52] demonstrated that non-collaborative processes block exposure to new ideas and comprehensive information sharing and engagement among all stakeholders. The lack of exposure to transdisciplinary ideas delays shared knowledge to avoid unintended consequences or opportunities to implement LSC.

Research for this paper highlighted the criticality of knowledge sharing through top-down-bottom-up engagement between all actors to achieve LSC for sustainability [13,27–29]. Hornsey et al. [33] described the complexity of intervening in a wicked system and the danger of creating a ripple effect without bottom-up knowledge.

Figure 3 illustrates the respondents' involvement in policy writing within their organisation from a top-down-bottom-up structure. Respondents who feel they are always involved are marginally highest within primary producers (23%), compared to respondents from government (17%) and retailers (17%). The majority of respondents across all stakeholder groups feel they are either 'somewhat' or 'mostly involved' in policy development within their organisation (government 75%; primary producers 49%; retailers 66%). The percentage of respondents with no involvement in policy for their organisation includes government at 8%, primary producer at 27%, and retailer at 17%.

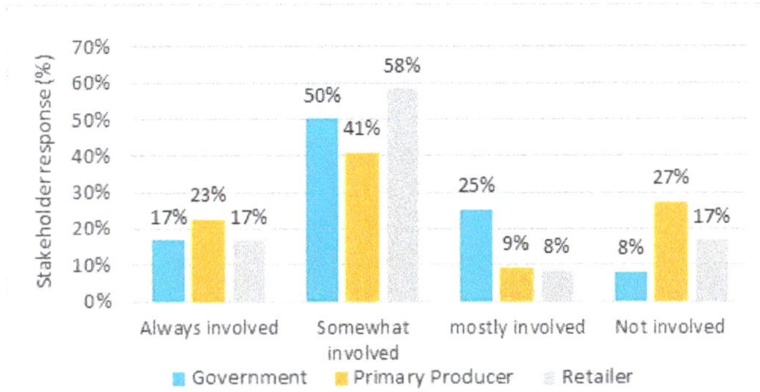

Figure 3. Respondents' involvement and knowledge of policy from a bottom-up–top-down perspective within their organisation.

Insights were sought through the survey on how internal policy related to sustainable change is implemented within organisations for the fresh produce sector. Respondents from the government show the highest knowledge of internal policy measures (77%), while responses from retailers and primary producers demonstrated lower levels of policy knowledge at 66% and 50%, respectively.

Table 5 shows participants' confidence in the policy written for the IFV 2030. It is noted that almost half of the respondents from the Retailer cohort have never heard of the IFV 2030 (47%). Respondents who show full confidence that the IFV 2030 will achieve all goals is low across all stakeholder groups (government (8%), primary producers (9%) and retailers (8%).

Table 5. Respondents' confidence and knowledge in LSC plans by policymakers.

Sector	Prefer Not to Say	IFV 2030 Will Not Achieve Any of Its Goals	IFV 2030 Will Achieve Its Most Important Goals	IFV 2030 Will Achieve All of Its Goals	Never Heard of the IFV 2030
Government	8.0%	33%	51%	8.0%	0%
Food Production	5.0%	31.%	41.%	9.0%	14.%
Retailer	0%	8.0%	37%	8.0%	47%

Results from Table 5 indicate a disconnect among the stakeholders regarding knowledge of the IFV 2030, potentially implying an unequal exposure to what the IFV 2030 is trying to achieve. This potentially implies a siloed implementation strategy when auctioning policy and sustainable vision of the IFV 2030 among the key stakeholders for LSC. Without holistic knowledge among all members of the supply chain regarding the IFV 2030s existence or intended vision for a sustainable food system, there is limited accountability and "buy-in" from all of the supply chain stakeholders.

Figure 4 shows declining levels of knowledge and involvement in the development of the IFV 2030 roadmap from government to primary producers to retailers. In terms of knowledge, the government (policy writers and implementation strategists) shows the highest understanding (71%), followed by the primary producer (46%) and retailers (38%). A similar pattern of knowledge decline can be seen when respondents were asked if they felt they were involved in the development of the IFV 2030 across government (28%), primary producer (25%), and retailer (23%) from a top-down-bottom-up perspective.

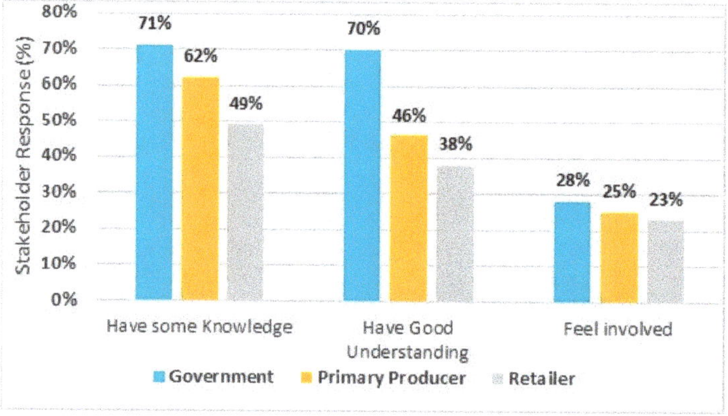

Figure 4. Respondents' knowledge and involvement in policy development.

47% of respondents from the government, 41% from primary producers and 52% from retailers perceived that the appropriate actors are included in the development of policy for LSC. This suggests that between 48% and 59% of respondents are either unsure or feel that the correct actors are not involved. This illustrates uncertainty and a lack of consensus across stakeholder groups in relation to which actors should be involved in policy development for sustainable change. This may suggest a gap in how actors and stakeholders understand the missions outlined in Table 2, suggesting a lack of recognition by policymakers for a bottom-up and collaborative culture for LSC. Without a bottom-up culture approach, a lack of "buy-in" creates barriers delaying sustainable change and the associated policy implementation.

Figure 5 shows that all respondents are willing to be involved in policy collaboration for their sector, with 0% showing no interest in policymaking. It is important to establish willingness in the context of a bottom-up-top-down collaboration among key stakeholders for co-creation within the fresh produce supply chain [53].

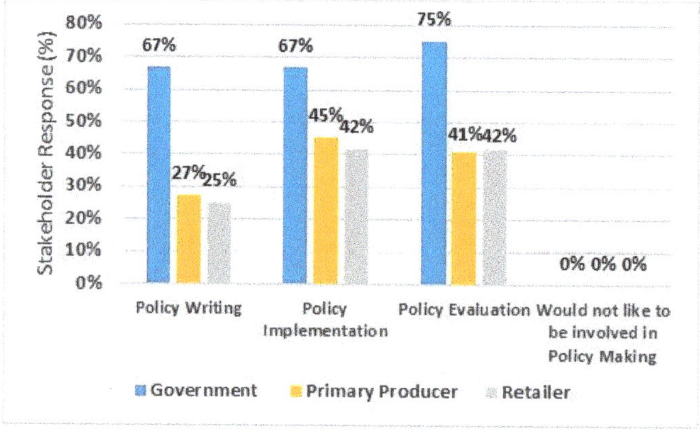

Figure 5. Respondents' willingness to be involved in policy strategies.

3.2. Design Framework Methods

The results from the survey and Foucault's genealogical methodology found similar patterns between historical and current policy strategies for the implementation of LSC.

Foucault's methodology (Table 1) demonstrated that the IFV 2030 implementation process follows similar political channels and processes when compared to historical Irish processes for LSC initiated by the EU. Brouwer et al. [39] demonstrated that the IFV 2030 procedures follow reactive and wasteful events, a similar description to Laffan's [37] analysis of historical Irish LSC events. Using Foucault's principles, given that historical LSC events have not successfully met targets, it can be surmised that the IFV 2030 will continue to follow the same course, and Ireland's sustainability targets will not be achieved.

Insights from systems thinking theory (Table 4), Foucault's methodology and Hornsey et al. [33] indicate that when faced with missed targets, the political arena is pressured to intervene. This type of intervention can be deemed as a retrospective reaction brought on by public pressure, forcing politicians to make quick decisions to solve complex problems (such as climate change, land, and biodiversity degradation) [33]. Hornsey et al. [33] demonstrated how such decisions, made without incorporating the necessary knowledge through collaborative channels, can create ripple effects that lead to unintended consequences.

3.2.1. System Archetypes

System archetypes were used to characterise barriers to the successful implementation of the IFV 2030 within the fresh produce supply chain. Archetypes were identified using insights from literature, Foucault's genealogical methodology, system thinking tools, and the stakeholder survey. Systems dynamics was used to visualise constraints in relation to the system as a whole. A dynamic map of archetypes was developed with a focus primarily on the ability of organisations to implement the IFV 2030 and secondly on the likely success of the IFV 2030 in relation to targets for sustainability (specifically greenhouse gas emissions, land use and biodiversity).

Fixes That Fail

Foucault's methodology (Table 1) identifies patterns in Ireland's current LSC events for sustainability. It was found that current structures for policy writing, implementation and evaluation are not a cohesive pathway. Instead, this falls under an acquisition archetype of "Fixes that fail" or "Sacrificing Quality" [13].

As demonstrated in Figure 6, "fixes that fail" [13] show a negative outcome despite the IFV 2030 increase in efforts to create a sustainable food system. The latest reports are showing that the current trajectory of GHG and biodiversity restoration is significantly off target (Table 1) [20,22]. Figure 6 shows how scheduled pressure and lack of cohesion are hindering the success of the IFV 2030 in implementing the LSC needed to offset the environmental issues.

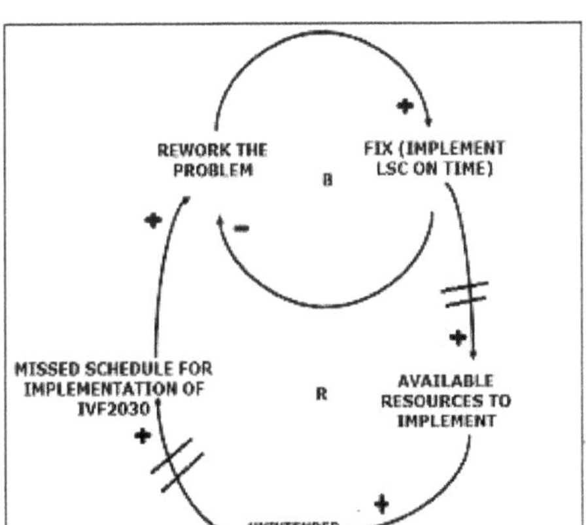

Figure 6. Illustration of the archetype "fixes that fail". With associated arrow (+) = increasing effect on variable; (−) = decreasing effect on variable.

Foucault's analysis (Table 1) demonstrated many repeated patterns of political discourse between historical policy implementation and the current implementation of the IFV 2030 in Ireland. As seen in Figure 6, these are associated with unintended consequences such as policy implementation through non-collaborative channels [37] (Table 1). The most significant consequence is system delays due to a lack of supporting knowledge from the bottom-up actors [13,46]. System constraints appear in the policy arena due to delays in learning across the system, which leads to missed targets for EGD-F2F and IFV 2030 [19,22].

Delays add political pressure to fix the problem to ensure targets are realigned to meet the 2030 deadline. Figure 6 demonstrates this as a retrospective reaction that leads policymakers to "rework the problem" (e.g., introduce a new policy, reform policy, extra funding), creating more fixes through policy to achieve the original goal [50]. Currently, the implementation of IFV 2030 is showing a reinforcing loop scenario, with imminent delays that require more resources to achieve the intended goals. This, in turn, increases the chance of unintended consequences.

A mitigating factor in balancing the system is to use collaborative stakeholder engagement for proactive problem-solving to ensure policy is co-created for a smooth LSC event. The survey results highlighted many knowledge gaps between stakeholders for the implementation of the IFV 2030s for LSC.

The survey further deep-dived beyond collaboration among the supply chain stakeholders and sought an understanding of collaboration within each of the stakeholder's respective organisations, depicted in Figure 3. The type of discourse looked at in Figure 3 involved the creation and implementation of policy for sustainable change from a top-down and bottom-up perspective (i.e., senior leadership to lower levels of the employment structure) internally within each stakeholder's organisation. Figure 3 demonstrates that the direction for sustainable restructuring within an organisation is directed from the top-down to the lower-level employment tiers. This implies the current process of managing policy change in the fresh produce supply chain is not collaborative both among the stakeholders of the fresh produce supply chain and within the culture of each of the stakeholder's organisations.

This study suggests that for a long-term and truly sustainable food system, the chain of information from the stakeholder level (government, primary producer, retailer) requires "bottom-up" transdisciplinary knowledge [13,46]. Stakeholder knowledge needs to be co-created within a system that is sufficiently agile and reflexive in order to be capable of responding to unforeseen consequences [21]. Figure 5 demonstrated that all stakeholder groups showed interest in co-creation for policy change and implementation for LSC to mitigate rising GHG land and biodiversity loss.

Limits to Success

Figure 7 demonstrates a "Limits to Success" [13] archetype scenario with a reinforcing loop (R) linking to a balancing loop (B). The constraint identified for the implementation of the IFV 2030 is the lack of cohesion among the supply chain stakeholders. Table 5 demonstrated significant gaps in information flow pertaining to the implementation of the IFV 2030. The results from the survey (Figure 4) also showed variation in awareness or knowledge of the IFV 2030s across the stakeholder groups. Respondents representing government organisations showed the most awareness and knowledge of the IFV 2030 (71%), while respondents in the retailer cohort demonstrated the least knowledge of the IFV 2030, with almost half of the respondents (47%) unaware of the IFV 2030 (Table 5). This limits success by creating a major delay due to an absence of equally shared information in relation to policy. As an example of this, a primary producer's cost of work is proportionately determined by standards of quality, both for conformance with policy and retailer demands. This is problematic since the survey results show that the retailer lacks knowledge of the IFV 2030 (e.g., 47% have never heard of the IFV 2030). This puts the primary producer in an isolated position among the stakeholders, as it must respond to the requirements of the IFV 2030 within its own organisation and effort, which is unrecognised and, therefore, undervalued by the retailer. A collaborative approach to IFV 2030 across the entire supply chain would help to mitigate this constraint.

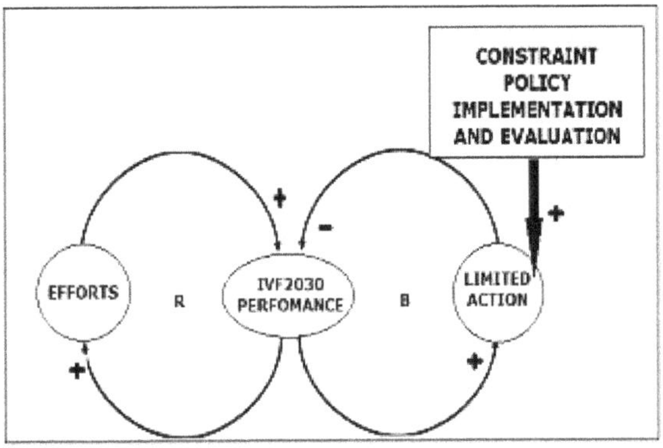

Figure 7. "Limits to success" archetype. With associated arrow (+) = increasing effect on variable; (−) = decreasing effect on variable.

In parallel with Figure 7, Foucault's analysis of the political arena (Table 1) found patterns between historically unsuccessful LSC events and the current implementation of the IFV 2030. Historically, Ireland has struggled to reach its green targets related to GHG, land and biodiversity [21]. Social Justice Ireland (SJI) reports that Ireland's climate action targets for 2030 rank 8th in the 2024 Sustainable Progression Index out of fourteen EU countries [21–23].

Foucault's analysis (Table 1), Figures 3 and 7 and Table 5 imply a delay in knowledge sharing due to lack of collaboration both at an EU level and national level. It was demonstrated that Ireland's response to meet EU policy has historically been slow. Ireland and the EU typically drive LSC through a series of overhauls supported by heavy funding, European Directives, and the reformation or introduction of new policies (e.g., CAP) [16,37,54].

Accidental Adversaries (Escalation)

Figure 8 shows an "Accidental Adversaries" structure [13]. This system archetype is synonymous with a lack of understanding between two (or more) stakeholders and illustrates how a lack of knowledge, understanding and buy-in can create accidental adversaries in the fresh produce supply chain. Figure 8 demonstrates how A (primary producer) is incurring costs through a new policy for sustainability, while B (retailer) is responsible for securing quality fresh produce at competitive pricing through a tendering process. This adds more pressure on the primary producer to maintain product standards and quality, lower prices and comply with sustainability targets related to the IFV 2030. Through competitive bidding and added costs to implement the IFV 2030, the primary producer receives less profit return and fails to invest in implementing innovations needed to drive change. This scenario can lead the primary producer to get caught into another archetype trap known as "drifting goals". The lack of funds for investment can lead to a lowering of the goal to meet the bidding demand from the retailer. In the long term, this has an adverse effect on the retailer as lowering the goal may reduce product quality, supply stability and overall yield availability.

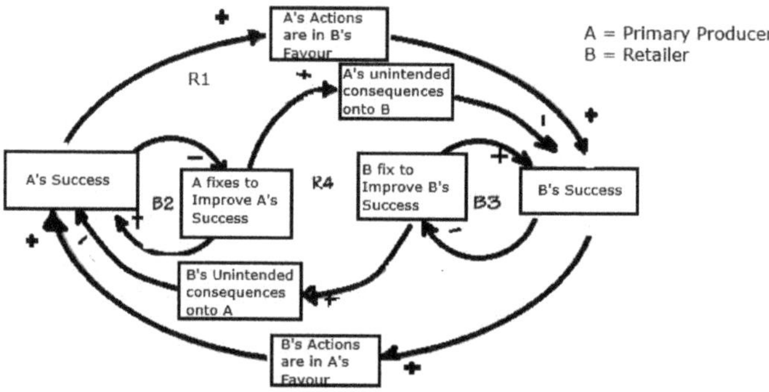

Figure 8. System archetype "Accidental Adversaries (Escalation)". With associated arrow (+) = increasing effect on variable; (−) = decreasing effect on variable.

Growth and Underinvestment

Figure 9 is an example of a system archetype where the main themes also align with "limits to success" and "accidental adversaries" archetypes [13]. "Growth" represents achievement and performance for a sustainable food system through the IFV 2030; "Underinvestment" is the lack of transparent and effective knowledge transfer from the IFV 2030 to the key stakeholders within the supply chain. A report by Jackson et al. [19] demonstrated how existing policy can hinder the success of sustainable implementation. The accidental adversaries' archetype showed how unequal policy disseminated between key stakeholders limits the success of the IFV 2030 and also limits, or hinders, the successful partnership of stakeholders within the supply chain. This can lead to perceived unfairness [52] and lack of buy-in from all the actors, creating an "accidental adversaries (escalation)" archetype.

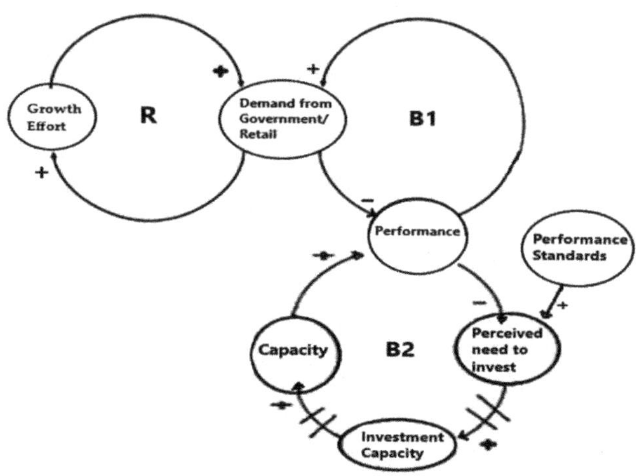

Figure 9. Archetype "Growth and underinvestment". With associated arrow (+) = increasing effect on variable; (−) = decreasing effect on variable.

3.3. Design Framework through Dynamic Systems

Systems archetypes identified in this study informed the creation of a design framework using the dynamics of a system (causal loop) diagram. Systems dynamics is a useful tool for interpreting the behaviour of a system. The causal loop diagrams below depict the current and future state of the Irish fresh produce food system in relation to the implementation of sustainability policy.

3.3.1. Conventional Agriculture Supply Chain

The literature researched for this study clearly outlined a current food system that is contributing to major global climate-related issues [31,32]. All parts of the food supply chain are contributors to land degradation issues (including biodiversity loss) and the release of anthropogenic GHG emissions (CO_2eq) into the atmosphere [8,9,35]. Studies by Pravalie [8] and Brouwer et al. [39] demonstrated how unsustainable land use is causing major annual economic losses through global crop losses owing to extreme weather events [9]. This signifies that all three pillars of sustainability are threatened by the global food system.

Figure 10 shows an example of a "Wicked System" involving a series of drivers creating positive and negative feedback loops within the system. The input dangle in this causal loop diagram is the current conventional supply chain. The main goal of the conventional fresh produce supply chain is to create economic growth and to supply food security for the short term. However, conventional agriculture is dependent on land use and contributes to a reduction in biodiversity. This has two causal effects: a reduced ability of the natural environment to absorb and sequester GHGs and a reduced capacity of living systems to support life and maintain resilience.

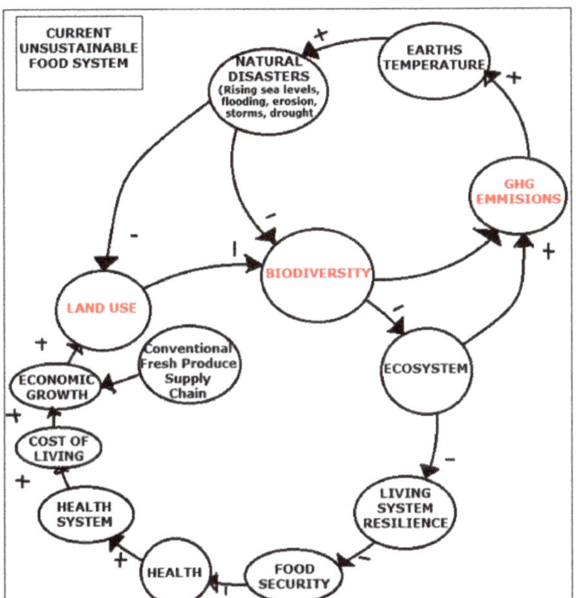

Figure 10. Current conventional food system pertaining to unsustainable economic, social, and environmental performance. With associated arrow (+) = increasing effect on variable; (−) = decreasing effect on variable.

Figure 10 illustrates an input dangle, titled "conventional fresh produce supply chain", where the elements of the supply chain are related to factor markets (Agri inputs) and primary production (farm) of fresh produce and including all inputs of downstream organisations to the retailer and post-consumption. The causal loop diagram demonstrates the consequences associated with the activities of the fresh produce supply chain on three major environmental variables (biodiversity, land use, and GHG emissions). As system resilience diminishes, the food system becomes less secure, driving the need for further land use change to produce food. As land becomes scarcer and environmental stability decreases, the production of healthy fresh produce decreases, which has negative consequences for human health and the cost of living [55,56]. This puts pressure on the economic pillar to increase its growth in this sector by creating more fresh produce using more land.

3.3.2. F2F and IFV 2030 LSC for Sustainability

Jackson et al. [19] discussed how EU policy initiatives are "key in transitioning to a sustainable food system". However, it was concluded that implementation was difficult due to several factors. Jackson et al. [19] described how political channels of communication are hindering implementation progress for a LSC event for a sustainable European food system. The report concluded that the F2F capability for LSC change was limited in detailing workable policy and will fail to reach 2030 targets.

As part of the EU's standards, Ireland is obliged to serve the F2F agenda through the 2030 IFV. Brouwer et al. [39] and Foucault's methodology both concluded that Irish political channels addressing climate and environmental issues are also hindering progress for LSC and are not meeting international targets. This type of communication implies that implementation of the F2F and IFV 2030 is hindered by the lack of transdisciplinary collaboration.

Figure 11 shows how a ripple effect creates a reinforcing loop by putting increasing pressure on the organisational economic and social pillars (e.g., supply chain instability). As food security declines and supply chains become more fragile, access to fresh food will be affected. Fresh food is critical to human health and well-being, and if it decreases, it will increase pressure on the health system. Added pressure on the health system will drive up the cost of living and require more funding from the economic pillar. In response, the economic pillar will be pressured to grow further to sustain the extra costs from the social pillar, thus requiring more of the environmental pillar, and a systems trap ensues.

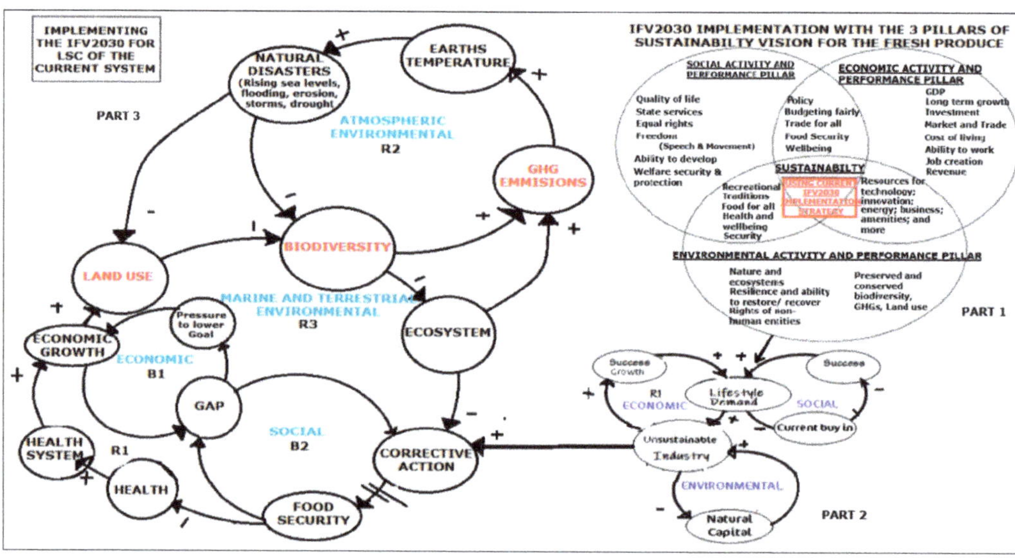

Figure 11. The food system causal loop diagram (Part 3) using current IFV 2030 implementation strategies (Part 1 and Part 2). With associated arrow (+) = increasing effect on variable; (−) = decreasing effect on variable.

Figure 11 shows the outcome of the implementation of the IFV 2030 strategy. The theoretical framework (systems thinking, Foucault's analysis of political discourse, and the survey) identified a lack of collaboration among key stakeholders as a major barrier to the implementation of a sustainable fresh produce food sector. Figure 11 demonstrates how the input dangle (Figure 11 (Part 1)) representing the IFV 2030 roadmap, leads to a "limits to success" archetype associated with the three pillars of the fresh food system (Figure 11 (Part 2)), with another archetype "Fixes that Fail" creating a ripple effect of social, economic, and environmental related issues. Figure 11 (Part 2) represents a dynamic system map of

Figure 11 (Part 2) in action for the implementation of the IFV 2030 roadmap. Figure 11 (Part 2) feeds into Figure 11 (Part 3), a causal loop diagram of the impact of the fresh produce industry and supply chains on societal social performance, economic performance, and effects on the environment through negative effects associated with three variables (depicted in red text) land use, biodiversity and GHG emissions. The marine and terrestrial variables of the causal loop diagram represent the ecosystems of land and water from the point of view of natural capital and the consequence of unsustainable action currently practised in the fresh produce supply chain to ensure its continued capacity to support it. According to Figure 11, using the current structure to implement the IFV 2030 roadmap to implement the LSC of the conventional fresh produce supply chain demonstrates a ripple effect. The ripple effect is evidence of a disconnect between critical stakeholders within the fresh produce supply chain and the unequal dissemination of policy across stakeholders in the sector. The cause of the ripple effect draws from archetypal behaviours brought on by the implementation of the IFV 2030 through repeated historical procedures, as demonstrated by Foucault's analysis (Table 1). If the wicked system continues to create ripple effects, it will contribute to additional pressure on the natural living system. Figure 11 demonstrates the criticality of collaboration between the variables and the level of structure to connect them. The level of collaboration is attributed to the implemented structure and mitigates through signalling unintended consequences unforeseen by the IFV 2030 of how a target variable changes.

3.3.3. A Sustainable Food System Map

Figure 12 outlines the main elements of a sustainable food system for the fresh produce supply chain centred on interdisciplinary co-creation through stakeholder engagement. The three pillars model described in Figure 12 demonstrates a resilient and robust food system accomplished through the collaborative implementation of the IFV 2030. The red text box at the core of the three pillars illustrates how transdisciplinary collaboration and co-creation intersect all pillars of a sustainable food system. Implementing the IFV 2030 through the concepts of Figure 12 implies a sustained anthropological system in balance with the environmental pillar [43].

Figure 12. Elements of a sustainable food system using the three pillars of sustainability with a top-down and bottom-up structure between relevant actors and supply chain stakeholders.

In the current food system, the three pillars of sustainability are imbalanced. Viewing each pillar through a system thinking lens of cause-and-effect highlights trade-offs active in each pillar. Three critical components are needed for the transition to a sustainable food system [32,46]:

I. Fresh produce economic value
II. Social importance
III. Environmental impact

The IFV 2030 views the commercial horticultural fresh produce sector as important for maintaining a healthy societal balance of economic, social, and environmental performance through actions and practices according to principles of the three pillars of sustainability (Figure 12). Using systems maps to view the three pillars of economic, social, and environmental sustainability demonstrates the relationships and interconnectedness of elements within the fresh produce supply chain. The anthropological pillars associated with socio and economic activities demonstrate the systems archetype "Limits to Growth" (Figure 7). Reinforcing feedback loops of economic growth and social need are linked to a balancing loop of environmental activity and performance. This reinforcing growth creates more success and increases performance, driving more growth. The balancing loop within the environmental pillar (e.g., limited resources) constrains the performance of the social and economic pillar (e.g., recession). The economic and social boom activity slows down in response to the limiting constraints.

Breaking the limiting factor regarding sustainability for the sector requires engagement and buy-in between all stakeholders in the sector [13,53]. The results from the survey demonstrated a perceived lack of co-creation, with less than 17% of respondents believing the process to be collaborative. This suggests that the process of policy development is missing key interdisciplinary contributions which could facilitate the transition required for IFV 2030. Thomas [18] demonstrated the complexity of introducing the missions of the IFV 2030, and Clark [21] postulates that the incorporation of interdisciplinary skills across the supply chain can inform policymakers on potential causes and consequences of barriers to implementation, ripple effects and unforeseen issues.

Figure 13 illustrates the three pillars of sustainability as a dynamic map, using the red box describing co-creation as an enabler for the IFV 2030 within the fresh produce sector. This figure demonstrates the importance of a combined effort across stakeholders invested in the product life cycle to create and apply appropriate interventions [53,57].

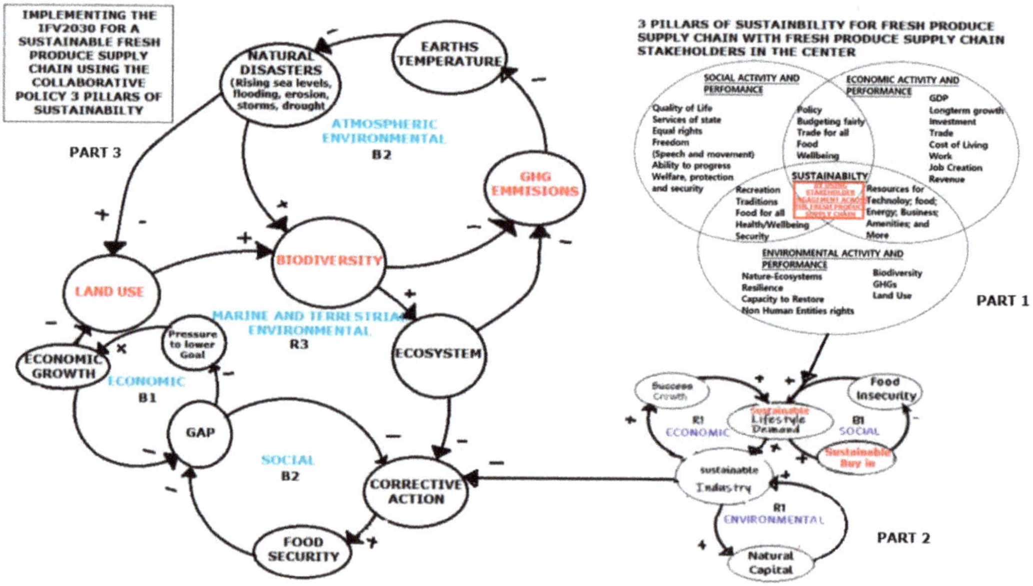

Figure 13. A concept map with the collaborative supply chain model at its centre.

3.4. The Design Framework Outcome

Figure 13 demonstrates the importance of adopting new political channels for writing and implementing sustainability policy to meet sustainability goals. Figure 12 depicts how the three pillars of sustainability conceptualise the transdisciplinary inputs of all stakeholders and respective actors within the fresh food supply chain. Ultimately, using a collaborative approach, implemented equally and with accountability across all stakeholders, will better support the delivery of LSC to achieve Ireland's national sustainability targets as intended by the IFV 2030 missions (Table 2).

Figure 13 demonstrates the concept of using a collaborative supply chain model based on the three pillars of sustainability to support the successful implementation of the IFV 2030. The red text box central to Figure 13 (Part 1) depicts the implementation of LSC for a sustainable supply chain using collaboration for co-creation and through organisation accountability for interconnected development to meet the intended environmental targets as outlined by the IFV 2030. Figure 13 (Part 2) depicts, through a dynamic map, the implementation of the IFV 2030 roadmap in practice. Figure 13 (Part 3) demonstrates the intended impact of meeting environmental targets. Using a collaborative and integrated implementation of LSC significantly reduces the amount of corrective action needed and mitigates any delay in progress towards sustainable fresh produce. Figure 13 (Part 3) implies positive consequences for the development of the commercial horticultural fresh produce industry as set out by the IFV 2030 [25]. All system components of Figure 13 (Part 3) benefit from sustainability targets implemented through collaborative channels as directed by the IFV 2030. As outlined by KPMG [25] and Story et al. [56], fresh produce consumption has increased benefits for the health system. Figure 13 (Part 3) demonstrates the importance of the horticultural fresh produce sector to maintain a healthy life of economic, social and environmental performance and actions the practices need to be incorporated into the fresh produce supply chains to ensure food is produced according to principles of the three pillars of sustainability.

4. Limitations

One of the main limitations of this study was the small number of participants. However, the findings of this position paper, supported by systems thinking frameworks, have given insights and actionable recommendations for LSC for the fresh produce supply chain, as described in the next section.

5. Conclusions and Recommendations

The aim of this study was to identify the potential of the IFV 2030, as directed by the EGD-F2F, as a roadmap for sustainable change for the Irish fresh produce sector, a sector that plays a significant role in the well-being of society. The literature reviewed for the theoretical framework identified major knowledge gaps and demonstrated a need for knowledge and expertise across multiple disciplines and organisations for a true long-term sustainability plan. This study identified non-collaborative and hierarchical direction as a knowledge gap associated with delaying sustainability progress in addressing climate-related issues such as rising GHG emissions, biodiversity loss and land degradation. The use of Foucault's genealogical methods highlighted a critical discourse where Ireland and EU communications are locked in repeating patterns of historical interactions. It was found that Ireland's inception into the EU was characterised by similar ad-hoc and wasteful interactions for large-scale change events, which is influencing current political discourse.

It was established that policy implementations are circulated through non-collaborative channels, which are missing the interdisciplinary connectedness of competent actors within the fresh produce supply chain. The data collected from stakeholders across the fresh produce sector, together with systems thinking methodologies, were used to diagnose barriers and unintended consequences for the implementation of the IFV 2030. This study found key issues with the implementation of the F2F and IFV 2030 commitments, identifying barriers and potential ripple effects.

Through the identification of system archetypes and illustrations using systems dynamics, the study showed that the EGD-F2F and IFV 2030 are not on target to reach their main objectives. The survey demonstrated that current stakeholder engagement, knowledge and understanding for a sustainable supply chain is fragmented. It is evident that the

EGD F2F and IFV 2030 implementation strategy does not follow an interdisciplinary implementation model, as described in the three pillars of the sustainability model. The current implementation strategy is still hierarchical among the stakeholders in the fresh produce supply chain. For critical large-scale change, the chain of information needs to be altered to allow critical feedback from all stakeholders and highlight unintended consequences through collaborative channels for policy evaluation.

This study highlighted the need for further research with a larger sample size of actors and stakeholders in the fresh produce chain to solve complex problems. Through knowledge sharing of everyday practices and through organisational learning and stakeholders' shared accountability of policy and sustainability standards, it is possible to remove unforeseen barriers pertaining to achieving critical environmental targets. It is critical that primary producers, retailers, and policymakers emphasise the value of the product, both in terms of the work performed in producing it in a sustainable manner and the value fresh produce has to society and the consumer. Restructuring to sustainable practice means reshaping and rethinking the value of how fresh produce is produced and marketed.

This study diagnosed real-world problems and provided potential solutions for the successful implementation of large-scale reform for environmental, economic, and social sustainability. Systems thinking highlighted how transdisciplinary collaboration and continuous stakeholder engagement can be performed to ensure Ireland's environmental targets are met. Drawing upon multiple stakeholder perspectives facilitates the successful delivery of new policies, innovative ideas, and solutions through cross-disciplinary participation, co-creation, and support.

Supplementary Materials: The following supporting information can be downloaded at: https://www.mdpi.com/article/10.3390/su16167237/s1, Table S1: Questions used in the protocol of the current study.

Author Contributions: Conceptualization D.K.; methodology, D.K. and F.B.; software, D.K., M.D. and F.B.; validation, D.K., F.B. and M.D.; formal analysis, D.K. and F.B.; investigation, D.K.; resources, D.K.; data curation, D.K.; writing—original draft preparation, D.K.; writing—review and editing, F.B.; visualisation, D.K.; supervision, F.B.; project administration, D.K. and F.B. All authors have read and agreed to the published version of the manuscript.

Funding: This research received no external funding.

Institutional Review Board Statement: The study was conducted in accordance with the Declaration of Helsinki and approved by the Research Ethics Committee of the Department of Environmental Sciences of Atlantic Technological University, Sligo (FSS202310 and 21 March 2023).

Informed Consent Statement: Written informed consent has been obtained from the patient(s) to publish this paper.

Data Availability Statement: Data are available upon request.

Acknowledgments: The authors would like to acknowledge both the Food Drink Ireland Skillnet and Atlantic Technological University (ATU) for supporting this research within the MSc in Sustainable Food Systems.

Conflicts of Interest: The first author declares he works in the soft fruit industry. The remaining authors declare that the research was conducted in the absence of any commercial or financial relationships that could be construed as a potential conflict of interest.

References

1. Mintz, S.W. *Tasting Food, Tasting Freedom: Excursions into Eating, Culture, and the Past*; Beacon Press: Boston, MA, USA, 1996; ISBN 0-8070-4628-0.
2. Tauger, M.B. Introduction: The Place of Agriculture and Farmers in World History. In *Agriculture in World History*; Routledge: London, UK, 2020. Available online: https://www.perlego.com/book/1608612/agriculture-in-world-history-pdf (accessed on 19 June 2023).

3. Dainese, M.; Martin, E.A.; Aizen, M.A.; Albrecht, M.; Bartomeus, I.; Bommarco, R.; Carvalheiro, L.G.; Chaplin-Kramer, R.; Gagic, V.; Garibaldi, L.A.; et al. A Global Synthesis Reveals Biodiversity-Mediated Benefits for Crop Production. *Sci. Adv.* **2019**, *5*, eaax0121. [CrossRef]
4. FAO. *Agricultural Cooperatives, Responsible Sourcing and Risk-Based Due Diligence*; FAO: Rome, Italy, 2022.
5. Anon European Commission. *Communication from the Commission to Farm to Fork Strategy for a Fair, Healthy and Environmentally Friendly Food System*; The European Parliament, The European Council, The Council, The European Economic and Social Committee and The Committee of the Regions: Brussels, Belgium, 2020. Available online: https://eur-lex.europa.eu/legal-content/EN/TXT/?uri=CELEX:52020DC0381 (accessed on 17 June 2024).
6. FAO: Sustainable Food and Agriculture. Land Use in Agriculture by the Numbers. 7 May 2020. Food and Agriculture Organization of the United Nations (2020). Available online: https://www.fao.org/sustainability/news/detail/en/c/1274219/ (accessed on 17 June 2024).
7. Attenborough, D. *A Life on Our Planet: My Witness Statement and a Vision for the Future*; Random House: New York, NY, USA, 2022; ISBN 1-4735-8488-4.
8. Prăvălie, R. Exploring the Multiple Land Degradation Pathways across the Planet. *Earth-Sci. Rev.* **2021**, *220*, 103689. [CrossRef]
9. Thiaw, I. *Land in Numbers 2019: Risks and Opportunities 2019*; UNCCD: Bonn, Germany, 2019.
10. Voulvoulis, N.; Giakoumis, T.; Hunt, C.; Kioupi, V.; Petrou, N.; Souliotis, I.; Vaghela, C. Systems Thinking as a Paradigm Shift for Sustainability Transformation. *Glob. Environ. Chang.* **2022**, *75*, 102544. [CrossRef]
11. Attenborough, D. We Need Immediate Action to Stop Extinction Crisis. *BBC News*, 2020.
12. Ericksen, P.J. Conceptualizing Food Systems for Global Environmental Change Research. *Glob. Environ. Chang.* **2008**, *18*, 234–245. [CrossRef]
13. Meadows, D.H. *Thinking in Systems: A Primer*; Chelsea Green Publishing: Chelsea, VT, USA, 2008; ISBN 1-60358-055-7.
14. Sherwood, D. *Seeing the Forest for the Trees: A Manager's Guide to Applying Systems Thinking*; Nicholas Brealey International: London, UK, 2011; ISBN 1-85788-497-3.
15. Pandit, R.; Scholes, R.; Montanarella, L.; Brainich, A.; Barger, N.; ten Brink, B.; Cantele, M.; Erasmus, B.; Fisher, J.; Gardner, T. *Summary for Policymakers of the Assessment Report on Land Degradation and Restoration of the Intergovernmental Science-Policy Platform on Biodiversity and Ecosystem Services*; USDA: Washington, DC, USA, 2018.
16. Arnold, T. *Research and Innovation for Sustainable Food Systems: Delivering on the Ambition of Food Vision 2030*; Report of the High-Level EU Committee on Food Systems Science Tom Arnold Chair; High Level EU Committee on Food Systems Science: Brussels, Belgium, 2022.
17. Department of Agriculture Food and the Marine (DAFM). *DAFM Food Vision 2030—A World Leader in Sustainable Food Systems*; Department of Agriculture, Food and the Marine: Dublin, Ireland, 2021. Available online: https://www.gov.ie/en/publication/c73a3-food-vision-2030-a-world-leader-in-sustainable-food-systems/ (accessed on 17 June 2024).
18. Thomas, I. The Irish Agri-Food Sector: Recent Developments. *Eur. Food Feed Law Rev.* **2021**, *16*, 505.
19. Jackson, P.; Candel, J.; Davies, A.; de Vries, H.; Derani, C.; Dragović-Uzelac, V.; Håkon Hoel, A.; Holm, L.; Morone, P.; Penker, M. *A Sustainable Food System for the European Union*; Elsevier: Amsterdam, The Netherlands, 2020.
20. CCAC. *CCAC Climate Change Advisory Council's Annual Review 2023*; Climate Change Advisory Council: Dublin, Ireland, 2023.
21. Clark, C.M.A. *Measuring Progress: Economy, Society and Environment in Ireland: Sustainable Progress Index 2022*; Social Justice Ireland: Dublin, Ireland, 2022.
22. Environmental Protection Agency. *EPA Ireland's Provisional Greenhouse Gas Emissions Report 2023*; Environmental Protection Agency: Washington, DC, USA, 2023.
23. Social Justice Ireland. *SJI Measuring Progress: Sustainable Progress Index 2024*; Social Justice Ireland: Dublin, Ireland, 2024.
24. Teagasc Innovation Drivers in Horticulture. 2023. Available online: https://www.teagasc.ie/news--events/daily/horticulture/innovation-drivers-in-horticulture.php (accessed on 1 July 2024).
25. KPMG. *Opportunities for the Irish Horticulture Sector Prepared for the Department of Agriculture, Food and the Marine (DAFM)*; KPMG: Amstelveen, The Netherlands, 2022.
26. Teagasc. *Unearthing the Value of Irish Fruit and Vegetables*; Teagasc: Dublin, Ireland, 2021.
27. Redman, C.L. Should Sustainability and Resilience Be Combined or Remain Distinct Pursuits? *Ecol. Soc.* **2014**, *19*, 37. [CrossRef]
28. Pereira, P.; Zhao, W.; Symochko, L.; Inacio, M.; Bogunovic, I.; Barcelo, D. The Russian-Ukrainian Armed Conflict Will Push Back the Sustainable Development Goals. *Geogr. Sustain.* **2022**, *3*, 277–287. [CrossRef]
29. Stroh, D.P. *Systems Thinking for Social Change: A Practical Guide to Solving Complex Problems, Avoiding Unintended Consequences, and Achieving Lasting Results*; Chelsea Green Publishing: Chelsea, VT, USA, 2015; ISBN 1-60358-581-8.
30. Rossi, R. EPRS Ideas Paper Thinking about Future EU Policy EPRS. European Parliamentary Research Service. 2020. Available online: https://www.europarl.europa.eu/RegData/etudes/BRIE/2020/652058/EPRS_BRI(2020)652058_EN.pdf (accessed on 17 June 2023).
31. El Bilali, H. Transition Heuristic Frameworks in Research on Agro-Food Sustainability Transitions. *Environ. Dev. Sustain.* **2020**, *22*, 1693–1728. [CrossRef]
32. Siddh, M.M.; Soni, G.; Jain, R.; Sharma, M.K.; Yadav, V. Agri-Fresh Food Supply Chain Quality (AFSCQ): A Literature Review. *Ind. Manag. Data Syst.* **2017**, *117*, 2015–2044. [CrossRef]

33. Hornsey, M.J.; Chapman, C.M.; Oelrichs, D.M. Ripple Effects: Can Information about the Collective Impact of Individual Actions Boost Perceived Efficacy about Climate Change? *J. Exp. Soc. Psychol.* **2021**, *97*, 104217. [CrossRef]
34. Rittel, H.W.; Webber, M.M. *Dilemmas in a General Theory of Planning*; IGP Stuttgart: Dusseldorf, Germany, 1977.
35. Stout, J. Human Nature: Opening the Front Gate to Biodiversity. *Hum. Nat.* **2023**.
36. Ferreira-Neto, J. Michel Foucault and Qualitative Research in Human and Social Sciences. *Forum Qual. Sozialforschung* **2018**, *19*, 1–18. [CrossRef]
37. Laffan, B. *Organising for a Changing Europe: Irish Central Government and the European Union*; Policy Institute Trinity College Dublin: Dublin, Ireland, 2001; Volume 7.
38. Matthews, A. Climate Mainstreaming the CAP in the EU Budget: Fact or Fiction. *Cap Reform*, 2020.
39. Brouwer, H.; Guijt, W.J.; Kelly, S.; Garcia-Campos, P. *Ireland's Journey towards Sustainable Food Systems. The Processes and Practices That Made a Difference*; FAO: Rome, Italy, 2021. [CrossRef]
40. Environmental Protection Agency (EPA). *EPA Data Shows Ireland's 2021 Greenhouse Gas Emissions above Pre-COVID Levels*; Environmental Protection Agency: Dublin, Ireland, 2022.
41. Adshead, M. EU Cohesion Policy and Multi-Level Governance Outcomes in Ireland: How Sustainable Is Europeanization? *Eur. Urban Reg. Stud.* **2014**, *21*, 416–431. [CrossRef]
42. Department of Agriculture Food and the Marine (DAFM). *Anon Executive Summary: Vision 2030—A World Leader in Sustainable Food Systems Vision*; Department of Agriculture, Food and the Marine: Dublin, Ireland, 2021. Available online: https://www.gov.ie/pdf/?file=https://assets.gov.ie/179696/6c6b405e-7c06-4f23-82c0-9edaf7d70a8a.pdf#page=null (accessed on 17 June 2024).
43. Purvis, B.; Mao, Y.; Robinson, D. Three Pillars of Sustainability: In Search of Conceptual Origins. *Sustain. Sci.* **2019**, *14*, 681–695. [CrossRef]
44. Ademi, B.; Sætre, A.S.; Klungseth, N.J. Advancing the Understanding of Sustainable Business Models Through Organizational Learning. *Bus. Strategy Environ.* **2024**. [CrossRef]
45. Fortis, Z.; Maon, F.; Frooman, J.; Reiner, G. Unknown Knowns and Known Unknowns: Framing the Role of Organizational Learning in Corporate Social Responsibility Development. *Int. J. Manag. Rev.* **2018**, *20*, 277–300. [CrossRef]
46. Mondini, G. Sustainability Assessment: From Brundtland Report to Sustainable Development Goals. *Valori Valutazioni* **2019**. Available online: https://siev.org/wp-content/uploads/2020/02/23_15-_-MONDINI_eng.pdf (accessed on 17 June 2024).
47. Brundtlant, C. Report of the World Commission on Environment and Development: Our Common Future. UN 20-03-1987. Available online: https://www.are.admin.ch/are/en/home/media/publications/sustainable-development/brundtland-report.html (accessed on 16 May 2024).
48. Richmond, B. System Dynamics/Systems Thinking: Let's Just Get on with It. *Syst. Dyn. Rev.* **1994**, *10*, 135–157. [CrossRef]
49. Goyal, C.; Jambur, M.A. Employee retention for sustainable business and development: Strategies and best practices. In *Sustainable Economic and Management Practices Challenges and Future Prospects Volume 1*; Anand, N., Sharma, S., Yadav, S., Eds.; Empyrea Publishing House: Ghaziabad, India, 2023; pp. 76–83. ISBN 978-93-93810-98-4. Available online: https://www.empyrealpublishinghouse.com/pdf/sustainable-economic-and-management-practices-challenges-and-future-prospects-vol-1.pdf#page=89 (accessed on 17 June 2024).
50. Petryk, I. Restructuring of Business Processes for Sustainability: Revealing the Potential of Reengineering and Kaizen. *Law Bus. Sustain. Her.* **2021**, *1*, 33–42. [CrossRef]
51. Forbes Employee Retention: A Worthwhile Long-Term Investment. Sean Manning Forbes Council Member. Forbes Business Council Post 2023. Available online: https://www.forbes.com/sites/forbesbusinesscouncil/2023/10/18/employee-retention-a-worthwhile-long-term-investment/ (accessed on 17 June 2024).
52. Skippari, M.; Laukkanen, M.; Salo, J. Cognitive Barriers to Collaborative Innovation Generation in Supply Chain Relationships. *Ind. Mark. Manag.* **2017**, *62*, 108–117. [CrossRef]
53. Moallemi, E.A.; Malekpour, S.; Hadjikakou, M.; Raven, R.; Szetey, K.; Ningrum, D.; Dhiaulhaq, A.; Bryan, B.A. Achieving the Sustainable Development Goals Requires Transdisciplinary Innovation at the Local Scale. *One Earth* **2020**, *3*, 300–313. [CrossRef]
54. Quill, P.; Teahon, P. Structural Economic Change in Ireland 1957-2006: Statistics, Context and Analysis. *J. Stat. Soc. Inq. Soc. Irel.* **2010**, *39*, 110–143.
55. Tarasuk, V.; Cheng, J.; de Oliveira, C.; Dachner, N.; Gundersen, C.; Kurdyak, P. Association between Household Food Insecurity and Annual Health Care Costs. *Can. Med. Assoc. J.* **2015**, *187*, E429. [CrossRef]
56. Story, M.; Kaphingst, K.M.; Robinson-O'Brien, R.; Glanz, K. Creating Healthy Food and Eating Environments: Policy and Environmental Approaches. *Annu. Rev. Public Health* **2008**, *29*, 253–272. [CrossRef]
57. Lynch, J.; Donnellan, T.; Finn, J.A.; Dillon, E.; Ryan, M. Potential Development of Irish Agricultural Sustainability Indicators for Current and Future Policy Evaluation Needs. *J. Environ. Manag.* **2019**, *230*, 434–445. [CrossRef]

sustainability

MDPI

Article

Enhancing the Sustainability of Food Supply Chains: Insights from Inspectors and Official Controls in Greece

Christos Roukos [1], Dimitrios Kafetzopoulos [2], Alexandra Pavloudi [1], Fotios Chatzitheodoridis [3] and Achilleas Kontogeorgos [1,*]

1 Department of Agriculture, International Hellenic University, 57001 Thessaloniki, Greece; roukxris@gmail.com (C.R.)
2 School of Business Administration, University of Macedonia, 54636 Thessaloniki, Greece
3 Laboratory of Sustainable Urban and Rural Development, Department of Management Science and Technology, University of Western Macedonia, 50100 Kozani, Greece; fxtheodoridis@uowm.gr
* Correspondence: akontoge@ihu.gr

Abstract

Food fraud represents a growing global challenge with significant implications for public health, market integrity, sustainability, and consumer trust. Beyond economic losses, fraudulent practices undermine the environmental and social sustainability of food systems by distorting markets, misusing natural resources, and weakening incentives for authentic and responsible production. Despite the establishment of harmonized frameworks of the European Union for official controls, the increasing complexity of food supply chains has exposed persistent gaps in fraud detection, particularly for high-value products such as those with PDO (Protected Designation of Origin) and PGI (Protected Geographical Indication) Certification. This study investigates the perceptions, attitudes, and experiences of frontline inspectors in Greece to assess current challenges and opportunities for strengthening official food fraud controls. Data were collected through a structured questionnaire, validated by experts and administered nationwide, involving 122 participants representing all major national food inspection authorities. Statistical analysis revealed significant institutional differences in perceptions of fraud prevalence, with mislabeling of origin, misleading organic claims, ingredient substitution, and documentation irregularities identified as the most common fraudulent practices. Olive oil, honey, meat, and dairy emerged as the most vulnerable product categories. Inspectors reported relying primarily on consumer complaints and institutional databases as key tools for identifying fraud risks. Food fraud was perceived to contribute strongly to losses in consumer trust in food safety and product authenticity, as well as to the erosion of sustainable production models that depend on transparency, fair competition, and responsible resource use. Overall, the findings highlight detection gaps, uneven resources across authorities, and the need for improved coordination and capacity-building to support more efficient, transparent, and sustainability-oriented food fraud control in Greece.

Keywords: food fraud; inspectors' perceptions; Greece; PDO; PGI

1. Introduction

Food fraud has emerged as one of the major global issues with profound impact on public health, market integrity, and consumer trust in the food system [1]. Recent studies on the economic impact of food fraud within the global food supply chain estimate annual costs ranging from $10 billion to $49 billion [2] and potentially between $10 billion and $65 billion [3]. These figures correspond to approximately 5–7% of global food trade [4].

Food fraud incidents, such as food adulteration and mislabeling, undermine the authenticity and safety of agri-food products throughout the supply chain [5]. These incidents have highlighted the significant gaps in traditional food control mechanisms, prompting CAs worldwide to enhance preventive strategies and surveillance systems [6,7].

Beyond regulatory and enforcement concerns, food fraud is increasingly recognized as a systemic threat to the sustainability of food supply chains as it disrupts fair market practices, weakens consumer confidence, and may enable environmentally harmful production practices [8].

In this context, food fraud is increasingly conceptualized not only as a compliance or enforcement issue, but also as a governance challenge with direct implications for the economic, social, and environmental dimensions of sustainability [9,10]. The increasing complexity and globalization of food supply chains have rendered conventional inspection methods insufficient for the timely and effective detection of fraudulent practices [11,12].

In response to these challenges, digital technologies, particularly artificial intelligence (AI), are increasingly employed to enhance food fraud detection and prevention. Beyond established applications of AI in food fraud detection, such as machine learning or big data analytics, AI can be utilized through a range of complementary approaches including predictive analytics, anomaly detection, the use of blockchain technology to ensure transparent records of product origin and movement, and automated analysis of large amounts of datasets derived from laboratory tests, commercial transactions, and customer complaints [1,13]. Moreover, AI-enabled controls contribute to sustainable food safety and authenticity by enhancing the transparency and efficiency of inspections, reducing information asymmetries and by strengthening the capacity of the food supply chains to recover from fraud-related disruptions [9,14,15].

In practice, the integration of AI into public control infrastructures remains limited, particularly within national authorities across the European Union. In Greece, the food control system operates through a multi-tiered governance structure involving central CAs, regional food safety units, and official laboratories. While the legislative and institutional framework is formally aligned with EU mandates, persistent resource availability, inspector training, and intergraded data platforms crucially affect the system's capacity to detect and respond to food fraud consistently [16–18]. These systemic limitations not only reduce the effectiveness of fraud prevention but also weaken the sustainability performance of the food supply chain by undermining governance coherence, limiting traceability, and eroding institutional trust [10,15].

These characteristics render the Greek case particularly suitable for examining how institutional design and inspectors' perceptions interact within sustainability-oriented food fraud control systems.

Despite the extended literature on food fraud and digitalization, limited attention has been paid to inspectors' perceptions as a critical governance layer capable of bridging the gap between regulatory framework, operational control practices, and sustainability outcomes. Understanding inspectors' perceptions will assist in identifying institutional weaknesses and provide a basis for developing a more cohesive and sustainable control strategy.

Accordingly, this study addresses the following research questions:

RQ1: How do official food inspectors perceive the prevalence and dominant forms of food fraud within the Greek food supply chain?

RQ2: Which product categories and fraud typologies are perceived as most vulnerable?

https://doi.org/10.3390/su18021101

RQ3: Which existing control tools are perceived as most effective for the detection of food fraud?

RQ4: How do inspectors perceive the potential role and institutional readiness for AI-enabled tools in supporting sustainable food supply chain governance?

The study adopts an exploratory, perception-based approach and does not seek to estimate objective fraud prevalence or establish causal relationships. Instead, it aims to provide governance-relevant empirical insights that can inform more coherent and sustainable food fraud control strategies.

2. Literature Review

2.1. Food Fraud as a Governance and Sustainability Challenge

The literature on food fraud has gradually moved from a narrow focus on food safety incidents, economic deception, and consumer protection to a much broader sustainability-oriented perspective [19,20]. Recent research on food fraud has focused on issues related to the governance of food supply chains, emphasizing their implications for environmental sustainability, social equity, market integrity, and consumer trust [1,8,21]. Thus, food fraud is increasingly viewed as the outcome of interactions between the structural characteristics of supply chains and regulatory systems, thereby affecting long-term sustainability outcomes rather than opposed to being viewed as discrete acts of non-compliance [17,22].

A comprehensive strategy to combat food fraud is essential not only to detect fraudulent activities by identifying and prosecuting fraudsters, but also to focus on preventive measures. The theory of situational crime prevention seeks to minimize opportunities and increase risks to deter potential offenders [12]. Traditionally, food policy has focused primarily on protecting public health. However, there is now a growing concern that the current risk analysis framework for food safety should be revised to provide evidence and guidance for the development of policies that effectively minimize incidents of food fraud [23]. Within this evolving policy landscape, the ability of food control systems to safeguard authenticity, promote transparency, and ensure accountability across all nodes of the supply chain is now closely linked to economic, social, and environmental sustainability objectives [14,20].

Studies have shown that products with Protected Designation of Origin (PDO) and Protected Geographical Indication (PGI) are particularly vulnerable to fraud due to their premium market value and their intrinsic association with specific regional characteristics [16,20,24], and fraud incidents significantly reduce consumer trust in these premium and certified products [22,25–27]. The integrity of these products is also central to rural economic sustainability, cultural heritage preservation, and environmentally differentiated production systems, making their protection a sustainability priority [20]. This erosion of trust destabilizes markets for sustainable products, weakens incentives for compliance, and threatens rural development models that rely on quality differentiation and territorial identity [28,29]. Consequently, food fraud is increasingly viewed as a structural sustainability risk, rather than a series of isolated illegal acts [1,30,31].

Taken together, food fraud is increasingly considered a structural threat to the sustainability of food supply chains, extending beyond immediate safety or economic concerns. By undermining consumer trust, distorting fair competition, and weakening incentives for certified and transparent production systems, food fraud challenges the environmental, social, and governance dimensions of sustainability [32–35]. However, while existing studies clearly establish these systemic effects, they primarily address food fraud at the level of markets, products, or consumers, offering limited insight into how sustainability risks are perceived and managed within official food control systems. This highlights the need for

https://doi.org/10.3390/su18021101

empirical research that links sustainability-oriented food fraud risks with the perspectives, capacities, and practices of regulatory authorities.

2.2. *Official Food Controls and Inspectors' Role in Fraud Detection*

Official food control systems are essential government mechanisms through which regulatory requirements related to food safety, integrity, and sustainability are translated into practice [33–35]. Official food controls function not only as compliance checks, but also as multi-level regulatory systems that rely on legal frameworks, information-sharing infrastructures, and inter-institutional cooperation [36,37]. Within this governance perspective, the effectiveness of food fraud prevention depends not only on formal regulations and technological tools, but also on the way control systems are designed, coordinated, and implemented across complex agri-food supply chains [37,38].

Regulation (EU) 2017/625 on Official Controls and Regulation (EU) 2019/1715 (IMSOC), together with their information systems and cooperation networks, such as the EU Food Fraud Network, provide the legal backbone for enforcing EU agri-food law, including the prevention and detection of food fraud [34,35]. This regulatory framework requires authorities to detect intentional deception for economic gain, extends official controls across the entire food chain, and strengthens cooperation among EU Member States through systems such as the EU Food Fraud Network (FFN), enabling information exchange and coordinated action against fraudulent practices [9,34,39].

The system of official controls is crucial for the sustainability of food systems, as it ensures compliance, transparency, and consumer protection across all stages of the supply chain [34]. In the context of Regulation (EU) No 2017/625, official controls enhance the ability of CAs to monitor the compliance of food businesses, collect reliable data, and support fair market practices [34,39]. The effective implementation of the Regulation provides a framework for a multi-level governance system that strengthens consumer confidence, combats fraudulent activities, and contributes to the development of a transparent food supply chain. Thus, official controls serve not only as a means of enforcement, but also as a cornerstone of sustainable agri-food chain governance, particularly in light of the significant sustainability challenges currently observed at the global level [33–35,39,40].

The effectiveness of official controls therefore depends not only on regulatory design, but also on institutional capacity, coordination mechanisms, and the operational practices of frontline inspectors. A critical challenge within the EU is the absence of a unified legal definition of food fraud, which creates inconsistencies in enforcement across member states [32]. The EU Food Fraud Network relies on operational criteria to distinguish fraud cases rather than a statutory definition, empowering but not obliging Member States to collaborate. The Rapid Alert System for Food and Feed (RASFF) serves as a key mechanism for reporting and analyzing food fraud incidents across the EU. However, its effectiveness is limited by its primary design focus on food safety rather than fraud detection [34].

Therefore, official food controls constitute a central governance mechanism for mitigating food fraud risks and supporting the sustainability of food supply chain [37,40]. Risk-based inspections, laboratory analyses, traceability requirements, and information-sharing systems are designed to reduce information asymmetries and enhance accountability across the food supply chain actors [31,32,36,39–42].

Nevertheless, empirical studies highlight significant variations in the effectiveness of official controls across authorities, often linked to differences in institutional capacity, inspector training, resource availability, and coordination mechanisms [9,34–36,38]. Fragmented governance structures and uneven enforcement practices tend to create regulatory blind spots that increase vulnerability to fraud, particularly in complex, multi-tiered food supply chains [13,40,43].

https://doi.org/10.3390/su18021101

Current research into governance-oriented practices emphasizes the role of inspectors' perceptions and their use of professional judgment in determining how enforcement outcomes are achieved. Inspectors act as "street-level bureaucrats" who assess risks and prioritize violations based upon their own interpretations of regulations and therefore play a significant role in shaping the practical effectiveness of official control systems [44–46].

Taken together, the literature positions official food controls as a central component of food fraud governance, highlighting their role in mitigating information asymmetries, coordinating enforcement actions, and supporting the sustainability of food supply chains. At the same time, empirical evidence reveals substantial variation in control effectiveness across authorities, shaped by institutional capacity, resource availability, coordination mechanisms, and inspector training [1,10,34,40].

Importantly, the above-mentioned governance-oriented research underscores that inspectors' perceptions and professional judgment play a decisive role in translating regulatory frameworks into enforcement outcomes. Despite this recognition, inspectors' perspectives remain comparatively underexplored in food fraud research, which has largely focused on legal instruments, technological solutions, or firm-level behavior. This research gap highlights the need for empirical investigation into how frontline enforcement actors perceive and enact official controls within sustainability-oriented governance systems.

2.3. Digitalization and Artificial Intelligence in Food Fraud Prevention

The literature on food fraud prevention increasingly highlights digitalization and artificial intelligence as key enablers of risk-based, data-driven governance in food supply chains. Rather than being viewed as stand-alone technical solutions, digital tools and AI-based applications are discussed within broader debates on transparency, traceability, and institutional capacity to manage fraud risks [35,36,47]. Accordingly, the potential contribution of digitalization to food fraud prevention depends not only on technological performance, but also on governance arrangements, organizational readiness, and the effective integration of digital tools into existing official control systems [10,19,27,39,48].

Digitalization has been widely promoted as a means to enhance transparency, traceability, and resilience in food supply chains. Technologies such as blockchain, integrated databases, and advanced data analytics have demonstrated significant potential to support food fraud detection, early warning systems, and targeted inspections [14,29,39,48].

AI-based applications, including machine learning techniques and anomaly detection methods, have shown promising results in experimental and pilot-level studies, particularly when combined with large-scale datasets derived from trade flows, laboratory results, and alert systems [49–51]. However, the majority of empirical evidence remains concentrated on technical feasibility rather than on institutional adoption within public authorities.

Previous studies indicate that technological solutions alone are insufficient to address food fraud risks without accompanying institutional reforms, capacity building, and ethical governance frameworks [41,50,52,53]. In official controls conducted by public authorities, the effectiveness of AI depends on inspector training, data quality, system interoperability, and trust in algorithmic decision-support systems [51,54–56]. Consequently, understanding the inspectors' perceptions of AI is critical for assessing its realistic contribution to sustainable food supply chain governance.

Overall, the reviewed literature indicates that digitalization and artificial intelligence are increasingly discussed as potential tools for supporting food fraud prevention through enhanced data integration, early warning systems, and more targeted inspection approaches. At the same time, existing studies emphasize important limitations on routine institutional adoption within public authorities. In the context of official food controls, research highlights that the use and perceived usefulness of AI-based tools depend on

https://doi.org/10.3390/su18021101

factors such as inspector training, data quality, system interoperability, and trust in algorithmic decision-support systems. Despite growing attention to these governance-related conditions, empirical insights into inspectors' perceptions of digitalization and AI remain limited, underscoring the need for further empirical investigation in this area.

2.4. Positioning and Contribution of the Present Study

Based on the above-mentioned literature, the present study is positioned as an exploratory, governance-oriented investigation focusing on inspectors' perceptions within official food control systems. The study adopts an institutional governance perspective that emphasizes institutional capacity, coordination mechanisms, and information asymmetries as key determinants of sustainability outcomes, rather than advancing a specific causal model or testing hypotheses derived from a single theoretical framework.

By empirically capturing inspectors' views on food fraud and its current detection tools, this research contributes novel insights to national and international debates on food fraud control. It complements existing firm- and technology-focused studies by highlighting the human and institutional dimensions that condition the effectiveness of regulatory interventions in complex food supply chains.

3. Materials and Methods

3.1. Research Design

The present study adopts a cross-sectional survey design to explore food inspectors' perceptions regarding food fraud, current detection methods, and digital tools for food fraud detection within the Greek official food control system. Data were collected through a structured questionnaire that was distributed to food inspectors employed by the CAs throughout the country.

The study is explicitly positioned as exploratory and descriptive, rather than confirmatory or explanatory. Its primary objective is not to test cause-and-effect relationships or to measure the objective incidence of food fraud, but to identify patterns in perception, institutional variations, and governance-relevant insights derived from frontline inspectors. Such an approach is considered appropriate in contexts where empirical evidence remains limited and where professional judgment plays a central role in regulatory effectiveness [57,58].

Given the limited availability of public datasets on food fraud detection practices within public authorities, and the absence of harmonized indicators across institutions, an exploratory survey approach was considered the most appropriate means to address the research objectives and research questions of the study. This methodological choice aligns with previous studies examining inspectors' perceptions, governance efficiency, and control system performance in relation to food safety and food fraud issues, which have likewise employed survey-based methodology [40,59–62].

3.2. Sampling Strategy

The target population consisted of official food inspectors employed by the CAs responsible for official food controls in Greece, in accordance with Regulation (EU) No 2017/625. These authorities include: (i) the Ministry of Rural Development and Food (MRDF), (ii) the Regional Agricultural Directorates (DAOK), (iii) the Hellenic Food Authority (EFET), and (iv) ELGO–DIMITRA, the designated authority for PDO/PGI controls.

A non-probability purposive sampling strategy, complemented by institutional snowball dissemination, was employed. This approach was selected due to the absence of a publicly accessible sampling frame of inspectors and the institutional sensitivity of the target population. Similar sampling strategies are commonly applied in expert-based

https://doi.org/10.3390/su18021101

research, where access constraints and professional specialization limit the feasibility of random sampling [63,64].

Participation criteria included: (a) active involvement in official food controls, (b) employment within a CA during the survey period, and (c) professional experience related to inspection, auditing, or managerial oversight of food controls. No exclusion criteria were applied, beyond non-involvement in official control activities.

3.3. Questionnaire Development

The questionnaire was based on more than 15 years of expertise in the implementation of EU and national legislation on official food controls. It was developed based on a comprehensive review of the relevant literature [49,54,59,65,66].

Structured into four sections, the questionnaire covered: (1) socio-demographic characteristics and occupational roles of respondents; (2) current food fraud detection practices and the effectiveness of official control systems; (3) a general evaluation of AI-based tools to strengthen official food controls; and (4) perceptions and attitudes towards the adoption of AI technologies in official food control activities.

The selection of food fraud categories and vulnerable product groups was theory-driven, drawing on established food fraud taxonomies and EU fraud reports [66,67]. The list of food fraud incidents included in the questionnaire was predefined by the authors based on an extensive review of the literature on food fraud typologies. The selected categories are representative of common fraudulent practices within official food control systems, including mislabeling, substitution, fraudulent claims, documentation irregularities, and other economically motivated practices, as identified in previous studies. The majority of attitudinal questions were measured using Likert-type scales, while selected items employed ranking formats to capture the perceived relative importance of each category.

Attitudinal and perceptual items were measured using a five-point Likert scale, ranging from 1 (strongly disagree/never) to 5 (strongly agree/always), consistent with established methodological practices. The choice of a five-point scale was guided by empirical evidence indicating that scales with five response categories provide an optimal balance between cognitive load, response reliability, and measurement validity in professional and expert surveys [68–70].

The initial version of the questionnaire was reviewed by 10 experts specializing in official food control from the Competent Food Control Authorities. Experts were selected through purposive sampling, and subsequently, other experts were recruited using snowball sampling techniques [58,63,71]. For the purposes of this study, experts were defined as professionals actively managing official controls at national, regional, or local levels, according to Regulation (EU) No 2017/625.

Experts were invited to provide feedback on the content, structure, and clarity of the questionnaire. They were also asked to provide suggestions for revisions and additions where appropriate. Based on their input, the questionnaire was revised and subsequently pilot-tested with the same group of experts, who voluntarily completed the survey using the SurveyMonkey® platform, an online tool designed for administering and collecting self-reported survey data.

3.4. Data Collection

Data were collected using the computer-assisted web interviewing (CAWI) method via the SurveyMonkey® platform. The CAWI approach was selected due to its suitability for the geographically dispersed nature of the target population, its efficiency, and its demonstrated suitability for use in food governance and sustainability research [72–75].

https://doi.org/10.3390/su18021101

The final version of the questionnaire was hosted on the SurveyMonkey® platform, and the survey link was emailed to Competent Food Control Authorities nationwide. These authorities were instructed to further disseminate the survey to their respective food control auditors.

Data were collected from November 2024 to January 2025. Although online data collection may introduce sampling bias, this approach aligns with contemporary practices reported in the literature, where convenience sampling is frequently employed [61,74].

Participation was entirely voluntary. Prior to completing the survey, participants were informed about the study's objectives and assured that their responses would remain anonymous and confidential, to be used exclusively for research purposes.

3.5. Sample Characteristics

Among the 122 participants, women accounted for 61.5% of the responses, while men accounted for 38.5%. The higher representation of women respondents could be attributable to either the gender distribution of the types of CAs who participated in the study, or a greater willingness of women to participate in food-related surveys [42] (Table 1).

Table 1. Sociodemographic characterization of the sample.

Variable	Groups	N	(%)
Gender	Male	47	38.52%
	Female	75	61.48%
Age	31–40	5	4.10%
	41–50	39	31.97%
	51–60	73	59.84%
	≥60	3	2.46%
Competent Authority	MRDF (Ministry of Rural Development and Food)	42	34.43%
	DAOK (Regional Agricultural Directorates)	45	36.89%
	EFET (Hellenic Food Authority)	23	18.85%
	ELGO-DIMITRA (PDO/PGI inspection authority)	12	9.84%
Level of education	University/Integrated master	28	22.95%
	Master	65	53.28%
	PhD	29	23.77%
Occupational role	Employee/Inspector	89	72.95%
	Head of Department	25	20.49%
	Head of Directorate	8	6.56%
Years of professional experience	≤5	23	18.85%
	5–10	28	22.95%
	≥10	71	58.20%

The distribution of respondents' allocation across Competent Authorities (MRDF—Ministry of Rural Development and Food; DAOK—Regional Agricultural Directorates; EFET—Hellenic Food Authority; ELGO-DIMITRA—PDO/PGI inspection authority) was aligned with the organizational structure of the official food control system in Greece, thereby supporting the representativeness of the sample.

In terms of educational level, 53.3% of participants held a master's degree and 23.8% held a doctorate, thus high educational attainment was also present in the sample. This is particularly relevant to the context of official food controls, where specialized scientific knowledge is critical.

Regarding occupational status, 73.0% of respondents were employed as inspectors, while 27.0% occupied managerial roles at the department or directorate level. This distribu-

https://doi.org/10.3390/su18021101

tion of respondents between non-managerial and managerial positions potentially reflects the administrative hierarchy of the CAs.

The distribution of professional experience indicates that 58.2% of participants reported more than 10 years of experience, 23.0% reported between 5 and 10 years, and 18.8% reported less than 5 years. This profile provides evidence of a sample predominantly composed of inspectors with moderate to extensive professional experience, thereby enhancing the validity and reliability of the data collected for this study.

3.6. Calculations and Data Analysis

The first section of the questionnaire collected socio-demographic information. Respondents' attitudes towards various statements regarding food fraud were assessed using a five-point Likert scale, where 1 indicated "strongly disagree" and 5 indicated "strongly agree" [68,69]. Statistical analyses were performed using IBM SPSS Statistics for Windows (version 23.0; IBM Corp., Armonk, NY, USA). Likert scale responses were treated as ordinal data. The internal consistency of the questionnaire was evaluated using Cronbach's alpha, which demonstrated good reliability, with coefficients ranging from 0.70 to 0.86.

Facts identified as food fraud by the respondents (Figure 1) were ranked according to the percentage of participants who selected each category as a case of fraud. A weighted ranking score was used to calculate the score of the most vulnerable product to food fraud (Figure 2) by assigning 10 points to the product ranked first, 9 points to the second, and progressively decreasing by one point per rank, with one point assigned to the lowest rank.

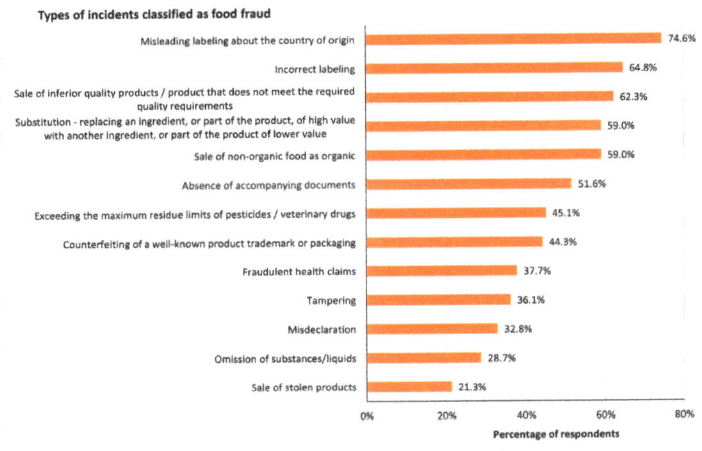

Figure 1. Facts identified as food fraud by the respondents (the ranking is based on the percentage of respondents who selected each category as a case of fraud).

The ranking of the main risk factors for food fraud detection by CAs, the perceived impacts of food fraud, and the effectiveness of existing control tools against food fraud (Figures 3–5) was based on the respondents' Likert-scale answers. For each item, mean values and standard deviations were calculated.

https://doi.org/10.3390/su18021101

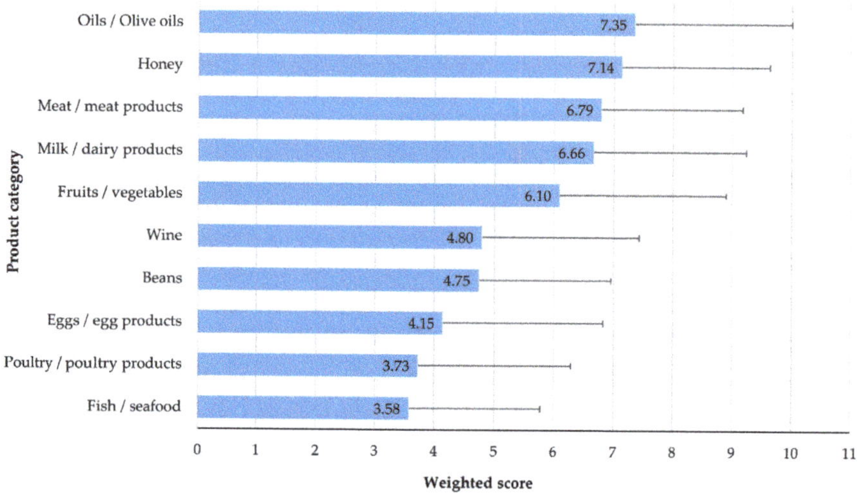

Figure 2. Ranking of the most vulnerable product to food fraud.

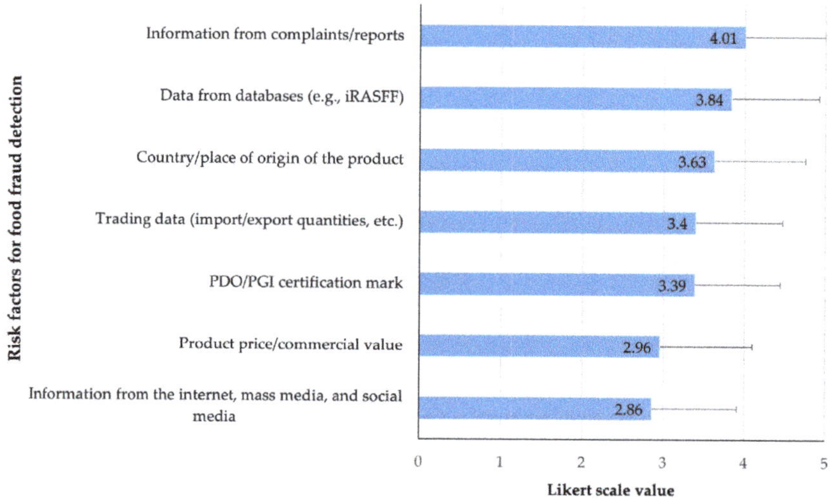

Figure 3. Ranking the main risk factors for food fraud detection from Competent Authorities (mean values ± standard deviation).

Non-parametric tests were employed to explore statistically significant differences between qualitative variables. The Chi-square test of independence was applied to examine associations between categorical variables. Where statistically significant relationships were identified, Cramér's V coefficient was calculated to assess the strength of association, with the following interpretations: $V \approx 0.1$ (weak association), $V \approx 0.3$ (moderate association), and $V \geq 0.5$ (strong association). Sociodemographic variables were considered potential predictors influencing responses to survey items. All statistical tests were conducted using a significance threshold of $p < 0.05$.

https://doi.org/10.3390/su18021101

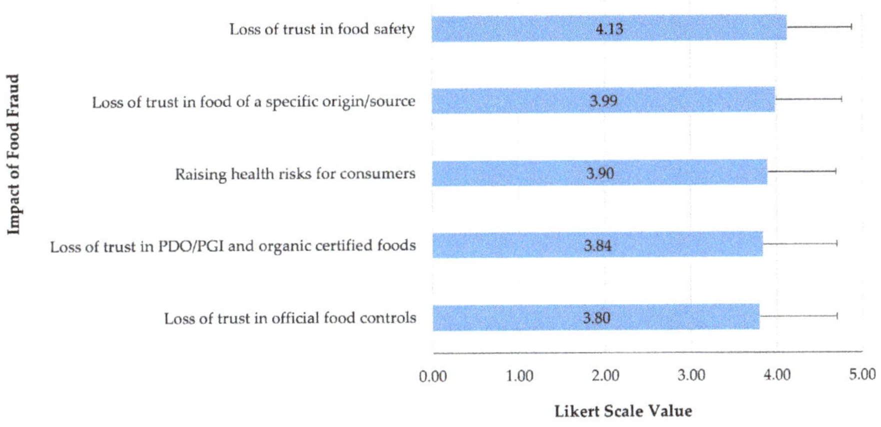

Figure 4. Ranking the impact of food fraud according to the participants' perception (mean value ± standard deviation).

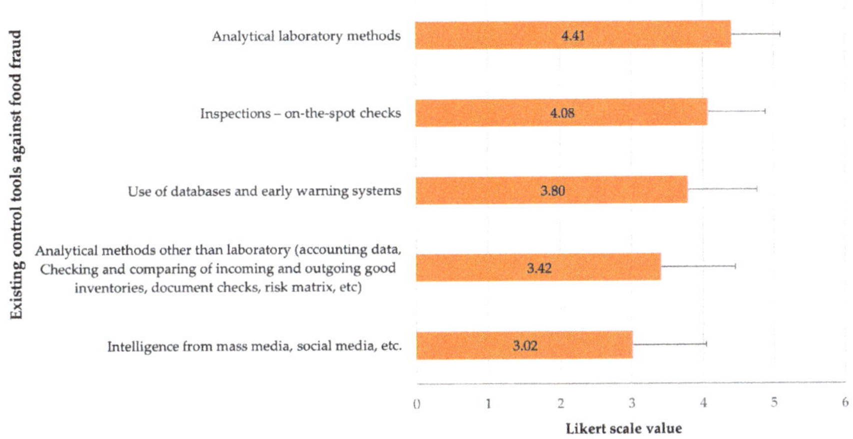

Figure 5. Ranking the effectiveness of existing control tools against food fraud according to the participants' perception (mean value ± standard deviation).

4. Results

4.1. Perceived Degree of Food Fraud

The analysis revealed (see Table A1 in the Appendix A) a statistically significant association between the respondents' perceptions of food fraud degree and their CA affiliation ($\chi^2 = 23.426$, $p = 0.024$), while individual characteristics such as gender, age, and educational level did not have a statistically significant impact. These results indicate differences in perceived food fraud across institutional contexts rather than objective differences in fraud prevalence.

Respondents from the MRDF predominantly perceived food fraud as a moderate issue, with 57.1% of participants ranking it accordingly, while 21.6% reported higher perceived levels of food fraud (Table 2). In the case of DAOK, 40.0% of participants perceived "some" fraud and 42.9% reported higher perceived levels. Among the EFET participants, concerns were more pronounced, with 40.9% rating food fraud as "high" and 18.2% as "very high". In contrast, participants from ELGO-DIMITRA mostly considered the problem to be moderate (50.0%), while only 8.3% perceived it as "very high".

https://doi.org/10.3390/su18021101

Table 2. Participants' perception on the extent of food fraud as a significant issue in their area of responsibility per Competent Authority (scale from 1 = not at all to 5 = very high).

Question: To What Extent Do You Consider Food Fraud to Be a Significant Issue in Your Area?	Answers According to Scale Points (%)				
	1	2	3	4	5
MRDF	4.8	16.7	57.1	14.3	7.1
DAOK	0.0	48.9	31.1	15.6	4.4
EFET	0.0	26.1	26.1	26.1	21.7
ELGO-DIMITRA	0.0	25.0	50.0	16.7	8.3
Overall Competent Authorities	1.6	31.1	41.0	17.2	9.0

The moderate association (Cramér's V = 0.438) suggests that the institutional framework exerts a meaningful influence on the inspectors' perception of food fraud within their authority operational areas. These findings should be considered as reflecting differences in perceived risk and exposure to food fraud, rather than as evidence of differential regulatory performance across CAs, which appear to differ in their perceived engagement with food fraud issues, potentially reflecting variations in mandates, operational focus, and inspection experience.

These findings are consistent with previous research suggesting that auditors' perceptions of food fraud within their work environment are pivotal to the capacity of CAs to combat fraud. Knowledge, training, and field experience influence auditors' ability to recognize and detect fraud and to implement effective controls [15,16,76].

Generally, more experienced auditors tend to adopt a more comprehensive approach to identify fraudulent practices, thereby enhancing audit effectiveness [76]. Enforcement style is also conditioned by auditors' sense of responsibility and accountability, which can influence their willingness to act against food fraud [43,77]. When inspectors perceive a higher risk of personal liability, they may adopt a more cautious enforcement, potentially allowing some level of fraud to persist.

In addition, clear and standardized definitions and terminology for food fraud are essential, as ambiguity can impede inspectors' ability to accurately identify and report fraudulent practices [66].

From a sustainability and governance perspective, the observed institutional variability reflects perceived differences in enforcement contexts rather than verified systemic failures. Variations in perceived fraud risk may undermine the cohesion and predictability required for effective and transparent control systems. Such perceptions can influence resource prioritization and the identification of emerging risks, highlighting the importance of coordination and a shared understanding across CAs within the broader framework of EU food system governance, including the Farm-to-Fork Strategy.

4.2. Types of Incidents Classified as Fraud

Among incidents classified as food fraud according to the respondents' perceptions (Figure 1), mislabeling of country of origin accounted for the largest share (71.1%), indicating the prominence of origin-related claims in inspectors' fraud risk assessments, rather than verified incident frequency.

Fraudulent practices are generally concentrated at points in a supply chain where there is an intersection of information asymmetry, traceability issues, and high value product claims [39].

For PDO and PGI products, the stakes are even higher, as these products command price premiums due to certified quality and geographic links [76]. Inspectors' classifica-

https://doi.org/10.3390/su18021101

tion of misleading origin-related claims reflects concerns that such practices may erode consumer trust, particularly in certified schemes [78].

The second most frequently cited issue was mislabeling, specifically marketing non-organic food as organic (64.7%). Misleading labeling is widely reported as the most prevalent type of food fraud [24], and many cases involve false organic claims [78]. In this study, the high frequency of this response reflects the inspectors' perceived exposure to such practices during official controls.

Ranked third among the respondents' choices was the sale of inferior-quality products or products that do not meet current standards (62.3%), as perceived by inspectors, reflecting concerns about passing off low-quality goods as premium. Strong economic incentives make this practice attractive, particularly for high-value categories such as PDO/PGI products [1], which may shape inspectors' heightened awareness of this fraud type.

The absence of accompanying product documentation was cited by 51.6% of respondents, suggesting, from inspectors' perspectives, possible intentional concealment of traceability information for financial gain [77]. Missing or falsified accompanying documentation substantially hinders the efforts of the CAs to combat fraud [79]. Notably, the EU network's 2020 report attributes 25% of cases to this category, encompassing forged documents and traceability failures [80–82].

Exceeding the maximum permitted residue limits for pesticides or veterinary drugs was identified as fraud by 45.1% of participants. Such violations are often indicative of fraudulent practices [1,81] and simultaneously raise serious public-health concerns [83].

Substitution, defined as the mixing or replacing of a high-value or high-quality ingredient with a lower-value or lower-quality alternative, was selected by 59.0% of respondents, consistent with the inspectors' perceptions of practice that directly degrade the product quality [83,84]. Such fraud is frequently reported for olive oil, honey, dairy, and meat [85].

Counterfeiting of well-known trademarks or packaging was identified less often (44.3%). The omission of substances or liquids—despite its prevalence in international markets [86]—was cited by only 28.7% of respondents, suggesting lower perceived exposure to this practice within the surveyed control contexts.

Other incidents, such as fraudulent health claims and the sale of stolen products, were selected by 37.7% and 21.3% of respondents, respectively. Although reported less frequently, these practices are perceived by inspectors as interconnected with misleading labeling and documentation issues, which can erode consumer confidence [6,30,87].

4.3. Vulnerable Products to Fraud

Figure 2 summarizes inspectors' perceptions of the food categories most vulnerable to fraud. According to the participants, olive oil and olives were the most vulnerable of the ten listed product categories. This may likely reflect both intrinsic vulnerabilities, such as the misuse of geographical indications, inferior physico-chemical characteristics, and unauthorized pesticide use, and the respondent pool, which was largely composed of staff from CAs responsible for this sector.

The relatively high mean value (7.35 $\pm$ 2.66) confirms that olive oil remains a major food category for food fraud detection efforts. Honey ranked second (7.14 $\pm$ 2.49), followed by meat and meat products (6.79 $\pm$ 2.39) and milk and dairy products (6.66 $\pm$ 2.58), indicating that products of animal origin are consistently perceived as high-risk. Fruits and vegetables (6.10 $\pm$ 2.80) were also considered moderately vulnerable. Legumes, poultry, fish/seafood, and eggs were reported as less frequently affected, with mean values below 4.8, which may indicate lower perceived exposure to fraud or fewer detected cases, rather than an absence of risk.

https://doi.org/10.3390/su18021101

These results align with previous studies that highlight olive oil as a globally adulterated product due to its high value and authentication challenges [25]. Similarly, meat and dairy are considered as high-risk sectors due to frequent mislabeling, substance substitution, and illegal production practices [67,88]. Fraud in the dairy sector is particularly concerning, as it may undermine consumer confidence and pose significant health risks, including allergen exposure and reduced traceability [2,79]. Moreover, the relatively higher variability (standard deviations above 2.5) indicates that perceptions of vulnerability may vary across product categories depending on the inspectors' experience of fraud cases.

A recent review highlights that vulnerability to fraud can be influenced by structural aspects of the food supply chain [13]. The authors note that products that are embedded in large and complex supplier networks with multiple tiers, especially where there are no standardized traceability systems, are at greater risk of being opaque, mislabeled, or subject to economically motivated adulteration. Fruits and vegetables are commonly reported as vulnerable to fraudulent claims regarding organic status, country of origin, and pesticide residue levels [89,90]. Honey is also a frequent target of adulteration, often through the addition of undeclared substances that degrade quality and may expose consumers to health risks by misleading them into believing they are purchasing pure honey [91].

4.4. Risk Factors for Food Fraud Detection

To evaluate the frequency with which particular criteria are reportedly used by CAs for food fraud detection, participants rated the use of five criteria on a Likert scale (Table 3). "Information from complaints/reports" had the highest frequency score (Table 3 and Figure 3). This finding indicates that complaints are perceived by inspectors as a key trigger for fraud investigations, rather than constituting direct evidence of fraud occurrence. Complaints, particularly those submitted by individuals with market knowledge, provide relevant, case-specific information, reducing reliance on secondary sources, and accelerating the potential for the identification and investigation of fraudulent activities [21]. "Data from databases (e.g., iRASFF)" ranked second (Table 3). This ranking reflects inspectors' perceptions of the growing importance of inter-authority information exchange and digital infrastructure, rather than a direct assessment of system effectiveness. Platforms such as iRASFF provide valuable data and enable CAs to analyze trends, assess vulnerabilities, and plan targeted interventions [15].

Table 3. Participants' perception on use of risk factors for food fraud detection from Competent Authorities (scale from 1 = never to 5 = always).

Question: Which of the Following Risk Factors Are Used to Food Fraud Detection from Your Authority:	**Answers According to Scale Points (%)**				
	1	**2**	**3**	**4**	**5**
Trading data (import/export quantities, etc.)	5.7	14.8	25.4	41.8	12.3
Country/place of origin of the product	4.9	12.3	21.3	37.7	23.8
PDO/PGI certification mark	4.9	15.6	27.9	39.3	12.3
Product price/commercial value	13.1	18.0	37.7	22.1	9.0
Information from the internet, mass media, and social media	13.9	17.2	41.0	24.6	3.3
Information from complaints/reports	0.8	9.0	16.4	36.1	37.7
Data from databases (e.g., iRASFF)	6.6	3.3	18.0	44.3	27.9

Furthermore, the ranking results (Figure 3) confirm that the two highest rated criteria—information from complaints/reports and data from databases—are perceived by respondents as the sources currently supporting proactive fraud detection. Their higher mean values indicate that CAs are perceived to rely on both reactive inputs and institutional data

https://doi.org/10.3390/su18021101

flows, such as RASFF notifications, when prioritizing fraud related inspections. Ranking third and fourth were the criteria "country/place of origin of the product" and "country/place of production or source", respectively. The prominence of these criteria reflects inspectors' perceptions of origin-related information as relevant indicators of food fraud risk. Prior studies similarly reported that many EU fraud incidents are associated with specific countries or regions, often linked to differences in regulatory oversight and enforcement capacity [92,93].

Country of origin has repeatedly been identified in the literature as salient for flagging potential food fraud [94,95]. Numerous cases reported in the EU Rapid Alert System for Food and Feed (RASFF) have been linked to specific countries [84], a pattern that inspectors may draw upon when assessing perceived fraud risks, including cases involving products originating from certain Asian countries [96].

The "presence of a PDO/PGI certification mark" ranked fifth, despite the fact that geographical indication labeling is widely discussed as a criterion for assessing fraud risk, and supporting product authenticity and consumer confidence [97]. In this study, the lower ranking suggests that PDO/PGI status is perceived as a secondary indicator, relative to more immediate information sources, such as complaints or database alerts. The criteria "information from the Internet, mass media, and social media" and "product price/commercial value" were reported as the least frequently used for fraud detection. This lower ranking (mean values of 2.86 and 2.96, respectively) suggests that more traditional and verifiable sources of information are preferred from CAs.

The low ranking of media-derived information likely reflects the complexity of fraud schemes, which typically requires a more comprehensive approach. In contrast, the limited use of price as a criterion appears at odds with studies showing that price strongly shapes consumer purchasing behavior, with higher prices often associated with signals of quality or authenticity and supporting consumers' willingness to pay [98].

4.5. The Impact of Food Fraud

Food fraud poses significant public-health risks, especially for vulnerable populations, such as children and older adults. Examples include milk being adulterated with sodium hydroxide [99] or the melamine adulteration incident in China [7], both of which led to significant food-safety issues. Global estimates indicate that approximately 10% of the food supply may be adulterated [100], reflecting a significant level of food fraud risk.

Incidents of fraud—including mislabeling and the use of harmful additives—erode consumer trust in food control systems. Empirical evidence shows that perceived fraud may reduce consumer confidence in regulatory institutions and fosters a broader environment of distrust [93,101]. This erosion of consumer trust is particularly salient for PDO and PGI products, as these high-value products are perceived as vulnerable to fraud due to supply chain complexity [63].

According to inspectors' perceptions (Table 4, Figure 4), the main consequence of food fraud was the loss of trust in food safety, which ranked first among all evaluated impacts (4.13 ± 0.75). This was followed by loss of trust in food of specific origin or source (3.99 ± 0.77) and raising health risks for consumers (3.90 ± 0.79). The relatively high mean values across these issues indicate that respondents primarily associate food fraud with reduced confidence in food safety, rather than solely with direct health risks. Moreover, the loss of trust in official food controls received the lowest rank (3.80 ± 0.90), suggesting that inspectors perceive consumer concerns to be more strongly linked to the reliability and integrity of food products themselves, rather than to control authorities per se.

https://doi.org/10.3390/su18021101

Table 4. Participants' perception on the effectiveness of official food control to combat food fraud (scale from 1 = strongly disagree to 5 = strongly agree).

Question: To What Extent Do You Believe That Food Fraud Contributes to:	Answers According to Scale Points (%)				
	1	2	3	4	5
Raising health risks for consumers	0.0	3.8	24.5	51.9	19.8
Loss of trust in food safety	0.0	3.8	15.1	50.0	31.1
Loss of trust in official food controls	4.7	0.9	23.6	51.9	18.9
Loss of trust in PDO/PGI and organic certified foods	0.9	6.6	22.6	48.1	21.7
Loss of trust in food of a specific origin/source	0.0	3.8	20.8	51.9	23.3

Limited consumer awareness of EU quality schemes can increase skepticism toward certified products, while counterfeit products further undermine perceived authenticity and safety [31]. These issues not only weaken consumer confidence but also threaten the economic viability of producers that rely on certification for market differentiation [102].

Fraudulent practices also reinforce the perception that CAs are incapable of preventing or reacting to incidents [103]. The increased complexity of food supply chains, coupled with perceived inconsistent enforcement and regulatory inertia, have expanded opportunities for fraud to occur [3]. As a result, consumers are increasingly convinced that official controls are insufficient, and this perception is heavily influenced by the perceived ineffectiveness of enforcement mechanisms [18].

In relation to this, Niu et al. [104] identified that current regulations on food safety often do not adequately address fraud, leading people to perceive greater exposure, even when strict food safety regulations are in place. This aligns with the survey findings, which indicate that the perceived inefficiency of official controls remains a critical factor in shaping public distrust, although the respondents' dominant concerns related to food-safety integrity rather than regulatory failure alone.

Furthermore, the associations presented in Table A1 (Appendix A) reveal significant relationships between respondents' characteristics and their perceptions of food fraud impacts. Specifically, respondents affiliated with CAs exhibited stronger concern regarding the development of health risks ($\chi^2 = 29.408$, $p = 0.001$, $V = 0.491$) and the loss of trust in food safety ($\chi^2 = 24.903$, $p = 0.003$, $V = 0.452$), suggesting heightened perceived sensitivity among those directly engaged in enforcement activities. Educational level also influenced perceptions, with higher-educated respondents showing greater awareness of the loss of trust in PDO/PGI and organic certified foods ($\chi^2 = 22.905$, $p = 0.003$, $V = 0.433$). Gender differences were evident for several factors, particularly health risk perception ($\chi^2 = 9.820$, $p = 0.020$, $V = 0.284$) and trust in official controls ($\chi^2 = 12.414$, $p = 0.015$, $V = 0.319$). These findings suggest that professional experience, educational background, and demographic factors shape the perceived consequences of food fraud, reinforcing the importance of targeted communication and training within food control authorities.

4.6. Perceived Overall Effectiveness of Competent Authorities Tools Against Food Fraud

Control authorities face substantial challenges in achieving effectiveness. Only 29.5% of respondents rated the current control procedures as "very" or "very highly" effective in combating food fraud (Table 5), indicating relatively limited perceived effectiveness among inspectors, rather than objective assessments of control performance. Perceived effectiveness also varies across authorities (Table 5). In DAOK, 37.7% of respondents judged the procedures to be only "low" or "not at all" effective, compared with 11.9% at MRDF and 4.3% at EFET.

https://doi.org/10.3390/su18021101

Table 5. Participants' perception on overall effectiveness of Competent Authorities' tools and methodologies against Food Fraud (scale from 1 = not at all to 5 = very high).

Question: How Effective Do You Consider the Existing Procedures Implemented by Your Authority to Be in Addressing Food Fraud Within Its Area of Competence?	Answers According to Scale Points (%)				
	1	2	3	4	5
MRDF (Ministry of Rural Development and Food)	2.4	9.5	42.9	38.1	7.1
DAOK (Regional Agricultural Directorates)	4.4	33.3	46.7	15.6	0.0
EFET (Hellenic Food Authority)	0.0	4.3	69.6	26.1	0.0
ELGO-DIMITRA (PDO/PGI inspection authority)	0.0	0.0	66.7	8.3	25.0
Overall Competent Authorities	2.5	16.4	51.6	24.6	4.9

Auditor competence and experience are important factors associated with effective fraud detection. More competent and experienced auditors implement fraud-oriented audit procedures more successfully [105]. Consistent with this, auditor competence is a strong driver of audit quality, which in turn facilitates the detection of fraudulent activities [106]. Taken together, these findings provide a relevant framework for understanding inspectors' perceptions and underscore that strengthening auditors' skills is critical for the successful implementation of procedures established by the CAs.

According to the associations presented in Table 5, the perceived overall effectiveness of food control shows a statistically significant relationship with respondents' CA affiliation ($\chi^2 = 38.353$, $p = 0.000$, V = 0.561), suggesting that institutional factors influence perceptions of effectiveness. Notably, participants from DAOK expressed significantly lower confidence in the adequacy of existing procedures. These differences reflect the uneven distribution of resources and specialized training across authorities, which may lead to inconsistencies in the capacity to combat fraud, rather than to confirmed differences in actual control outcomes.

Beyond technical competence, the ethical environment in which auditors operate is a key determinant of effectiveness. Ethical leadership strengthens auditors' intentions to report detected fraud, indicating that a supportive ethical framework is necessary for the successful implementation of detection procedures [107]. Consistent with this view, Ode et al. [108] found that auditors' ethical principles and professionalism indirectly enhanced their ability to detect fraud. Based on the inspectors' perceptions of effectiveness, cultivating an ethics-oriented culture within inspection teams may therefore improve the effectiveness of existing procedures.

Resources and training are likewise pivotal to the performance of official control systems against fraud. Uneven resourcing and training across CAs can produce inconsistent implementation of food-safety regulations, undermine the consistency and effectiveness of controls, and create opportunities for fraud [109]. From the perspective of respondents, such disparities may influence how the effectiveness of control tools is perceived, potentially shaping confidence in existing procedures.

Some control authorities may underestimate the prevalence of food fraud, when existing controls are perceived as sufficient [110]. Such perceptions can foster complacency and ultimately weaken efforts to combat fraud. The resources and training available to auditors are likewise critical to the effectiveness of control systems. Variation in resourcing and training across CAs can lead to inconsistent implementation of food-safety regulations, undermining the consistency and effectiveness of controls and creating opportunities for fraud [109].

4.7. Perceived Effectiveness of Existing Control Tools Against Food Fraud

Participants' responses showed differences in the perceived effectiveness of existing control tools against food fraud among CAs (Table 6 and Figure 5). Analytical laboratory methods received the highest rating, indicating that inspectors perceive these tools as particularly effective, consistent with evidence that techniques such as mass spectrometry and hyperspectral imaging spectroscopy offer high sensitivity and specificity across commodities. These methods are the most reliable for confirming suspicions raised through other monitoring methods [41].

Table 6. Participants' perception on effectiveness of the existing food control tools against food fraud (scale from 1 = strongly disagree to 5 = strongly agree).

Question: How Effective Do You Consider the Following Existing Food Control Tools Against Food Fraud to Be:	Answers According to Scale Points (%)				
	1	2	3	4	5
Analytical laboratory methods	0.0	0.0	11.5	36.1	52.5
Use of databases and early warning systems	1.6	6.6	28.7	36.9	26.2
Non laboratory analytical methods (accounting data, Checking and comparing of incoming and outgoing good inventories, document checks, risk matrix, etc)	4.1	13.1	34.4	33.6	14.8
Inspections—on-the-spot checks	0.8	1.6	18.0	47.5	32.0
Intelligence from mass media, social media, etc.	8.2	18.0	44.3	22.1	7.4

Databases and early warning systems (e.g., RASFF) also rated highly, reflecting respondents' perceptions of their usefulness, supported by studies suggesting that such systems enable horizon scanning, predictive analytics, and prioritization for targeted checking [90,111]. Their impact is enhanced when accompanied by confirmatory laboratory analysis.

Analytical methods other than laboratory-based techniques were rated moderately high, suggesting that inspectors perceive them as functional, scalable, and cost-effective tools for identifying anomalies prior to laboratory confirmation. The literature indicates their effectiveness in vulnerability-based programs, especially when enhanced with digital traceability tools [17,112].

Inspections scored slightly lower, indicating that respondents perceived untargeted checks as having limited capacity for fraud detection. In contrast, risk-based inspections, on the other hand, can enhance fraud detection by relying on vulnerability assessments and historical data [113]. In the present study, these distinctions reflect perceived differences in inspection approaches rather than measured detection outcomes.

Media and social media intelligence received the lowest ratings, suggesting lower perceived reliability among inspectors, consistent with studies finding that their value as supplementary tools require a follow-up verification [114].

Overall, the results support a layered, intelligence-informed method approach in which high-specificity laboratory tests are deployed based on information provided by early warning systems, administrative verification, and on-the-spot checks, with media monitoring serving a complementary role [17].

Statistical associations revealed that perceived effectiveness varies significantly across professional and sociodemographic groups. Specifically, respondents affiliated with CAs reported a significantly higher perception of the effectiveness of non-laboratory analytical methods (χ^2 = 25.317, p = 0.013, V = 0.456) and on-the-spot inspections (χ^2 = 28.561, p = 0.005, V = 0.484) compared to other respondent groups. These associations suggest that practical enforcement experience and direct involvement in control operations may shape the perceived usefulness of specific control tools.

https://doi.org/10.3390/su18021101

Moreover, occupational role was significantly associated with the perceived usefulness of databases and early warning systems (χ^2 = 10.245, p = 0.036, V = 0.290), suggesting that data-driven tools are more highly valued by respondents with analytical or policy-related responsibilities. A moderate gender-related difference was also observed in the evaluation of information derived from media and social networks (χ^2 = 9.449, p = 0.049, V = 0.278), indicating varying levels of trust in informal intelligence sources. Overall, these associations underscore that professional background influences how different control tools are perceived in terms of their effectiveness against food fraud.

5. Further Discussion: Sustainability of Food Supply Chain Implications

The findings of this study suggest that food fraud is perceived by inspectors not merely as a regulatory challenge, but as a structural risk to the sustainability of the Greek food supply chain. Inspectors highlighted widespread mislabeling, ingredient substitution, and fraudulent organic claims, particularly in high-value sectors such as olive oil, honey, meat, and dairy. From the perspective of respondents, these practices undermine environmental sustainability by weakening incentives for producers to adhere to resource-efficient, authentic, and certified production models.

As suggested in the literature, fraudulent substitution distorts the competitive landscape, enabling unsustainable producers to externalize environmental and social costs while undermining those who comply with certification and traceability norms [8,18]. The inspectors' strong perception that fraud erodes trust in PDO/PGI and organic products further illustrates how fraud disrupts sustainability-oriented value chains built on quality differentiation and regional identity, and may be perceived as vulnerable to fraud-related disruptions.

It should be noted that these findings reflect inspectors' perceptions rather than objective measurements of fraud incidence or sustainability performance. Nevertheless, inspectors' assessments provide governance-relevant insights into where sustainability risks are perceived to be most acute within official control systems.

Within this context, the typology of food fraud incidents reported in this study (see Figure 1) shows that food fraud encountered by official control authorities is predominantly associated with labeling and documentation practices, indicating that fraud is largely driven by information manipulation, rather than by technologically complex adulteration. This pattern reflects underlying governance weaknesses related to information asymmetry, fragmented documentation, and limited traceability, particularly in high-value and certified food markets. Accordingly, the findings suggest that critical vulnerabilities in food fraud control are rooted more in administrative and informational gaps than in analytical capacity alone. By reflecting inspectors' experiential knowledge as street-level regulators, the results point to institutional coordination and data integration as priority areas for strengthening sustainability-oriented enforcement.

The results of the ranking of the most vulnerable products to food fraud (Figure 2) further indicate that inspectors perceive fraud vulnerability to be focused on specific high-value product categories, notably olive oil, honey, meat, and dairy products. These sectors combine price premiums and certification complexity, increasing exposure to mislabeling and fraudulent claims, and indicating that fraud risks are structurally embedded in specific segments of the supply chain. At the same time, significant institutional disparities in perceived fraud prevalence and control effectiveness point to a fragmented governance landscape. According to inspectors, reliance on reactive mechanisms and the absence of integrated digital infrastructure limit coordination, transparency, and traceability, thereby constraining the capacity of food supply chains to address the sustainability impacts of fraud.

https://doi.org/10.3390/su18021101

Moreover, the study's evidence of significant institutional disparities—both in inspectors' perceptions of fraud prevalence and in the effectiveness of existing controls—points to a fragmented governance landscape as experienced by respondents. Such fragmentation reduces the ability to coordinate responses, share intelligence, and ensure uniform enforcement, conditions known to heighten system vulnerability to sustainability shocks [22]. According to inspectors, fraud detection in Greece still relies heavily on reactive mechanisms such as consumer complaints and manual documentation checks, rather than on predictive analytics or integrated early warning systems. This perceived governance gap prevents supply chains from meeting core sustainability principles such as transparency, traceability, and equitable risk distribution—elements accentuated in frameworks like the EU Farm-to-Fork Strategy. The lack of centralized digital infrastructure, as highlighted by inspectors, directly constrains the capacity to mitigate the economic, social, and environmental consequences of fraud.

From a sustainability governance perspective, such perceived fragmentation represents a structural weakness rather than a series of isolated operational shortcomings. Consistent enforcement, shared risk intelligence, and institutional coordination are widely recognized as prerequisites for resilient and sustainable food supply chains.

The survey findings also highlight that trust—both in food safety and in certified food categories—is perceived as the sustainability dimension most affected by food fraud. Loss of trust undermines consumer willingness to purchase premium, sustainable products, thereby destabilizing markets for organic and PDO/PGI goods. Similar dynamics have been documented in international markets, where perceived fraud significantly reduces consumer engagement with sustainable labels and disrupts responsible procurement behaviors [115,116]. The loss of confidence for producers threatens long-term investment in sustainable production systems, as incentives to maintain higher quality standards diminish when consumers do not trust product claims. Inspectors' perceptions that fraud causes greater damage to reputation than to health underscore the systemic nature of food fraud, suggesting that sustainability is closely linked not only to safety and quality, but also to the reliability of information flows that enable markets to function effectively.

These findings suggest that reputational and trust-related impacts may represent a critical pathway through which food fraud is perceived to undermine sustainability, even in the absence of immediately observable health effects.

The introduction of AI-enabled tools into official controls—a field in which inspectors expressed interest but reported low levels of preparedness—has been discussed in the literature as a challenge for strengthening supply chain sustainability. The use of predictive analytics, digital traceability, and anomaly detection can provide an improvement over current levels of information asymmetry and allow for the early identification of high-risk transactions, thereby enhancing the ability to plan risk-based inspections [64,117]. In addition, the use of AI systems can contribute to greater environmental sustainability by enhancing transparency within value chains and thereby rewarding authentic producers and limiting the availability of counterfeit goods produced using unsustainable methods. However, it is important to recognize that for technological solutions such as AI to be successful, institutional reforms are required, including capacity development and the creation of ethical governance structures consistent with the EU's Artificial Intelligence Act. Without such accompanying reforms, respondents expressed concern that digitalization could exacerbate existing inequalities in control capacity and potentially introduce new trust-related challenges.

Accordingly, the contribution of AI to food supply chain sustainability should be interpreted as conditional and complementary, supporting—rather than substituting—human expertise, institutional capacity, and coordinated governance.

https://doi.org/10.3390/su18021101

6. Policy Recommendations

Several policy options can be derived from the empirical findings and the sustainability-related implications identified in the research. The first is for Greece to develop a centralized digital platform can interoperate inspection data, traceability information, laboratory test results, and AI-based fraud-risk indicators. Platforms of this nature have been demonstrated to be successful in other parts of the EU and can assist in the coordination of efforts between regions, eliminate duplication of work, and provide an early warning system for detecting fraudulent activity. Such a platform would require clear institutional ownership, standardized data protocols, and robust safeguards for data protection and accountability, in order to ensure interoperability across CAs and avoid reinforcing existing governance fragmentation.

Second, there is a need for tailored training programs to be developed to address the diverse professional backgrounds of inspectors involved in the inspection of different product categories. These training programs should include modules on food fraud types, digital traceability, and the ethical use of AI. Such capacity-building programs should place particular emphasis on regional authorities, such as DAOK, which was identified by inspectors as having less effective existing procedures. Training initiatives should be differentiated according to operational role and product specialization and supported by continuous professional development schemes rather than one-off interventions, in order to ensure sustained institutional capacity building

Third, the sustainability of the food supply chain can be enhanced through the reinforcement of certification integrity via systematic verification of PDO/PGI and organic claims, combined with sanctions proportional to the environmental and social harms caused. Such measures may strengthen deterrence, while simultaneously protecting compliant producers who rely on certification schemes as a basis for sustainable value creation and market differentiation.

Fourth, when designing policies related to fraud prevention, it is important to incorporate a sustainability-based risk analysis, acknowledging that fraud poses not only risks to food safety, but also risks to environmental stewardship, fair competition, and consumers' welfare. Incorporating sustainability criteria into fraud prevention strategies will enable national fraud control measures to be aligned with the EU's long-term objectives of achieving climate neutrality, developing resilient food systems and creating sustainable rural development. In this context, sustainability-oriented risk analysis should be integrated into existing risk-based inspection frameworks rather than treated as a parallel policy agenda, ensuring coherence between food safety enforcement and broader sustainability objectives.

7. Conclusions

This study shows that food fraud remains a persistent and multifaceted challenge in Greece, affecting the sustainability of agri-food supply chains. This conclusion reflects inspectors' perceptions derived from the survey data rather than objective measurements of food fraud prevalence or intensity.

The most common perceived fraudulent practices identified by inspectors include the mislabeling of food products, use of lower-cost ingredients or substitutes for higher-cost ingredients, and false labeling of products as "organic". A significant variation exists among the CAs responsible for enforcing regulations related to official control activities, as they possess different level of resources and operational capacity. These variations are perceived to create challenges for the consistent implementation of official controls, rather than providing definitive evidence of differences in regulatory effectiveness across authorities.

With regard to digitalization, inspectors identified artificial intelligence as a potentially useful tool for supporting food fraud detection and enhancing supply chain transparency,

https://doi.org/10.3390/su18021101

particularly through improved traceability and data integration. These views should be interpreted as expectations and perceived opportunities, rather than as evidence of implemented AI systems or demonstrated impacts within official food controls. At the same time, respondents reported limited preparedness to effectively utilize AI-based tools, highlighting perceived needs related to training, data quality, interoperability, and institutional support.

Overall, the findings underscore the importance of institutional readiness, capacity building, and appropriate governance frameworks as conditions for the responsible integration of digital tools into public control systems. Within the empirical scope of this study, these considerations should be understood as policy-relevant implications informed by inspectors' perceptions, rather than as directly observed outcomes. Future research combining perception-based data with objective performance indicators and comparative institutional analysis would be valuable for further assessing the role of official food controls and digitalization in supporting sustainable and transparent food supply chains.

8. Limitations and Suggestions for Future Research Directions

This study has several limitations that should be considered when interpreting the findings. First, the analysis was based on the inspectors' perceptions derived from a survey and does not provide objective measurements of food fraud prevalence or regulatory effectiveness. Consequently, the results reflect perceived patterns and challenges rather than empirically verified impacts.

Second, the use of a non-probability sampling strategy limits the generalizability of the findings beyond the specific national and institutional context examined. In addition, the exploratory nature of the analysis, which relies primarily on descriptive and non-parametric statistics, does not allow for the identification of causal relationships.

With regard to digitalization and artificial intelligence, the study examined perceived potential and preparedness, rather than actual implementation or performance within official control systems. As a result, conclusions related to digital tools should be interpreted cautiously.

Future research could address these limitations by combining perception-based data with objective indicators, adopting comparative cross-country designs, and employing mixed-method or longitudinal approaches. Such research would contribute to a more comprehensive understanding of how official food controls and digitalization support sustainability-oriented food fraud governance.

Author Contributions: Conceptualization, C.R., D.K. and A.K.; methodology, C.R.; software, C.R.; validation, A.P., F.C. and A.K.; formal analysis, A.P. and C.R.; investigation, C.R.; data curation, C.R.; writing—original draft preparation, C.R. and A.P.; writing—review and editing, A.P.; visualization, D.K.; supervision, F.C. and A.K.; project administration, A.K. and F.C. All authors have read and agreed to the published version of the manuscript.

Funding: This research received no external funding.

Institutional Review Board Statement: This study was conducted in accordance with the Declaration of Helsinki, and the protocol used was approved by the Ethics Committee of International Hellenic University on 10 March 2025 Approval Code: 2025-16.

Informed Consent Statement: Informed consent was obtained from all subjects involved in the study.

Data Availability Statement: The raw data supporting the conclusions of this article will be made available by the authors on request.

Conflicts of Interest: The authors declare no conflicts of interest.

https://doi.org/10.3390/su18021101

Abbreviations

The following abbreviations are used in this manuscript:

CA	Competent Authority
CAs	Competent Authorities
MRDF	Ministry of Rural Development and Food
EFET	Hellenic Food Authority
DAOK	Regional Agricultural Directorates
ELGO-DIMITRA	Designated authority for PDO/PGI controls

Appendix A

Table A1. Associations between (food fraud-related perceptions, impacts, and control effectiveness and respondents' sociodemographic and professional attributes).

	Gender			Competent Authority			Occupational Role			Educational Level		
	χ^2 *	p **	V ***	χ^2 *	p **	V ***	χ^2 *	p **	V ***	χ^2 *	p **	V ***
To what extent do you consider food fraud to be a significant issue in your area?				23.426	0.024	0.438						
Which of the following risk factors are used to detect food fraud from your Authority:												
Trading data (import/export quantities, etc.)				22.429	0.033	0.248						
Country/place of origin of the product				24.326	0.018	0.258						
PDO/PGI certification mark				29.013	0.004	0.282						
Product price/commercial value				28.631	0.004	0.280						
Information from the internet, mass media, and social media	14.699	0.005	0.347	24.072	0.020	0.256						
Information from complaints/reports				35.742	0.000	0.312						
Data from databases (e.g., iRASFF)				35.482	0.000	0.311						
Impact of food fraud												
Health Risks development for Consumers	9.820	0.020	0.284	29.408	0.001	0.491						
Loss of trust in food safety				24.903	0.003	0.452						
Loss of trust in official food controls	12.414	0.015	0.319									
Loss of trust in PDO/PGI and organic certified foods				26.576	0.009	0.467				22.905	0.003	0.433
Loss of trust in food of a specific origin/source												
How effective do you consider the existing procedures implemented by your Authority to be in addressing food fraud within its area of competence				38.353	0.000	0.561						
How effective do you consider the following existing food control tools against food fraud to be?												
Analytical laboratory methods												
Use of databases and early warning systems							10.245	0.036	0.290			
Non laboratory analytical methods (accounting data, Checking and comparing of incoming and outgoing good inventories, document checks, risk matrix, etc)				25.317	0.013	0.456						
Inspections—on-the-spot checks				28.561	0.005	0.484						
Intelligence from mass media, social media, etc.	9.449	0.049	0.278									

* Chi-square test, ** Level of significance of 5%: $p < 0.05$, *** Cramer's coefficient.

References

1. Giannakas, K.; Yiannaka, A. Food Fraud: Causes, Consequences, and Deterrence Strategies. *Annu. Rev. Resour. Econ.* **2023**, *15*, 85–104. [CrossRef]
2. Soon, J.M.; Nyarugwe, S.P.; Jack, L. Food fraud and mitigating strategies of UK food supply chain during COVID-19. *Food Control* **2023**, *148*, 109670. [CrossRef] [PubMed]
3. Robson, K.; Dean, M.; Haughey, S.; Elliott, C. A Comprehensive Review of Food Fraud Terminologies and Food Fraud Mitigation Guides. *Food Control* **2021**, *120*, 107516. [CrossRef]
4. Food Standards Agency. *The Cost of Food Crime*; Rep. FS 301065; Food Standards Agency: London, UK, 2020. Available online: https://www.food.gov.uk/sites/default/files/media/document/the-cost-of-food-crime.pdf (accessed on 7 December 2025).
5. Spink, J.; Moyer, D.C. Defining the public health threat of food fraud. *J. Food Sci.* **2011**, *526*, 157–162. [CrossRef]
6. Barnett, J.; Begen, F.; Howes, S.; Regan, A.; McConnon, A.; Marcu, A.; Rowntree, S.; Verbeke, W. Consumers' confidence, reflections and response strategies following the horsemeat incident. *Food Control* **2016**, *59*, 721–730. [CrossRef]
7. Xiu, C.; Klein, K.K. Melamine in milk products in China: Examining the factors that led to deliberate use of the contaminant. *Food Policy* **2010**, *35*, 463–470. [CrossRef]
8. Manning, L. Chapter Eight–Food Supply Chain Fraud: The Economic, Environmental, and Sociopolitical Consequences. *Adv. Food Secur. Sustain.* **2018**, *3*, 253–276. [CrossRef]
9. Rossi, A.; Rossi, G.; Rosamilia, A.; Micheli, M.R. Official controls on food safety: Competent Authority measures. *Ital. J. Food Saf.* **2020**, *9*, 8607. [CrossRef]
10. Keller, J.; Jung, M.; Lasch, R. Sustainability Governance: Insights from a Cocoa Supply Chain. *Sustainability* **2022**, *14*, 10763. [CrossRef]
11. Lawrence, S.J.; Elliott, C.; Huisman, W.; Dean, M.; van Ruth, S. The 11 sins of seafood: Assessing a decade of food fraud reports in the global supply chain. *Compr. Rev. Food Sci. Food Saf.* **2022**, *21*, 3746–3769. [CrossRef]
12. Lord, N.; Flores Elizondo, C.J.; Spencer, J. The dynamics of food fraud: The interactions between criminal opportunity and market (dys-) functionality in legitimate business. *Criminol. Crim. Justic.* **2017**, *17*, 605–623. [CrossRef]
13. Adams, D.; Donovan, J.; Topple, C. Achieving sustainability in food manufacturing operations and their supply chains: Key insights from a systematic literature review. *Sustain. Prod. Consum.* **2021**, *28*, 1491–1499. [CrossRef]
14. Amentae, T.K.; Gebresenbet, G. Digitalization and Future Agro-Food Supply Chain Management: A Literature-Based Implications. *Sustainability* **2021**, *13*, 12181. [CrossRef]
15. De Silvo, F.D.E. Brief Notes on the European Geographical Indication Law: Among Sustainability Implications and Artificial Intelligence Applications. *Int. J. Manag. Know. Learn.* **2024**, *13*, 105–111. [CrossRef]
16. Gracia, G.; Kurnia, R. The determinant factors affecting auditors' ability to detect fraud: Empirical study at public accounting firms in Jakarta and Tangerang. *Econ. Manag. Sustain.* **2021**, *6*, 132–145. [CrossRef]
17. Popping, B.; Buck, N.; Bánáti, D.; Brereton, P.; Gendel, S.; Hristozova, N.; Chaves, S.M.; Saner, S.; Spink, J.; Willis, C.; et al. Food inauthenticity: Authority activities, guidance for food operators, and mitigation tools. *Compr. Rev. Food Sci. Food Saf.* **2022**, *21*, 4776–4811. [CrossRef]
18. Wu, W.; Zhang, A.; van Klinken, R.D.; Schrobback, P.; Muller, J.M. Consumer Trust in Food and the Food System: A Critical Review. *Foods* **2021**, *18*, 2490. [CrossRef]
19. Otter, V.; Robinson, D. Transparency and changing stakeholder roles in the digital age of sustainable agri-food supply chain networks. *Front. Sustain. Food Syst.* **2024**, *8*, 1449684. [CrossRef]
20. León-Bravo, V.; Caniato, F.; Caridi, M. Sustainability assessment in the food supply chain: Study of a certified product in Italy. *Prod. Plan. Control.* **2021**, *32*, 567–584. [CrossRef]
21. Manning, L.; Soon, J.M. Food fraud vulnerability assessment: Reliable data sources and effective assessment approaches. *Trends Food Sci. Technol.* **2019**, *91*, 159–168. [CrossRef]
22. Xue, Y.; Yan, J.; Mohsin, M.; Mehak, A. Supply chain risks in agri-food systems: A comprehensive review of economic vulnerabilities and mitigation approaches. *Front. Sustain. Food Syst.* **2025**, *9*, 1649834. [CrossRef]
23. Spink, J.; Vincent Hegarty, P.; Fortin, N.D.; Elliott, C.T.; Moyer, D.C. The application of public policy theory to the emerging food fraud risk: Next steps. *Trends Food Sci. Technol.* **2019**, *85*, 116–128. [CrossRef]
24. Charlebois, S.; Schwab, A.; Henn, R.; Huck, C.W. Food fraud: An exploratory study for measuring consumer perception towards mislabeled food products and influence on self-authentication intentions. *Trends Food Sci. Technol.* **2016**, *50*, 211–218. [CrossRef]
25. Agnusdei, G.P.; Coluccia, B. Sustainable agrifood supply chains: Bibliometric, network and content analyses. *Sci. Total Environ.* **2022**, *824*, 153704. [CrossRef] [PubMed]
26. Han, Q.; Erasmus, S.W.; Elliott, C.T.; van Ruth, S.M. A sense of ginger fraud: Prevalence and deconstruction of the China-European union supply chain. *npj Sci. Food* **2022**, *6*, 51. [CrossRef]

https://doi.org/10.3390/su18021101

27. Vasileiou, M.; Kyrgiakos, L.S.; Kleisiari, C.; Lappas, P.Z.; Tsinopoulos, C.; Kleftodimos, G.; Ntemou, A.; Kateris, D.; Moulogianni, C.; Vlontzos, G. Digital Transformation of Food Supply Chain Management Using Blockchain: A Systematic Literature Review Towards Food Safety and Traceability. *Bus. Inf. Syst. Eng.* **2025**. [CrossRef]
28. Kendall, H.; Clark, B.; Rhymer, C.; Kuznesof, S.; Hajslova, J.; Tomaniova, M.; Brereton, P.; Frewer, L. A systematic review of consumer perceptions of food fraud and authenticity: A European perspective. *Trends Food Sci. Technol.* **2019**, *94*, 79–90. [CrossRef]
29. Glogovețan, A.I.; Pocol, C.B. The Role of Promoting Agricultural and Food Products Certified with European Union Quality Schemes. *Foods* **2024**, *13*, 970. [CrossRef]
30. Savelli, E.; Bravi, L.; Francioni, B.; Murmura, F.; Pencarelli, T. PDO labels and food preferences: Results from a sensory analysis. *Br. Food J.* **2021**, *123*, 1170–1189. [CrossRef]
31. Magarelli, M.; Novielli, P.; De Filippis, F.; Magliulo, R.; Di Bitonto, P.; Diacono, D.; Bellotti, R.; Tangaro, S. Explainable artificial intelligence and microbiome data for food geographical origin: The Mozzarella di Bufala Campana PDO Case of Study. *Front. Microbiol.* **2024**, *15*, 1393243. [CrossRef]
32. Manning, L.; MacLeod, A.; James, C.; Thompson, M.; Oyeyinka, S.; Cowen, N.; Skoczylis, J.; Onarinde, B.A. Food fraud prevention strategies: Building an effective verification ecosystem. *Compr. Rev. Food Sci. Food Saf.* **2024**, *23*, e70036. [CrossRef] [PubMed]
33. Al Busaidi, M.A.; Rahman, M.S.; Al Masroori, H.S. Transitioning from a Multi-Agency to an Integrated Food Control System: A Case Study from the Sultanate of Oman. *Foods* **2025**, *14*, 2618. [CrossRef] [PubMed]
34. Conter, M.; Rega, M.; Lamperti, L.; Andriani, L.; Bacci, C.; Bonardi, S. Comparative analysis of official controls and voluntary certifications in ensuring food safety compliance: A review. *Ital. J. Food Saf.* **2025**, *14*, 13452. [CrossRef] [PubMed]
35. Abid, H.M.R.; Aslam, S.; Alwan, N.; Khalid, N. Current readiness on food fraud risk mitigation in developing countries: A review. *Agric. Food Secur.* **2025**, *14*, 9. [CrossRef]
36. Fernando, I.; Fei, J.; Cahoon, S.; Close, D.C. A review of the emerging technologies and systems to mitigate food fraud in supply chains. *Crit. Rev. Food Sci. Nutr.* **2025**, *65*, 5108–5135. [CrossRef]
37. Demeshko, A.; Clifford Astbury, C.; Lee, K.M.; Clarke, J.; Cullerton, K.; Penney, T.L. The role of corruption in global food systems: A systematic scoping review. *Global Health* **2024**, *20*, 48. [CrossRef]
38. Mu, W.; Kleter, G.A.; Bouzembrak, Y.; Dupouy, E.; Frewer, L.J.; Radwan Al Natour, F.N.; Marvin, H.J.P. Making food systems more resilient to food safety risks by including artificial intelligence, big data, and internet of things into food safety early warning and emerging risk identification tools. *Compr. Rev. Food Sci. Food Saf.* **2024**, *23*, e13296. [CrossRef]
39. Grau-Noguer, E.; Rodríguez-Sanz, M.; Suppi, R.; Serratosa, J.; Lundén, J.; Bolao, A.; Cedano, D.; Portaña, S. Effectiveness of official food safety control in Barcelona city: Digital and traditional inspections. *Food Control* **2024**, *165*, 110655. [CrossRef]
40. Joenperä, J.; Lundén, J. Food fraud detection and reporting by food control officers in Finland. *Int. J. Environ. Health Res.* **2024**, *34*, 2230–2247. [CrossRef]
41. Vinothkanna, A.; Dar, O.I.; Liu, Z.; Jia, A.Q. Advanced detection tools in food fraud: A systematic review for holistic and rational detection method based on research and patents. *Food Chem.* **2024**, *446*, 138893. [CrossRef]
42. Coral, C.; Mithöfer, D. Integrating social vulnerability into food fraud vulnerability assessment: Policy implications for authenticity in Spanish honey. *Food Policy* **2025**, *136*, 102954. [CrossRef]
43. Manning, L. Fraud in the food system: Critiquing the 'bad apple' perspective. *Trends Food Sci. Technol.* **2024**, *149*, 104563. [CrossRef]
44. Borraz, O.; Beaussier, A.-L.; Demeritt, D.; Hermans, M.; Huber, M.; Paul, R.; Rothstein, H.; Wesseling, M. Why regulators assess risk differently: Regulatory style, business organization, and the varied practice of risk-based food safety inspections across the EU. *Regul. Gov.* **2020**, *16*, 274–292. [CrossRef]
45. Winter, S.C.; May, P.J. Eight: Street-level bureaucrats and regulatory deterrence. In *Understanding Street-Level Bureaucracy*; Policy Press: Bristol, UK, 2015. [CrossRef]
46. Klijn, E.; Eshuis, J.; Opperhuizen, A.; Boer, N.d. Blaming the bureaucrat: Does perceived blame risk influence inspectors' enforcement style? *Int. Rev. Adm. Sci.* **2020**, *88*, 283–301. [CrossRef]
47. Marín, X.; Grau-Noguer, E.; Gervilla-Cantero, G.; Ripolles-Avila, C.; Castillo, M. Emerging Technologies for Detecting Food Fraud: A Review of the Current Landscape in the 2020s. *Trends Food Sci. Technol.* **2025**, *165*, 105313. [CrossRef]
48. Duan, K.; Onyeaka, H.; Pang, G. Leveraging blockchain to tackle food fraud: Innovations and obstacles. *J. Agric. Food Res.* **2024**, *18*, 101429. [CrossRef]
49. Rossi, S.; Gemma, S.; Borghini, F.; Perini, M.; Butini, S.; Carullo, G.; Campiani, G. Agri-Food Traceability Today: Advancing Innovation towards Efficiency, Sustainability, Ethical Sourcing, and Safety in Food Supply Chains. *Trends Food Sci. Technol.* **2025**, *163*, 105154. [CrossRef]
50. Manning, L.; Brewer, S.; Craigon, P.J.; Frey, J.; Gutierrez, A.; Jacobs, N.; Kanza, S.; Munday, S.; Sacks, J.; Pearson, S. Reflexive governance architectures: Considering the ethical implications of autonomous technology adoption in food supply chains. *Trends Food Sci. Technol.* **2023**, *133*, 114–126. [CrossRef]

https://doi.org/10.3390/su18021101

51. Bhargava, A.; Bester, M.; Bolton, L. Employees' Perceptions of the Implementation of Robotics, Artificial Intelligence, and Automation (RAIA) on Job Satisfaction, Job Security, and Employability. *J. Technol. Behav. Sci.* **2021**, *6*, 106–113. [CrossRef]
52. Goyal, K.; Kumar, P.; Verma, K. Food Adulteration Detection using Artificial Intelligence: A Systematic Review. *Arch. Computat. Methods Eng.* **2022**, *29*, 397–426. [CrossRef]
53. Van de Poel, I. Embedding Values in Artificial Intelligence (AI) Systems. *Minds Mach.* **2020**, *30*, 385–409. [CrossRef]
54. Mirzaei, A.; Hajizade, M.; Hajizade, H. Studying the effect of artificial intelligence on improvement of various quality criteria in relation to audit work in Iran. *Int. J. Health Sci.* **2022**, *6*, 12623–12635. [CrossRef]
55. Odeyemi, O.; Awonuga, K.F.; Mhlongo, N.Z.; Ndubuisi, N.L.; Olatoye, F.O.; Daraojimba, A.I. The role of AI in transforming auditing practices: A global perspective review. *World J. Adv. Res. Rev.* **2023**, *21*, 359–370. [CrossRef]
56. Hamdan, S.A.R.; Al Habashneh, A.K. The Advantages and Difficulties of Using AI and BT in the Auditing Procedures: A Literature Review. In *Artificial Intelligence-Augmented Digital Twins. Studies in Systems, Decision and Control*; Musleh Al-Sartawi, A.M.A., Al-Qudah, A.A., Shihadeh, F., Eds.; Springer: Cham, Switzerland, 2024; Volume 503. [CrossRef]
57. Creswell, J.W.; Clark, V.L.P. *Designing and Conducting Mixed Methods Research*, 3rd ed.; SAGE Publications: Thousand Oaks, CA, USA, 2018.
58. Schreier, M. Sampling and generalization. In *The SAGE Handbook of Qualitative Data Collection*, 1st ed.; Flick, U., Ed.; SAGE Publications: Thousand Oaks, CA, USA, 2018.
59. Wisniewski, A.; Buschulte, A. How to tackle food fraud in official food control authorities in Germany. *J. Consum. Prot. Food Saf.* **2019**, *14*, 319–328. [CrossRef]
60. Kosola, M.; Kiviniemi, K.; Lundén, J. Factors affecting effectiveness of food control inspections in food production establishments in Finland. *Sci. Rep.* **2022**, *12*, 4230. [CrossRef]
61. Skalkos, D.; Kosma, I.S.; Vasiliou, A.; Guine, R.P.F. Consumers' Trust in Greek Traditional Foods in the Post COVID-19 Era. *Sustainability* **2021**, *13*, 9975. [CrossRef]
62. Piira, N.; Marami, E.; Lunden, J. Official food control inspectors' perceptions of remote food control in Finland. *Food Control* **2025**, *171*, 111128. [CrossRef]
63. Marcus, B.; Weigelt, O.; Hergert, J.; Gurt, J.; Gelléri, P. The use of snowball sampling for multi source organizational research: Some cause for concern. *Pers. Psychol.* **2017**, *70*, 635–673. [CrossRef]
64. Buyuktepe, O.; Catal, C.; Kar, G.; Bouzembrak, Y.; Marvin, H.; Gavai, A. Food fraud detection using explainable artificial intelligence. *Expert Syst.* **2023**, *42*, e13387. [CrossRef]
65. Ulberth, F. Tools to combat food fraud—A gap analysis. *Food Chem.* **2020**, *330*, 127044. [CrossRef]
66. Moore, J.C.; Spink, J.; Lipp, M. Development and application of a database of food ingredient fraud and economically motivated adulteration from 1980 to 2010. *J. Food Sci.* **2012**, *77*, R118–R126. [CrossRef]
67. Everstine, K.D.; Chin, H.B.; Lopes, F.; Moore, J.C. Database of Food Fraud Records: Summary of Data from 1980 to 2022. *J. Food Prot.* **2024**, *87*, 100227. [CrossRef]
68. Joshi, A.; Kale, S.; Chandel, S.; Pal, D.K. Likert Scale: Explored and Explained. *Curr. J. Appl. Sci. Technol.* **2015**, *7*, 396–403. [CrossRef]
69. Likert, R. A technique for the measurement of attitudes. *Arch. Psychol.* **1932**, *140*, 44–53.
70. Revilla, M.; Saris, W.E.; Krosnick, J.A. Choosing the Number of Categories in Agree–Disagree Scales. *Sociol. Methods Res.* **2014**, *43*, 73–97. [CrossRef]
71. Parker, C.; Scott, S.; Geddes, A. *Snowball Sampling*; Atkinson, P., Delamont, S., Cernat, A., Sakshaug, J.W., Williams, R.A., Eds.; SAGE Research Methods Foundations: London, UK, 2019. [CrossRef]
72. Wright, K.B. Researching Internet-Based Populations: Advantages and Disadvantages of Online Survey Research. *J. Comput.-Mediat. Commun.* **2017**, *22*, 408–425. [CrossRef]
73. Evans, J.R.; Mathur, A. The Value of Online Surveys: A look back and a look ahead. *Internet Res.* **2018**, *28*, 854–887. [CrossRef]
74. Palmieri, N.; Perito, M.A.; Lupi, C. Consumer acceptance of cultured meat: Some hints from Italy. *Br. Food J.* **2021**, *123*, 109–123. [CrossRef]
75. Field, A. *Discovering Statistics Using IBM SPSS Statistics*, 5th ed.; SAGE Publications: London, UK, 2018.
76. Kizos, T.; Kohsaka, R.; Penker, M.; Piatti, C.; Vogl, C.R.; Uchiyama, Y. The governance of geographical indications: Experiences of practical implementation of selected case studies in Austria, Italy, Greece and Japan. *Br. Food J.* **2017**, *119*, 2863–2879. [CrossRef]
77. Tibola, C.S.; da Silva, S.A.; Dossa, A.A.; Patrício, D.I. Economically Motivated Food Fraud and Adulteration in Brazil: Incidents and Alternatives to Minimize Occurrence. *J. Food Sci.* **2018**, *83*, 2028–2038. [CrossRef]
78. Arfini, F.; Antonioli, F.; Cozzi, E.; Donati, M.; Guareschi, M.; Mancini, M.C.; Veneziani, M. Sustainability, Innovation and Rural Development: The Case of Parmigiano-Reggiano PDO. *Sustainability* **2019**, *11*, 4978. [CrossRef]
79. Bouzembrak, Y.; Steen, B.; Neslo, R.; Linge, J.; Mojtahed, V.; Marvin, H.J.P. Development of food fraud media monitoring system based on text mining. *Food Control* **2018**, *93*, 283–296. [CrossRef]

https://doi.org/10.3390/su18021101

80. European Union. *The EU Agri-Food Fraud Network and the Administrative Assistance and Cooperation System. 2020 Annual Report*; Publications Office of the European Union: Luxembourg, 2021. Available online: https://food.ec.europa.eu/document/download/5135ace4-2a9d-4bf7-afad-574621b43b1c_en?filename=ff_ffn_annual-report_2020_1.pdf (accessed on 7 December 2025).
81. Li, D.; Zang, M.; Li, X.; Zhang, K.; Zhang, Z.; Wang, S. A study on the food fraud of national food safety and sample inspection of China. *Food Control* **2020**, *116*, 107306. [CrossRef]
82. Winter, C.K. Chronic dietary exposure to pesticide residues in the United States. *Int. J. Food Contam.* **2015**, *2*, 11. [CrossRef]
83. Soman, M.; Paul, R.J.; Antony, M.; Sasidharan, S.P. Detecting mislabelling in meat products using PCR-FINS. *J. Food Sci. Tech.* **2020**, *57*, 4286–4292. [CrossRef]
84. Se, K.W.; Wahab, R.A.; Syed Yaacob, S.N.; Ghoshal, S.K. Detection Techniques for Adulterants in Honey: Challenges and Recent Trends. *J. Food Compos. Anal.* **2019**, *80*, 16–32. [CrossRef]
85. Everstine, K.; Spink, J.; Kennedy, S. Economically motivated adulteration (EMA) of food: Common characteristics of EMA incidents. *J. Food Protect.* **2013**, *76*, 723–735. [CrossRef]
86. Ng, S.; Shao, S.; Ling, N. Food safety risk-assessment systems utilized by China, Australia/New Zealand, Canada, and the United States. *J. Food Sci.* **2022**, *87*, 4780–4795. [CrossRef]
87. Bannor, K.R.; Arthur, K.; Oppong, D.; Oppong-Kyeremeh, H. A comprehensive systematic review and bibliometric analysis of food fraud from a global perspective. *J. Agric. Food Res.* **2023**, *14*, 100686. [CrossRef]
88. Montgomery, H.; Haughey, S.A.; Elliott, C.T. Recent food safety and fraud issues within the dairy supply chain (2015–2019). *Glob. Food Secur.* **2020**, *26*, 100447. [CrossRef]
89. Johnson, R. *Food Fraud and "Economically Motivated Adulteration" of Food and Food Ingredients*; Report No. R43358; Congressional Research Service: Washington, DC, USA, 2014. Available online: https://blog.foodfraudpreventionthinktank.com/wp-content/uploads/2021/02/CRS-Food-Fraud-and-EMA-2014-R43358-2.pdf (accessed on 7 December 2025).
90. Bouzembrak, Y.; Marvin, H.J.P. Impact of drivers of change, including climatic factors, on the occurrence of chemical food safety hazards in fruits and vegetables: A Bayesian Network approach. *Food Control* **2019**, *97*, 67–76. [CrossRef]
91. Fakhlaei, R.; Selamat, J.; Khatib, A.; Razis, A.F.A.; Sukor, R.; Ahmad, S.; Babadi, A.A. The Toxic Impact of Honey Adulteration: A Review. *Foods* **2020**, *9*, 1538. [CrossRef]
92. Bouzembrak, Y.; Marvin, H.J.P. Prediction of food fraud type using data from Rapid Alert System for Food and Feed (RASFF) and Bayesian network modelling. *Food Control* **2016**, *61*, 180–187. [CrossRef]
93. Djekic, I.; Dimitrijevic, B.; Smigic, N. Consumer complaints associated with food quality. *J. Consum. Prot. Food Saf.* **2023**, *18*, 57–69. [CrossRef]
94. Marvin, H.J.P.; Bouzembrak, Y.; Janssen, E.M.; van der Fels- Klerx, H.J.; van Asselt, E.D.; Kleter, G.A. A holistic approach to food safety risks: Food fraud as an example. *Food Res. Int.* **2016**, *89*, 463–470. [CrossRef] [PubMed]
95. Aboah, J.; Lees, N. Consumers use of quality cues for meat purchase: Research trends and future pathways. *Meat Sci.* **2020**, *166*, 108142. [CrossRef]
96. Kemsawasd, V.; Jayasena, V.; Karnpanit, W. Incidents and potential adverse health effects of serious food fraud cases originated in Asia. *Foods* **2023**, *12*, 3522. [CrossRef]
97. Krajnc, B.; Bontempo, L.; Araus, J.L.; Giovanetti, M.; Alegria, C.; Lauteri, M.; Ogrinc, N. Selective methods to investigate authenticity and geographical origin of mediterranean food products. *Food Rev. Int.* **2020**, *37*, 656–682. [CrossRef]
98. Marozzo, V.; Meleddu, M.; Abbate, T. Sustainability and authenticity: Are they food risk relievers during the COVID-19 pandemic? *Br. Food J.* **2018**, *124*, 4234–4249. [CrossRef]
99. Van Ruth, S.M.; de Pagter-de Witte, L. Integrity of Organic Foods and Their Suppliers: Fraud Vulnerability Across Chains. *Foods* **2020**, *9*, 188. [CrossRef]
100. Fritsche, J. Recent developments and digital perspectives in food safety and authenticity. *J. Agric. Food Chem.* **2018**, *66*, 7562–7567. [CrossRef] [PubMed]
101. Moreira, M.J.; García-Díez, J.; de Almeida, J.M.M.M.; Saraiva, C. Consumer Knowledge about Food Labeling and Fraud. *Foods* **2021**, *15*, 1095. [CrossRef] [PubMed] [PubMed Central]
102. Lawrence, S.; Elliott, C.; Huisman, W.; Dean, M.; van Ruth, S. Food fraud threats in UK post-harvest seafood supply chains; an assessment of current vulnerabilities. *NPJ Sci. Food* **2024**, *8*, 30. [CrossRef] [PubMed]
103. Franc-Dąbrowska, J.; Ozimek, I.; Pomianek, I.; Rakowska, J. Young consumers' perception of food safety and their trust in official food control agencies. *Br. Food J.* **2021**, *123*, 2693–2704. [CrossRef]
104. Niu, L.; Chen, M.; Chen, X.; Wu, L.; Tsai, F. Enterprise food fraud in china: Key factors identification from social co-governance perspective. *Front. Public Health* **2021**, *9*, 752112. [CrossRef]
105. Pramesti, D.S.P.; Koeswayo, P.S.; Devano, S. Understanding how investigative auditors' competence, independence, and experience affect the efficiency with which audit procedures are implemented in fraud proof. *J. Akunt dan Sist. Teknologi Inf.* **2023**, *7*, 366–377. [CrossRef]

https://doi.org/10.3390/su18021101

106. Kertarajasa, A.Y.; Marwa, T.; Wahyudi, T. The effect of competence, the effect of competence, experience, independence, due professional care, and auditor integrity on audit quality with auditor ethics as moderating variable. *J. Account. Financ. Audit. Stud.* **2019**, *5*, 80–99. [CrossRef]
107. Anggraini, F.R.R.; Siswanto, F.A.J. Ethical leadership for internal auditor: An examination of social cognitive theory. *J. Akunt. Keuangan Ind.* **2019**, *16*, 165–179. [CrossRef]
108. Ode, A.L.; Wahyuniati, H.; Ángela, F.; Oktri, S. Auditor's Ability to Detect Fraud: Independence, Audit Experience, Professional Skepticism, and Work Load. *Russ. J. Agric. Soc.-Econ. Sci.* **2020**, *107*, 192–205. [CrossRef]
109. Svrčinová, P.; Janout, V. Comparison of official food safety control systems in member states of the European Union. *Cent. Eur. J. Public Health* **2018**, *26*, 321–325. [CrossRef]
110. Lane, S.W. Fraud in London local authorities: A comparative appraisal. *J. Financ. Crime* **2010**, *17*, 387–403. [CrossRef]
111. Marvin, H.J.P.; Bouzembrak, Y.; van der Fels-Klerx, H.J.; Kempenaar, C.; Veerkamp, R.; Chauhan, A.; Stroosnijder, S.; Top, J.; Simsek-Senel, G.; Vrolijk, H.; et al. Digitalisation and Artificial Intelligence for sustainable food systems. *Trends Food Sci. Technol.* **2022**, *120*, 344–348. [CrossRef]
112. Soon, J.M.; Krzyzaniak, S.C.; Shuttlewood, Z.; Smith, M.; Jack, L. Food fraud vulnerability assessment tools used in food industry. *Food Control* **2019**, *101*, 225–232. [CrossRef]
113. van Asselt, E.D.; Hoffmans, Y.; Hoek-van den Hil, E.F.; van der Fels-Klerx, H.J. Methods to perform risk-based inspections of food companies. *J. Food Sci.* **2021**, *86*, 5078–5086. [CrossRef] [PubMed]
114. Tao, D.; Yang, P.; Feng, H. Utilization of text mining as a big data analysis tool for food science and nutrition. *Compr. Rev. Food Sci. Food Saf.* **2020**, *19*, 875–894. [CrossRef]
115. Garaus, M.; Treiblmaier, H. The influence of blockchain-based food traceability on retailer choice: The mediating role of trust. *Food Control* **2021**, *129*, 108082. [CrossRef]
116. Tran, D.; Schouteten, J.; Gellynck, X.; De Steur, H. How do consumers value food traceability?—A meta-analysis. *Food Control* **2024**, *162*, 110453. [CrossRef]
117. Qian, C.; Murphy, S.I.; Orsi, R.H.; Wiedmann, M. How Can AI Help Improve Food Safety? *Annu Rev Food Sci Technol.* **2023**, *14*, 517–538. [CrossRef]

https://doi.org/10.3390/su18021101

sustainability

Article

Young Consumers' Price Perceptions in Purchasing Foods: Evidence from Greece

Zoi C. Kalyva, Ioanna S. Kosma and Dimitris Skalkos *

Laboratory of Food Chemistry, Department of Chemistry, University of Ioannina, 45110 Ioannina, Greece; zoikal@uoi.gr (Z.C.K.); i.kosma@uoi.gr (I.S.K.)
* Correspondence: dskalkos@uoi.gr; Tel.: +30-2651008345

Abstract: The recent consecutive economic and social crises impose sustainable "from farm to fork" food chain management to feed the global population. In this study, we investigated the price perceptions of young consumers (Gen Z) in purchasing foods in Greece to find out the determinants ensuring sustainable, future food consumption. We used eight overall price perception determinants, five with negative roles, namely value and price consciousness, coupon and sales proneness, and price mavenism, and three with positive roles, namely price–quality, price–value, and prestige–sensitivity for the formation of the study's questionnaire. A total of 514 students (Gen Z, 85%) answered the questionnaire, promoted through the Google platform during September and October 2023. The data were analyzed with statistical tools, combining cross and chi-square tests. Between the negative determinants, the "value consciousness" price perceptions (71.02%) were the most important parameters in purchasing food, followed by "price consciousness" (55.02%) parameters. "Coupon proneness", 48.4%, and "sales proneness", 49%, were equally lower, while "price mavenism" parameters were minimally preferred by only 26.4% of the participants. Participants exhibited a major preference for the "value to price" interconnection (66.7%), such as good value for money, value exceeding a product's price, and overvalued low-priced foods, while their preference for the "quality to price" interconnection was significantly lower (48.8%), such as in terms of getting what you pay for, more money for better quality, and priced, quality foods. The "prestige–sensitivity" price perception was outside of their preferences in terms of food purchasing (only 7.1%). Our findings indicate that young consumers (Gen Z) pay more attention to the values of negative and positive parameters concerning price perceptions when purchasing food rather than quality, coupons and sales, low prices, and mavenism, or even the prestige of the foods. This means that value issues such as the perceived environmental impact (green value), the climate crisis, the social signaling potential, and others are significant concerns, including their price perceptions for food purchases.

Keywords: food choice motives (FCM); value consciousness; price consciousness; sales and coupon proneness; price mavenism; value-price; quality-price; Generation Z (Gen Z)

1. Introduction

Daily lifestyle habits have changed in a significant manner due to the global burden of COVID-19, which continues to redefine parts of our daily habits [1]. Changes vary from country to country and include, among others, time spent with family, physical activity, office work, sleeping behavior, mental health, eating habits, etc. Changes have been recorded in the food choice motives (FCM) of consumers, too, as evidenced in recent literature which was systematically reviewed by our group last year [2]. FCM, namely health—convenience—sensory appeal—nutritional quality—ethical concerns—weight control—mood—familiarity—price—shopping frequency behavior, in the new era, are perceived differently by consumers depending on their age, country, sex, and culture [2]. "Health" refers to the link of food consumption with chronic food-related diseases, "convenience foods" refers to those foods prepared and made available for easy and quick consumption, "sensory appeal" is the taste, smell, texture, and appearance of foods, and "nutritional quality" refers to the food combinations that affect overall diet quality and health [2]. "Ethical concern" refers to the impact of food production and consumption on the environment or society, "weight control" refers to the diets and exercise programs controlling body weight, "mood and stress" refers to the mood and emotional eating which influences the quantity and frequency of meals, and "familiarity" is the cognitive ability to apply knowledge acquired via experience [2]. Finally, "price" refers to the selection of foods based on their sale prices, and "shopping frequency behavior" refers to the frequency of shopping based on, among others, the sustainability and shelf-life of perishable foods [2].

Changes due to the pandemic are still underway; therefore, definite answers defining the "new" index of consumer satisfaction cannot be given yet for the "from farm to fork" food consumption process, which is an important aspect of sustainable development, especially due to new global crises caused by political instability and conflict around the world [3]. The "farm to fork" agri-food chain's hidden, external costs of USD 12 trillion illustrate the need to make the food process more sustainable to overcome the planetary boundaries responsible for the climate crisis and biodiversity loss [4].

Since the young generation is the "future", comprising consumers forming the future index of food satisfaction, we exploited the impact of the COVID-19 pandemic on college students of Greece regarding FCM for sustainable eating behavior [5]. Most college students (18 to 32 years old) by far belong to the newest generation, referred to as Generation Z (12–28 years old), which is very different from earlier generations in terms of their preferences and characteristics, shaping the global future in a unique way, including in terms of food consumption [6]. We found that students have already returned to their previous motives for food selection engendered by the period before COVID-19, as most of the 10 parameters studied, except for "home-cooked food", now rank higher in their preferences, and "eating at restaurants" and "eating fast food" ranked lower in their preferences. The "shopping frequency" which changed during the pandemic has now returned to the preferences of the pre-pandemic period. The study showed that the motive that continues to be of the highest concern for students before and after the pandemic is price, with students looking for good value, inexpensive foods [5].

Literature Review

The marketing literature, for a long time now, has shown that consumer knowledge, including price, plays an important role in purchase behavior [7–9]. Price is an important factor in food choice, especially for low-income consumers [10], who are significantly more conscious of value and price than higher-income consumers [11]. The most attractive strategies, according to the consumers' opinions so far, are discounting healthy food more often and applying a lower VAT (value-added tax) rate on them. Pricing strategies (e.g., price reductions/increases, the "buy one get two" strategy, bonus systems, etc.) are seen as a promising approach because sales promotions form an important part of the marketing mix [12,13]. The price gradient more favorable to large unit sizes receives wide criticism because it can trigger consumers to over-purchase and eventually waste food [14]. However, recent research indicates that this relationship is not as straightforward as the criticism implies [15,16]. Two systematic reviews on the effects of price perceptions and consumer shopping behavior highlight the importance of assessing possible different parameters of pricing strategies on dietary behaviors, and the limited evidence available addressing these parameters [17,18]. Investigating if pricing interventions differentially affect subgroups of the population is important, especially in studying new generations such as Gen Z, since these interventions may alter their food disparities [17,19]. The consumers' pricing perceptions may differ across socio-economic positions or person-related factors such as Body Mass Index and sex [20,21]. To date, limited research results have been published on the potential differential effects of pricing attitudes in terms of personal characteristics, including targeted subgroups, impulsivity, decision-making styles, price sensitivity, and food choice motives [22]. Even though price sensitivity is related to individuals' decision-making processes, evidence shows that individuals who highly value "health", "natural content", and "weight control" tend to purchase foods with high prices compared to individuals who find these motives of less importance [22].

Currently, studies are targeting trust and consumers' acceptance of food products incorporating social and environmental costs into the price of the food, i.e., "True price food products" [23]. Among the rather novel approach of the economic instrument of "true price food", another possible measure is cost accounting [24], and ecological and sometimes social implications from agricultural production are monetized and internalized into the price of foods. Consumers show interest in true food pricing, even though there are concerns that many of them might not be able to afford to pay the true prices. The more consumers that perceive themselves as gaining value from true food pricing as it pertains to social status and green value (positive environmental impact), the greater the consumers' trust in true pricing characteristics and in organizations that implement true pricing, and therefore the higher the consumers' intentions to purchase true price foods [25]. True pricing levels the food's market prices and true costs of food production [26], encouraging the food industry to come up with more beneficial externalities in food production and to provide more transparency about the true price or even charge for it [27].

Recent studies show that the current continuing global economic crises are causing increased prices for all economic activities [28]. Not only the agricultural products of the farm-to-fork chain are dramatically affected [29], but also the food prices [30], with inflation increasing worldwide [31]. Therefore, studying youngsters' (Gen Z) price perceptions in purchasing their foods is an urgent research topic for shaping the future of the sustainable "farm to fork" food chain in such OKturbulent periods.

In this study, we exploited the Greek students' responses about their perceptions of food prices when deciding to choose their food. To accomplish this research, according to the literature on food pricing [32], our work tested the following determinants regarding purchasing food:

Determinants with a negative role of price on food selection:

- Value consciousness;
- Price consciousness;
- Coupon consciousness;
- Sales proneness;
- Price mavenism (maven).

Determinants with a positive role of price in food selection:

- Price–quality;
- Value–price;
- Prestige–sensitivity.

2. Materials and Methods

2.1. Data Collection and Sample Characterization

A questionnaire was prepared to investigate the students' food price perceptions; it was composed of nine parts, based on the parts presented for the first time by Lichtenstein et al. in 1993 [32] (Table S1). The questions were initially formed in English, as presented in Table S1, and then were translated into Greek for the promotion of the questionnaire to the Greek students. The social/demographic characteristics of the respondents were obtained in the first part (gender, age, civil state, employment status, and permanent residency). Parts 2–8 consisted of four questions each designed to assess the perceptions of students regarding their consciousness of value, price, coupon proneness, sales proneness, price mavenism, the price–quality relationship, and the value–price relationship, while part 9 consisted of eight questions regarding the prestige–sensitivity relation.

The initial testing of the questionnaire as well as the method used for its distribution was conducted as described by Skalkos et al. in the first paper regarding students' questionnaires [5].

The survey took place during the period of September to October 2023. The research was conducted through the online Google Forms distributed to the students of the University of Ioannina, Greece, which has seven schools, fifteen departments covering all subject matters, and more than 30,000 active students from all over Greece. GDPR approval was granted by the University's Bureau of Personal Data Protection and the students were reached afterward through their academic e-mails. In the survey, 514 students of the University responded, a survey population comprising 1.7% of the 30,000 enrolled students. The sociodemographic characterization of the perticipants is shonw in Table 1 below.

Table 1. Sociodemographic characterization of the sample.

Variable	Groups	%
Gender	Male	27.9
	Female	72.1
Age	18–20	46.7
	21–25	33.7
	26–30	8.1
	31–35	11.4
Civil state	Single	89.5
	Married	7.9
	Divorced	2.6
Job situation	Employed student	30
	Student exclusively	70
Permanent residency (among the Greek regions)	NORTH GREECE (regions of Macedonia—Thrace)	27.5
	WEST GREECE (region of Epirus—Aitoloakarnania prefecture)	35.4
	CENTRAL GREECE (including Athens)	24.2
	SOUTH GREECE (region of Peloponnese)	6.1
	ISLANDS	6.8

In terms of geographical distribution, participants, students studying in the Epirus region of Greece but residing permanently in other regions were 35.4% permanent residents of west Greece, 27.5% of north Greece, 24.2% residents of Central Greece, 6.8% residents of the Greek islands, and 6.1% of South Greece, a well-balanced national distribution based on the population of each region. Most of the participants were aged between 18 and 20 and between 21 and 25 years old (46.7% and 33.7%, respectively), and less between 26 and 30 and 31 and 35 years (8.1% and 11.4%, respectively). Therefore, Generation Z (18–28 years old) comprised more than 85% of the participants. Regarding the employment status category, students (70%) dominated the respondents, which is also representative for the Gen Z population.

2.2. Data Analysis

The questionnaire was built up on a five-point Likert scale (1 = not at all important, 2 = less important, 3 = moderately important, 4 = quite important, and 5 = very important) [33] to measure the students' perceptions of price. Statistical treatment of data was performed using IBM SPSS Statistics for Windows (Version 25.0, IBM Corp., Armonk, NY, USA). Nonparametric tests were used. Nonparametric testing was performed to test the distribution of the variables of each group and response based on the hypothesized equal proportions for each variable. The Chi-Square Independence Test was used to determine whether there was an association between the variables. Cramer's V coefficient was used to analyze the strength of the significant relations found between some of the variables in the study. This coefficient ranged from 0 to 1 and can be interpreted as follows: $V \approx 0.1$, the association is considered weak; $V \approx 0.3$, the association is moderate; and $V \approx 0.5$ or over, the association is strong. Sociodemographic characteristics were considered as predictor variables that could affect the other responses to the questionnaire. In all of the tests performed, the level of significance considered was 5% ($p < 0.05$), as described by Skalkos et al. [34].

3. Results

The results of the negative role of price perceptions on food purchase answered by the participants of the study are presented in Table 2. As shown, based on the "quite" and "very important" answers, the most important negative price determinant for food purchase was "value consciousness", for which it was "quite" or "very important" in the "worth for money" selection criterion (77.7%), followed by "shopping around" for lower prices (71.9%), the connection between "quality and low price" (69.1%), and "price per Kg" (65.4%) among the available foods for purchase.

Table 2. Young consumers' perceptions of the negative role of price on food selection regarding consciousness of value and price, proneness toward coupons and sales, and price mavenism (Values represent %).

THE NEGATIVE ROLE OF PRICE IN PURCHASING FOOD					
PREFERENCE REGARDING **VALUE CONSCIOUSNESS** IN PURCHASING FOOD					
How important is the criterion for your purchase of FOOD	Not at all important	Less important	Moderately important	Quite important	Very important
The low prices in connection with the food quality	2.8	7.3	20.9	37.2	31.9
The "shopping around" for lower prices of food	0.8	6.1	21.3	40.2	31.7
The "worth of money" selection criteria	0.6	4.1	17.6	41.4	36.3
The comparison of the "price per Kg" between the available foods for purchase	3.1	9.8	21.6	37.6	27.8
PREFERENCE REGARDING **PRICE CONSCIOUSNESS** IN PURCHASING FOOD					
How important is the criterion for your purchase of FOOD					
Not to go to extra effort to find lower prices.	10.2	16.5	28.9	28.5	15.7
To shop at more than one store to take advantage of low prices.	9.1	18.5	26.0	29.5	16.9
The time it takes to find low prices.	6.3	12.4	31.4	31.8	18.1
The money saved by finding low prices.	1.8	3.9	14.7	34.3	45.3
PREFERENCE REGARDING **COUPON PRONENESS** ON PURCHASING FOOD					
How important is the criterion for your purchase of FOOD					
To redeem coupons in order to feel good.	13.6	14.2	21.1	26.0	25.2
To enjoy clipping coupons out of different sources.	21.5	21.9	22.0	22.2	12.4
To feel you are getting a good deal using coupons.	13.4	14.8	21.1	29.5	21.3
To enjoy using coupons regarding the amount of money saved by doing so.	13.9	9.9	19.0	27.9	29.3
PREFERENCE REGARDING **SALES PRONENESS** ON PURCHASING FOOD					
How important is the criterion your purchase of FOOD					
The food is on sale.	2.0	5.1	20.1	33.7	39.2
The selection of the food brand because it is on sale.	2.2	11.2	25.1	36.5	25.1
The selection of a favorite food brand regarding the sale status.	5.3	15.1	37.6	30.7	11.4
The negative attitude toward purchasing food brands that are on sale.	26.8	26.2	27.2	15.2	4.7

Table 2. *Cont.*

PREFERENCE REGARDING **PRICE MAVENISM** ON PURCHASING FOOD					
How important is the criterion your purchase of FOOD					
Searching for information in advance about prices for different types of food.	13.9	23.2	28.7	22.0	12.3
Being well-informed constantly as an expert on food prices.	19.2	26.1	28.1	17.0	9.7
Asking an expert that you know about food prices before purchasing the food.	31.0	24.5	25.7	12.6	6.1
Trusting the internet as a reliable source about the prices of foods.	20.0	25.7	28.1	18.4	7.7

The second important determinant was "price consciousness", for which it was "quite" or "very important" for the participants that the food they purchase helped them "save money by finding low prices" (79.6%), followed by "the time that it takes to find lower prices" (49.9%), "shopping in more stores for lower prices" (46.4%), and "not expend extra effort to find lower prices" (44.2%).

The third important determinant for the participants was "coupon proneness", for which was is "very" and "quite important" that consumers are "enjoying using coupons regarding the saving of money" (57.2%), followed by "redeeming coupons to feel good" (51.2%), "the feeling of getting a good deal with the coupons" (50.8%), and "less extend enjoying clipping coupons of different sources" (34.6%).

The fourth important determinant, almost equal to the third one, was "sales proneness", for which it was "quite" or "very important" for the participants that "the food be on sale" (72.9%), followed by "the selection of the food brand be on sale" 61.6%); important to a lesser extent were the "the selection of food brand regarding the sales status" (42.1%) and "the negative attitude for food brand on sale" criteria (29.9%).

The fifth negative important determinant, by far the last one in the participants' price perceptions, was "price mavenism", for which it was "quite" and "very important" that the students "search for information in advance about prices" for different types of food, 34.3%, "ask experts for food prices", 28.7%, and "be well informed about food prices", 26.7%, followed by "trust the internet for food prices", 26.1%. Price mavens, coined by Feick and Price in 1987 [35], like their market maven counterparts, collect price information in order to share it with others and obtain social returns from their searching behavior [36].

Table S2 depicts the significant ($p < 0.05$) associations between participants' perceptions of negative food pricing determinants and sociodemographic variables. Specifically, regarding the topic of value consciousness, associations were observed between gender, age, civil state, job situation and residency (connection of low prices and food quality: age ($x^2 = 23.672$, $p = 0.023$), comparison of the "price per Kg" between the available foods: gender ($x^2 = 12.739$, $p = 0.013$), age ($x^2 = 35.417$, $p = 0.000$), job situation ($x^2 = 13.930$, $p = 0.008$)), the price convenience topic showed significant associations between age, job situation and residency (no extra effort to find lower prices: job situation ($x^2 = 11.050$, $p = 0.026$), shop to more than one stores to find lower prices: gender ($x^2 = 11.106$, $p = 0.025$), saving money by finding lower prices: job situation ($x^2 = 13.405$, $p = 0.009$), residency ($x^2 = 26.649$, $p = 0.046$)). The coupon proneness showed statistically significant associations ($p < 0.05$) between gender and residency (redeem coupons to feel good: residency ($x^2 = 26.255$, $p = 0.050$), enjoy clipping coupon from different sources: residency ($x^2 = 27.667$, $p = 0.035$), getting a good deal: residency ($x^2 = 29.751$, $p = 0.019$) and enjoy using coupons regarding the amount of money saved by doing so: gender ($x^2 = 11.214$, $p = 0.024$), residency ($x^2 = 26.308$, $p = 0.050$)), while the sales proneness topic showed associations with most of the sociodemographic variables (food on sale: gender ($x^2 = 18.123$, $p = 0.001$), age ($x^2 = 26.593$, $p = 0.009$), selection of a food brand on sale: gender ($x^2 = 15.402$, $p = 0.004$), residency ($x^2 = 27.623$, $p = 0.035$), selection of the favor food brand regarding the sale status: gender ($x^2 = 10.130$, $p = 0.038$), negative attitude toward purchasing a food brand which is on sale:

civil state ($x^2 = 31.716$, $p = 0.000$)). Finally, the price mavenism topic showed associations between the sociodemographic variables regarding the trust in the internet as a reliable source about the prices of foods: gender ($x^2 = 11.729$, $p = 0.019$), age ($x^2 = 27.213$, $p = 0.007$), and residency ($x^2 = 39.460$, $p = 0.001$).

The results of the positive role of price on food selection and purchase answered by the participants of the study are presented in Table 3. The most important determinant was the "value–price" interconnection, for which it was "quite" or "very important" for the participants to receive "good value for money food", 80.6%, "not an undervalued food because of its low price", 72.2%, "value exceeding its price", 60.3%, and "price base on foods' exact value, 53.8%.

Table 3. Young consumers' perceptions of the positive role of price on food selection regarding the connections of price–quality, value–price, and prestige–sensitivity (Values represent %).

THE POSITIVE ROLE OF PRICE IN PURCHASING FOOD					
PREFERENCE REGARDING **PRICE–QUALITY** WHEN PURCHASING FOOD					
How important is the criterion for your purchase of FOOD	Not at all important	Less important	Moderately important	Quite important	Very important
The higher the price of a food, the higher its quality.	9.4	21.0	35.4	19.3	14.9
The common phrase "you get what you pay for" is generally true.	4.9	16.7	28.7	31.4	18.3
The price of food is a good indicator of its quality.	5.5	15.7	25.3	28.5	25.0
You must pay a bit more for the best food.	3.6	11.5	27.1	35.0	22.9
PREFERENCE REGARDING **VALUE–PRICE** WHEN PURCHASING FOOD					
How important is the criterion for your purchase of FOOD					
To be priced based on its exact value.	3.0	13.0	30.2	34.5	19.3
To be a "good value for money" food.	0.6	4.1	14.7	40.8	39.8
To have a value exceeding its price.	4.3	8.3	27.2	33.9	26.4
Not to be undervalued because of its low price.	2.9	4.7	20.2	40.6	31.6
PREFERENCE REGARDING THE **PRESTIGE–SENSITIVITY** WHEN PURCHASING FOOD					
How important is the criterion for your purchase of FOOD					
To pay attention when you buy the most expensive brand of food.	42.5	31.8	19.9	3.7	2.1
To feel better buying a high-priced food brand.	38.8	30.2	19.5	8.2	3.3
To feel classy buying the most expensive food brand.	58.7	20.9	11.5	6.0	2.9
To enjoy the prestige of buying a high-priced food brand.	53.4	22.6	12.5	8.0	3.5
To have your friends consider you are cheap if you consistently buy the lower priced version of a food.	64.1	20.5	6.2	5.8	3.3
To buy the most expensive food brand just because your friends will notice it.	78.6	14.4	3.5	2.1	1.4
To buy the kinds of foods and food brands based on the judgments others will make about you because of the specific selections.	78.0	13.8	4.5	2.1	1.6
To select a costly food brand versus a relatively inexpensive food since it is impressive.	81.1	12.7	3.3	1.6	1.4

The second most important determinant was the "quality–price" interconnection, for which it was "quite" or "very important" for the participants to "pay a bit more for the best food", 57.9%, "get a price indicator of the food's quality", 53.5%, "get what you pay for", 49.7%, and "get a higher price with higher quality", 34.2%.

The third and least important determinant was the "prestige–sensitivity" interconnection, for which all questions had a very low percentage of "quite" or "very important" responses, including "feeling better buying high-priced food brands", 11.5%, "enjoying the prestige of buying high-priced food brands", 11.5%, "having friends considering you cheap buying constantly lower-priced versions of food", 9.1%, "feeling classy buying the most expensive food brand", 8.9%, "paying attention when buying the most expensive food brand", 5.8%, "buying the specific food brand based on the judgment of others will make about you", 3.7%, "buying the most expensive food brand for friends' attention", 3.5%, and "selecting a costly food brand since it is impressive", 3%.

Table S3 shows the statistically significant ($p < 0.05$) associations between participants' perceptions on the remaining topics of the food pricing questionnaire and sociodemographic variables. Regarding the connection between price and quality, significant associations were found between civil state and gender (the higher the price of a food, the higher its quality: civil state ($x^2 = 17.232$, $p = 0.028$), the common phrase "you get what you pay for" to be generally true: civil state ($x^2 = 16.786$, $p = 0.032$), and one must pay a bit more for the best food: gender ($x^2 = 12.790$, $p = 0.012$)). The connection between value and price showed significant associations for two of the questions with the sociodemographic variables (to be priced based on its exact value: age ($x^2 = 25.368$, $p = 0.013$), and residency ($x^2 = 26.675$, $p = 0.045$), to be a "good value for money" food: civil state ($x^2 = 18.174$, $p = 0.020$)). Finally, for the connection between prestige and sensitivity, the significant associations were the following: between paying attention when you buy the most expensive brand of food and age ($x^2 = 30.044$, $p = 0.003$), between feeling better when buying a high-priced food brand and age ($x^2 = 23.711$, $p = 0.022$), and between feeling classy buying the most expensive food brand and age ($x^2 = 22.745$, $p = 0.030$), and civil state ($x^2 = 15.391$, $p = 0.050$).

4. Discussion

The results presented above indicate that young consumers' price perceptions for the purchase of their foods vary depending on the determinant (parameter) chosen for the food selection.

Between the negative determinants, the "value consciousness" price perception on purchasing food was the most important parameter for the participants of the study (average 71.02% of "quite" and "very important" answers based on the five questions included in the questionnaire). Our results agree with the reported literature indicating that initial value sources can potentially contribute to promoting trust and consumer acceptance of the true pricing of foods [25]. Wikstrom et al. reported that, often, consumers' biggest problem is how to integrate available resources and to make trade-offs between different value dimensions in a way so as to contribute to a good price of food [37].

The second most important negative determinant based on participants' answers was been "price consciousness", providing an average of 55.02% of "quite" and "very important" answers. The importance of low pricing was addressed by Afshin et al., who systematically reviewed existing literature on the prospective impact of food pricing on improving food consumption (an action that follows the purchase of foods) [38]. They indicated that, according to existing literature, a 10% decrease in the price of food increases consumption by 12%, and a 10% increase in price decreases consumption by 6%.

The two determinants with equal negative importance for price perceptions recorded, third and fourth in a row, were "coupon proneness" with a 48.4% average of "quite" and "very important" answers and "sales proneness" with a 49% average. Our results agree with the findings of Yen-Ting et al. [39], who studied the effects of price discounts and bonus packs together on consumers. The authors reported that either for vice foods (pearl milk tea) or virtue foods (sugar-free tea), a price discount is as effective as a bonus pack. They contended that consumers would prefer a price discount when purchasing pearl milk tea, but a bonus pack when purchasing sugar-free tea.

The last negative price determinant for the participants' preference for food purchase, with a very low average percentage of "quite" and "very important answers", was "price mavenism", with only 26.4%. Feick and Price introduced the concept of market mavens (MM) to describe a unique pattern of consumer behavior wherein a minority of retail consumers disproportionately influences the behavior of other consumers [35]. Goldsmith et al. showed that mavenism is positively associated with brand engagement in self-concept, status consumption, and materialism [40]. Somers et al. studied the association of mavenism and pleasure with food involvement in older adults and found that food mavenism and pleasure motivation are stronger predictors of food involvement than demographic factors [41].

From the three determinants with positive affects on price perceptions recorded by the young participants, the most important was "value–price" with an average of 66.7% of "quite" and "very important" answers to the four questions asked. The importance of the value-to-price connection by consumers for food purchase has been emphasized by many scholars [42–45]. Taufik et al. recently studied consumer value for true-price food products and found that value sources can potentially contribute to promoting consumer acceptance of true pricing in the food domain, with various other factors being relevant as well [25].

The determinant with second most positive importance for the young consumers on purchasing food recorded was "quality–price", with an average of 48.8% of "quite" and "very important" answers, significantly lower than the "value–price" answers. Food quality as a major parameter for consumers' food perception has been studied extensively for more than 20 years [46,47]. Studies have focused recently on purchase decisions based on quality and price for selected foods such as fast food [48], organic food [49], and others. Nabila and Tambunan recently indicated that customers in making purchases are influenced by the quality of food, service levels, prices, and the store environment [50]. Our results indicated, however, that value assets are much more important than quality for price perceptions in food purchasing for young consumers, which may include assets such as the perceived positive environmental impact (green value), the social signaling potential [25], and others.

The determinant with no positive importance on purchasing food by the young consumers of our study was "prestige–sensitivity", with a low 7.1% average of "quite" and "very important" answers. Based on the eight questions used in this parameter and the answers received, young consumers do not pay attention to expensive brands when purchasing their food, even when they are persuaded by their friends. Even though personal branding is highly important for Gen Z youngsters for their own activities [51,52], apparently it is not important for their food choice, even when it has to do with specific food brand groups such as halal foods [53].

5. Conclusions

As Generation Z (Gen-Z) consumers currently constitute approximately 40% of global consumers and are projected to become the largest consumer segment worldwide by 2030 [54], their burgeoning spending power has become increasingly evident. They are now moving to the next phase in which they will constitute the predominant majority of the incoming workforce bringing a distinct set of characteristics into the workplace and marketplace, including the purchase and consumption of foods. The current work on young consumers' perceptions is the first study ever that systematically examines Gen Z's price determinants in purchasing foods. It is the research extension of our earlier findings indicating students' preference for value for money, inexpensiveness, and cheap foods as part of their food choice motives [5].

Our current findings indicated that youngsters are positively affected primarily by the "value to price" interconnection for the food they buy, and secondarily by the "quality to price" relationship. Interestingly, they do not purchase expensive, high-priced food brands, neither as a prestigious, impressive projection for friends nor as a prompt from friends.

On the other hand, our findings showed that youngsters are negatively affected by the "value consciousness" of the food price they select, shopping around to receive proper value for their money and low-priced, and priced-per-Kg foods. Secondarily, they pay attention to the "price consciousness" of foods, evaluating the time they spend, the extra effort they take, the stores they visit, and the money they save searching for the lowest price of each food. Interestingly, they are not affected by "coupon and sales proneness" as much as expected, such as redeeming coupons or selecting food brands on sale, except for finding food and food brands on sale. Lastly, "price mavenism" is the price perception that does not interest the young participants of this study significantly, and they are affected minimally by advanced information and expert opinions when purchasing foods.

The study has two limitations concerning the participants' group. The first is the female participation of 72.1%, exceeding by far the male participation, which is only 27.9% (a discrepancy typical of most online studies). The second is the participation of the Gen Z participants of Greece only (extension to other countries should be conducted in the future).

This research has not only managerial and policy implications for marketing but also poses a theoretical contribution for marketing researchers studying Gen Z's behavior. The results are very helpful for the food industry and those organizations which participate in the farm-to-fork process overall, ensuring a successful path to market for foods. With this research work, the industry has a first indication of the price perceptions of future adults in order to be prepared in advance for the food market of the near future.

Future research as a continuation of the current study will include an examination of youngsters' price perceptions of selected groups of daily purchased foods such as dairy, fruits and vegetables, etc. and a further investigation of the various determinants affecting the value-to-price and value consciousness criteria food-purchasing behavior, since value appears to be the most important criterion.

Supplementary Materials: The following supporting information can be downloaded at https://www.mdpi.com/article/10.3390/su16135752/s1, Table S1: Questionnaire food price perception by Greek students for sustainable food consumption, Table S2: Associations between students' perception of food pricing regarding value and price consciousness, coupon and sales proneness and price mavenism and the sociodemographic variables, Table S3: Associations between students' perception on food pricing regarding the connections of price-quality, value–price and prestige–sensitivity and the sociodemographic variables.

Author Contributions: Conceptualization, methodology, D.S. and Z.C.K., writing—original draft preparation, D.S., Z.C.K. and I.S.K., supervision and editing, D.S. All authors have read and agreed to the published version of the manuscript.

Funding: This research received no external funding.

Institutional Review Board Statement: No ethical approval was required for this type of study according to the GDPR (General Data Protection Regulation) of the European Union, adapted by the Greek legislation by the law 4624/2019. Only approval by the Bureau of Personal Data Protection of the University of Ioannina was required and obtained (3995/24-10-2023 in Greek) prior to the distribution of the questionnaire through Google Forms within the university community, as a questionnaire with no commercial interest.

Informed Consent Statement: Not applicable based on the GDPR European Union law, adapted by the Greek law 4624/2019 for this case.

Data Availability Statement: The data presented in this study are available on request from the corresponding author.

Conflicts of Interest: The authors declare no conflicts of interest.

References

1. Radhika, V.; Kumari, R. A Study on Life Style Changes of Households Due to COVID-19. *Int. J. Multidiscip. Res.* **2023**, *5*, 1–8. [CrossRef]
2. Skalkos, D.; Kalyva, Z.C. Exploring the Impact of COVID-19 Pandemic on Food Choice Motives: A Systematic Review. *Sustainability* **2023**, *15*, 1606. [CrossRef]
3. Rejman, K.; Kaczorowska, J.; Halicka, E.; Laskowski, W. Do Europeans Consider Sustainability When Making Food Choices? A Survey of Polish City-Dwellers. *Public Health Nutr.* **2019**, *22*, 1–10. [CrossRef]
4. National Library of Medicine. Counting the Hidden $12-Trillion Cost of a Broken Food System. *Nature* **2019**, *574*, 296. [CrossRef] [PubMed]
5. Skalkos, D.; Kalyva, Z.C.; Kosma, I.S. The Impact of the COVID-19 Pandemic on College Students' Food Choice Motives in Greece. *Sustainability* **2023**, *15*, 9865. [CrossRef]

6. Pichler, S.; Kohli, C.; Granitz, N. DITTO for Gen Z: A Framework for Leveraging the Uniqueness of the New Generation. *Bus. Horiz.* **2021**, *64*, 599–610. [CrossRef]
7. Basu, A.; Vitharana, P. Impact of Customer Knowledge Heterogeneity on Bundling Strategy. *Mark. Sci.* **2009**, *28*, 792–801. [CrossRef]
8. Alba, J.W.; Hutchinson, J.W. Dimensions of Consumer Expertise. *J. Consum. Res.* **1987**, *13*, 411–454. [CrossRef]
9. Sujan, M. Consumer Knowledge: Effects on Evaluation Strategies Mediating Consumer Judgments. *J. Consum. Res.* **1985**, *12*, 31–46. [CrossRef]
10. De Irala-Estévez, J.; Groth, M.; Johansson, L.; Oltersdorf, U.; Prättälä, R.; Martínez-González, M.A. A Systematic Review of Socio-Economic Differences in Food Habits in Europe: Consumption of Fruit and Vegetables. *Eur. J. Clin. Nutr.* **2000**, *54*, 706–714. [CrossRef]
11. Steenhuis, I.H.M.; Waterlander, W.E.; De Mul, A. Consumer Food Choices: The Role of Price and Pricing Strategies. *Public Health Nutr.* **2011**, *14*, 2220–2226. [CrossRef]
12. Hawkes, C. Sales Promotions and Food Consumptionnure. *Nutr. Rev.* **2009**, *67*, 333–342. [CrossRef] [PubMed]
13. Han, S.; Gupta, S.; Lehmann, D.R. Consumer Price Sensitivity and Price Thresholds. *J. Retail.* **2001**, *77*, 435–456. [CrossRef]
14. Hegnsholt, E.; Unnikrishnan, S.; Pollmann-Larsen, M.; Askelsdottir, B.; Gerard, M. *Tackling the 1.6-Billion-Ton Food Loss and Waste Crisis*; The Boston Consulting Group: London, UK, 2018.
15. Tsalis, G.; Boutrup Jensen, B.; Aschemann-Witzel, J. The Relationship between Retail Price Promotions and Household-Level Food Waste: Busting the Myth with Behavioural Data? *Waste Manag.* **2024**, *173*, 29–39. [CrossRef] [PubMed]
16. Tsalis, G.; Jensen, B.B.; Wakeman, S.W.; Aschemann-Witzel, J. Promoting Food for the Trash Bin? A Review of the Literature on Retail Price Promotions and Household-Level Food Waste. *Sustainability* **2021**, *13*, 4018. [CrossRef]
17. Mizdrak, A.; Scarborough, P.; Waterlander, W.E.; Rayner, M. Differential Responses to Food Price Changes by Personal Characteristic: A Systematic Review of Experimental Studies. *PLoS ONE* **2015**, *10*, e0130320. [CrossRef]
18. Epstein, L.H.; Jankowiak, N.; Nederkoorn, C.; Raynor, H.A.; French, S.A.; Finkelstein, E. Experimental Research on the Relation between Food Price Changes and Food-Purchasing Patterns: A Targeted Review. *Am. J. Clin. Nutr.* **2012**, *95*, 789–809. [CrossRef] [PubMed]
19. Hartmann-Boyce, J.; Bianchi, F.; Piernas, C.; Riches, S.P.; Frie, K.; Nourse, R.; Jebb, S.A. Grocery Store Interventions to Change Food Purchasing Behaviors: A Systematic Review of Randomized Controlled Trials. *Am. J. Clin. Nutr.* **2018**, *107*, 1004–1016. [CrossRef]
20. Darmon, N.; Lacroix, A.; Muller, L.; Ruffieux, B. Food Price Policies May Improve Diet but Increase Socioeconomic Inequalities in Nutrition. *World Rev. Nutr. Diet.* **2016**, *115*, 36–45. [CrossRef]
21. Blakely, T.; Mhurchu, C.N.; Jiang, Y.; Matoe, L.; Funaki-Tahifote, M.; Eyles, H.C.; Foster, R.H.; McKenzie, S.; Rodgers, A. Do Effects of Price Discounts and Nutrition Education on Food Purchases Vary by Ethnicity, Income and Education? Results from a Randomised, Controlled Trial. *J. Epidemiol. Commun. Health* **2011**, *65*, 902–908. [CrossRef]
22. Naughton, P.; McCarthy, S.N.; McCarthy, M.B. The Creation of a Healthy Eating Motivation Score and Its Association with Food Choice and Physical Activity in a Cross Sectional Sample of Irish Adults. *Int. J. Behav. Nutr. Phys. Act.* **2015**, *12*, 1–10. [CrossRef] [PubMed]
23. Michalke, A.; Stein, L.; Fichtner, R.; Gaugler, T.; Stoll-Kleemann, S. True Cost Accounting in Agri-Food Networks: A German Case Study on Informational Campaigning and Responsible Implementation. *Sustain. Sci.* **2022**, *17*, 2269–2285. [CrossRef]
24. Kennedy, E.; Webb, P.; Block, S.; Griffin, T.; Mozaffarian, D.; Kyte, R. Transforming Food Systems: The Missing Pieces Needed to Make Them Work. *Curr. Dev. Nutr.* **2021**, *5*, nzaa177. [CrossRef] [PubMed]
25. Taufik, D.; van Haaster-de Winter, M.A.; Reinders, M.J. Creating Trust and Consumer Value for True Price Food Products. *J. Clean. Prod.* **2023**, *390*, 136145. [CrossRef]
26. Pieper, M.; Michalke, A.; Gaugler, T. Calculation of External Climate Costs for Food Highlights Inadequate Pricing of Animal Products. *Nat. Commun.* **2020**, *11*, 1–13. [CrossRef]
27. Hendriks, S.; de Groot Ruiz, A.; Acosta, M.H.; Baumers, H.; Galgani, P.; Mason-D'Croz, D.; Godde, C.; Waha, K.; Kanidou, D.; von Braun, J.; et al. The True Cost of Food: A Preliminary Assessment. In *Science and Innovations for Food Systems Transformation*; Springer: Berlin/Heidelberg, Germany, 2023.
28. Walters, E. Skyrocketing Home Prices and The Global Housing Crisis Today. *J. Manag. Train. Ind.* **2022**, *9*, 21–39. [CrossRef]
29. Dejanović, M. The influence of economic and energy crisis on price of agricultural products. *Ekon. Poljopr.* **2023**, *70*, 253–266. [CrossRef]
30. Adeosun, O.A.; Olayeni, R.O.; Tabash, M.I.; Anagreh, S. Revisiting the Oil and Food Prices Dynamics: A Time Varying Approach. *J. Bus. Cycle Res.* **2023**, *19*, 275–309. [CrossRef]
31. Zhou, Y.; Chen, K.Z. Food Price Inflation in East and Southeast Asia: Situation, Driving Forces, and the Outlook. *Stud. Agric. Econ.* **2023**, *125*, 77–86. [CrossRef]
32. Lichtenstein, D.R.; Ridgway, N.M.; Netemeyer, R.G. Price Perceptions and Consumer Shopping Behavior: A Field Study. *J. Mark. Res.* **1993**, *30*, 234. [CrossRef]
33. Likert, R. A Technique for the Measurement of Attitudes. *Arch. Psychol.* **1932**, *140*, 44–53.
34. Skalkos, D.; Kosma, I.S.; Chasioti, E.; Skendi, A.; Papageorgiou, M.; Guiné, R.P.F. Consumers' Attitude and Perception toward Traditional Foods of Northwest Greece during the COVID-19 Pandemic. *Appl. Sci.* **2021**, *11*, 4080. [CrossRef]

35. Feick, L.F.; Price, L.L. The Market Maven: A Diffuser of Marketplace Information. *J. Mark.* **1987**, *51*, 83–97. [CrossRef]
36. Vazifedoost, H.; Charsetad, P.; Akbari, M.; Akbari, J.A. Studying the Effects of Negative and Positive Perceptions of Price on Price Mavenism. *Res. J. Appl. Sci. Eng. Technol.* **2013**, *5*, 3986–3991. [CrossRef]
37. Wikstrom, S.R.; Hedbom, M.; Thuresson, L. Value Creation from a Consumer Perspective. *Mercat. Compet.* **2021**, *1*, 55–81. [CrossRef]
38. Afshin, A.; Peñalvo, J.L.; Del Gobbo, L.; Silva, J.; Michaelson, M.; O'Flaherty, M.; Capewell, S.; Spiegelman, D.; Danaei, G.; Mozaffarian, D. The Prospective Impact of Food Pricing on Improving Dietary Consumption: A Systematic Review and Meta-Analysis. *PLoS ONE* **2017**, *12*, e0172277. [CrossRef]
39. Chen, Y.T.; Lan, L.C.; Fang, W.C. What Do Customers Want? The Impact of Pricing Tactic Persuasion Knowledge and Frequency of Exposure. *Br. Food J.* **2020**, *123*, 2321–2334. [CrossRef]
40. Goldsmith, R.E.; Flynn, L.R.; Clark, R.A. Motivators of Market Mavenism in the Retail Environment. *J. Retail. Consum. Serv.* **2012**, *19*, 390–397. [CrossRef]
41. Somers, J.; Worsley, A.; McNaughton, S.A. The Association of Mavenism and Pleasure with Food Involvement in Older Adults. *Int. J. Behav. Nutr. Phys. Act.* **2014**, *11*, 60. [CrossRef]
42. Wenzig, J.; Gruchmann, T. Consumer Preferences for Local Food: Testing an Extended Norm Taxonomy. *Sustainability* **2018**, *10*, 1313. [CrossRef]
43. Zander, K.; Feucht, Y. Consumers' Willingness to Pay for Sustainable Seafood Made in Europe. *J. Int. Food Agribus. Mark.* **2018**, *30*, 251–275. [CrossRef]
44. Li, S.; Kallas, Z. Meta-Analysis of Consumers' Willingness to Pay for Sustainable Food Products. *Appetite* **2021**, *163*, 105239. [CrossRef] [PubMed]
45. Priem, R.L. A Consumer Perspective on Value Creation. *Acad. Manag. Rev.* **2007**, *32*, 219–235. [CrossRef]
46. Röhr, A.; Lüddecke, K.; Drusch, S.; Müller, M.J.; Alvensleben, R.V. Food Quality and Safety—Consumer Perception and Public Health Concern. *Food Control.* **2005**, *16*, 649–655. [CrossRef]
47. Grunert, K.G. Food quality and safety: Consumer perception and demand. *Eur. Rev. Agricult. Econ.* **2005**, *32*, 369–391. [CrossRef]
48. Riszaini, V.A.; Indayani, L. Fast-Food Consumer Purchasing Decisions: Quality, Price, and Service Impact. *Acad. Open* **2023**, *8*, 44. [CrossRef]
49. Singh, S.; Alok, S. Drivers of Repurchase Intention of Organic Food in India: Role of Perceived Consumer Social Responsibility, Price, Value, and Quality. *J. Int. Food Agribus. Mark.* **2022**, *34*, 246–268. [CrossRef]
50. Nabila, N.A.; Tambunan, D.B. The Effect of Food Quality, Service Quality, Price and Store Atmosphere on Consumers' Buying Interest. *Asian J. Eng. Soc. Health* **2023**, *2*, 76–90.
51. Viţelar, A. Like Me: Generation Z and the Use of Social Media for Personal Branding. *Manag. Dyn. Knowl. Econ.* **2019**, *7*, 257–268. [CrossRef]
52. Trang, N.M.; McKenna, B.; Cai, W.; Morrison, A.M. I Do Not Want to Be Perfect: Investigating Generation Z Students' Personal Brands on Social Media for Job Seeking. *Inf. Technol. People* **2024**, *37*, 793–814. [CrossRef]
53. Krishnan, S.; Musa, C.; Omar, C.; Zahran, I.; Syazwan, N.; Alyaa, S. The Awareness of Gen Z's toward Halal Food Industry. *Management* **2017**, *2017*, 44–47.
54. Aimee, K.; Paul, M.; Thomas, S.; Naomi, Y. *What Makes Asia-Pacific's Generation Z Different?* McKinsey & Company: London, UK, 2020.

sustainability

MDPI

Article

Australian Consumers' Drivers and Barriers to Purchasing Local Food from Alternative Agri-Food Networks

Amy D. Lykins [1,*], Nicolette Larder [2], Cassandra Sundaraja [1] and Lucie Newsome [3]

1 School of Psychology, University of New England, Armidale, NSW 2351, Australia; csundar2@une.edu.au
2 Department of Geography and Planning, School of Humanities, Arts, and Social Sciences, University of New England, Armidale, NSW 2351, Australia; nlarder@une.edu.au
3 UNE Business School, University of New England, Armidale, NSW 2351, Australia; lnewsom3@une.edu.au
* Correspondence: alykins@une.edu.au

Abstract: Greater engagement with alternative food supply chains is considered a key factor in reducing a range of environmental and social harms associated with the global agri-food system. However, consumer engagement with these supply chains is low, and little research has investigated this issue in the Australian context. This study aimed to identify Australian consumers' drivers and barriers in procuring food grown locally from alternative grocery retailers. Self-reported primary or co-equal grocery shoppers (n = 325) completed measures of drivers and barriers to shopping for locally produced food (within 200 km) from alternative retailers, as well as current behavioural engagement with such. An exploratory factor analysis revealed four key drivers (Food Shopping as an Expression of Values, Food Shopping as a Socio-Emotional Experience, Avoiding "Unnatural" Food, Protesting the Duopoly) and two key barriers (It's All Too Hard, Local Food Scepticism). Multiple regression analysis demonstrated that together, these drivers and barriers explained a significant 9% of the variance in the frequency of alternate shopping practices, of which only the barrier It's All Too Hard accounted for a significant amount of unique variance. Findings point to ways to encourage engagement with sustainable food systems, as well as critical barriers to overcoming disengagement.

Keywords: alternative agri-food supply chains; consumer behaviour; sustainable food consumption; local food; climate change

1. Introduction

Supply chain consolidation in the agri-food sector has been one of the most important structural changes in the sector since the 1950s [1]. Arguably, the most consequential aspect of the Australian food system has been domestic vertical integration by food retailers, namely the two major supermarket corporations—Coles and Woolworths—which control 67% of supermarket retail sales nationally [2]. These retailers have amassed political, economic, and regulatory control up and down supply chains, which has given them considerable power to influence the discursive space around food, as well as material patterns of retailing and food production and consumption [3–7]. For close to three decades, researchers have reported on the negative impacts of unequal power relations between supermarkets and other actors in the supply chain (see, for example, [4,8–12]). Despite inquiries into the effects of grocery market concentration on food prices (see, for example, [13]), the market regulator has failed to take substantial action to disrupt the market-distorting effects of the duopoly [14].

For Australian consumers, there is ample evidence that shopping for groceries outside the supermarket duopoly—that is, at alternative food retailers such as farmers' markets and independently owned retailers such as greengrocers, butchers, bakers, and ethnic food stores—is worthwhile. From a price perspective, fruit and vegetables are significantly cheaper at greengrocers compared with the supermarket duopoly [15,16], and consumers also report feeling socially connected when food shopping at farmers' markets compared with feeling alienated at the major supermarkets [17]. Further, the power of the Australian supermarket duopoly has also been identified for some time as an ongoing public health issue due to the types of food they sell, their lack of genuine commitment to contributing to improving population health, and the sales strategies they use [18–20]. For instance, from a consumer trust perspective, Coles and Woolworths have been accused by market watchdogs of lying to consumers about so-called "discount pricing". At the time of writing, the Australian Competition & Consumer Commission is alleging both Coles and Woolworths spiked prices by at least 15% before "dropping" prices to the same as, or higher than, the regular price before the spike.

The purpose of this study was to investigate grocery shopping practices among Australian consumers. Specifically, it explores the factors that both drive and prevent consumers from shopping for locally produced food at alternative food retailers. A better understanding of the drivers and barriers shaping consumer grocery shopping practices will inform the future of the Australian agri-food system through elucidating the challenges for consumers in engaging in alternative agri-food supply chains. Beyond the noted benefits for consumers, alternative agri-food supply chains are associated with a range of important environmental outcomes, including improved biodiversity, an increase in sustainable production methods, and reduced pollution [21–23]. They also engender significant social benefits, such as greater opportunities for rural development [24], larger income dividends for producers [25], and a more stable safety net for food security and nutrition during times of crisis [26]. Thus, diversity in the food system has emerged as a critical element of a resilient food system that will ensure food security [27]. As such, promoting and supporting greater consumer engagement with alternative food systems supports several of the UN's Sustainable Development Goals and, consequently, greater global food security. Understanding factors related to consumer engagement, as well as barriers to such, is crucial in the movement towards sustainable food systems [28].

1.1. Brief Literature Review on Drivers and Barriers to Shopping for Locally Grown Food

In recent decades, many consumers have moved away from purchasing decisions based on price and brand loyalty and towards those made on personal values. In the case of food consumption, this shift in priorities manifests as a preference for sustainable produce based on the individual's morals, ethics, and social views [29,30], in addition to perceptions that these choices assist in mitigating climate change [31]. Following shocks to the Australian food system due to the COVID-19 pandemic, consumers have engaged in a range of strategies to improve the sustainability and resilience of the food system, including strengthening local food systems [32]. Research indicates unequivocally that consumers, irrespective of income and age, are willing to pay a premium for what they perceive to be sustainable produce (e.g., [33–35]); specifically, consumers are willing to pay more for both locally sourced and organically grown food than conventionally produced and sourced food [36,37].

Examinations of the underlying motivations for these shifting consumption patterns have revealed some interesting factors. In an extensive review of 73 internationally based publications, Feldmann and Hamm [38] concluded that attitudes are an important predictor of food purchasing, with consumers' beliefs that locally grown food was of higher quality and better taste supporting their engagement with local food networks. This research was supported by Watts et al. [39], who found that consumers believed that food from alternative food networks was of better quality than food from mainstream supermarkets. Research on the Australian context [40] found that the perception of the freshness of locally grown fruit and vegetables is a key enabler. In contrast, some research from Germany [41] and Finland [42] did not show perceived higher quality as a factor, though the German participants did perceive local food to be more "natural" in content.

Beyond perceptions of higher quality and better taste, research has also pointed to the role of trust in locally sourced food, revealing higher reported trust in "food from somewhere" than in the "food from nowhere" sold by the corporate-industrial food system [39,43,44]. The literature examining local food consumption in the United Kingdom (UK) identified the shortening of relations between consumer and producer and the associated role of food's embeddedness in place (e.g., [24,45,46]). Scholars suggested that the observed turn to local food in the UK was part of a re-spatialisation of the social relations of agriculture and food that followed a series of food scares (e.g., foot-and-mouth disease) through the 1990s (e.g., [45,47–49]). The implication is that locally grown food sold through alternative food retailers feels more trustworthy to consumers than the faceless, locationless "food from nowhere" sold by supermarkets with respect to safety, and that this is a driving factor in its purchase.

Research has also demonstrated that consumers seek to purchase from alternative food retailers because it is seen both as more ethical and as a protest against the perceived social, political, and environmental ills of the conventional food system and major supermarkets. In doing so, consumers are constructing alternative economic imaginaries to the dominant food system (e.g., [50–52]). More recently, Watts et al. [39] confirmed this motivation, reporting that consumers purchase from alternative food networks as a form of protest against the market power of supermarkets and the perceived social, political, and environmental problems associated with conventional food systems. Godrich et al. [40] found that consumers were motivated to purchase food locally to support their communities and local farmers.

Others have argued that locally grown and sold foods, as symbols, are imbued with normative characteristics that signal consumers' valued socio-political positions and/or ideologies (e.g., [53]). This characterisation occurs because producers and marketers present their items with valued qualities, such as rarity and simplicity, and consumers believe it [54]. Winter [49] noted that these characteristics support a belief in the higher quality of these items than those conventionally sourced, irrespective of whether the claims of sustainable production, low environmental impact, and safety were valid. Again, it is the consumers' beliefs in these qualities of food from alternative networks that drive their purchasing behaviour.

Finally, research has shown that the practices of shopping at alternative food retailers, particularly at farmers' markets, are tied to the sociality of the shopping experience itself. Studies by both McEachern et al. [55] and Albrecht and Smithers [56] have shown that for some consumers, the practice of grocery shopping at alternative retailers is driven by the symbolic aspects of the experience of shopping—in particular, the cultural capital associated with the novelty and sociality of farmers' markets. That is, shopping at these markets may be both a reflection of a particular cultural practice associated with leisure as much as an attempt to practice a particular food-based ethic.

Much of the research investigating consumer behaviour around shopping at alternative food retailers has focused on motivations or intentions; relatively less interest has been paid to the real, practical behaviour of shopping. Results from those studies have shown that even for those who are motivated to diversify their food purchasing practices and who are willing to pay more for food from alternative retailers, this may not translate into actual behaviour [37]. Noting that food purchasing intention and behaviour are never perfectly correlated [57], it is important that we understand not only why people procure food from alternative retailers but also what factors may make it challenging to do so.

Some evidence points to potential barriers to the purchasing of food from alternative retailers. Higher perceived or actual prices of food from alternative retailers are regularly identified by participants as a barrier to their consumption [33,37,38,40,56–59], as is the perceived (or real) inconvenience of sourcing it [38,56–60]. Less common, barriers include not recognising or knowing how to prepare unfamiliar produce [56,59,61], not having ready access to local producers' markets [37,57,59], the limited seasonality of produce [40], and having a limited understanding of the benefits of supporting these producers and suppliers [57] have also been reported.

1.2. Beyond the Duopoly in Rural and Urban Australia

To date, there have been few studies of Australian consumers' motivations to shop for local food at alternative food retailers. The work of Lockie et al. [62] on consumer motivation to purchase organic food was seminal. The researchers concluded that health and the nature of the content of the food were the most important motivators for the purchasing of organic food, followed by price. This finding was supported by more recent research by Birch et al. [47], who found that Australian consumers were motivated to purchase local food primarily by self-interest related to personal health and well-being, concerns around food safety, and lastly, the construction of an ethical personal identity. Other research has found that consumer approaches depend on what type of shopping the person is doing, whether that be "main" shopping (i.e., where most of the groceries are purchased) or "top-up" shopping (i.e., where the consumer may purchase other items forgotten or to supplement items purchased during the main shopping). In Australia, the main shopping tended to occur at one of the two primary supermarkets, whereas top-up shopping more often occurred at shops that were smaller and more conveniently located [63]. These differences were also reflected in the consumer approach, where ethically farmed produce had the most influence on store choice when doing main shopping, and fair trading and environmentally responsible policies had a greater influence on selection when top-up shopping [63].

More recently, Godrich et al. [40] examined barriers and enablers to the consumption of regionally grown fresh fruit and vegetables in south Western Australia and Tasmania. Enablers included the perception of freshness and the desire to support local farmers and communities, whereas barriers included price and availability of produce. Altruism and civic environment concerns were not associated with the purchasing of local food in this study. In contrast, Barraket et al. [64] investigated rural-dwelling Australian consumer engagement with local social enterprises, concluding that these individuals are largely motivated to engage with these providers by both ethical and instrumental consumer concerns, including the personal relationships and connections they have with the providers. Taken together, drivers for explicitly engaging with local food suppliers are likely motivated by a number of different factors, which may vary depending on whether the population under examination lives in an urban or a rural environment [65]. Given the somewhat unique ecological and agri-food corporate environments of Australia and the relative dearth of data in this space on Australian consumers, this issue deserves further investigation.

The major conclusion that can be drawn from this literature is that the practice of food purchasing is not tied to one particular motivating factor. Instead, it is likely the result of complex and interrelated factors, which may be a key explanation for the intention–behaviour gap observed in many studies of ethical and/or sustainable consumption. If the aim is to encourage and support consumer engagement with alternative agri-food supply chains, both significant drivers of and barriers to this behaviour need to be understood and addressed in a comprehensive and holistic context, particularly as they relate to one's local setting. This is more so the case where very little research on consumer attitudes towards and engagement with alternative agri-food supply chains exists, such as in Australia.

1.3. Aims of Current Study

Previous research has identified a number of factors that motivate consumers to shop for local food at alternative food retailers; however, a number of barriers have been noted as well, and the intention–behaviour gap persists. To date, there has been little examination of consumer engagement with alternative food retailers within Australia, particularly among people living outside urban centres.

The current study aimed to assess Australian consumers' engagement with alternative food retailers, how this varies depending on geographic location (i.e., urban vs. rural/regional), and drivers and barriers towards procurement of local food from these outlets. We respond to the call from Nemes et al. [66] for research that focuses on specific geographic contexts to understand national differences in attitudes towards sustainable food consumption. To do this, we first reviewed the literature on all known potential drivers and barriers around alternative food consumption and developed a novel questionnaire comprising these items. Following an exploratory factor analysis, the identified drivers and barriers were used in a multiple regression analysis to assess their respective contributions to the purchasing of food from alternative retailers. As this study was exploratory, we had no specific hypotheses about the predicted relationships among our variables of interest.

2. Materials and Methods

2.1. Participants

The sample consisted of 325 adult Australians who self-reported being either the primary food shopper in their household or that food shopping was an equally shared role. A target sample size was determined by a power analysis. A study that examined drivers and barriers associated with the adoption of sustainable palm oil purchasing practices among Australian residents, and thus had some meaningful parallels to the proposed study with respect to methodology and analytic approach, found small to medium effect sizes for their psychological variables (squared semi-partial correlations ranging from <0.01 to 0.18; [67]). Based on this research, a small to medium effect size of f2 = 0.10 [68,69] was predicted. Assuming a target power of 0.90, 10 predictors, and an α level of 0.01, a power analysis using G*Power [70] suggested a minimum sample size of 282 participants.

All participants were sourced using a survey panel from Qualtrics™, an online database and survey administrator. The final sample was representative across adult age groups, mapped on the national representative census data, and drew from both regional and urban New South Wales (51% urban dwelling). Participants were predominantly female (69%), likely due to the screening procedures utilised to survey members of households who primarily do grocery shopping. Although trends are changing, grocery shopping traditionally has been viewed as a female-centric gendered role, and recent surveys continue to indicate that women are more likely than men to perform routine grocery purchases [71,72]. Seventy-nine per cent of participants reported being the primary grocery shoppers in their household, with the remaining 21% reporting that it is equally shared.

Respondents had a mean age of 52.67 years (SD = 17.39, range = 18 to 85 years). With respect to education, 27% had a college certificate/diploma, 17% said they had completed an undergraduate degree, 17.5% reported completing year 12, and 15% had an education level of year 10 or less. The median annual household income reported was between

50,000 and 59,000 AUD, which is lower than the average Australian household income for 2021 at approximately 92,000 AUD [73]. In terms of ethnicity, most of the sample (72%) identified as European Australian. While 59% of the respondents did not identify as migrants to Australia, 21.5% identified as being first-generation migrants, and 19.4% as being second-generation migrants. Finally, almost half the sample (43%) reported growing some of their own food (which included herbs, green leafy vegetables, root vegetables, tomatoes, and fruits).

2.2. Measures

The measures used in this study included an indication of the existing frequency of food shopping behaviour across a range of locations (e.g., large retail supermarkets, local butchers, farmers' markers, etc.) and a specially designed survey to capture factors influencing local food purchasing behaviour derived from the existing literature.

The frequency of food shopping behaviour was estimated as follows. Participants were asked to indicate all the locations where they shopped for food, and this list contained the following options: major/large retail supermarkets (e.g., Coles and Woolworths), other supermarkets (e.g., ALDI and IGA—Independent Grocers of Australia), farmers' markets, local fruit and vegetable shops, local butchers' shops, local bakeries, organic shop, community supported agriculture/food box scheme, ethnic/culture-specific stores/markets, and direct from producers outside of farmers' markets. For each of the locations that participants selected, they were asked to provide an indication of the frequency of each behaviour (either in-person or online) over the past month on an 11-point scale, where 0 = "never" and 10 = "10 or more times".

The frequency of shopping at these locations in person was examined using Cronbach's α to ascertain whether there were consistencies in patterns across shopping at locations other than the major supermarkets (i.e., whether it made sense to group the shopping locations together in a particular way or not). Frequencies across all locations apart from supermarkets (which, although geographically "local", mainly rely on long, non-diverse supply chains) were summed (farmer's markets, local fruit and vegetable shops, local butchers' shops, local bakeries, organic shops, community supported agriculture/food box schemes, ethnic/culture-specific stores/markets, and direct from producers outside of farmers' markets), which resulted in a Cronbach's α of 0.69. These frequencies were added together to provide a single, comprehensive measure of the frequency of the alternative shopping practices and were used in subsequent analyses. An attempt to sum the frequencies relating to shopping at supermarkets yielded a Cronbach's α of 0.10, which was very low. Hence, the frequencies of shopping in person at large retail supermarkets vs other supermarkets (e.g., ALDI and IGA) were considered separately in subsequent analyses.

Factors influencing local food shopping survey. Based on a detailed literature review of research investigating engagement with diverse agri-food supply chains (e.g., [24,33,36–38,42,56–58,61,74–78]) and adding onto an existing survey that explored factors influencing local food shopping in the UK [59], potential barriers and drivers of purchasing local food were identified. These were then incorporated into a survey of 61 driver items and 34 barrier items that included items about price, knowledge (on availability, production practices, etc.), convenience or lack of it (in terms of distance, availability, seasonal variability, etc.), perceived health benefits, and wishing to demonstrate support for local producers, among others (including open-ended "other" items for participants to write any other reasons they did not think had been captured in the survey items). For a complete list of all of the items, please see Supplementary Materials. Though we endorse the broader understanding of short supply chains provided by Renting et al. [24] and others, we elected to define "local food" in the instructions as having been produced within a 200-kilometre radius of the participant's home to ensure that all participants were using the same definition in answering the barrier and driver items. All items were rated on a 7-point scale of 1 = "strongly disagree" to 7 = "strongly agree". These items were subjected to an exploratory factor analysis, the details of which are summarised in Section 3. Cronbach's α for the scaled factors ranged from 0.87 to 0.96.

2.3. Procedure

Participants were recruited via a Qualtrics™ online panel in 2022. The online survey began with information about the study, after which they could provide consent and then complete the questionnaires. Those who were below 18 years of age and those who reported that someone else (apart from the participant themselves) primarily did the grocery and/or supermarket shopping for the household were screened out of the survey. In the survey, all questions were mandatory (although participants could select "rather not say" for the questions about ethnicity and annual household income). The socio-demographic questions and frequency of local food shopping behaviour were first presented, followed by the survey on factors influencing local food purchasing (driver items and then barrier items). As attention-checks, three instructed-response items (e.g., "In order to check for attention, please answer '5' for this question") were incorporated into the survey on factors influencing local food purchasing. These instructed-response items have been known to be useful in screening out careless responders while still protecting the validity of the scale [79,80]. Qualtrics™ screened out participants who failed any of the attention checks or provided only partial responses. Additionally, a speed-checker was incorporated into the online survey. Participants whose response times were approximately below one-half of the median time taken to complete the survey in a soft launch (i.e., less than or equal to six minutes and 50 s) were automatically screened out as well to ensure good data quality. This study was approved by the Human Research Ethics Committee of the University of New England (HE21-214) and was conducted in compliance with the approved research ethics procedure.

2.4. Data Analysis

All data analyses were run using IBM SPSS Statistics v. 28 [81]. Further information on selected statistical analyses is presented below.

3. Results

Twenty-four per cent of participants reported that they obtained their food from one primary store, and on average, the sample purchased food from three different sources. Ninety per cent of the sample reported that they shop at major/large retail supermarkets at least some of the time, followed by 55% who reported shopping at other supermarkets (ALDI and IGA). The percentages decreased after that, with 47% who reported shopping at local fruit and vegetable shops, 40% at local bakeries, 37% at local butchers, and 21.5% at farmers' markets. The remaining shopping locations were shopped at by less than 10% of the sample. The selection of shopping locations was then compared for participants from regional versus urban geographic locations. Those in regional areas tended to shop significantly more frequently at local fruit and vegetable shops, $t(323) = 2.196$, $p = 0.029$, 95% CI (0.01, 0.23), while those in urban areas tend to shop significantly more at ethnic/culture-specific shops, $t(323) = 4.269$, $p < 0.001$, 95% CI (0.07, 0.18). At all other shopping locations, purchasing patterns across urban and regional consumers in the current sample were not significantly different. Finally, there was no significant difference between those in regional and urban areas in terms of growing one's own food, X^2 (1) = 2.883, $p = 0.090$, $\Phi = -0.09$.

3.1. Exploratory Factor Analysis to Identify Potential Drivers and Barriers

The survey on factors influencing local food shopping consisted of 61 driver items and 34 barrier items. These driver items and barrier items were separately subjected to exploratory factor analysis, using the maximum likelihood extraction method, to determine the underlying structure of the variables and to reduce the data into more manageable units.

Drivers. For the exploratory factor analysis run with the driver items, the Kaiser–Meyer–Olkin measure of sampling adequacy was 0.96, and Bartlett's test of sphericity had a p-value of less than 0.001, which indicated that there were strong linear relationships within the data set. The number of factors to retain was decided based on Cattell's [82] scree plot and Kaiser's rule (of eigenvalues greater than one). The scree plot distinctly indicated that three factors should be retained, whereas Kaiser's rule suggested nine. All possible solutions for three to nine factors were run using the direct oblimin rotation with Δ set to 0. A four-factor solution was the most interpretable and accounted for 59% of the overall response variance. Factor solutions of more than four factors had a high number of cross-loading items across two or more factors, resulting in fewer items per factor. Additionally, there was a notable conceptual overlap between the additional factors generated, and hence, the four-factor solution was selected.

Items that loaded greater than 0.50 on one factor with a cross-loading of 0.30 or less were used to define each factor. Scale scores for each of the retained factors were computed by taking the average across the selected items for each factor and were used for subsequent analysis. Table 1 lists the items included under each of the four driver factors, the mean and standard deviation, and the internal reliability score for each factor.

Table 1. Exploratory factor analysis pattern matrix loadings for drivers (n = 325).

Driver Items	*M (SD)*	Factor Loading			
		1	2	3	4
Factor 1—Food Shopping as an Expression of Values (α = 0.96)					
I can buy the amount I want.	2.64 (1.45)	0.57		0.25	
It supports local producers.	1.96 (1.20)	0.88			
It supports local retailers.	2.02 (1.20)	0.88			
I know where it comes from.	2.34 (1.38)	0.68		0.23	
It is ethical.	2.81 (1.33)	0.53	0.24		
It tastes good.	2.45 (1.34)	0.71			
Fair trade is important.	2.72 (1.46)	0.60			
It uses less packaging.	2.78 (1.54)	0.63			
It is fresh.	2.06 (1.28)	0.85			
It is healthy.	2.36 (1.38)	0.70			
It involves "friendly" farming methods (e.g., grass-fed cows).	2.68 (1.51)	0.51		0.24	
It is of high quality.	2.22 (1.22)	0.69			
I think it is the right thing to do.	2.25 (1.27)	0.61			
It is safe.	2.42 (1.26)	0.53		0.24	
I trust the producers.	2.68 (1.31)	0.61			
There is transparency in food production.	3.00 (1.42)	0.53	0.25		
It is sourced directly from the producer (there are no intermediates).	2.57 (1.35)	0.68			
It is important to preserve agricultural traditions.	2.61 (1.48)	0.67			0.30
It is important to preserve local seeds and varieties.	2.79 (1.44)	0.59			0.26

Table 1. *Cont.*

Driver Items	M (SD)	Factor Loading			
		1	2	3	4
Factor 2—Food Shopping as a Socio-Emotional Experience (α = 0.87)					
Shopping for it brings back memories of the past.	3.60 (1.64)		0.65		
It is fun.	3.51 (1.58)	0.24	0.67		
It is nostalgic.	3.96 (1.47)		0.64		
I feel guilty if I do not.	4.42 (1.55)		0.58		0.28
It is more affordable.	3.45 (1.63)	0.24	0.57		
The products are unique.	3.55 (1.61)		0.60		
Many people in my social circle do so.	4.68 (1.67)		0.62		
Factor 3—Avoiding "Unnatural" Foods (α = 0.92)					
It is free from preservatives.	2.81 (1.50)	0.24		0.72	
It is free from chemicals (e.g., pesticides, herbicides).	3.06 (1.51)			0.70	
It doesn't use GMO (genetically-modified organisms).	3.04 (1.53)			0.69	
The production methods don't use antibiotics.	3.01 (1.56)			0.77	
The production methods don't use hormones.	3.07 (1.51)			0.83	
It is organic.	3.54 (1.66)			0.60	
Factor 4—Protesting the Duopoly (α = 0.89)					
I do not trust the large retailers (e.g., supermarkets like Coles and Woolworths).	4.22 (1.66)				0.68
I dislike the shopping experience at large retailers like Coles and Woolworths.	4.42 (1.68)				0.70
I am ethically opposed to buying from large retailers like Coles and Woolworth.	4.75 (1.66)				0.73

M = mean, *SD* = standard deviation; all items were rated on a 7-point scale of 1 = "strongly disagree" to 7 = "strongly agree".

Barriers. For the exploratory factor analysis run with the barrier items, the Kaiser–Meyer–Olkin measure of sampling adequacy was 0.97, and Bartlett's test of sphericity had a p-value of less than 0.001, which once again indicated that there were strong linear relationships within the dataset. The number of factors to retain was decided based on Cattell's [82] scree plot and Kaiser's rule (of eigenvalues greater than one). The scree plot distinctly indicated that two to three factors should be retained, whereas Kaiser's rule suggested three. Solutions for both two and three factors were run using the direct oblimin rotation with Δ set to 0. A two-factor solution was the most interpretable and accounted for 61% of the overall response variance. The three-factor solution had items from the third factor with low factor loadings and a high number of cross-loading items across the other two factors, so this was not utilised.

As with the driver items, barrier items that loaded greater than 0.50 on one factor with a cross-loading of 0.30 or less were used to define each factor; scale scores for each of the retained factors were computed by taking the average across the selected items for each factor and were used for subsequent analysis. Table 2 lists the items included under each of the two barrier factors, the mean and standard deviation, and the internal reliability score for both factors.

Table 2. Exploratory factor analysis pattern matrix loadings for barriers (n = 325).

Barrier Items	M (SD)	Factor Loadings	
		1	2
Factor 5—It's All Too Hard (α = 0.97)			
The range of products is limited.	5.02 (1.58)	0.68	
Food produced elsewhere is sometimes better.	5.07 (1.50)	0.52	0.25
It is not well promoted.	4.86 (1.75)	0.70	
The price is not always clear.	5.17 (1.56)	0.64	
It is not readily available.	4.84 (1.73)	0.91	
It is expensive.	4.58 (1.77)	0.77	
To do so is time-consuming.	5.09 (1.54)	0.85	
It requires extra effort.	5.02 (1.67)	0.88	
It is inconvenient.	5.17 (1.65)	0.87	
I have to travel farther to do so.	4.94 (1.79)	0.90	
I do not know where to get it from.	5.19 (1.69)	0.62	
It is not part of my normal/regular shopping routine	4.88 (1.78)	0.94	
It is challenging to plan for.	5.25 (1.53)	0.69	
I prefer to complete all my purchases at one location (i.e., a large retail supermarket).	4.53 (1.89)	0.75	
It is difficult to access places to do so.	4.86 (1.78)	0.86	
There is not much food produced in my local area.	4.97 (1.72)	0.69	
Factor 6—Local Food Scepticism (α = 0.94)			
I do not trust the producers.	5.93 (1.17)		0.84
I don't trust the safety of local food.	5.92 (1.12)		0.78
I do not recognise some of the food that is sold.	5.55 (1.40)		0.69
I rarely cook.	5.80 (1.33)		0.61
I do not know how to cook/prepare it.	5.88 (1.26)		0.79
I like cooking meals that use products that are not available locally.	5.31 (1.41)		0.53
It is not important to me.	5.66 (1.39)	0.29	0.56
I do not know why I should.	5.79 (1.24)		0.78
I am not convinced of its benefits of local food.	5.69 (1.28)		0.77
I do not like the way it looks.	5.89 (1.20)		0.83
I don't think much about where food comes from.	5.53 (1.44)		0.63
I prefer to invest in other sustainability initiatives (e.g., decreasing energy use, reducing plastic, etc.).	5.43 (1.33)		0.68
I feel out of place (uncomfortable) at farmers' markets.	5.77 (1.41)		0.64

M = mean, SD = standard deviation; all items were rated on a 7-point scale of 1 = "strongly disagree" to 7 = "strongly agree".

3.2. Multiple Regression to Predict Frequency of Alternative Shopping Practices

A multiple regression analysis was conducted to predict the frequency of various shopping practices. As described above, the frequency of alternative shopping experiences was taken to include in-person shopping at farmers' markets, local fruit and vegetable shops, local butchers' shops, local bakeries, organic shops, community-supported agriculture/food box schemes, ethnic/culture-specific stores/markets, and direct from producers outside of farmers' markets. As there was a reasonably large number of participants who shopped at mainstream supermarkets and other supermarkets (i.e., ALDI and IGA), the frequency of shopping at these locations was used separately in the regression analysis.

Together, the four driver factors and two barrier factors explained 9% of the variance in the frequency of alternative shopping practices. A summary of the regression analysis is presented in Table 3. Examining the beta-coefficients of the six factors, it is apparent that only *It's All Too Hard* explained a statistically significant amount of unique variance (2%) in the frequency of alternative shopping practices. Therefore, these results indicate that it is likely that the perceived barriers relating to difficulty and inconvenience are the main influence on consumers' decisions to shop outside of mainstream supermarkets (at least of the variables assessed in this study).

Table 3. Predicting frequency of shopping practices from the four driver factors and two barrier factors influencing local food shopping.

Predictors	*M* (*SD*)	B	95% CI for B		*r*	sr^2
			LB	UB		
Food Shopping as an Expression of Values	2.49 (1.05)	−1.09	−2.60	0.41	−0.23 ***	0.01
Food Shopping as A Socio-Emotional Experience	3.88 (1.20)	−0.91	−1.99	0.17	−0.24 ***	0.01
Avoiding "Unnatural" Foods	3.09 (1.30)	0.80	−0.24	1.85	−0.13 **	0.01
Protesting the Duopoly	4.46 (1.51)	−0.50	−1.19	0.19	−0.19 ***	0.01
It's All Too Hard	4.96 (1.37)	1.18	0.19	2.17	0.25 ***	0.02 *
Local Food Scepticism	5.70 (1.01)	−0.15	−1.53	1.23	0.15 **	0.00

M = mean, *SD* = standard deviation, B = unstandardised beta, CI = confidence interval, LB = lower bound, UB = upper bound, *r* = correlation coefficient, sr^2 = squared semipartial correlation coefficient. * $p < 0.05$, ** $p < 0.01$, *** $p < 0.001$, $R = 0.33$, $R^2 = 0.11$, $Adj\ R^2 = 0.09$.

4. Discussion

To our knowledge, this is the first systematic assessment of drivers and barriers to engagement with local short supply chains in the Australian population. A full 90% of our sample reported that they purchased food from the major/large retail supermarkets at least some of the time, whereas just over half (55%) reported shopping at other supermarkets. Just under half of the sample also shop at local fruit and vegetable shops, just over one-third at local bakeries and butchers, and about 20% at local farmers' markets. Our results identified four main drivers for purchasing local food—an expression of values, the socio-emotional experience of local food shopping, wishing to avoid foods produced "unnaturally", and as a protest to the Australian supermarket duopoly—and two main barriers, including difficulty/inconvenience, and scepticism about local food. Together, these six factors accounted for 9% of the total variance in explaining local food purchasing behaviour, with only the difficulty/inconvenience factor contributing significant unique variance. Furthermore, we did not find meaningful differences in purchasing patterns between our urban and rural participants. This study provides new data about why Australian shoppers may or may not engage with diverse agri-food supply chains, critical information to have if we wish to encourage broader adoption to support small businesses and local suppliers, contribute to rural development, enhance global food security, and combat climate change.

4.1. What Motivates Australian Consumers to Engage in Sustainable Food Systems: Identified Drivers

The first major driver identified in our study was Food Shopping as an Expression of Values, with the key underlying theme that purchasing local food aligned with people's values and ethics in meaningful ways. Items that fell onto this factor covered a lot of ground, including an emphasis on ethical purchasing, trust in local producers and a desire to have a direct relationship with them, as well as beliefs that local food is healthy, safe, fresh, and of high quality. Much of the research on engagement with short supply chains has been framed as "ethical consumption," so a values-based driver emerging is not especially surprising, and many of the contributors to this factor have been observed in previous studies (though not often clustered together).

Pro-environmental attitudes and valuing sustainability have encouraged local food purchasing in a number of studies [38,57–59,61,74,75,77], as has the desire for a relationship with the producer [37,58,61,64,75] and a desire to support local/regional businesses and economies [38,40,57,58,61,64]. Furthermore, perceptions of better taste, freshness, safety, healthiness, and overall higher quality have also been observed in other studies [24,37,38, 40,42,57,58,61], though why these perceptions loaded on the ethical/values-based factor is not immediately obvious. Interestingly, this factor appears to be a combination of the "Local Support and Provenance" and "Ethical Sustainability" factors derived from the factor analysis conducted by Megicks et al. [59] in their sample from the UK. Future research would benefit from assessing the items falling on this factor in different samples to ascertain whether they are meaningfully different components from each other (as observed in other studies) or to establish that they do have a common underlying theme, as our data indicate.

Related to the motivations of health, freshness, and safety in food, the Avoiding "Unnatural" Foods factor identified drivers of local food purchasing as wishing to avoid chemicals (e.g., pesticides, herbicides), preservatives, antibiotics, hormones, and genetically modified organisms (GMOs), as well as wanting food that is organically produced. These kinds of motivations have been observed in several other studies [24,57,77] and largely map onto the "Intrinsic Quality" factor observed in Megicks et al.'s [59] UK study. We found it interesting that health, which had been previously found to be one of the most important motivators among Australian consumers of chemical-free organic foods [62], did not load onto this factor. Similarly, safety did cross-load onto this factor but was primarily associated with the ethics/values factor. This finding suggests that another factor, such as aversion to perceived risk in food consumption (e.g., orthorexia nervosa [83]), may drive the desired avoidance of chemically laden food. Another relevant point is that simply because food is farmed and sold locally provides no guarantee that it has been farmed organically [84], suggesting a potential mismatch between consumer expectations and reality. This characteristic is an important driver for some people in purchasing local foods, which supports the value of certification schemes and clear labelling to allow consumers to make informed purchasing decisions.

Food Shopping as a Socio-Emotional Experience was another major driver that focused on the shopping experience, with some components of affordability and uniqueness of products included. Both positive (e.g., finding the experience fun/nostalgic, social circle peer influences) and negative (e.g., feeling guilty if they do not purchase local foods) reinforcers were evident in this factor, showing some parallels with, as well as some distinctions from, the "Shopping Benefits" factor observed in the Megicks et al. [59] study. The endorsement of items on this factor was quite high, suggesting that the social and experiential value of local food shopping was particularly relevant for our participants. Others have also noted the power of the hedonic experience and personal well-being derived by "doing good" [64] via engaging with local food suppliers, which, combined with our results, points to a potentially important driver to emphasise in supporting engagement with diverse agri-food supply chains.

Finally, and potentially unique to the Australian food landscape, Protesting the Duopoly was the last major factor observed as a driver of local food purchasing. As noted previously, two major supermarket chains dominate the food market in Australia, and this duopoly and their associated practices have garnered significant social criticism. As with the previous factor, there was a high level of endorsement of the items loading on this factor, suggesting a general dissatisfaction with the shopping experience offered by these two supermarket chains, ethical opposition to shopping at them, and an expressed lack of trust in these venues. This factor may provide a regional example of food activism (e.g., [39,61]), which includes components of anti-capitalist, anti-industrial, and anti-concentrated production methods sentiment related to the globally integrated agri-food system and serves to support engagement with alternative, diverse food networks. However, even despite the relatively high endorsement of the items on this factor, the vast majority of our participants continued to shop at one or both of these supermarkets at least occasionally. It is possible that this represents an issue of easy access and lack of alternative, convenient local options, as one or more of these supermarkets is often present even in regional towns of a certain size. Notably, though, this value/intention–behaviour gap has been observed in other studies (e.g., [37,57]), and its presence highlights the need to understand potential barriers to local food purchasing, as well as associated drivers.

4.2. What Makes This Engagement Challenging: Identified Barriers

All of the relevant barrier items fell into one of two factors. The first major factor, *It's All Too Hard*, highlighted challenges with (in)convenience of and difficulties (genuine or perceived) with sourcing local food and encompassed items related to expense/price sensitivity, feeling that it was time-consuming to access and/or not readily available, that accessing local food required travelling farther, that the product range was limited, that it required extra effort to access, and/or participants simply did not know where to buy local food—that it was just "harder." Inconvenience as a major barrier to purchasing local food has been found in a number of studies [38,56–60], as have (lack of) access and extra time and effort required [37,38,56,57,60]. Interestingly, at least for fruit and vegetables, any price differences between supermarkets and farmers' markets in Australia are negligible, with supermarkets often being more expensive [15,85]. This finding suggests that better advertising of local foods may assist with their consumption if price-conscious consumers were aware of these price trends.

Of all the factors derived from the factor analysis, this one was the most important of the six, as it was the only one that contributed unique variance to predicting local food purchasing behaviour. This result suggests that addressing inconvenience and lack of access is imperative in encouraging purchasing from diverse agri-food supply chains. No matter what reasons people may have to engage with local food suppliers, if this barrier outweighs them, habitual behaviour is unlikely to change. We suggest that diverse agri-food businesses, policymakers, and advocates engage in three key strategies. First, interventions to support new habit formation should be designed and tested (e.g., [86]). Second, better advertising of these suppliers should be conducted so that people know they exist, that the products meet the needs of consumers identified in the survey, where they are, how to access them, and have a general sense of product pricing. For example, one could launch a marketing campaign that details a day in the life of a local producer through photos/videos, from the production of their product to its delivery to consumers. Third, availability should be increased, potentially by increasing the days or times the suppliers are open and/or offering purchasing online. Wills and Arundel [87] found in their analysis of Canadian and Australian consumer engagement with local food systems that online retailing did not compromise food quality and had the potential to broaden access to local food systems.

Lastly, the second barrier and last major factor amounted to Local Food Scepticism—emphasising that (dis)trust can go both ways (i.e., towards the major supermarket chains or towards local food suppliers), with a strong endorsement of items related to scepticism about local food. Participants reported not trusting producers with respect to safety, that they are not familiar with the products or how to prepare them, and/or that they do not like the way they look. Providing a counterpoint to the socio-emotional driver factor, some participants did not feel comfortable at farmers' markets, and some did not endorse any particular ethic or value motivating them to engage with local food suppliers, reflecting some barriers noted by Vermeir and Verbeke [57]. Suggestions for helping consumers overcome aspects of this major barrier may include educational campaigns on the benefits of local food and short/diverse supply chains, having local food suppliers provide printed recipes with their products that guide shoppers on how to use and/or prepare unfamiliar foods, and encouraging better labelling to increase trust in producers and their products. A recent initiative in New South Wales, Australia, to digitise local food environments and enable consumers to filter results by how local food is to the individual, as well as healthiness, may enable greater local and alternative food production [88].

Interestingly, essentially all of the items included in the original survey that referenced animal welfare motivations—which conceptually might have loaded onto an ethical/values-based factor—were weeded out in the factor analysis; they did not load onto any of the four drivers. This finding contrasts with other research (e.g., [24,38,59,77]), where animal welfare was found to be an important driver of local food procurement. The loss of animal welfare items may be reflective of a separation between humans and systems of food production, such that animal welfare has become detached from food practices in Australia in ways that it has not in other countries [89]. For example, in Sweden, farm animals in the environment closely align with values of environmental care; in contrast, in Australia, agriculture is understood (in part) through a narrative of environmental damage, and farm animals are seen as inimical to the Australian ecology [90]. This rejection of farm animals as "natural" in Australia may translate into a separation of these animals from the environment in which they are raised, which may have contributed to the lack of relationship between our values-based factor, which included aspects of environmental care, and the animal welfare items in the original survey.

4.3. Urban vs. Rural Consumers

The current study also aimed to assess differences between urban- and rural-dwelling shoppers' local food procurement, with the expectation that there would be significant differences between these two groups on alternative shopping practices as per [65]. However, despite a significant difference in shopping at cultural/ethnic food locations (endorsed to a greater degree by our urban participants) and a barely significant difference in shopping at local fruit and vegetable markets (endorsed to a greater degree by our rural participants), there were no significant differences in reported shopping behaviour between these two groups. This finding is particularly interesting given the relative lack of alternative food purchasing options in rural areas [15], which may suggest an over-engagement in local food purchasing from our rural participants relative to overall access.

4.4. Strengths, Limitations, and Future Directions

Noted strengths of the current study include the large and diverse sample recruited, as well as focusing only on adults who actually participate in food shopping. We also intentionally over-sampled participants from outside of major metropolitan areas to provide a balanced perspective on this issue, given that much of the research in this space has focused on urban consumers and access to local food suppliers and the overall diversity of foods available varies widely depending on geographic location [15]. The systematic assessment of a comprehensive list of both drivers and barriers also provides new data from the Australian population with respect to engagement with diverse agri-food supply chains. The resulting questionnaire, both in its original form and as derived from the factor analyses, may be useful to other researchers investigating these issues in Australia and potentially beyond.

The current study also has several limitations worth mentioning. The final sample was somewhat older than anticipated, so it would be worth recruiting younger people in future research to assess whether the current factor structure holds. Also, in the interest of scale validity, we elected to provide a relatively narrow definition of "local food" (i.e., produced within a 200-kilometre radius of one's home) to our participants so that everyone was working from the same understanding in responding to the questionnaire items. The trade-off, of course, is that short supply chains encompass more than simply geographic distance [24], and our definition did not support this broader understanding. Future research may wish to provide a more nuanced description of "local food" to further enhance our understanding of these relationships. Furthermore, since the data were collected in 2022, Australia (like much of the world) has experienced significant inflationary pressures on the economy, although supermarket food prices have outpaced inflation in recent years [91,92]. While we believe that the data collected likely represent the purchasing landscape in "normal" economic periods, it may be worth assessing whether price serves as a stronger barrier now than it was observed pre-2023, given rising inflation and prices. Moreover, although our factors explained a significant amount of variance in local food shopping behaviour, 91% of the variance was unaccounted for by these variables. Future research would benefit from investigating other constructs (e.g., identity, cultural worldviews, etc.) that may also contribute to food purchasing behaviour so that targeted interventions to promote local food purchasing are better refined (and, thus, more likely to succeed). Michie et al.'s [93] Behaviour Change Wheel may be particularly useful in addressing both barriers and drivers in developing new interventions that have empirical support. Finally, whilst also a strength of the study given the relative dearth of information on this issue in Australia, it is unclear how well these findings would generalise outside of the country. As mentioned above, future research could test the utility of the original and shortened versions of this questionnaire to see how well the factors obtained in the Australian sample replicate in other countries.

5. Conclusions

Changing food demand has been identified as key to achieving transformation of the agri-food system [94], which is essential to supporting an expanded version of global food security, particularly as climate change advances. If we want to encourage consumer engagement with short/diverse agri-food supply chains, we urgently must understand both why people do (or would) purchase from local food suppliers, as well as why they do (or would) not, so that evidence-based interventions can be developed and trialled for efficacy in promoting behaviour change.

The current study goes some way to providing new, comprehensive information on both important drivers (e.g., values and ethics, enjoying the social and emotional experience of local food shopping, avoiding "unnatural" foods, and a protest against the dominance of the Australian supermarket duopoly), as well as barriers (e.g., scepticism around local food and a lack of understanding why people should care, as well as, very broadly, inconvenience). Among these, beyond value-based motivation, it was perceived difficulty and inconveniences around product availability, costs, and the efforts required to plan one's shopping that was most significant in determining where Australians shop. However, given the significant but somewhat small amount of variance accounted for in current shopping behaviour by these factors, further research is needed. Future research could trial the questionnaire we developed to assess its utility in other populations.

Finally, convenience/inconvenience around shopping is related to a whole set of multi-scalar factors that include interpersonal (e.g., socio-economic status, age, gender, health, education), interpersonal (e.g., family structure, peer pressure/support, parenting practices), and meso-scale settings (e.g., retail and urban environments) and policies (e.g., nutrition and labelling standards, advertising and marketing, food system and supply chain regulation). Those interested in encouraging behaviour change with respect to local food consumption could focus on addressing the "inconvenience" factor that most directly influenced local food procurement through a wide variety of interventions across these multiple scales.

Supplementary Materials: The following supporting information can be downloaded at https://www.mdpi.com/article/10.3390/su17073093/s1, Table S1: Drivers for Local Food Purchasing Survey (Original); Table S2: Barriers to Local Food Purchasing Survey (Original).

Author Contributions: Conceptualisation, A.D.L., N.L., C.S. and L.N.; data curation, A.D.L. and C.S.; formal analysis, C.S.; funding acquisition, L.N.; investigation, A.D.L. and C.S.; methodology, A.D.L. and C.S.; project administration, A.D.L. and L.N.; writing—original draft, A.D.L., N.L., C.S. and L.N. All authors have read and agreed to the published version of the manuscript.

Funding: This work was supported by the University of New England Centre for Agribusiness. The Centre had no involvement in the study's design, data collection, analysis or interpretation of the data, or in the writing of the report.

Institutional Review Board Statement: The study was conducted according to the guidelines of the Declaration of Helsinki and approved by the Human Research Ethics Committee of the University of New England (HE21-214, 1 November 2021).

Informed Consent Statement: Informed consent was obtained from all subjects involved in the study.

Data Availability Statement: The raw data supporting the conclusions of this article will be made available by the authors on request.

Conflicts of Interest: The authors declare no conflicts of interest.

References

1. Merrett, D.T. The making of Australia's supermarket duopoly. *Aust. Econ. Hist. Rev.* **2019**, *60*, 301–321. [CrossRef]
2. Australian Competition & Consumer Commission. ACCC Supermarket Inquiry Moves into Next Phase After Hearing Consumer and Supplier Concerns. Australian Government, 2024. Available online: https://www.accc.gov.au/media-release/accc-supermarkets-inquiry-moves-into-next-phase-after-hearing-consumer-and-supplier-concerns (accessed on 31 January 2025).
3. Bailey, M. Retail suburbanization, modernization, and growth in Sydney during Australia's postwar boom. *J. Urban Hist.* **2023**, *49*, 844–864. [CrossRef]
4. Burch, D.; Dixon, J.; Lawrence, G. Introduction to symposium on the changing role of supermarkets in global supply chains: From seedling to supermarket: Agri-food supply chains in transition. *Agric. Hum. Values* **2013**, *30*, 215–224. [CrossRef]
5. Lang, T.; Heasman, M. *Food Wars: The Global Battle for Mouths, Minds and Markets*; Earthscan: London, UK, 2004.
6. Parker, C.; Scrinis, G. Out of the cage and into the barn: Supermarket power food system governance and the regulation of free range eggs. *Griffith Law Rev.* **2014**, *23*, 318–347. [CrossRef]
7. Richards, C.; Bjorkhaug, H.; Lawrence, G.; Hickman, E. Retailer-driven agricultural restructuring—Australia, the UK and Norway in comparison. *Agric. Hum. Values* **2013**, *30*, 235–245.
8. Burch, D.; Rickson, R.; Lawrence, G. *Globalization and Agri-Food Restructuring: Perspectives for the Australasia Region*; Avebury: Aldershot, UK, 1996.
9. Burch, D.; Lawrence, G. Supermarket own brands, supply chains and the transformation of the agri-food system. *Int. J. Sociol. Food Agric.* **2005**, *13*, 1–18. [CrossRef]
10. Burch, D.; Lawrence, G. *Supermarkets and Agri-Food Supply Chains: Transformations in the Production and Consumption of Foods*; Edward Elgar: Cheltenham, UK, 2007.

11. Messner, R.; Johnson, H.; Richards, C. From surplus-to-waste: A study of systemic overproduction, surplus and food waste in horticulture supply chains. *J. Clean. Prod.* **2021**, *278*, 123952. [CrossRef]
12. Singh-Peterson, L.; Lieske, S.; Underhill, S.J.R.; Keys, N. Food security, remoteness and consolidation of supermarket distribution centres: Factors contributing to food pricing inequalities across Queensland, Australia. *Aust. Geogr.* **2016**, *47*, 89–102. [CrossRef]
13. Australian Competition & Consumer Commission. Report of the ACCC Inquiry into the Competitiveness of Retail Prices for Standard Groceries. Commonwealth of Australia. 2008. Available online: https://www.accc.gov.au/about-us/publications/report-of-the-accc-inquiry-into-the-competitiveness-of-retail-prices-for-standard-groceries (accessed on 31 January 2025).
14. Richards, C.; Lawrence, G.; Loong, M.; Burch, D. A toothless chihuahua? The Australian Competition and Consumer Commission, neoliberalism and supermarket power in Australia. *Rural Soc.* **2012**, *21*, 250–263. [CrossRef]
15. Abley, S.; Cassar, O.; Khinsoe, E.; Marks, L.; Vanderzwan, O.; Palermo, C.; Kleve, S. Do farmers' markets offer consumers an available and affordable supply of fresh fruit and vegetables compared to other retail outlets in Australia? *J. Hunger Environ. Nutr.* **2020**, *15*, 827–834. [CrossRef]
16. Williams, P.; James, Y.; Kwan, J. The Illawarra Healthy Food Price Index 2. Pricing methods and index trends from 2000–2003. *Nutr. Diet.* **2004**, *61*, 208–214. Available online: https://ro.uow.edu.au/hbspapers/13 (accessed on 5 March 2024).
17. O'Kane, G.M.; Pamphilon, B. 'My lifestyle kind of locks me into supermarket shopping': Narratives of reflexivity and routines from supermarket shoppers in Australia. *J. Hunger Environ. Nutr.* **2020**, *15*, 372–387. [CrossRef]
18. Pulker, C.E.; Trapp, G.S.A.; Scott, J.A.; Pollard, C.M. What are the position and power of supermarkets in the Australian food system, and the implications for public health? A systematic scoping review. *Obes. Rev.* **2018**, *19*, 198–218. [CrossRef] [PubMed]
19. Pulker, C.E.; Trapp, G.S.A.; Scott, J.A.; Pollard, C.M. The nature and quality of Australian supermarkets' policies that can impact public health nutrition, and evidence of their practical application: A cross-sectional study. *Nutrients* **2019**, *11*, 853. [CrossRef] [PubMed]
20. Wardle, J.; Baranovic, M. Is lack of retail competition in the grocery sector a public health issue? *Aust. N. Z. J. Public Health* **2009**, *33*, 477–481. [CrossRef] [PubMed]
21. Forssell, S.; Lankoski, L. The sustainability promise of alternative food networks: An examination through "alternative" characteristics. *Agric. Hum. Values* **2015**, *32*, 63–75. [CrossRef]
22. Kumar, V.; Wang, M.; Kumari, A.; Akkaranggoon, S.; Garza-Reyes, J.A.; Neutzling, D.; Tupa, J. Exploring short food supply chains from Triple Bottom Line lens: A comprehensive systematic review. In Proceedings of the International Conference on Industrial Engineering and Operations Management, Bangkok, Thailand, 5–7 March 2019; pp. 728–738.
23. Schmitt, E.; Galli, F.; Menozzi, D.; Maye, D.; Touzard, J.-M.; Marescotti, A.; Six, J.; Brunori, G. Comparing the sustainability of local and global food products in Europe. *J. Clean. Prod.* **2017**, *165*, 346–359. [CrossRef]
24. Renting, H.; Marsden, T.K.; Banks, J. Understanding alternative food networks: Exploring the role of short food supply chains in rural development. *Environ. Plan. A* **2003**, *35*, 393–411. [CrossRef]
25. Andrée, P.; Dibden, J.; Higgins, V.; Cocklin, C. Competitive productivism and Australia's emerging 'alternative' agri-food networks: Producing for farmers' markets in Victoria and beyond. *Aust. Geogr.* **2010**, *41*, 307–322. [CrossRef]
26. Food and Agriculture Organisation (FAO). Impact of COVID-19 on Food Security and Nutrition (FSN). 2018. Available online: http://www.fao.org/fileadmin/templates/cfs/Docs1920/Chair/CFS_Chair_Statement_HLPE_COVID.pdf (accessed on 27 April 2020).
27. Smith, K.; Lawrence, G.; MacMahon, A.; Muller, J.; Brady, M. The resilience of long and short food chains: A case study of flooding in Queensland, Australia. *Agric. Hum. Values* **2016**, *33*, 45–60. [CrossRef]
28. Hoek, A.C.; Malekpour, S.; Raven, R.; Court, E.; Byrne, E. Towards environmentally sustainable food systems: Decision-making factors in sustainable food production and consumption. *Sustain. Prod. Consum.* **2021**, *26*, 610–626. [CrossRef]
29. Gilg, A.; Barr, S.; Ford, N. Green consumption or sustainable lifestyles? Identifying the sustainable consumer. *Futures* **2005**, *37*, 481–504.
30. Griskevicius, V.; Tybur, J.M.; van den Bergh, B. Going green to be seen: Status, reputation, and conspicuous conservation. *J. Personal. Soc. Psychol.* **2010**, *98*, 392–404. [CrossRef]
31. European Commission. Special Eurobarometer 459—Climate Change Report. 2018. Available online: https://europa.eu/eurobarometer/surveys/detail/2140 (accessed on 11 September 2018).
32. Kent, K.; Gale, F.; Penrose, B.; Auckland, S.; Lester, E.; Murray, S. Consumer-driven strategies towards a resilient and sustainable food system following the COVID-19 pandemic in Australia. *BMC Public Health* **2022**, *22*, 1539. [CrossRef]
33. Adalja, A.; Hanson, J.; Towe, C.; Tselepidakis, E. An examination of consumer willingness to pay for local products. *Agric. Resour. Econ. Rev.* **2015**, *44*, 253–274. [CrossRef]
34. De Magistris, T.; Gracia, A. Do consumers care about organic and distance labels? An empirical analysis in Spain. *Int. J. Consum. Stud.* **2014**, *38*, 660–669. [CrossRef]
35. Hu, W.; Batte, M.T.; Woods, T.; Ernst, S. Consumer preferences for local production and other value-added label claims for a processed food product. *Eur. Rev. Agric. Econ.* **2012**, *39*, 489–510. [CrossRef]

36. Bazzani, C.; Caputo, V.; Nayga, R.M.; Canavari, M. Revisiting consumers' valuation for local versus organic food using a non-hypothetical choice experiment: Does personality matter? *Food Qual. Prefer.* **2017**, *62*, 144–154. [CrossRef]
37. Kiss, K.; Ruszkai, C.; Szucs, A.; Koncz, G. Examining the role of local products in rural development in the light of consumer preferences—Results of a consumer survey from Hungary. *Sustainability* **2020**, *12*, 5473. [CrossRef]
38. Feldmann, C.; Hamm, U. Consumers' perceptions and preferences for local food: A review. *Food Qual. Prefer.* **2015**, *40*, 152–164. [CrossRef]
39. Watts, D.; Little, J.; Ilbery, B. "I am pleased to shop somewhere that is fighting the supermarkets a little bit". A cultural political economy of alternative food networks. *Geoforum* **2018**, *91*, 21–29. [CrossRef]
40. Godrich, S.; Kent, K.; Murray, S.; Auckland, S.; Lo, J.; Blekkenhorst, L.; Penrose, B.; Devine, A. Australian consumer perceptions of regionally grown fruits and vegetables: Importance, enablers, and barriers. *Int. J. Environ. Res. Public Health* **2019**, *17*, 63. [CrossRef] [PubMed]
41. Hasselbach, J.L.; Roosen, J. Motivations behind preferences for local or organic food. *J. Int. Consum. Mark.* **2015**, *27*, 295–306. [CrossRef]
42. Kumpulainen, T.; Vainio, A.; Sandell, M.; Hopia, A. How young people in Finland respond to information about the origin of food products: The role of value orientations and product type. *Food Qual. Prefer.* **2018**, *68*, 173–182. [CrossRef]
43. Campbell, H. Breaking new ground in food regime theory: Corporate environmentalism, ecological feedbacks and the "food from somewhere" regime? *Agric. Hum. Values* **2009**, *26*, 309–319. [CrossRef]
44. Friedmann, H. From colonialism to green capitalism: Social movements and the emergence of food regimes. In *New Directions in the Sociology of Global Development*; Buttel, F., McMichael, P., Eds.; Elsevier: Amsterdam, The Netherlands, 2005.
45. Ilbery, B.; Kneafsey, M. Producer constructions of quality in regional specialty food production: A case study from south west England. *J. Rural Stud.* **2000**, *16*, 217–230.
46. Ilbery, B.; Maye, D. Alternative (shorter) food supply chains and specialist livestock products in the Scottish-English borders. *Environ. Plan. A* **2005**, *37*, 823–844. [CrossRef]
47. Birch, D.; Memery, J.; De, M.; Kanakaratne, S. The mindful consumer: Balancing egoistic and altruistic motivations to purchase local food. *J. Retail. Consum. Serv.* **2018**, *40*, 221–228.
48. Goodman, D. The quality 'turn' and alternative food practices: Reflections and agenda. *J. Rural Stud.* **2003**, *19*, 1–7.
49. Winter, M. Embeddedness, the new food economy and defensive localism. *J. Rural Stud.* **2003**, *19*, 23–32. [CrossRef]
50. Blake, M.D.; Mellor, J.; Crane, L. Buying local food: Shopping practices, place, and consumption networks in defining food as "local". *Ann. Assoc. Am. Geogr.* **2010**, *100*, 409–426. [CrossRef]
51. Jackson, P. Food stories: Consumption in an age of anxiety. *Cult. Geogr.* **2010**, *17*, 147–165. [CrossRef]
52. Little, J.; Ilbery, B.; Watts, D. Gender, consumption and the relocalisation of food: A research agenda. *Sociol. Rural.* **2009**, *49*, 201–217. [CrossRef]
53. Kim, S.-H.; Huang, R. Understanding local food consumption from an ideological perspective: Locavorism, authenticity, pride and willingness to visit. *J. Retail. Consum. Serv.* **2021**, *58*, 102330. [CrossRef]
54. Guthman, J. *Agrarian Dreams: The Paradox of Organic Farming in California*; UC Press: Berkeley, CA, USA, 2004.
55. McEachern, M.G.; Warnaby, G.; Carrigan, M.; Szmigin, I. Thinking locally, acting locally? Conscious consumers and farmers' markets. *J. Mark. Manag.* **2010**, *26*, 395–412. [CrossRef]
56. Albrecht, C.; Smithers, J. Reconnecting through local food initiatives? Purpose, practice and conceptions of 'value'. *Agric. Hum. Values* **2018**, *35*, 67–81. [CrossRef]
57. Vermeir, I.; Verbeke, W. Sustainable food consumption: Exploring the consumer "attitude—Behavioral intention" gap. *J. Agric. Environ. Ethics* **2006**, *19*, 169–194. [CrossRef]
58. Kummer, S.; Milestad, R. The diversity of organic box schemes in Europe—An exploratory study in four countries. *Sustainability* **2020**, *12*, 2734. [CrossRef]
59. Megicks, P.; Memery, J.; Angell, R.J. Understanding local food shopping: Unpacking the ethical dimension. *J. Mark. Manag.* **2012**, *28*, 264–289. [CrossRef]
60. Byker, C.; Rose, N.; Serrano, E. The benefits, challenges, and strategies of adults following a local food diet. *J. Agric. Food Syst. Community Dev.* **2010**, *1*, 125–137. [CrossRef]
61. Papaoikonomou, E.; Ginieis, M. Putting the farmer's face on food: Governance and the producer-consumer relationship in local food. *Agric. Hum. Values* **2017**, *34*, 53–67. [CrossRef]
62. Lockie, S.; Lyons, K.; Lawrence, G.; Mummery, K. Eating "green": Motivations behind organic food consumption in Australia. *Sociol. Rural.* **2002**, *42*, 23–40. [CrossRef]
63. Williams, J.; Memery, J.; Megicks, P.; Morrison, M. Ethics and social responsibility in Australian grocery shopping. *Int. J. Retail. Distrib. Manag.* **2010**, *38*, 297–316. [CrossRef]
64. Barraket, J.; McKinnon, K.; Brennan-Horley, C.; de Cotta, T. Motivations and effects of ethical purchasing from social enterprise in a regional city. *Soc. Enterp. J.* **2022**, *18*, 643–659. [CrossRef]

65. Weatherall, C.; Tregear, A.; Allinson, J. In search of the concerned consumer: UK public perceptions of food, farming and buying local. *J. Rural Stud.* **2003**, *19*, 233–244. [CrossRef]
66. Nemes, G.; Chiffoleau, Y.; Zollet, S.; Collison, M.; Benedek, Z.; Colantuono, F.; Dulsrud, A.; Fiore, M.; Holtkamp, C.; Kim, T.-Y.; et al. The impact of COVID-19 on alternative and local food systems and the potential for the sustainability transition: Insights from 13 countries. *Sustain. Prod. Consum.* **2021**, *28*, 591–599. [CrossRef]
67. Sundaraja, C.S.; Hine, D.W.; Lykins, A.D. Palm oil: Understanding barriers to sustainable consumption. *PLoS ONE* **2021**, *16*, e0254897.
68. Cohen, J. *Statistical Power Analysis for the Behavioral Sciences*; Lawrence Erlbaum Associates: Hillsdale, NJ, USA, 1988.
69. Henseler, J.; Ringle, C.M.; Sinkovics, R.R. The use of partial least squares path modeling in international marketing. In *New Challenges to International Marketing (Advances in International Marketing)*; Sinkovics, R.R., Ghauri, P.N., Eds.; Emerald Group Publishing Limited: Warrington, UK, 2009.
70. Faul, F.; Erdfelder, E.; Buchner, A.; Lang, A.G. Statistical power analyses using G*Power 3.1: Tests for correlation and regression analyses. *Behav. Res. Methods* **2009**, *41*, 1149–1160.
71. Bailey, M. Consumer profiles and behavior in Australian shopping centers, new benchmarks for assessing mall shopping patterns. *Retail. Prop. Insights* **2013**, *20*, 4–11.
72. Inside FMCG. *Women Chief Grocery Buyers*; Inside FMCG: Sydney, Australia, 2015.
73. Australian Bureau of Statistics. New Census Insights on Income in Australia Using Administrative Data. 2023. Available online: https://www.abs.gov.au/articles/new-census-insights-income-australia-using-administrative-data (accessed on 21 October 2024).
74. Beingessner, N.; Fletcher, A.J. "Going local": Farmers' perspectives on local food systems in rural Canada. *Agric. Hum. Values* **2020**, *37*, 129–145. [CrossRef]
75. Giampietri, E.; Verneau, F.; del Giudice, T.; Carfora, V.; Finco, A. A Theory of Planned Behaviour perspective for investigating the role of trust in consumer purchasing decision related to short food supply chains. *Food Qual. Prefer.* **2018**, *64*, 160–166. [CrossRef]
76. Head, L.; Klocker, N.; Dun, O.; Waitt, G.; Goodall, H.; Aguirre-Bielschowsky, I. Barriers to and enablers of sustainable practices: Insights from ethnic minority migrants. *Int. J. Justice Sustain.* **2021**, *26*, 595–614. [CrossRef]
77. Mazzocchi, C.; Orsi, L.; Sali, G. Consumers' attitudes for sustainable mountain cheese. *Sustainability* **2021**, *13*, 1743. [CrossRef]
78. Scalco, A.R.; Devos Ganga, G.M.; de Oliveira, S.C.; Baker, G. Development and validation of a scale for identification of quality attributes of agri-food products in short chains. *Geoforum* **2020**, *111*, 165–175. [CrossRef]
79. Kung, F.Y.H.; Kwok, N.; Brown, D.J. Are attention check questions a threat to scale validity? *Appl. Psychol.* **2018**, *67*, 264–283.
80. Meade, A.W.; Craig, S.B. Identifying careless responses in survey data. *Psychol. Methods* **2012**, *17*, 437–455.
81. IBM Corp. *IBM SPSS Statistics for Windows*; Version 28.0; IMB Corp: Armonk, NY, USA, 2021.
82. Cattell, R.B. The scree test for the number of factors. *Multivar. Behav. Res.* **1966**, *1*, 245–276.
83. Koven, N.S.; Abry, A.W. The clinical basis of orthorexia nervosa: Emerging perspectives. *Neuropsychiatr. Dis. Treat.* **2015**, *11*, 385–394.
84. Born, B.; Purcell, M. Avoiding the local trap: Scale and food systems in planning research. *J. Plan. Educ. Res.* **2006**, *26*, 195–207. [CrossRef]
85. O'Kane, G.M.; Richardson, A.; D'Almeida, M.; Wei, H. The cost, availability, cultivars, and quality of fruit and vegetables at farmers' markets and three other retail streams in Canberra, ACT, Australia. *J. Hunger Environ. Nutr.* **2019**, *14*, 643–661. [CrossRef]
86. Carden, L.; Wood, W. Habit formation and change. *Curr. Opin. Behav. Sci.* **2018**, *20*, 117–122. [CrossRef]
87. Wills, B.; Arundel, A. Internet-enabled access to alternative food networks: A comparison of online and offline food shoppers and their differing interpretations of quality. *Agric. Hum. Values* **2017**, *34*, 701–712. [CrossRef]
88. Jia, S.S.; Luo, X.; Gibson, A.A.; Partridge, S.R. Developing the DIGIFOOD Dashboard to monitor the digitalization of local food environments: Interdisciplinary approach. *JMIR Public Health Surveill.* **2024**, *10*, e59924. [CrossRef] [PubMed]
89. Evans, A.B.; Miele, M. Enacting public understandings: The case of farm animal welfare. *Geoforum* **2019**, *99*, 1–10. [CrossRef]
90. Saltzman, K.; Head, L.; Stenseke, M. Do cows belong in nature? The cultural basis of agriculture in Sweden and Australia. *J. Rural Stud.* **2011**, *27*, 54–62. [CrossRef]
91. Ainsworth, K. Coles and Woolworths Food Prices Rise by 9.6% Per Cent in Past Year, Outpacing Inflation Rate. ABC News. 2023. Available online: https://www.abc.net.au/news/2023-05-23/supermarket-prices-increase-coles-woolworths-inflation/102380456 (accessed on 31 January 2025).
92. LaFrenz, C. Fresh Food Prices Spike in March: UBS. Australian Financial Review. 2023. Available online: https://www.afr.com/companies/retail/fresh-food-prices-spike-in-march-ubs-20230420-p5d20s (accessed on 31 January 2025).

93. Michie, S.; van Stralen, M.M.; West, R. The behaviour change wheel: A new method for characterising and designing behaviour change interventions. *Implement. Sci.* **2011**, *6*, 42. [CrossRef]
94. Aschemann-Witzel, J.; de Hooge, I.; Amani, P.; Bech-Larsen, T.; Oostindjer, M. Consumer-related food waste: Causes and potential for action. *Sustainability* **2015**, *7*, 6457–6477. [CrossRef]

sustainability

MDPI

Review

The Necessary Transition Towards Healthier Diets: An Assessment of Replacing Meat and Refined Wheat Flour with a Mixture of Different Plant-Based Foods

Diego Luna * and Vicente Montes

Departamento de Química Orgánica, Instituto Químico para la Energía y el Medioambiente (IQUEMA), Universidad de Córdoba, E-14071 Córdoba, Spain; q22mojiv@uco.es

* Correspondence: qo1lumad@uco.es

Abstract

Currently, at least one third of greenhouse gas (GHG) emissions come from the agricultural sector, with meat production making a particularly significant contribution. Therefore, alongside the ongoing efforts to transform transport and cut its emissions, it is essential to adopt urgent measures that limit GHG emissions from food production, consumption and distribution. Without them, the Paris Agreement goal of net-zero GHG emissions by 2050 cannot be met, and the most severe impacts of climate change will not be avoided. In principle, lowering emissions from the global food system may appear simple, as no new technology (for example, electric cars or carbon-neutral fuels) is required to decarbonize transport. However, since meat consumption accounts for the majority of food related GHG emissions, it must be coupled with a sharp reduction in the large-scale production and consumption of animal foods. Encouragingly, a growing number of consumers already choose diets that are both healthy and environmentally sustainable. As meat reduction gains popularity in these groups, plant-based products are expanding in the marketplace, mainly in the form of snacks, pasta, pizzas and especially vegan or vegetarian burgers. Thus, almost spontaneously, components of the Westernized diet, rich in ultra-processed foods, salt, sugar and animal protein, are gradually being replaced by plant-derived nutrients that are healthier and more environmentally friendly. To accelerate this trend, legal measures could be introduced to improve the nutritional quality of widely consumed, low-nutrient snacks and to promote agricultural reforms that encourage the production of nutrient-dense legumes and pseudocereals.

Keywords: smart food; Westernized diet; plant-based foods; GHG emissions; planetary health plate

1. Introduction

1.1. Current Panorama of Food Production and Consumption All over the World

According to a recent report from the World Health Organization (WHO) [1], obesity and other disorders related to the metabolic syndrome now constitute the deadliest global pandemic, claiming at least 2.8 million lives each year [2]. The crisis is no longer confined to high income nations; in 2016, more than 1.9 billion adults were overweight worldwide, and 650 million of them were classified as obese [3]. Indeed, the WHO regards obesity as the most serious public health challenge of the twenty first century, noting that the majority of the population of the world lives in countries where

 https://doi.org/10.3390/su17188357

overweight and obesity cause more deaths than undernutrition linked to insufficient food intake [4]. Alarmingly, the situation continues to deteriorate, as the global prevalence of obesity has tripled since 1975 [5]. At present, nearly one third of all people can be categorized as overweight or obese. Rates have increased across every age group, sex, country, ethnic background, and socioeconomic stratum, although prevalence remains highest among older adults and women [6].

Thus, an excessive or unbalanced dietary intake is associated with numerous chronic conditions, including coronary heart disease, stroke, type 2 diabetes, and several forms of cancer. Because maintaining a preventive diet proves extremely difficult for many people, once a pathology develops, they often rely on multiple medications [7,8]. This dependence imposes very high costs on national health systems and markedly reduces quality of life for extended periods [9].

At the same time, environmental pressures such as water scarcity, soil degradation, and related challenges threaten food security worldwide and act as additional drivers of climate change [10]. Consequently, the functioning of the global food system itself represents a significant climate risk; ensuring its sustainability is crucial for safeguarding both urban populations and the agricultural landscapes that supply their food [11].

Replacing the ultra-processed foods that dominate the westernized diet, now consumed worldwide, with healthier and more organic products would deliver a dual benefit. First, it would lower the incidence of disorders linked to obesity; second, it would reduce environmental pressure. A food pattern centered on minimally processed, largely plant-based items limits demand for meat and industrially manufactured products, thereby cutting the volumes of waste and packaging generated by intensive processing [12]. At the global scale, today's excessive and nutritionally unbalanced intake drives oversupply, energy-intensive manufacture, and complex waste management, all of which release avoidable carbon dioxide. In high-income economies, the prevailing menu depends heavily on meat, so shifting from animal to plant protein would both improve the health of citizens and curb greenhouse gas emissions associated with cattle raising. Moreover, farmland currently dedicated to crops for feed could be restored to natural vegetation, enhancing carbon sequestration and recovering ecosystem services [13].

Given the current growth in the consumption of meat from intensive livestock systems, this production model is clearly unviable and unsustainable. The concerns extend beyond its documented harm to human health; large-scale industrial farming also accelerates biodiversity loss across vast regions and makes a major contribution to climate change. Livestock-oriented agriculture already accounts for roughly one third of global greenhouse gas emissions [14]. Moreover, total agricultural output has more than doubled since 1970, and with land-use change included, agriculture is now responsible for about one quarter of all emissions [15]. Dietary patterns are therefore a key driver of climate change: as per-capita incomes rise and populations urbanize, traditional menus centered on staple starches, legumes, and vegetables are increasingly replaced by energy-intensive foods such as refined sugars, fats, oils, and meat [15,16].

1.2. *Current Perspectives for Measures Planned to Reduce Emissions from the World Food System in the Coming Decades*

It is important to note that, despite significant governmental efforts to promote renewable energy in transport, policy measures aimed at reducing the climate impact of food and agriculture remain virtually absent [17]. Yet meeting the Paris Agreement targets [18] will require a sharp decline in emissions from the global food system over the coming decades, in parallel with the ongoing transformation of the transport sector [19].

Given the scale of current food sector emissions, any meaningful reduction must combine several strategies: modifying dietary patterns in both quantity and composition, cutting the vast amounts of food that are wasted, and improving agricultural practices [20]. Rationalizing diets at a global level would yield substantial greenhouse gas savings because foods of animal origin generate far more emissions than plant products. Excessive consumption of protein and meat calories not only harms public health but also amplifies pollution, since foods derived from animals generally demand more resources and impose a greater environmental burden than those from plants. For example, beef generates the highest emissions, with greenhouse gases per kilogram roughly ten times higher than chicken and up to twenty times higher than plant foods such as nuts, seeds, or legumes [21]. Figure 1 illustrates the emission intensity range (form low to high environmental impact) of representative animal and plant foods that dominate the Westernized diet, a pattern typically low in vegetables and rich in animal protein, ultra-processed items, sugar, and salt [22]. The average CO_2 emissions in modern diet (2500 cal/day) can be estimated to be between 2000 and 15,000 g of CO_2 equivalent per day. Within this context, beef production stands out as the leading source of methane, a potent greenhouse gas [23], and its CO_2 equivalent emissions could be reduced only partially to 50%, if the meat is raised under a low environmental impact.

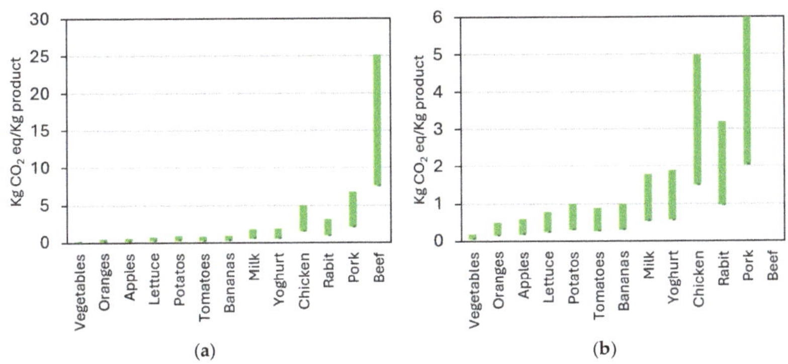

Figure 1. Greenhouse gas emissions per kilogram of several food products measured in carbon dioxide equivalents (CO_2eq), from beginning-to-consumer based on data from [20] in two scales on y axes, from 0 to 30 (**a**) and from 0 to 6 (**b**).

The rationalization of global dietary patterns could be achieved relatively easily because it requires no new technology; the main challenge is altering cultural habits that are deeply embedded in local customs [24]. It is therefore both feasible and urgent to identify dietary models and production practices compatible with the United Nations Sustainable Development Goals (SDGs) and the Paris climate targets. In this context, the EAT-Lancet Commission on Healthy Diets from Sustainable Food Systems has proposed the Planetary Health Diet as an optimal pattern for both people and the environment [25]. The commission argues that a projected world population of ten billion can be nourished within the biophysical limits assigned to anthropogenic greenhouse gas (GHG) emissions, provided that intake of animal protein is cut by at least half and consumption of vegetables, legumes, and nuts is doubled [20,26].

The Planetary Health Diet is a worldwide reference for adults; it counteracts the harmful effects of the westernized diet. Figure 2 illustrates the concept as a plate half filled with fruits and vegetables. The other half consists mainly of whole grains, plant proteins (beans, lentils, pulses, nuts), and unsaturated plant oils, complemented by modest amounts of meat and dairy plus small quantities of added sugars and starchy vegetables. This framework is sufficiently flexible to accommodate diverse nutritional needs, personal preferences, and cultural traditions, including fully vegetarian patterns [25].

Global adoption of the Planetary Health Diet would yield substantial reductions in agricultural GHG emissions in at least 101 countries [27]. The average CO_2 emissions for a Planetary Health Diet (2500 cal/day) can be estimated to be between 500 and 3000 g of CO_2 equivalent per day. Comparison with the modern diet represents a percentage of reduction in CO_2 equivalent emissions around 30 to 80%. A simple calculation using these numbers and the amount of population in the first level world can give a rough idea of the magnitude on CO_2 emissions that the shift in the diet represents. In fact, dietary change may prove more decisive than any other single measure for meeting the climate targets set for 2050 [28–31].

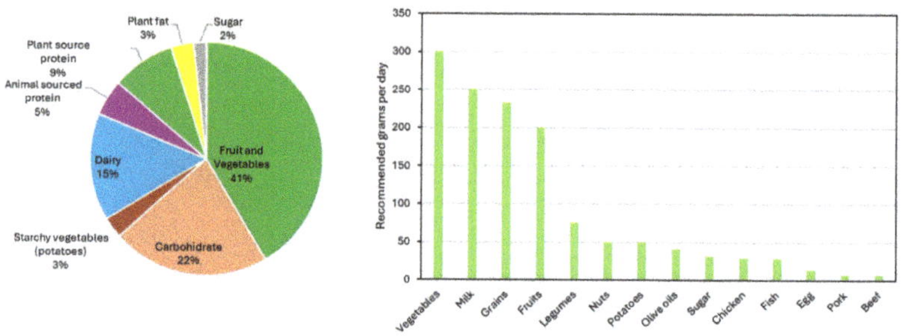

Figure 2. Weight percentage of different types of food based on the EAT-Lancet Commission planetary health plate [25] and one example of the food required for this diet on a basis of 2500 calories per day.

Consequently, the transition from animal-based to plant-based foods should begin as soon as possible, because products of animal origin demand more resources and generate a larger environmental footprint than those of plant origin.

Nevertheless, policies that encourage a reduction in meat consumption can face two major objections. First, many health professionals and large segments of the public believe that meat guarantees superior dietary quality, especially with respect to protein and essential minerals and amino acid [32]. Second, constructing a calorie-balanced, nutritionally adequate menu based mainly on plant foods, as envisaged in the Planetary Health Diet, demands more forethought than the prevailing Westernized pattern, which still dominates the eating habits of most people. The pressures of urban living therefore pose a significant barrier to adopting healthy plant-centered diets such as the planetary, Mediterranean, DASH, or Harvard plate models [33]. The Westernized diet, which underlies both widespread health problems and excessive greenhouse gas emissions, is thus not merely a matter of individual preference; it also reflects practical constraints that limit alternative choices within modern lifestyles [34]. Even so, interest is growing in substituting meat and refined wheat flour with commonly called smart foods that offer higher nutritional and environmental value [35–37].

2. Some Possible Measures to Move Towards a Healthier and More Sustainable Future

2.1. Implement New Strategies to Increase the Proportion of Plant Foods in the Diet of the Current Urban Population, Within the Concept of "Smart Food"

To increase the proportion of plant foods in the diets of urban populations, it is essential to design strategies that genuinely fit modern city life. The poor nutritional quality of the Westernized diet arises largely from the challenge of accommodating healthy eating within demanding work schedules. Consequently, city dwellers often turn to a wide range of snacks, Italian pasta and pizzas as quick substitutes for a main meal. These items are typically highly processed and provide minimal nutritional value, serving mainly as time-saving replacements. They therefore play a significant role in the poor quality of the current Westernized diet [38–40].

However, a promising strategy would be to leverage these fast-food formats to enhance the nutritional quality of meals consumed under current lifestyle constraints. Significant gains could be achieved by upgrading the nutritional profile of popular snacks and pasta dishes [41–43]. For example, an innovative baked and UVB-irradiated snack made from Pleurotus eryngiums, an edible mushroom native to the Mediterranean basin, has been proposed as a convenient vehicle for increasing nutrient intake [44]. In line with this approach, many research efforts now focus on fortifying snacks with essential vitamins, amino acids, minerals, and dietary fiber [45–48]. Parallel studies have improved the nutritional value of pasta and pizza by incorporating whole-grain flours, legumes, and other functional ingredients [49–51]. Replacing conventional snacks and pasta with these nutrient-dense alternatives appears feasible, given the widespread acceptance of such foods. In the United States, for instance, nearly one quarter of daily energy intake comes from snacks [41]; upgrading their composition would therefore deliver a substantial improvement in overall diet quality and, by extension, public health.

These healthy snacks would rely mainly on plant-based ingredients, the most effective option for improving both human and planetary health. They should integrate easily into meals that also include a variety of vegetables, thereby aligning daily intake with the Planetary Health Diet, the Harvard plate, or the DASH model, each closely linked to the traditional Mediterranean pattern [33]. Pasta products reformulated with unconventional flours and functional components in place of refined wheat likewise become healthy snack alternatives [49–54]. Many authors classify such items as "Smart Food" because they benefit consumers by delivering essential nutrients, benefit the planet through lower environmental impact, and benefit farmers by creating new markets and potentially higher revenues [53–57]. The Smart Food concept therefore represents a future-oriented blueprint for food systems that provide healthy diets, preserve natural resources, and remain economically viable for producers [58–61].

Production and consumption of vegetable and vegan burgers can follow the same Smart Food approach, replacing large amounts of meat with a diverse range of plant ingredients. These burgers are increasingly common in fast-food chains as alternatives to classic beef patties. Formulations typically employ tofu, seitan, lentils, and other legumes that provide amino acids comparable to those in meat but with much lower fat content while preserving sensory qualities similar to conventional hamburgers [62–64]. Their rapid market acceptance has even sparked controversy within the European Union over the naming of these meat-substitute products [65].

Smart Food therefore links a healthy, environmentally sustainable diet with farming systems capable of producing nutrient-dense ingredients in an economically viable manner. At present, however, agricultural production is dominated by a narrow set of crops—mainly wheat, maize, barley, and soybeans—that supply most nutrients for both people and livestock. This supply is controlled by a few large corporations that provide low-quality products at very low prices, limiting dietary diversity and hindering the expansion of alternative Smart Food crops.

However, this supply strategy delivers only limited nutritional value for the billions of citizens who depend on it in many different food formats. The deficit in essential amino acids and micronutrients is clear, given the narrow set of plant sources employed and the heavy reliance on refined wheat flour. Meat therefore remains a dominant feature of the Westernized diet because it supplies indispensable nutrients that could, in principle, be obtained from plant foods. Abrupt measures that simply slash meat intake could lower the availability of critical nutrients, especially essential amino acids, currently provided by animal products.

Consequently, any plan to reduce meat consumption must both raise the overall intake of plant foods and improve their amino-acid profile. This improvement can be achieved by replacing refined wheat flour with a wider range of legumes, which complement cereal proteins and furnish key micronutrients. Substituting meat with diverse pulses would not only cut greenhouse gas emissions and enhance the sustainability of agricultural production but also strengthen public health by providing the vitamins and minerals required for an adequate diet.

At present, the idea of a healthy diet is usually framed in terms of calories and macronutrients, proteins, carbohydrates, and fats. Yet micronutrients, which include trace minerals, vitamins, and enzyme cofactors, act as biocatalysts that enable proper assimilation of those macronutrients. Adequate intake of carbohydrates, proteins, and fats alone is therefore insufficient; health also depends on obtaining appropriate quantities of micronutrients. Numerous studies have linked deficiencies in specific micronutrients to a wide range of pathologies. Plant-based foods offer a clear advantage in this regard, as they often contain larger and more diverse supplies of essential micronutrients than commonly consumed meats.

Public authorities should therefore give high priority to improving the nutritional quality of widely consumed plant-based items such as vegetable and vegan burgers, snack products, and convenience pastas and pizzas, which are particularly popular among younger urban consumers. A straightforward first step would be to replace refined wheat flour with whole grains blended with pseudocereals and legumes. Such reformulations would markedly enhance the nutritional profile by supplying all essential amino acids together with significant amounts of fiber, vitamins, and minerals. Production lines for plant-based burgers, snacks, and pasta could incorporate, alongside wheat, a broad range of grains, rice, maize, barley, oats, rye, sorghum, and millet, together with pseudocereals such as quinoa, chia, amaranth, and buckwheat. Most important, a variety of legumes (for example, lentils, chickpeas, black or white beans, pinto beans, broad beans, soy, lupins, or peanuts) should be included, since the amino-acid complementarity between cereals and legumes provides a full profile of indispensable amino acids as well as additional fiber and micronutrients.

Numerous studies have documented innovative applications of legumes in familiar formats such as burgers, pasta, and bakery items [44–56,62–64]. Because these products resemble foods that consumers already recognize, they are commercially attractive. Unlike current equivalents, legume-based versions supply a complete profile of essential amino acids, comparable to meat, while containing far less saturated fat and considerably more dietary fiber. This composition is expected to improve health outcomes and reduce obesity among consumers. Encouragingly, several of these products are already on the market. In Spain, for instance, the Pastas Gallo company sells noodles, spaghetti, macaroni, spirals, and pizza bases made entirely from chickpeas, lentils, or peas. A range of legume-rich snacks also aims to balance essential amino acids, including Falafel in Israel, Doushabao in China, Bindaetteok in Korea, Butsi in the Philippines, Mame daifuku in Japan, Batagor in Indonesia, Bolani in Afghanistan, as well as Pé-de-moleque, Acarajé, and Arrumadinho in Brazil.

Although these products are very popular in their countries of origin, they are neither widely known nor readily available internationally. The same applies to the traditional Mediterranean diet, which offers thousands of recipes that combine legumes with other functional ingredients; however, modern urban lifestyles make regular preparation of such dishes difficult. The most practical strategy is therefore to incorporate legumes and other functional ingredients into food categories that are already consumed on a massive scale, namely vegetable and vegan burgers, snack products, and convenience pasta. To realize this potential, public authorities at all levels should actively support commercial initiatives that promote Smart Food, given its clear environmental advantages and its capacity to improve public health.

2.2. Reduce the Environmental Impact of Food Production

According to United Nations estimations [66], food production accounts for roughly one third of global greenhouse gas emissions. Countries that aim to lead in climate-change mitigation must therefore adopt measures for the food sector comparable to the steps already being taken to curb fossil-fuel use. Within the European Union (EU) an intense debate is under way on the role carbon-neutral fuels might play in the transition envisaged by the European Green Deal, whose ultimate goal is to make Europe the first climate-neutral continent [67]. Draft legislation now targets a 55 percent cut in passenger-car emissions and a 50 percent reduction for vans by 2030 [68].

The Green Deal also pledges to "lead a global transition towards competitive sustainability from farm to fork" [69], thereby improving the environmental performance of food production as part of a broader effort to reduce the overall environmental impact of human activity (see Figure 3). Yet, despite this stated aim, the European Union has so far introduced no specific actions in the food sector, even though the Green Deal lists among its principal objectives the improvement of citizens' well-being and health by ensuring access to healthy and affordable food while enhancing biodiversity [70].

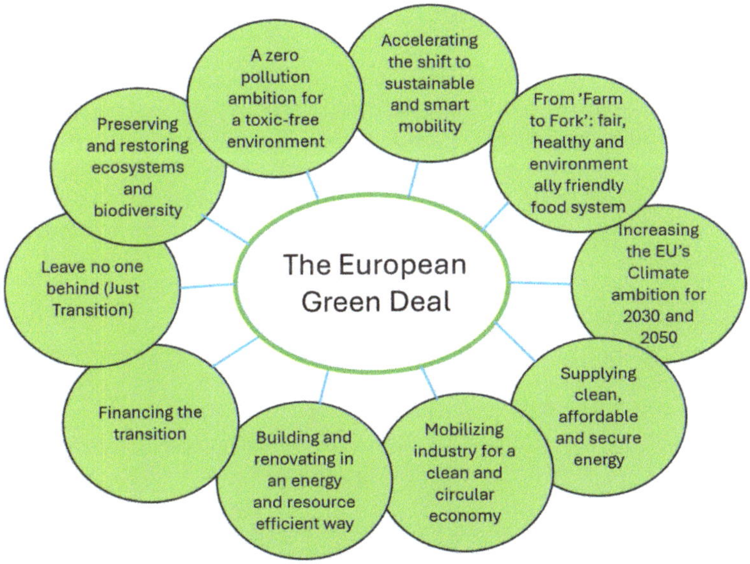

Figure 3. Elements of The European Green Deal. Source: European Commission (2019) [67].

In fact, this green plan (Figure 3) considers dedicating adequate financing to obtain a green transition, empowering European industry and small- and medium-sized companies, boosting the circular economy, creating a sustainable food system, and preserving biodiversity. The absence of concrete food-sector policies among the member states of the European Union may reflect cultural barriers to a circular food economy, limited consumer awareness, and low business engagement [71]. By contrast, firm deadlines have been set for phasing out internal-combustion engines in favor of electric powertrains, even though full consensus on the optimal technology is still lacking [72].

Unlike the decarbonization of transport, rationalizing food supply chains to improve public health and environmental safety does not depend on new technologies or additional scientific breakthroughs. What is required is the introduction of coherent policies at local, national, and global levels that promote dietary models with less meat and refined wheat and greater use of legumes and pseudocereals. Policy action, cultural change, and financial incentives therefore represent the main levers for overcoming the current inertia and advancing the Smart Food agenda on a worldwide scale.

While a growing segment of the population recognizes the value of adding legumes and other functional ingredients to popular plant-based burgers, pasta and snack foods in order to improve diet quality, enhance health and curb obesity, voluntary private initiatives alone cannot address the urgency of the challenge. The climate emergency and the worsening health of millions call for swift action by public authorities. In the European Union, food production accounts for almost one third of the ecological footprint of the region and uses more than half of its biocapacity; about a quarter of the biocapacity embodied in EU food consumption comes from outside the Union. Citizens of the EU-27 therefore withdraw more resources from nature than local ecosystems can regenerate, which underscores the need for stronger food and trade policies that can guide a transition to sustainable food systems in Europe [73].

The Sustainable Development Goals adopted by the United Nations in September 2015 remain in force, and Goal 2 calls on every country to secure food security and sound nutrition through sustainable food systems [74]. After nearly ten years, progress is still limited. Failure to achieve the Sustainable Development Goals and the Paris Agreement would accelerate environmental degradation and expose an ever larger share of the global population to malnutrition and preventable diseases linked to metabolic syndrome.

Consequently, measures on food-related emissions that parallel those already applied to transport are now unavoidable. In this case, no new technology is needed; rather, policy makers in the most developed nations must establish regulations that foster a Smart Food system capable of keeping emissions on track for net-zero by 2050. This aligns with the European Commission objective of leading a global shift toward competitive sustainability "from farm to fork" under the Green Deal. Improving the environmental performance of food production is therefore essential for reducing the overall impact of human activity.

Strong action is needed without delay to curb the consumption of animal-derived foods. Production of these foods uses more than three quarters of global agricultural land and generates about two thirds of agriculture-related greenhouse gas emissions, yet supplies only forty percent of the protein people consume each year. The main reason is the heavy reliance on, and low efficiency of, converting crops into animal feed. Raising cattle or sheep for meat can emit up to 250 times more greenhouse gases per gram of protein than producing legumes that deliver the same amount of protein [75].

Given the urgency of current environmental and public-health challenges and the absence of concrete food policies from the European Commission, the Union could look to recent reforms in the United States, where national, state, and municipal initiatives are beginning to support a shift toward plant-based diets and to curb large-scale production of animal foods [76]. Comparable proposals are now emerging at supranational level in Europe [77–79].

Effective action should combine positive standards for raw materials used in popular foods such as plant-based burgers, snacks, and pasta with disincentives similar to those already applied to fossil fuels. One option is to adjust value-added tax and other fees according to the climate footprint of individual foods, which varies widely, as illustrated in Figure 1.

Educational programs are equally essential. Consumers must understand the benefits of dietary patterns that prioritize plant products and limit meat, since these changes improve both human and planetary health [80]. Within this framework, the Smart Food concept can play a central role: it promotes crops and products that are nutritious for people, sustainable for the environment, and economically viable for farmers. Clear communication is needed to show that today's epidemic of metabolic diseases, including obesity, cardiovascular disease, diabetes, hypertension, dementia, and many cancers, stems largely from the Westernized diet [81–87].

3. Conclusions

Current meat consumption in high-income countries produces greenhouse gas emissions on the same scale as those generated by the entire fleet of transport vehicles, once livestock statistics are combined with all relevant emission factors [88]. Direct and indirect emissions from the roughly thirty billion animals slaughtered for food each year contribute about fourteen to sixteen percent of the global total. When methane, nitrous oxide, and land-use change linked to pasture conversion and feed crops are included, livestock-related warming rises to roughly twenty-three percent [89]. Achieving international climate goals therefore requires interventions that target activities with the largest carbon footprints. A review of the literature identifies three domains with the highest emissions: private vehicle use, meat consumption, and household energy demand [90].

Although every country has been committed for more than a decade to the Sustainable Development Goals and the Paris Agreement [91], most concrete measures to date focus on transport [92] and domestic energy use [93]. Food systems are widely acknowledged as a critical sector for reaching the SDG targets by 2030, yet action in this area is lagging, a delay that is particularly serious for the meat supply chain [94,95].

Although the European Green Deal sets out clear objectives for a sustainable and competitive global transition, including lower-impact food production as shown in Figure 3 [69], no concrete measures have yet been adopted to curb large-scale animal-based agriculture [76]. One likely reason is the profound cultural change that would be needed for society to reduce meat consumption and choose plant-based foods [96–100]. Over the past five years, a vast body of research has suggested that the most practical approach to lowering meat intake focuses on the development and widespread consumption of vegetarian and vegan burgers [62–65,101–125].

Alongside the extensive literature exploring vegetarian burgers as a tool for shifting consumption from meat to plant foods, an expanding body of research now targets the reformulation of snacks, pizzas and pasta with whole grains, pseudocereals and legumes in order to raise dietary quality through a broader range of plant ingredients [41–55,61,126–131]. Within this context, incorporating insects into the food chain is also gaining momentum, since insects already feature in the traditional diets of about two billion people worldwide [132–140]. The European Union has recognized this potential by authorizing insects as novel foods in Regulation (EU) 2015/2283, thereby acknowledging their advantages [141]. The main benefits include the provision of high-quality protein and micronutrients, very high production efficiency compared with other animal protein sources and greatly reduced water use and greenhouse-gas emissions [132].

In summary, a rising share of consumers now pays close attention to the health and sustainability of their diets. As a result, reducing meat intake is becoming popular in certain groups, and plant-based products are proliferating on the market. While many consumers are motivated primarily by the personal health gains that come from lowering or eliminating meat, these dietary shifts also deliver environmental advantages by cutting greenhouse gas emissions and easing pressure on agricultural land. Governments, however, have yet to adopt decisive policies in this area; food-related emissions, driven largely by meat consumption, remain effectively unmanaged and jeopardize the climate targets set for 2030 and 2050.

Any legal framework designed to limit meat in the Westernized diet must recognize recent changes in eating habits. Home cooking is less common, the consumption of ready-made meals is rising, and a new convenience culture built around delivered fast food and street food (hamburgers, pizzas, pasta and ice cream) has emerged, along with new venues for eating outside the home [136]. Regulations should therefore retain the familiar formats consumers already prefer while improving their composition, increasing both the quantity and the diversity of plant ingredients. This objective can be met by replacing a significant share of refined wheat flour with a broader range of legumes and whole grains, which are currently under represented in daily intake.

Because these reformulated foods, namely plant-enriched burgers, snacks and pasta, would remain recognizable and easy to prepare, there should be few obstacles to enforcing standards that require the food industry to manufacture them. Such measures align with the Smart Food concept, which links a nutritious diet and environmental sustainability to farming systems capable of producing healthful foods through economically viable enterprises.

Funding: This research received no external funding.

Conflicts of Interest: The authors declare no conflicts of interest.

References

1. Rutter, H.; Cavill, N.; Bauman, A.; Bull, F. Systems approaches to global and national physical activity plans. *Bull. World Health Organ.* **2019**, *97*, 162–165. [CrossRef]
2. Ellulu, M.; Abed, Y.; Rahmat, A.; Ranneh, Y.; Ali, F. Epidemiology of obesity in developing countries: Challenges and prevention. *Glob. Epidemic Obes.* **2014**, *2*, 2. [CrossRef]
3. Aziz, R.; Sherwani, A.Y.; Mahri, S.A.; Malik, S.S.; Mohammad, S. Why Are Obese People Predisposed to Severe Disease in Viral Respiratory Infections? *Obesities* **2023**, *3*, 46–58. [CrossRef]
4. Boutari, C.; Mantzoros, C.S. A 2022 update on the epidemiology of obesity and a call to action: As its twin COVID-19 pandemic appears to be receding, the obesity and dysmetabolism pandemic continues to rage on. *Metabolism* **2022**, *133*, 155217. [CrossRef]
5. Gallagher, E.J.; LeRoith, D. Obesity and cancer. *Cancer Metastasis Rev.* **2022**, *41*, 463–464. [CrossRef] [PubMed]
6. Chooi, Y.C.; Ding, C.; Magkos, F. The epidemiology of obesity. *Metab. Clin. Exp.* **2019**, *92*, 6–10. [CrossRef]
7. Rehman, F.; Khalid, O.; Haq, N.U.; Khan, A.U.R.; Bilal, K.; Madani, S.A. Diet-Right: A Smart Food Recommendation System. *KSII Trans. Internet Inf. Syst.* **2017**, *11*, 2910–2925. [CrossRef]
8. Gerhart, J.G.; Balevic, S.; Sinha, J.; Perrin, E.M.; Wang, J.; Edginton, A.N.; Gonzalez, D. Characterizing Pharmacokinetics in Children with Obesity—Physiological, Drug, Patient, and Methodological Considerations. *Front. Pharmacol.* **2022**, *13*, 818726. [CrossRef]
9. Busutil, R.; Espallardo, O.; Torres, A.; Martínez-Galdeano, L.; Zozaya, N.; Hidalgo-Vega, Á. The impact of obesity on health-related quality of life in Spain. *Health Qual. Life Outcomes* **2017**, *15*, 197. [CrossRef]
10. Li, X.; Siddique, K.H. Future Smart Food: Rediscovering Hidden Treasures of Neglected and Underutilized Species for Zero Hunger in Asia. *Matern. Child. Nutr.* **2020**, *16*, e13008. [CrossRef]
11. Zou, T.; Dawodu, A.; Mangi, A.; Cheshmehzangi, A. Exploring Current Trends, Gaps & Challenges in Sustainable Food Systems Studies: The Need of Developing Urban Food Systems Frameworks for Sustainable Cities. *Sustainability* **2023**, *15*, 10248. [CrossRef]
12. Popkin, B.M.; Ng, S.W. The nutrition transition to a stage of high obesity and noncommunicable disease prevalence dominated by ultra-processed foods is not inevitable. *Obes. Rev.* **2022**, *23*, 13366. [CrossRef] [PubMed]
13. Sun, Z.; Scherer, L.; Tukker, A.; Spawn-Lee, S.A.; Bruckner, M.; Gibbs, H.K.; Behrens, P. Dietary change in high-income nations alone can lead to substantial double climate dividend. *Nat. Food* **2022**, *3*, 29–37. [CrossRef] [PubMed]

14. Crippa, M.; Solazzo, E.; Guizzardi, D.; Monforti-Ferrario, F.; Tubiello, F.N.; Leip, A. Food systems are responsible for a third of global anthropogenic GHG emissions. *Nat. Food* **2021**, *2*, 198–209. [CrossRef]
15. Bennetzen, E.H.; Smith, P.; Portera, J.R. Agricultural production and greenhouse gas emissions from world regions—The major trends over 40 years. *Glob. Environ. Change* **2016**, *37*, 43–55. [CrossRef]
16. Lamb, W.F.; Wiedmann, T.; Pongratz, J.; Andrew, R.; Crippa, M.; Olivier, J.G.J.; Wiedenhofer, D.; Mattioli, G.; Al Khourdajie, A.; House, J.; et al. A review of trends and drivers of greenhouse gas emissions by sector from 1990 to 2018. *Environ. Res. Lett.* **2021**, *16*, 073005. [CrossRef]
17. Willits-Smith, A.; Aranda, R.; Heller, A.R.; Rose, D. Addressing the carbon footprint, healthfulness, and costs of self-selected diets in the USA: A population-based cross-sectional study. *Lancet Planet Health* **2020**, *4*, 98–106. [CrossRef]
18. Clark, M.A.; Domingo, N.G.G.; Colgan, K.; Thakrar, S.K.; Tilman, D.; Lynch, J.; Azevedo, I.L.; Hill, J.D. Global food system emissions could preclude achieving the 1.5° and 2 °C climate change targets. *Science* **2020**, *370*, 705–708. [CrossRef]
19. Fawzy, S.; Osman, A.I.; Doran, J.; Rooney, D.W. Strategies for mitigation of climate change: A review. *Environ. Chem. Lett.* **2020**, *18*, 2069–2094. [CrossRef]
20. Lucas, E.; Guo, M.; Guillén-Gosálbez, G. Low-carbon diets can reduce global ecological and health costs. *Nat. Food* **2023**, *4*, 394–406. [CrossRef]
21. Heller, M.C.; Willits-Smith, A.; Meyer, R.; A Keoleian, G.; Rose, D. Greenhouse gas emissions and energy use associated with production of individual self-selected US diets. *Environ. Res. Lett.* **2018**, *13*, 044004. [CrossRef] [PubMed]
22. Batlle-Bayer, L.; Bala, A.; García-Herrero, I.; Lemaire, E.; Song, G.; Aldaco, R.; Fullana-Palmer, P. The Spanish Dietary Guidelines: A potential tool to reduce greenhouse gas emissions of current dietary patterns. *J. Clean. Prod.* **2019**, *213*, 588–598. [CrossRef]
23. Pena-Bermudez, Y.A.; Vincenzi, R.; Meo-Filho, P.; Sakamoto, L.S.; Lobo, R.; Benetel, G.; Lobo, A.; Matos, C.; Benetel, V.; Lima, C.G.; et al. Effect of Yerba Mate Extract as Feed Additive on Ruminal Fermentation and Methane Emissions in Beef Cattle. *Animals* **2022**, *12*, 2997. [CrossRef] [PubMed]
24. Yang, M.; Zhang, Z.; Wang, Z. Does Internet use connect smallholder farmers to a healthy diet? Evidence from rural China. *Front. Nutr.* **2023**, *10*, 1122677. [CrossRef]
25. Willett, W.; Rockstrom, J.; Loken, B.; Springmann, M.; Lang, T.; Vermeulen, S.; Garnett, T.; Tilman, D.; DeClerck, F.; Wood, A. Food in the Anthropocene: The EAT–Lancet Commission on healthy diets from sustainable food systems. *Lancet* **2019**, *393*, 447–492. [CrossRef]
26. Lawrence, M.A.; Baker, P.I.; Pulker, C.E.; Pollard, C.M. Sustainable, resilient food systems for healthy diets: The transformation agenda. *Public Health Nutr.* **2019**, *22*, 2916–2920. [CrossRef]
27. Semba, R.D.; de Pee, S.; Kim, B.; McKenzie, S.; Nachman, K.; Bloem, M.W. Adoption of the 'planetary health diet' has different impacts on countries' greenhouse gas emissions. *Nat. Food* **2020**, *1*, 481–484. [CrossRef]
28. Comerford, K.B.; Miller, G.D.; Kapsak, W.R.; Brown, K.A. The Complementary Roles for Plant-Source and Animal-Source Foods in Sustainable Healthy Diets. *Nutrients* **2021**, *13*, 3469. [CrossRef]
29. Hennessy, D.P.; Shalloo, L.; van Zanten, H.H.E.; Schop, M.; De Boer, I.J.M. The net contribution of livestock to the supply of human edible protein: The case of Ireland. *J. Agric. Sci.* **2021**, *159*, 463–471. [CrossRef]
30. Meyer, N.; Reguant-Closa, A. "Eat as If You Could Save the Planet and Win!" Sustainability Integration into Nutrition for Exercise and Sport. *Nutrients* **2017**, *9*, 412. [CrossRef]
31. Theurl, M.C.; Lauk, C.; Kalta, G.; Mayer, A.; Kaltenegger, K.; Morais, T.G.; Teixeira, R.F.M.; Domingos, T.; Winiwarter, W.; Erba, K.H.; et al. Food systems in a zero-deforestation world: Dietary change is more important than intensification for climate targets in 2050. *Sci. Total Environ.* **2020**, *735*, 139353. [CrossRef]
32. Binnie, M.A.; Barlow, K.; Johnson, V.; Harrison, C. Red meats: Time for a paradigm shift in dietary advice. *Meat Sci.* **2014**, *98*, 445–451. [CrossRef] [PubMed]
33. Tangney, C.C.; Staffileno, B.A.; Rasmussen, H.E. Healthy Eating: How Do We Define It and Measure It? What's the Evidence? *J. Nurse Pract.* **2017**, *13*, 7–15. [CrossRef]
34. Kopp, W. How Western Diet and Lifestyle Drive the Pandemic of Obesity and Civilization Diseases. *Diabetes Metab. Syndr. Obes. Targets Ther.* **2019**, *12*, 2221–2236. [CrossRef] [PubMed]
35. Svend Daverkosen, S.; Mouritsen, O.G. Effects of specially designed meal boxes on plant-forward dietary choice. *Int. J. Gastron. Food Sci.* **2025**, *39*, 101079. [CrossRef]
36. Faris, M.E.; Hasan, H.; Ismail, L.C.; Jahrami, H.; Rajab, D.; Almashgouni, A.A.; Alshehhi, A.; Aljabry, A.; Aljarwan, M.; Alnaqbi, M.; et al. Assessment of nutritional quality of snacks and beverages sold in university vending machines: A qualitative assessment. *Br. Food J.* **2021**, *123*, 2449–2460. [CrossRef]
37. Rizzolo-Brime, L.; Orta-Ramirez, A.; Martin, Y.P.; Jakszyn, P. Nutritional Assessment of Plant-Based Meat Alternatives: A Comparison of Nutritional Information of Plant-Based Meat Alternatives in Spanish Supermarkets. *Nutrients* **2023**, *15*, 1325. [CrossRef]

38. Marquardt, S.G.; Joyce, P.J.; Rigarlsford, G.; Dötsch-Klerk, M.; van Elk, K.; Doelman, J.; Daioglou, V.; Huijbregts, M.A.J.; Sim, S. Prospective life cycle assessment of climate and biodiversity impacts of meat-based and plant-forward meals A case study of Indonesian and German meal options. *J. Ind. Ecol.* **2024**, *28*, 1598–1611. [CrossRef]
39. Sanders, L.M.; Slavin, J. Impact of Pasta Intake on Body Weight and Body Composition: A Technical Review. *Nutrients* **2023**, *15*, 2689. [CrossRef]
40. Adjibade, M.; Mariotti, F.; Leroy, P.; Souchon, I.; Saint-Eve, A.; Fagherazzi, G.; Soler, L.G.; Huneau, J.F. Impact of intra-category food substitutions on the risk of type 2 diabetes: A modelling study on the pizza category. *Br. J. Nutr.* **2022**, *127*, 1240–1249. [CrossRef]
41. Altamore, L.; Ingrassia, M.; Columba, P.; Chironi, S.; Bacarella, S. Italian Consumers' Preferences for Pasta and Consumption Trends: Tradition or Innovation? *J. Int. Food Agribus. Mark.* **2019**, *32*, 337–360. [CrossRef]
42. Assassi, P.; Selwyn, B.J.; Lounsbury, D.; Chan, W.; Harrell, M.; Wylie-Rosett, J. Baseline dietary patterns of children enrolled in an urban family weight management study:associations with demographic characteristics. *Child Adolesc. Obes.* **2021**, *4*, 37–59. [CrossRef]
43. Hess, J.M.; Slavin, J.L. The benefits of defining "snacks". *Physiol. Behav.* **2018**, *193*, 284–287. [CrossRef]
44. Amerikanou, C.; Tagkouli, D.; Tsiaka, T.; Lantzouraki, D.Z.; Karavoltsos, S.; Sakellari, A.; Kleftaki, S.-A.; Koutrotsios, G.; Giannou, V.; Zervakis, G.I.; et al. *Pleurotus eryngii* Chips—Chemical Characterization and Nutritional Value of an Innovative Healthy Snack. *Foods* **2023**, *12*, 353. [CrossRef] [PubMed]
45. Hess, J.; Rao, G.; Slavin, J. The Nutrient Density of Snacks: A Comparison of Nutrient Profiles of Popular Snack Foods Using the Nutrient-Rich Foods Index. *Glob. Pediatr. Health* **2017**, *4*, 2333794X17698525. [CrossRef]
46. Tyl, C.; Bresciani, A.; Marti, A. Recent Progress on Improving the Quality of Bran-Enriched Extruded Snacks. *Foods* **2021**, *10*, 2024. [CrossRef] [PubMed]
47. Li, X.; Guillermic, R.M.; Nadimi, M.; Paliwal, J.; Koksel, F. Physical and microstructural quality of extruded snacks made from blends of barley and green lentil flours. *Cereal Chem.* **2022**, *99*, 1112–1123. [CrossRef]
48. Sissons, M. Development of Novel Pasta Products with Evidence Based Impacts on Health—A Review. *Foods* **2022**, *11*, 123. [CrossRef] [PubMed]
49. Alam, S.S.; Bharti, D.; Pradhan, B.K.; Sahu, D.; Dhal, S.; Kim, N.M.; Jarzebski, M.; Pal, K. Analysis of the Physical and Structure Characteristics of Reformulated Pizza Bread. *Foods* **2022**, *11*, 1979. [CrossRef]
50. Pasqualone, A.; Costantini, M.; Faccia, M.; Difonzo, G.; Caponio, F.; Summo, C. The Effectiveness of Extruded-Cooked Lentil Flour in Preparing a Gluten-Free Pizza with Improved Nutritional Features and a Good Sensory Quality. *Foods* **2022**, *11*, 482. [CrossRef]
51. Nikinmaa, M.; Mustonen, S.A.; Huitula, L.; Laaksonen, O.; Linderborg, K.M.; Nordlund, E.; Nesli Sozer, N. Wholegrain oat quality indicators for production of extruded snacks. *LWT-Food Sci. Technol.* **2023**, *174*, 114457. [CrossRef]
52. Chriqui, J.F.; Lina, W.; Leidera, J.; Shangc, C.; Pernad, F.M. The Harmonizing Effect of Smart Snacks on the Association between State Snack Laws and High School Students' Fruit and Vegetable Consumption, United States—2005–2017. *Prev. Med.* **2020**, *139*, 106093. [CrossRef]
53. Mann, G.; Lambert, L.G.; Gupta, K.; Partacz, M. Smart snacks in universities: Possibilities for university vending. *Health Promot. Perspect.* **2020**, *10*, 393–400. [CrossRef]
54. Ciurzynska, A.; Ciesluk, P.; Barwinska, M.; Marczak, W.; Ordyniak, A.; Lenart, A.; Janowicz, M. Eating Habits and Sustainable Food Production in the Development of Innovative "Healthy" Snacks. *Sustainability* **2019**, *11*, 2800. [CrossRef]
55. Turnwald, B.P.; Crum, A.J. Smart food policy for healthy food labeling: Leading with taste, not healthiness, to shift consumption and enjoyment of healthy foods. *Prev. Med.* **2019**, *119*, 7–13. [CrossRef] [PubMed]
56. Ashaolu, T.J.; Ashaolu, J.O. Perspectives on the trends, challenges and benefits of green, smart and organic (GSO) foods. *Int. J. Gastron. Food Sci.* **2020**, *22*, 100273. [CrossRef] [PubMed]
57. Hawkes, C.; Smith, T.G.; Jewell, J.; Wardle, J.; Hammond, R.A.; Friel, S.; Thow, A.M.; Kain, J. Smart food policies for obesity prevention. *Lancet* **2015**, *385*, 2410–2421. [CrossRef]
58. Brouwer, I.D.; van Liere, M.J.; de Brauw, A.; Dominguez-Salas, P.; Herforth, A.; Kennedy, G.; Lachat, C.; Omosa, E.B.; Talsma, E.F.; Vandevijvere, S.; et al. Reverse thinking: Taking a healthy diet perspective towards food systems transformations. *Food Secur.* **2021**, *13*, 1497–1523. [CrossRef]
59. Ikegwu, T.M.; Balogu, T.V.; Iroagba, N.L.; Okoyeuzu, C.F.; Obiora, C.U.; Balogu, D.O.; Agu, H.O. Food Security in Emerging Global Situations-Functional Foods and Food Biotechnology Approaches: A Review. *J. Adv. Food Sci. Technol.* **2023**, *10*, 46–74. [CrossRef]
60. Kennedy, E.T.; Buttriss, J.L.; Bureau-Franz, I.; Wigger, P.K.; Drewnowski, A. Future of food: Innovating towards sustainable healthy diets. *Nutr. Bull.* **2021**, *46*, 260–263. [CrossRef]
61. Cortesi, A.; P'enicaud, C.; Saint-Eve, A.; Soler, L.G.; Souchon, I. Does environmental impact vary widely within the same food category? A case study on industrial pizzas from the French retail market. *J. Clean. Prod.* **2022**, *336*, 130128. [CrossRef]

62. Latunde-Dada, G.O.; Kajarabille, N.; Rose, S.; Arafsha, S.M.; Kose, T.; Aslam, M.F.; Hall, W.L.; Sharp, P.A. Content and Availability of Minerals in Plant-Based Burgers Compared with a Meat Burger. *Nutrients* **2023**, *15*, 2732. [CrossRef]
63. Greene, D.; Zhu, O.Y.; Dolnicar, S. Vegan burger, no thanks! Juicy American burger, yes please! The effect of restaurant meal names on affective appeal. *Food Qual. Prefer.* **2024**, *113*, 105042. [CrossRef]
64. Herawati, H.; Kamsiati, E. Characteristics of vegetarian patties burgers made from tofu and tempeh. *IOP Conf. Ser. Earth Environ. Sci.* **2021**, *653*, 012103. [CrossRef]
65. Bánáti, D. Veggie burgers, vegan meats? The ruling of the European Parliament paved the way for meat substitutes with meat denominations. *J. Food Investig.* **2020**, *66*, 3166–3174.
66. Filipovic, S.; Lior, N.; Radovanovic, M. The green deal—Just transition and sustainable development goals Nexus. *Renew. Sustain. Energy Rev.* **2022**, *168*, 112759. [CrossRef]
67. Paltsev, S.; Chen, Y.H.H.; Karplus, V.; Kishimoto, P.; Reilly, J.; Löschel, A.; von Graevenitz, K.; Koesler, S. Reducing CO_2 from cars in the European Union. *Transportation* **2018**, *45*, 573–595. [CrossRef]
68. Cifuentes-Faura, J. European Union policies and their role in combating climate change over the years. *Air Qual. Atmos. Health* **2022**, *15*, 1333–1340. [CrossRef]
69. Rosamond, J.; Dupont, C. The European Council, the Council, and the European Green Deal. *Politics Gov.* **2021**, *9*, 348–359. [CrossRef]
70. Delouyi, F.L.; Ranjbari, M.; Esfandabadi, Z.S. A Hybrid Multi-Criteria Decision Analysis to Explore Barriers to the Circular Economy Implementation in the Food Supply Chain. *Sustainability* **2023**, *15*, 9506. [CrossRef]
71. Estevez, R.; Aguado-Deblas, L.; López-Tenllado, F.J.; Bautista, F.M.; Romero, A.A.; Luna, D. Internal Combustion Engines and Carbon-Neutral Fuels: A Perspective on Emission Neutrality in the European Union. *Energies* **2024**, *17*, 1172. [CrossRef]
72. Galli, A.; Antonelli, M.; Wambersie, L.; Bach-Faig, A.; Bartolini, F.; Caro, D.; Iha, K.; Lin, D.; Mancini, M.S.; Sonnino, R.; et al. EU-27 ecological footprint was primarily driven by food consumption and exceeded regional biocapacity from 2004 to 2014. *Nat. Food* **2023**, *4*, 810–822. [CrossRef]
73. Fanzo, J. Healthy and Sustainable Diets and Food Systems: The Key to Achieving Sustainable Development Goal 2? *Food Ethics* **2019**, *4*, 159–174. [CrossRef]
74. Gardner, C.D.; Hartle, J.C.; Garrett, R.D.; Offringa, L.C.; Wasserman, A.S. Maximizing the intersection of human health and the health of the environment with regard to the amount and type of protein produced and consumed in the United States. *Nutr. Rev.* **2019**, *77*, 197–215. [CrossRef] [PubMed]
75. Espinosa-Marrón, A.; Adams, K.; Sinno, L.; Cantu-Aldana, A.; Tamez, M.; Marrero, A.; Bhupathiraju, S.N.; Mattei, J. Environmental Impact of Animal-Based Food Production and the Feasibility of a Shift Toward Sustainable Plant-Based Diets in the United States. *Front. Sustain.* **2022**, *3*, 841106. [CrossRef]
76. Olivier De Schutter, O.; Jacobs, N.; Clément, C. A 'Common Food Policy' for Europe: How governance reforms can spark a shift to healthy diets and sustainable food systems. *Food Policy* **2020**, *96*, 101849. [CrossRef]
77. Mozaffarian, D.; Angell, S.Y.; Lang, T.; Rivera, J.A. Role of government policy in nutrition—Barriers to and oppor-tunities for healthier eating. *Sci. Politics Nutr. BMJ* **2018**, *361*, k2426. [CrossRef]
78. Zarbà, C.; Chinnici, G.; La Via, G.; Bracco, S.; Pecorino, B.; D'Amico, M. Regulatory elements on the circular economy: Driving into the agri-food system. *Sustainability* **2021**, *13*, 8350. [CrossRef]
79. Poore, J.; Nemecek, T. Reducing food's environmental impacts through producers and consumers. *Science* **2018**, *360*, 987–992. [CrossRef]
80. Wangari, C.; Mwema, C.; Siambi, M.; Silim, S.; Ubwe, R.; Malesi, K.; Anitha, S.; Kane-Potaka, J. Changing perception through participatory approach by in-volving adolescent school children in evaluating Smart Food dishes in school feeding program—Real time experience from Central Tanzania. *Ecol. Food Nutr.* **2020**, *59*, 472–485. [CrossRef]
81. Anitha, S.; Htut, T.T.; Tsusaka, T.W.; Jalagam, A.; Kane-Potaka, J. Potential for smart food products in rural Myanmar: Use of millets and pigeonpea to fill the nutrition gap. *J. Sci. Food Agric.* **2019**, *100*, 394–400. [CrossRef]
82. Bhatia, M.; Ahanger, T.A. Intelligent decision-making in Smart Food Industry: Quality perspective. *Pervasive Mob. Comput.* **2021**, *72*, 101304. [CrossRef]
83. Stevens, H.; Ruperti, Y. Smart food: Novel foods, food security, and the Smart Nation in Singapore. *Food Cult. Soc.* **2023**, *27*, 754–774. [CrossRef]
84. Halgamuge, M.N.; Bojovschi, A.; Fisher, P.M.J.; Le, T.C.; Adeloju, S.; Murphy, S. Internet of Things and autonomous control for vertical cultivation walls towards smart food growing: A review. *Urban For. Urban Green.* **2021**, *61*, 127094. [CrossRef]
85. Challinor, A.J.; Arenas-Calles, L.N.; Whitfield, S. Measuring the Effectiveness of Climate-Smart Practices in the Context of Food Systems: Progress and Challenges. *Front. Sustain. Food Syst.* **2022**, *6*, 853630. [CrossRef]
86. Mustafa, M.A.; Mabhaudhi, T.; Massawe, F. Building a resilient and sustainable food system in a changing world—A case for climate smart and nutrient dense crops. *Glob. Food Secur.* **2021**, *28*, 100477. [CrossRef]

87. Altamura, C.; Cecchi, G.; Bravo, M.; Brunelli, N.; Laudisio, A.; Di Caprio, P.; Botti, G.; Paolucci, M.; Khazrai, Y.M.; Vernieri, F. The Healthy Eating Plate Advice for Migraine Prevention: An Interventional Study. *Nutrients* **2020**, *12*, 1579. [CrossRef]
88. Barthelmie, R.J. Impact of Dietary Meat and Animal Products on GHG Footprints: The UK and the US. *Climate* **2022**, *10*, 43. [CrossRef]
89. Reisinger, A.; Clark, H. How much do direct livestock emissions actually contribute to global warming? *Glob. Change Biol.* **2018**, *24*, 1749–1761. [CrossRef]
90. Wynes, S.; Nicholas, K.A.; Zhao, J.; Donner, S.D. Measuring what works: Quantifying greenhouse gas emission reductions of behavioral interventions to reduce driving, meat consumption, and household energy use. *Environ. Res. Lett.* **2018**, *13*, 113002. [CrossRef]
91. Brecha, R.J.; Ganti, G.; Lamboll, R.D.; Nicholls, Z.; Hare, B.; Lewis, J.; Meinshausen, M.; Schaeffer, M.; Smith, C.J.; Gidden, M.J. Institutional decarbonization scenarios evaluated against the Paris Agreement 1.5 °C goal. *Nat. Commun.* **2022**, *13*, 4304. [CrossRef]
92. Collaço, F.M.A.; Teixeira, A.C.R.; Machado, P.G.; Borges, R.R.; Brito, T.L.F.; Mouette, D. Road Freight Transport Literature and the Achievements of the Sustainable Development Goals—A Systematic Review. *Sustainability* **2022**, *14*, 3425. [CrossRef]
93. Kee, K.K.; Ting, H.H.; Lim, Y.S.; Ting, J.T.W.; Peter, M.; Ibrahim, K.; Show, P.L. Feasibility of UTS Smart Home to Support Sustainable Development Goals of United Nations (UN SDGs): Water and Energy Conservation. *Sustainability* **2022**, *14*, 12242. [CrossRef]
94. Wattiaux, M.A. Sustainability of dairy systems through the lenses of the sustainable development goals. *Front. Anim. Sci.* **2023**, *4*, 1135381. [CrossRef]
95. Djekic, I.V. Meat supply chain in the perspective. of UN SDGS. *Theory Pract. Meat Process.* **2021**, *6*, 242–247. [CrossRef]
96. Nevalainen, E.; Niva, M.; Vainio, A. A transition towards plant-based diets on its way? Consumers' substitutions of meat in their diets in Finland. *Food Qual. Prefer.* **2023**, *104*, 104754. [CrossRef]
97. Fresán, U.; Errendal, S.; Craig, W.J. Influence of the Socio-Cultural Environment and External Factors in Following Plant-Based Diets. *Sustainability* **2020**, *12*, 9093. [CrossRef]
98. Milfont, T.L.; Satherley, N.; Osborne, D.; Wilson, M.S.; Sibley, C.G. To meat, or not to meat: A longitudinal investigation of transitioning to and from plant-based diets. *Appetite* **2021**, *166*, 105584. [CrossRef]
99. Bryant, C.; Sanctorum, H. Alternative proteins, evolving attitudes: Comparing consumer attitudes to plant-based and cultured meat in Belgium in two consecutive years. *Appetite* **2021**, *161*, 105161. [CrossRef]
100. Jahn, S.; Furchheim, P.; Strässner, A.M. Plant-Based Meat Alternatives: Motivational Adoption Barriers and Solutions. *Sustainability* **2021**, *13*, 13271. [CrossRef]
101. Tarrega, A.; Rizo, A.; Murciano, A.; Laguna, L.; Fiszman, S. Are mixed meat and vegetable protein products good alternatives for reducing meat consumption? A case study with burgers. *Curr. Res. Food Sci.* **2020**, *3*, 30–40. [CrossRef]
102. Boukid, F.; Castellari, M. Veggie burgers in the EU market: A nutritional challenge? *Eur. Food Res. Technol.* **2021**, *247*, 2445–2453. [CrossRef]
103. Cole, E.; Goeler-Slough, N.; Cox, A.; Nolden, A. Examination of the nutritional composition of alternative beef burgers available in the United States. *Int. J. Food Sci. Nutr.* **2022**, *73*, 425–432. [CrossRef]
104. Abd-Elhak, N.A. Preparation and Evaluation of Different Nutritive Vegetarian Burger for Females and Women. *Egypt. J. Food. Sci.* **2021**, *49*, 107–123. [CrossRef]
105. Michel, F.; Knaapila, A.; Hartmann, C.; Siegrist, M. A multi-national comparison of meat eaters' attitudes and expectations for burgers containing beef, pea or algae protein. *Food Qual. Prefer.* **2021**, *91*, 104195. [CrossRef]
106. Smetana, S.; Profeta, A.; Voigt, R.; Kircher, C.; Heinz, V. Meat substitution in burgers: Nutritional scoring, sensorial testing, and Life Cycle Assessment. *Future Foods* **2021**, *4*, 100042. [CrossRef]
107. Costa-Catala, J.; Toro-Funes, N.; Comas-Basté, O.; Hernández-Macias, S.; Sánchez-Pérez, S.; Latorre-Moratalla, M.L.; Veciana-Nogués, M.T.; Castell-Garralda, V.; Vidal-Carou, M.C. Comparative Assessment of the Nutritional Profile of Meat Products and Their Plant-Based Analogues. *Nutrients* **2023**, *15*, 2807. [CrossRef]
108. Hielkema, M.H.; Onwezen, M.C.; Reinders, M.J. Veg on the menu? Differences in menu design interventions to increase vegetarian food choice between meat-reducers and non-reducers. *Food Qual. Prefer.* **2022**, *102*, 104675. [CrossRef]
109. Sousa, R.; Portmann, R.; Recio, I.; Dubois, S.; Egger, L. Comparison of in vitro digestibility and DIAAR between vegan and meat burgers before and after grilling. *Food Res. Int.* **2023**, *166*, 112569. [CrossRef]
110. Harnack, L.; Mork, S.; Valluri, S.; Weber, C.; Schmitz, K.; Stevenson, J.; Pettit, J. Nutrient Composition of a Selection of Plant-Based Ground Beef Alternative Products Available in the United States. *J. Acad. Nutr. Diet.* **2021**, *121*, 2401–2408. [CrossRef]
111. Fernandes, W.D.; Pinto, F.R.; Barroso, S.; Gil, M.M. Development, Characterization, and Consumer Acceptance of an Innovative Vegan Burger with Seaweed. *Sustainability* **2023**, *15*, 10869. [CrossRef]
112. Rajaretnam, S.; Malik, N.H. Physical and Sensory Properties of Vegetarian Burger Patty. *Enhanc. Knowl. Sci. Technol.* **2023**, *3*, 422–431.

113. Bouwman, E.P.; Bolderdijk, J.W.; Onwezen, M.C.; Taufik, D. "Do you consider animal welfare to be important?" activating cognitive dissonance via value activation can promote vegetarian choices. *J. Environ. Psychol.* **2022**, *83*, 101871. [CrossRef]
114. Ingenbleek, P.T.M.; Zhao, Y. The Vegetarian Butcher: On its way to becoming the world's biggest 'meat' producer? *Int. Food Agribus. Manag. Rev.* **2019**, *22*, 1–14. [CrossRef]
115. Kim, S.; Chung, S.J. Hedonic plasticity of vegan burger patty in implicit or explicit reference frame conditions. *J. Sci. Food Agric.* **2023**, *103*, 2641–2652. [CrossRef]
116. Rousta, N.; Hellwig, C.; Wainaina, S.; Lukitawesa, L.; Agnihotri, S.; Rousta, K.; Taherzadeh, M.J. Filamentous Fungus Aspergillus oryzae for Food: From Submerged Cultivation to Fungal Burgers and Their Sensory Evaluation—A Pilot Study. *Foods* **2021**, *10*, 2774. [CrossRef]
117. Franca, P.; Pierucci, A.P.; Boukid, F. Analysis of ingredient list and nutrient composition of plant-based burgers available in the global market. *Int. J. Food Sci. Nutr.* **2024**, *75*, 159–172. [CrossRef]
118. Wang, L.; Li, W.; Zheng, Y. Does the advertising of plant-based burgers attract meat consumers? The influence of new product advertising on consumer responses. *Agribusiness* **2024**, *40*, 680–698. [CrossRef]
119. Rosenfeld, D.L.; Rothgerber, H.; Tomiyama, A.J. When meat-eaters expect vegan food to taste bad: Veganism as a symbolic threat. *Group Process. Intergroup Relat.* **2024**, *27*, 453–468. [CrossRef]
120. Shen, Y.C.; Chen, H.S. Exploring Consumers' Purchase Intention of an Innovation of the Agri-Food Industry: A Case of Artificial Meat. *Foods* **2020**, *9*, 745. [CrossRef]
121. Tuomisto, H.L. The eco-friendly burger Could cultured meat improve the environmental sustainability of meat products? *EMBO Rep.* **2019**, *20*, e47395. [CrossRef]
122. Besson, T.; Bouxom, H.; Jaubert, T. Halo It's Meat! the Effect of the Vegetarian Label on Calorie Perception and Food Choices. *Ecol. Food Nutr.* **2020**, *59*, 3–20. [CrossRef]
123. Schillaci, E.; Gràcia, A.; Capellas, M.; Rigola, J. Numerical modeling and experimental validation of meat burgers and vegetarian patties cooking process with an innovative IR laser system. *J. Food Process Eng.* **2022**, *45*, e14097. [CrossRef]
124. Slegers, P.M.; Helmes, R.J.K.; Draisma, M.; Broekema, R.; Vlottes, M.; van den Burg, S.W.K. Environmental impact and nutritional value of food products using the seaweed Saccharina latissimi. *J. Clean. Prod.* **2021**, *319*, 128689. [CrossRef]
125. Kustar, A.; Patino-Echeverri, D. A Review of Environmental Life Cycle Assessments of Diets: Plant-Based Solutions Are Truly Sustainable, even in the Form of Fast Foods. *Sustainability* **2021**, *13*, 9926. [CrossRef]
126. Cappelli, A.; Cini, E. Challenges and Opportunities in Wheat Flour, Pasta, Bread, and Bakery Product Production Chains: A Systematic Review of Innovations and Improvement Strategies to Increase Sustainability, Productivity, and Product Quality. *Sustainability* **2021**, *13*, 2608. [CrossRef]
127. Segovia-Siapco, G.; Burkholder-Cooley, N.; Tabrizi, S.H.; Sabaté, J. Beyond Meat: A Comparison of the Dietary Intakes of Vegetarian and Non-vegetarian Adolescents. *Front. Nutr.* **2019**, *6*, 86. [CrossRef] [PubMed]
128. Guess, N.; Klatt, K.; Wei, D.; Williamson, E.; Ulgenalp, I.; Trinidade, O.; Kusaslan, E.; Yildirim, A.; Gowers, C.; Guard, R.; et al. Cross-Sectional Analysis of Products Marketed as Plant-Based Across the United States, United Kingdom, and Canada Using Online Nutrition Information. *Curr. Dev. Nutr.* **2023**, *7*, 100059. [CrossRef] [PubMed]
129. Noguerol, A.T.; Págan, M.J.; García-Segovia, P.; Varela, P. Green or clean? Perception of clean label plant-based products by omnivorous, vegan, vegetarian and flexitarian consumers. *Food Res. Int.* **2021**, *149*, 110652. [CrossRef]
130. Lindke, A.R.; Travis, A.; Smith, T.A.; Cotwright, C.J.; Morris, D.; Cox, G.O. Plate Waste Evaluation of Plant-Based Protein Entrees in National School Lunch Program. *J. Nutr. Educ. Behav.* **2022**, *54*, 12–19. [CrossRef]
131. Corvo, P.; Fontefrancesco, M.F.; Matacena, R. Eating at Work: The Role of the Lunch-Break and Canteens for Wellbeing at Work in Europe. *Soc. Indic. Res.* **2020**, *150*, 1043–1076. [CrossRef]
132. Cappelli, A.; Oliva, N.; Bonaccorsi, G.; Lorini, C.; Cini, E. Assessment of the rheological properties and bread characteristics obtained by innovative protein sources (*Cicer arietinum*, *Acheta domesticus*, *Tenebrio molitor*): Novel food or potential improvers for wheat flour? *LWT Food Sci. Technol.* **2020**, *118*, 108867. [CrossRef]
133. Galli, V.; Venturi, M.; Coda, R.; Maina, N.H.; Granchi, L. Isolation and characterization of indigenous Weissella confusa for in situ bacterial exopolysaccharides (EPS) production in chickpea sourdough. *Food Res. Int.* **2020**, *138*, 109785. [CrossRef]
134. Roncolini, A.; Milanović, V.; Aquilanti, L.; Cardinali, F.; Garofalo, C.; Sabbatini, R.; Clementi, F.; Belleggia, L.; Pasquini, M.; Mozzon, M.; et al. Lesser mealworm (*Alphitobius diaperinus*) powder as a novel baking ingredient for manufacturing high-protein, mineral-dense snacks. *Food Res. Int.* **2020**, *131*, 109031. [CrossRef]
135. García-Segovia, P.; Igual, M.; Martínez-Monzó, J. Physicochemical Properties and Consumer Acceptance of Bread Enriched with Alternative Proteins. *Foods* **2020**, *9*, 933. [CrossRef]
136. Cappelli, A.; Cini, E.; Lorini, C.; Oliva, N.; Bonaccorsi, G. Insects as food: A review on risks assessments of Tenebrionidae and Gryllidae in relation to a first machines and plants development. *Food Control* **2020**, *108*, 106877. [CrossRef]
137. García-Segovia, P.; Igual, M.; Noguerol, A.T.; Martínez-Monzó, J. Use of insects and pea powder as alternative protein and mineral sources in extruded snacks. *Eur. Food Res. Technol.* **2020**, *246*, 703–712. [CrossRef]

138. van Huis, A. Prospects of insects as food and feed. *Org. Agric.* **2021**, *11*, 301–308. [CrossRef]
139. Acosta-Estrada, B.A.; Reyes, A.; Rosell, C.M.; Rodrigo, D.; Ibarra-Herrera, C.C. Benefits and Challenges in the Incorporation of Insects in Food Products. *Front. Nutr.* **2021**, *8*, 687712. [CrossRef]
140. Alhujaili, A.; Nocella, G.; Macready, A. Insects as Food: Consumers' Acceptance and Marketing. *Foods* **2023**, *12*, 886. [CrossRef]
141. European Parliament and Council of the European Union. Regulation (EU) 2015/2283 of the European parliament and of the council of 25 November 2015 on novel foods, amending regulation (EU) No 1169/2011 of the European parliament and of the Council and repealing regulation (EC) No 258/97 of the European parliament and of the Council and commission regulation (EC) No 1852/2001. *Off. J. Eur. Union L* **2015**, *327*, 1–22.

sustainability

MDPI

Article

Exploring Honey Consumption and Sustainable Practices in a Segment of Algerian Households

Rifka Nakib [1,2,*], Sonia Harbane [1,2], Asma Ghorab [1], Yasmine Saker [1], Olga Escuredo [1,2], María Shantal Rodríguez-Flores [1,2] and María Carmen Seijo-Coello [1,2]

[1] Department of Plant Biology and Soil Sciences, Universidade de Vigo, Campus As Lagoas, 32004 Ourense, Spain; sonia.harbane@uvigo.gal (S.H.); asma.ghorab@uvigo.gal (A.G.); yasminesaker97@gmail.com (Y.S.); oescuredo@uvigo.gal (O.E.); mariasharodriguez@uvigo.gal (M.S.R.-F.); mcoello@uvigo.gal (M.C.S.-C.)

[2] Instituto de Agroecoloxía e Alimentación (IAA), Universidade de Vigo, Campus Agua, 32004 Ourense, Spain

* Correspondence: nakib.rifka@gmail.com or rifka.nakib2@uvigo.gal

Abstract

In Algeria, honey plays an important role in nutrition, traditional medicine and sustainable food practices. However, little is known about how consumers perceive and use this product in their daily lives. This study aims to explore how honey consumption patterns among a specific segment of Algerian households, mainly young, educated, and digitally active individuals, relate to traditional practices and contribute to sustainable food systems and cultural heritage. An online survey remained open for four months, and the final number of participants was 770 individuals from 51 wilayas, using convenience sampling through academic and social media networks. As this was an exploratory study, no fixed statistical population was defined. Chi-square tests revealed significant associations between age and honey consumption frequency ($\chi^2 = 45.33$, $p = 0.0010$), annual purchase quantity ($\chi^2 = 111.49$, $p < 0.0001$), and buying frequency ($\chi^2 = 47.26$, $p < 0.0001$), as well as between climatic zone and buying source ($\chi^2 = 34.90$, $p = 0.0097$). The findings highlight honey's multifunctional role, not only as a food product, but also as a traditional remedy and cosmetic ingredient, embedded in cultural routines and health practices. Consumer preferences are shaped by sensory attributes such as taste, type, and appearance, while purchasing decisions are strongly influenced by trust-based relationships, with most respondents favoring direct acquisition from beekeepers or known individuals. These informal sourcing habits reflect sustainable traditions that support local producers and reinforce consumer confidence. However, widespread misconceptions, such as the belief that crystallized honey is adulterated, reveal a need for targeted consumer education. To promote sustainable honey consumption, the study recommends clearer labeling, school-based programs, and public awareness campaigns.

Keywords: sustainable consumption; cultural heritage; household behavior; Algerian consumer; questionnaire

1. Introduction

Beekeeping has emerged as a vital pillar of sustainable development, offering a unique intersection between environmental stewardship, economic resilience, and cultural heritage within sustainable food systems, which aim to ensure food security and nutrition while preserving environmental, economic, and social resources for future generations. As global awareness of biodiversity loss and food insecurity intensifies, apiculture is increasingly recognized not only for its production of honey and other hive products, but also for its essential role in pollination, ecosystem services, and rural livelihoods [1]. Honey, in particular, is a multifunctional product valued for its nutritional richness, therapeutic properties, and symbolic significance across cultures, rich in antioxidants, enzymes, and trace minerals. It has been used for centuries to treat respiratory ailments, digestive issues, and skin conditions [2], and Algerian honeys have demonstrated strong antioxidant and antimicrobial properties, reinforcing their role in traditional medicine [3]. Despite this potential, Algeria's honey sector faces persistent challenges: climate change, habitat degradation, pesticide use, and diseases like Varroa mite infestation threaten bee populations and reduce honey yields [4]. A national survey conducted in 2021 across 19 wilayas in Algeria revealed that most beekeepers practiced sedentary beekeeping, while a smaller proportion adopted migratory practices to follow seasonal floral availability [4]. These findings highlight the need for improved disease management, technical training, and youth engagement to ensure long-term sustainability [5]. In Algeria, however, consumer behavior remains underexplored. Misconceptions about crystallized honey, for example, often lead to product rejection and waste, underscoring the need for public education and awareness campaigns [6]. Furthermore, the interplay between traditional knowledge, regional identity, and sustainability-oriented consumption has not been adequately studied. According to recent reports [7,8], demand for honey is rising due to its perceived health benefits and its use as a natural alternative to refined sugar. However, this surge in demand has also led to increased adulteration and counterfeit products, posing risks to consumer health and undermining trust in the industry [9]. Despite the recognized importance of honey, existing research has primarily focused on production practices and physicochemical quality [3–5], while consumer behavior, traditional uses, and sustainability perspectives remain underexplored, representing a clear theoretical and methodological gap.

To guide the analysis and reflect the thematic structure of the questionnaire, the study is framed around the following key research questions. These questions represent a synthesis of the main topics explored in the survey:

Q1: What are the consumption patterns, preferences, and traditional uses of honey among digitally active and educated segment Algerian households?

Q2: What factors—sensory, economic, and perceptual—influence consumer attitudes toward honey, including crystallized honey?

2. Literature Review

Honey consumption has been widely studied in different cultural and economic contexts, highlighting its nutritional, therapeutic, and symbolic roles [2,3]. Algerian honeys, for example, are rich in antioxidants and antimicrobial compounds, reinforcing their importance in traditional medicine [3]. Beekeeping practices vary globally, but in Algeria, ecological diversity from the humid Mediterranean coast to the arid Sahara supports distinct floral resources and native subspecies such as *Apis mellifera intermissa* and *Apis mellifera sahariensis*, which contribute to biodiversity and resilience [3,10]. Traditional methods, including clay and straw hives, remain common in rural areas, offering low-impact and sustainable approaches aligned with ecological goals [3].

In Algeria, honey production was estimated at 5165 tons in 2021, with average yields of 4–8 kg per hive, a modest output given the country's ecological diversity [11]. Domestic production remains insufficient to meet demand, leading to imports of up to 150,000 tons annually [11]. A national survey revealed that 69% of beekeepers practice sedentary beekeeping, while 31% adopt migratory practices [4]. Despite these figures, per capita consumption is relatively low, around 0.2 kg per year, and purchasing habits are dominated by informal channels, with 58.3% buying from trusted individuals and only 18.3% directly from beekeepers [5]. These patterns highlight structural challenges and cultural preferences that shape the Algerian honey market.

Studies in Europe and North Africa show strong cultural ties to honey consumption. In Morocco, consumers favor informal channels based on trust [5], while in Slovenia and Italy, labels and certifications play a central role in purchasing decisions [9], and recent research emphasizes the health-promoting properties of honey and bee products [12]. Mediterranean consumers often associate honey with health and sustainability values [6,13], and willingness to pay for organic or local honey is well documented in Serbia and Italy, where premiums range from 20% to 30% above conventional prices [14,15]. Similar trends appear in Mexico, where education and income strongly influence honey preferences [16], and in Australia, where origin and brand reputation drive choices [17]. In China, health benefits are the primary motivation for 74% of consumers [18], confirming the global perception of honey as a functional food.

Honey consumption aligns with sustainable food practices by promoting short supply chains and preserving traditional knowledge [2,3]. This perspective is consistent with broader research on mindful and responsible consumption, which emphasizes reducing environmental impact and supporting local economies [19]. Informal networks reduce packaging and transport emissions, while emerging innovations such as plant-based honey alternatives address environmental and ethical concerns [20]. These behaviors support SDG 12 (Responsible Consumption) and SDG 15 (Life on Land) by encouraging biodiversity-friendly practices [21]. Similar findings in Europe and North America show that consumers increasingly value natural, traceable, and ethically produced food products [9,21].

Despite honey's recognized benefits, misconceptions persist. Crystallization is often perceived as adulteration, leading to product rejection and waste [6]. Similar gaps in consumer education have been reported in Europe [9]. Addressing these issues through labeling and awareness campaigns is essential to reduce waste and strengthen trust. Studies recommend school-based programs and public outreach to correct these misconceptions [7,8,21].

Although demand for honey is rising due to health benefits and its role as a natural sugar alternative [7,8], this trend has also led to adulteration and counterfeit products, undermining trust [9]. Most research focuses on production and physicochemical quality [3–5], while consumer behavior, traditional uses, and sustainability perspectives remain underexplored, representing a clear theoretical and methodological gap. This study addresses this gap by analyzing consumption patterns, cultural practices, and sustainability perceptions among Algerian households.

3. Materials and Methods

3.1. *Survey Composition and Thematic Focus*

As part of a survey on honey-related practices in Algerian households, a structured online questionnaire was developed to comprehensively capture consumer behavior, purchasing habits, perceptions, and traditional uses of honey. The instrument was organized into two main sections. The first section collected demographic information, including age, gender, education level, professional status, and region of residence. The second section explored various aspects of honey consumption, such as purchase frequency, periods of consumption, preferred points of purchase (e.g., direct purchases from producers, local markets, supermarkets), typical quantities purchased, key product attributes considered during purchase, price perceptions, and opinions regarding crystallized honey—a characteristic often associated with purity or authenticity. In addition, this section addressed methods of consumption, cultural and medicinal uses, and consumer attitudes toward honey quality. The questionnaire combined multiple-choice and open-ended questions, enabling respondents to provide both structured responses and nuanced insights into their experiences and beliefs. The complete list of questions and research fields is provided in Supplementary Materials for full transparency and replicability, it was designed to address two central research questions which are outlined at the end of the introduction.

To ensure content validity, the questionnaire was reviewed by three experts in food science and apiculture. A pilot test with 20 participants was conducted to refine wording and structure. Reliability was assessed using Cronbach's alpha for attitude-related items ($\alpha = 0.82$), indicating good internal consistency. These steps confirm that the instrument was both clear and robust for capturing the intended constructs.

3.2. Sample Description

The national survey collected responses from 770 individuals across 51 wilayas in Algeria (Table 1). The sample was predominantly female (71.2%) and notably well-educated, with 60% holding a university degree. The Tell region was the most represented (41.18%), followed by the High Plateaux (33.33%), the Saharan region (15.69%), and the Saharan Atlas (9.8%). In terms of age, the largest group was 20–30 years old (44.3%), followed by 30–40 years old (33.5%). The least represented were those under 20 and over 50.

Table 1. Sociodemographic characteristics of the survey respondents.

Variable	Categories	Frequency
Gender	Female	548 (71.2%)
	male	222 (28.8%)
Gender (Mean ± SD)	Not applicable	
Education level	University degree	462 (60.0%)
	Other	308 (40.0%)
Education level (Mean ± SD)	Not applicable	
Age group	<20	22 (3.9%)
	20–30	341 (44.3%)
	30–40	258 (33.5%)
	40–50	83 (15.6%)
	>50	66 (2.7%)
Age (Mean ± SD)	32.8 ± 9.8	

This demographic profile reflects the nature of online survey distribution and should be considered when interpreting the findings. The results are indicative of behaviors within this segment, rather than the general Algerian population.

3.3. Data Collection

Data collection was carried out over a four-month period, from February to May 2024. The online questionnaire was disseminated through academic and professional networks, as well as social media platforms, allowing for broad participation across Algeria. Prior to its launch, the survey was pilot-tested with a small group of honey consumers to ensure clarity and relevance. Feedback from this phase helped refine the structure and wording of the questions.

3.4. Statistical Analysis

The data were analyzed using descriptive statistics to summarize demographic characteristics, consumption patterns, and purchasing preferences. To assess relationships between categorical variables, chi-square tests of independence were applied. These tests evaluated whether age was associated with consumption frequency, annual buying quantity, and perception of crystallized honey, as well as whether climatic zone influenced buying source. This approach allowed us to identify significant associations and confirm where consumer behaviors varied meaningfully across demographic and geographic factors. Additionally, to explore the relationships among multiple categorical variables, a Multiple Correspondence Analysis (MCA) was performed. This technique is suitable for qualitative data and allows visualization of associations between different modalities in a reduced-dimensional space.

4. Results

4.1. Honey Consumption Patterns and Preferences

The findings provide insight into the cultural and practical dimensions of honey use among Algerian consumers. The primary motivations include medicinal use (43%), culinary enjoyment (27%), and health benefits (17%), while cosmetic applications represented (13%). Medicinal use was particularly prominent, especially for treating respiratory ailments, digestive issues, and general immune support. Regarding purchasing behavior, most consumers preferred informal and trusted sources. Consumers emphasized trust, authenticity, and product quality as key factors in their choices. While price was considered, origin and purity were consistently prioritized. The survey also revealed honey's strong cultural and symbolic significance.

4.2. Sustainable Consumption and Buying Patterns

The results reveal a pattern of moderate honey consumption among Algerian households, which aligns with principles of sustainable food use. Honey consumption patterns differ noticeably across age categories. Figure 1 illustrates these differences, showing the distribution of consumption frequencies (daily, often, occasionally, rarely, never) across six age groups.

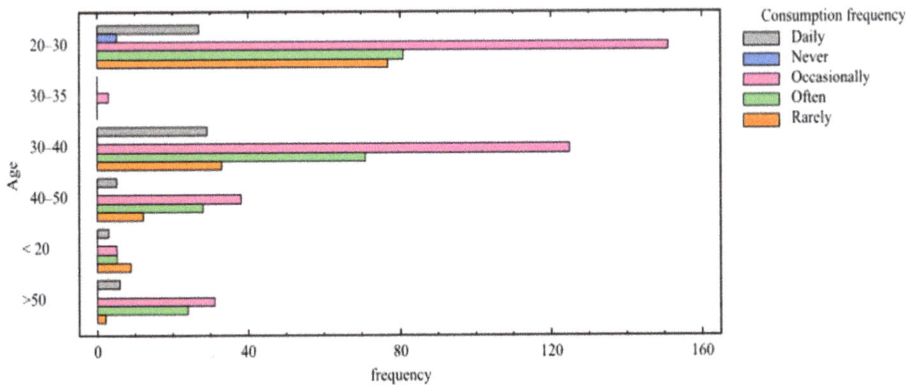

Figure 1. Distribution of Honey Consumption Frequencies across Age Groups.

To verify whether these differences are statistically significant, a chi-square test of independence was conducted. The results confirm a significant association between age and consumption frequency (Chi^2 = 45.33, df = 20, p = 0.0010), indicating that honey consumption habits vary meaningfully across age groups.

The analysis shows clear differences in the quantity of honey purchased across age groups. Young adults and the 30–40 age group are the most likely to buy moderate quantities, typically between 250–500 g or 500–1000 g per year. Respondents over 50 years display a tendency toward larger purchases (>1000 g), while the under 20 and 40–50 groups mostly buy smaller amounts (<250 g). These patterns suggest that younger and middle-aged consumers maintain sustainable buying habits, while older consumers may stock larger quantities, possibly for traditional or medicinal uses. Figure 2 illustrates these differences, showing the distribution of annual honey purchase quantities (<250 g, 250–500 g, 500–1000 g, >1000 g) across six age groups.

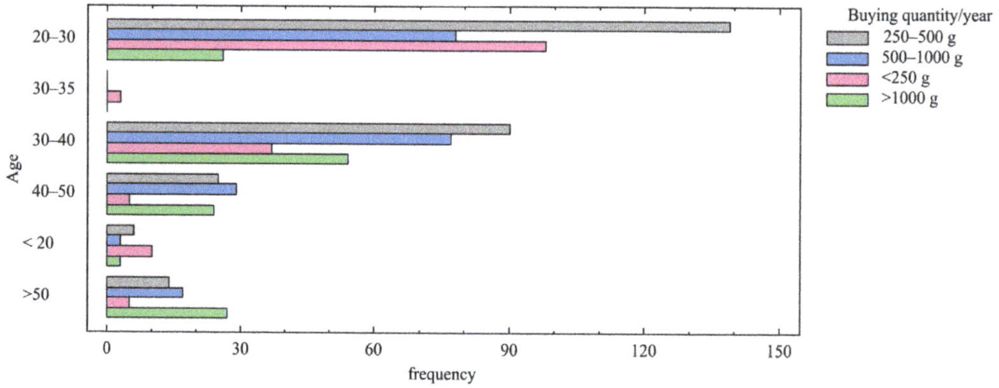

Figure 2. Distribution of annual honey purchase quantities across age groups.

The chi-square statistical test yielded $\chi^2 = 111.493$ with 15 degrees of freedom and a p-value < 0.0001. Since the p-value is less than 0.05, we reject the null hypothesis of independence at the 95% confidence level. This indicates that the observed buying quantity is significantly associated with age group. In other words, the amount of honey purchased per year varies meaningfully across different age categories.

Honey purchasing habits differ across age categories. Young adults (20–30 years) and the 30–40 age group show the highest frequency of buying honey "occasionally" or "often." Respondents over 50 years also demonstrate regular purchases, though less frequent compared to younger groups. The 40–50 and under–20 categories exhibit lower buying frequencies, often classified as "rarely" or "occasionally." These patterns indicate that trust-based and sustainable sourcing behaviors are maintained across generations, with younger consumers actively engaging in honey purchases. Figure 3 illustrates these differences, showing the distribution of buying frequencies (never, occasionally, often, rarely) across six age groups.

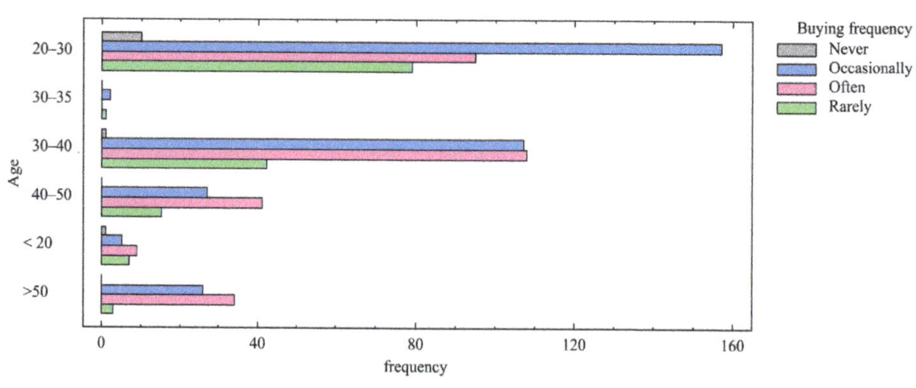

Figure 3. Distribution of buying frequencies across age groups.

The chi-square test of independence was conducted to examine the relationship between age and honey-buying frequency. The results confirm a significant association ($Chi^2 = 47.26$, df = 15, $p < 0.0001$), indicating that purchasing habits differ meaningfully across age groups.

4.3. Influence of Climatic Zone on Honey Buying Sources

The survey results show clear differences in honey purchasing habits across Algeria's four major climatic zones: Tell, High Plateau, Saharian Atlas, and Sahara. Consumers in the Tell region, which is the most populated and agriculturally diverse, reported the highest reliance on trusted individuals and local markets, reflecting strong informal networks and cultural traditions. In contrast, respondents from the Saharan and Saharian Atlas zones exhibited a stronger preference for direct purchases from beekeepers, likely due to limited market infrastructure and closer ties to primary producers. The High Plateau presented a mixed pattern, balancing informal trust-based sourcing with occasional market purchases. These variations suggest that geographic and socio-economic factors significantly influence sourcing behaviors, reinforcing the role of local identity and accessibility in shaping sustainable consumption practices.

Figure 4 illustrates the predominance of informal networks in all zones, with notable regional differences in the share of purchases from beekeepers and markets.

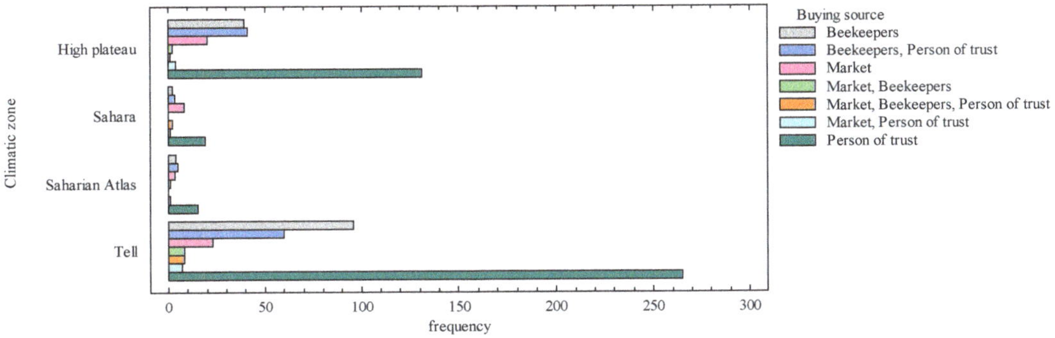

Figure 4. Distribution of Honey Buying Sources across Algeria's Climatic Zones.

The statistical test confirmed that the relationship between climatic zone and buying source is statistically significant ($\chi^2 = 34.90$, df = 18, $p = 0.0097$). This indicates that purchasing habits vary meaningfully across climatic zones, supporting the hypothesis that regional context influences consumer behavior.

A mosaic plot was generated to visualize the relationships among three categorical variables: climatic zone, buying source, and age group (Figure 5). The size of each rectangle represents the proportion of respondents within the corresponding combination of categories. The plot reveals clear patterns: Respondents from the Tell region show a higher proportion of purchases from trusted individuals and local markets, particularly among younger age groups (20–30 and 30–40 years). In contrast, respondents from Saharan and Saharian Atlas zones exhibit a stronger tendency to buy directly from beekeepers, with notable representation among older age groups (>40 years). Purchases from markets are more evenly distributed across regions but remain less frequent compared to informal sources.

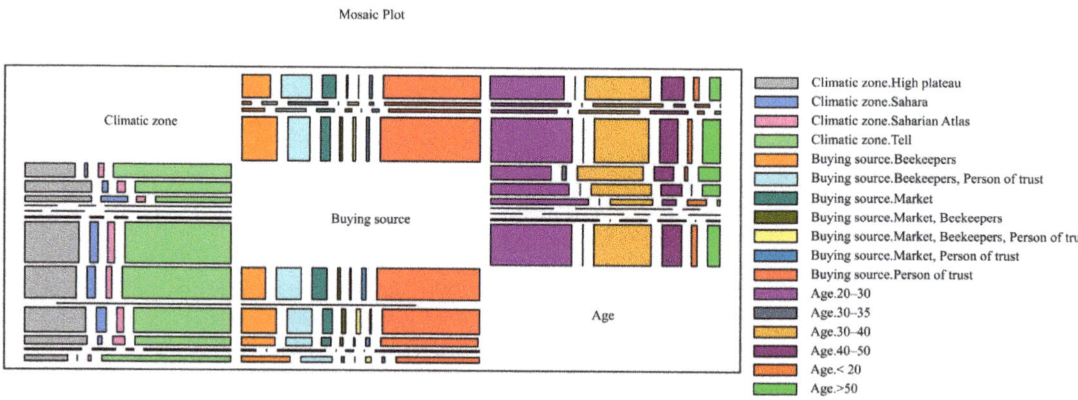

Figure 5. Cross-Analysis of Honey Purchasing Channels by Age and Climatic Region.

4.4. Preservation of Traditional Knowledge

The traditional use of honey in Algerian households goes far beyond consumption frequency. It encompasses a rich set of cultural practices, therapeutic applications, and sourcing habits that reflect inherited knowledge and sustainable values. Survey data show that older respondents (particularly those aged 40–50 and over 50) are more likely to use honey for medicinal purposes, such as treating respiratory, digestive, and skin conditions (Figure 6). This indicates that ancestral knowledge about honey's healing properties remains actively practiced among older generations. However, younger adults (especially those under 30) also demonstrate significant engagement with traditional uses, particularly in cosmetic applications and natural wellness routines. This suggests a revival or reinterpretation of traditional practices among younger demographics, possibly influenced by modern interest in natural products. Traditional knowledge is also reflected in sourcing behaviors. Many respondents prefer to buy honey from trusted individuals or directly from beekeepers, avoiding industrial supply chains. This trust-based acquisition method is not only culturally rooted but also supports local economies and aligns with sustainable consumption principles. Furthermore, beliefs about honey's physical properties, such as crystallization, serve as indicators of traditional understanding. Respondents who correctly identify crystallization as a natural process tend to be those with stronger ties to traditional knowledge, while misconceptions persist among others. In summary, traditional honey use in Algeria is a multifaceted phenomenon involving therapeutic, cosmetic, and cultural dimensions, as well as sourcing preferences and product perceptions. While older generations remain key custodians of this heritage, younger groups are increasingly adopting and adapting these practices, offering hope for their preservation and evolution.

Although not directly measured in the survey, the preference for natural honey and trust in local sources imply a consumer base that values authenticity and potentially supports biodiversity. Promoting honey from local beekeepers who use sustainable, pollinator-friendly methods can enhance ecosystem services, such as pollination, and contribute to the conservation of Algeria's diverse floral landscapes.

The results show that many respondents prefer natural honey and buy it directly from beekeepers, reflecting environmental awareness and support for sustainable practices. This preference contributes to the preservation of biodiversity by promoting short supply chains and local producers, while strengthening ecosystem services related to beekeeping.

The age groups most committed to this approach are 30–40-year-olds and 20–30-year-olds, followed by 40–50-year-olds, indicating intergenerational adoption of environmentally friendly practices. This suggests that awareness of biodiversity is well established among young adults, while also being supported by older generations.

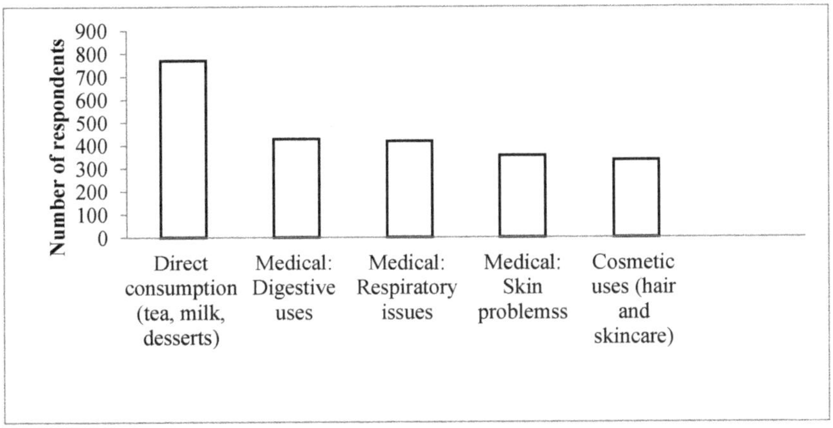

Figure 6. The reported uses of honey in Algerian households.

4.5. Biodiversity and Ecosystem Services

4.6. Consumer Education

The results indicate notable gaps in the knowledge of Algerian consumers regarding the characteristics of honey. Regarding crystallization, 40.52% of respondents recognised it as a natural process, 32.47% associated it with adulteration and 27.01% were unaware of its meaning. When it came to evaluation criteria, taste was the most frequently mentioned factor, cited by around 500 respondents. This was followed by type (monofloral or multifloral) and physical appearance (liquid or crystallized), which were mentioned by around 400 respondents each. Color was cited by 346 respondents and price (in Algerian dinars) received the fewest mentions at around 300. Furthermore, 399 respondents identified the type of honey as a determining factor in their purchasing decisions. The data also show that consumer perceptions are influenced by visual characteristics, oral traditions and family habits (Figure 7). The common misconceptions about honey crystallization often arise from a lack of consumer education, unclear labeling, and a reliance on informal knowledge handed down through families. These misunderstandings can result in customers rejecting products and lead to food waste, which undermines efforts toward sustainable consumption.

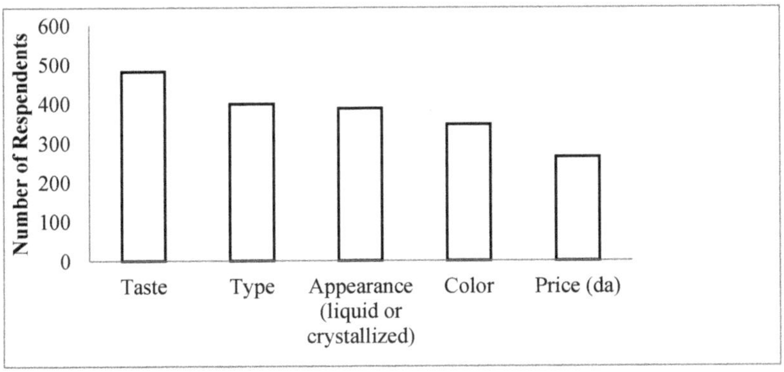

Figure 7. Primary criteria influencing honey purchase decisions.

Following this, a chi-square test was also conducted to examine whether age group influences perceptions of crystallized honey. The result (χ^2 = 17.47, df = 10, p = 0.0646) indicates no significant association, meaning attitudes toward crystallization are relatively consistent across age categories.

5. Discussion

The study reveals how Algerian consumers use honey in ways that reflect their cultural traditions, daily habits, and personal values. It highlights that people, often rely on trusted sources, such as family or local producers, and use honey not only as food but also for health and cosmetic purposes. These behaviors are shaped by long-standing traditions and practical knowledge passed down through generations. When compared with other countries, Algerian consumers show both similarities and unique patterns, especially in how they connect honey use with well-being and sustainability, often without being fully aware of it. The differences and similarities between Algerian honey consumption and other regions may be due to cultural habits, trust in informal networks, and how food is sold or labeled. In Algeria, people often buy honey from someone they know and use it for traditional health and beauty purposes. In Europe, consumers may rely more on labels and certifications. These factors help explain the unique patterns found in our study.

To better understand these behaviors, it is important to first look at who the consumers are and the cultural context in which they use honey.

5.1. Cross-Cultural and Demographic Insights

This study offers a detailed overview of honey consumption patterns among a specific segment of Algerian consumers, based on a diverse sample from 51 wilayas (Towns), based on a sample of 770 respondents. These findings should be interpreted with caution, as they reflect the views of a digitally engaged and educated population, rather than the full demographic spectrum of Algeria. Compared to previous national studies, such as Haderbach et al. (2015) [10], who surveyed 800 individuals from 20 wilayas, our research offers broader geographic coverage and more recent insights. Both studies highlight the cultural and medicinal importance of honey; however, our findings indicate emerging patterns in sourcing, consumer awareness, and the diverse applications of honey. Demographically, the sample was predominantly female (71.2%) and concentrated in the 20–40 age range. This contrasts with findings from [22], who observed higher honey consumption among older adults in Europe. Kleisiari et al. (2023) [9] also noted gender differences, with men consuming more honey in the Balkans and Western Europe. In our case, women appear more engaged in honey-related decisions, possibly due to their role in household health and food choices, also the demographic skew of our study might reflect the nature of online survey distribution, which tends to engage younger and more digitally active populations. While this may limit the generalizability of the findings, the data still provide valuable insights into honey consumption patterns among a key segment of Algerian households. Similar cultural contrasts were observed in Western Australia, where Batt and Liu (2012) [17] found that brand reputation, product origin, and value for money were the key drivers of honey purchasing decisions. Their study also highlighted that Asian consumers placed more emphasis on value and brand recognition, while Anglo-Saxon consumers prioritized origin. Future research should consider more balanced sampling strategies, including stratified or mixed-method approaches, to ensure broader representation of older adults and male respondents. Although chi-square tests confirmed significant associations, these results should be interpreted as indicative rather than causal. Future research should apply multivariate techniques to control for confounding factors such as age and education, providing a more robust understanding of the determinants of honey consumption. Similar findings were observed in Mexico, where Ávila Ramos et al. (2022) [16] identified three consumer profiles based on educational attainment and income. Middle-income individuals were the most frequent consumers of honey. These individuals preferred buying honey directly from beekeepers and recognized its health benefits. In contrast, younger, low-income consumers primarily used honey as a sugar substitute and preferred to buy it from the market. In Italy, Blanc et al. (2021) [23] identified four distinct consumption profiles among millennials, highlighting their strong preference for sustainability, label information, and local origin rather than intrinsic characteristics such as taste or texture. These findings underscore the importance of extrinsic cues and demographic factors, such as gender, urban origin, or sports participation, in shaping honey consumption behaviors.

Moreover, the survey results show that honey consumption in Algeria reflects a mindful and purposeful pattern that aligns with sustainable food practices. Moderate annual purchase volumes and restrained daily use suggest a conscious approach to consumption, often reserved for specific culinary or therapeutic purposes. Notably, honey also plays a central role in traditional Algerian pastries and festive desserts such as Makrout and Tamina, highlighting its cultural significance during special occasions. This pattern might demonstrate careful use that helps prevent overconsumption and supports the sustainable management of resources. Some findings also align with previous research conducted in Algeria, which reported an average annual honey consumption of approximately 0.2 kg per person. In these studies, honey was frequently regarded as a medicinal product and was predominantly purchased through informal, trust-based channels [10]. Similar trends are observed in Tunisia, where honey production is primarily dedicated to domestic use, and beekeeping practices are shaped by climate conditions and traditional transhumance [24].

The multifunctional use of honey—as food, medicine, and in cosmetics—not only increases its overall value but also decreases dependence on synthetic products, thereby supporting both environmental and public health sustainability [2]. These practices mirror sustainable behaviors observed in other Mediterranean contexts, where natural products are valued for their versatility and cultural significance, which is consistent with recent research by Herreros & Ali [25], which highlights practical approaches to sustainability in honey production, reinforcing the importance of environmentally responsible practices in the honey sector. In Greece, consumers showed a high willingness to purchase honey perceived as rich in antioxidants and vitamins, confirming the central role of health consciousness in honey consumption. A large-scale European study also confirms that health benefits are the main driver of honey consumption. According to Kleisiari et al. (2025), consumers perceive honey as a therapeutic and nutritious food and incorporate it into their diet as a healthy habit [9].

Figure 5 above, illustrating the interaction between climatic zone, age group, and honey buying source, reveals how geographic and demographic factors jointly shape consumer behavior. Respondents from the Tell region show a clear preference for purchases through trusted individuals and local markets, particularly among younger age groups (20–30 and 30–40 years). This pattern likely reflects the dense social networks and strong cultural traditions in this agriculturally rich zone, where informal trust-based channels substitute for formal certification. In contrast, consumers in the Saharan and Saharian Atlas zones exhibit a stronger tendency to buy directly from beekeepers, especially among older respondents (>40 years), which may be explained by limited market infrastructure and closer proximity to primary producers. These findings suggest that sourcing behaviors are not only age-dependent but also context-specific, influenced by accessibility, cultural norms, and perceived authenticity. From a sustainability perspective, these informal and direct channels reduce packaging and transport emissions, reinforcing short supply chains and supporting local economies. However, the reliance on informal networks also underscores the need for targeted education and labeling initiatives to ensure quality assurance and consumer confidence across regions.

5.2. Informal and Local Market Channels

Informal sourcing networks, particularly purchases from trusted individuals such as family members or local beekeepers, dominate acquisition practices. Among our respondents, 58.3% reported buying honey from a person of trust, while only 18.3% purchased directly from beekeepers. These trust-based relationships reinforce consumer confidence, reduce dependence on industrial supply chains, and minimize packaging and transport-related emissions. According to Zanchini et al. (2021) [2], consumers who purchase honey at local markets or directly from producers are more likely to associate it with health benefits. This suggests that short supply chains not only strengthen trust but also reinforce the perception of honey as a natural and therapeutic product. In Hungary, consumers show a strong preference for honey purchased directly from beekeepers or farmers' markets. This direct relationship not only builds trust but also reinforces the perception of honey as an authentic, high-quality product. Certification marks play a crucial role in guiding informed consumers to safe and authentic sources of honey [16]. This sourcing behavior supports local economies and reflects deep-rooted cultural traditions. However, the relatively low rate of direct purchases from beekeepers highlights an untapped opportunity; similar trends were observed in Greece, where over 77% of consumers preferred buying conventional honey directly from beekeepers. This reinforces the importance of direct sourcing in building trust and ensuring product authenticity, especially for organic varieties [15]. Strengthening direct links between consumers and producers could enhance traceability, encourage pollinator-friendly practices, and provide economic incentives for sustainable beekeeping. A similar trend was observed in Croatia, where 75% of consumers preferred buying honey directly from producers. This behavior was driven by trust and the perceived health benefits of domestic honey, with Protected Designation of Origin PDO labels reinforcing product authenticity and regional identity [26].

5.3. Traditional Knowledge and Environmental Sustainability

In Algeria, traditional knowledge continues to guide honey use, with older generations emphasizing medicinal purposes and younger adults favoring cosmetic and wellness applications. This intergenerational transmission is complemented by emerging innovations such as plant-based honey alternatives, which aim to address sustainability and ethical concerns [20]. Honey is also used in traditional ceremonies and festivals, reinforcing its role as a culturally embedded product. These practices contribute to the preservation of intangible heritage and support sustainable consumption rooted in local identity. In this context, consuming honey sustainably entails supporting small-scale beekeepers, choosing locally sourced products, and using honey sparingly and mindfully. These actions support local economies, protect traditional knowledge, and lessen their negative effects on the environment. By reducing packaging and transportation-related emissions and preserving close cultural and social ties, the use of unofficial, trust-based networks also promotes sustainability.

5.4. Sustainable Food Practices, Consumer Awareness, and SDG Integration

Beyond honey, Algerian households engage in sustainable consumption behaviors through other traditional foods such as olive oil, dates, legumes, and herbal products. These foods share similar cultural and multifunctional roles, often used in culinary, medicinal, and ceremonial contexts. Olive oil, for instance, is a staple in Mediterranean diets and is increasingly valued for its health benefits and sustainability attributes. Studies show that consumers are willing to pay more for olive oil with sustainability labels, although their motivations are often linked more to perceived quality and origin than to environmental concerns [16,27]. This parallels honey consumption, where trust and traditional sourcing outweigh formal certifications. Legumes also play a vital role in sustainable diets due to their low environmental footprint and high nutritional value. Their integration into daily meals supports biodiversity and reduces reliance on animal protein. Similarly, native foods and traditional crops contribute to food security and cultural preservation, especially when promoted through community-based interventions [27]. These findings suggest that Algerian food practices—though often informal and culturally driven—align with global sustainability goals. By recognizing and supporting these behaviors, policymakers can leverage traditional knowledge to promote resilient food systems across the region [27].

Regarding Consumer education, it has emerged as a critical issue. Misunderstandings about crystallization—only 40.52% recognized it as a natural process—affect purchasing decisions and trust. In Algeria, crystallized honey is often perceived as adulterated, typically associated with the addition of artificial sugars. These misconceptions, if not addressed, can lead to product rejection and food waste, undermining sustainability goals. Based on descriptive trends, younger consumers and individuals with limited awareness appear more prone to these beliefs, suggesting that targeted education campaigns could be more effective than generic interventions. Similar gaps were noted by Kleisiari et al. (2023) [9] in Europe. Addressing these misconceptions through labeling, outreach, and school programs could enhance consumer autonomy and reduce waste. Other sensory attributes, such as color, texture, and floral origin, also influence purchasing decisions. Recent studies on caper honey (*Capparis spinosa* L.) have shown that its aroma evolves over time, with vegetal notes perceived first, and followed by floral and sweet caramel sensations. This dynamic sensory profile, evaluated by analyzing temporal intensity, highlights the complexity and richness of certain monofloral honeys, which can appeal to experienced consumers [28]. However, many consumers lack the knowledge to interpret these characteristics accurately. Educational initiatives could empower consumers to choose honey based on specific needs—such as digestion, respiratory health, or skincare—while promoting local Algerian varieties.

It is noted also that the respondents are from diverse professional backgrounds, including employed individuals, students, and retirees. Although not analyzed in depth, this diversity may influence purchasing power, health awareness, and sustainability values. Mascarello et al. (2024) [15] found that employed individuals and retirees in Italy showed greater interest in traceability and were more likely to engage with digital tools such as QR codes. Future research could explore how occupational status correlates with sustainable purchasing behaviors in Algeria. By framing honey consumption within a sustainability context, this study aligns with and contributes to multiple United Nations Sustainable Development Goals (SDGs), these findings align with broader calls for robust metrics to evaluate sustainability and resilience in food systems, as highlighted by Hassan et al. (2025), who emphasize the importance of context-specific indicators to guide evidence-based decision-making [29]. Specifically, it supports SDG 3 (Good Health and Well-being) by highlighting the nutritional and medicinal benefits of honey; SDG 12 (Responsible Consumption and Production) through the promotion of environmentally conscious consumer behavior; and SDG 15 (Life on Land) by emphasizing the role of sustainable apiculture in preserving biodiversity and ecosystems.

5.5. Policy Implications and Recommendations

Although most consumers prefer informal and local channels, the Algerian market remains exposed to imports of foreign honey, which is sometimes cheap but of uncertain quality. This competition can undermine small local producers. According to the World Beekeeping Organization [28], traceability and certification of origin are key levers for promoting local honey on national and international markets. Encouraging regional labels or protected geographical indications (PGIs) could strengthen the competitiveness of Algerian honey while supporting sustainable practices. According to Zeng et al. (2023) [30], packaging also plays a crucial role in consumer perception. Unique jar shapes can significantly increase willingness to pay, suggesting that design and presentation are essential components of product differentiation in the honey market. These recommendations are consistent with findings from Uganda, where Amuko et al. (2023) [31] demonstrated that timely, accurate, credible, and usable market information significantly enhances entrepreneurial orientation among smallholder honey producers. Their study highlights how access to relevant market intelligence fosters innovation, proactiveness, and risk-taking, ultimately improving product development and competitiveness. In light of these findings, several recommendations can be made: integrate education on sustainable consumption into school curricula, support small-scale beekeepers through targeted subsidies and training in sustainable beekeeping, promote awareness campaigns on the benefits of local honey and quality criteria, and strengthen links between scientific research, producers, and consumers. These actions would help to build a more resilient beekeeping ecosystem, in line with sustainable development goals. These recommendations are supported by findings from Indonesia, where Febrianto et al. (2023) [32] demonstrated that product quality and promotional efforts are the most influential factors in honey-purchasing decisions. The study also confirmed that repeat purchases are a strong indicator of consumer loyalty, underlining the importance of maintaining product standards and effective communication strategies.

5.6. Technological Innovations and Future Directions

A recent study employing a multi-omic approach demonstrated that environmental conditions and agricultural practices markedly influence honeybee health—through mechanisms such as protein depletion and metal regulation—which subsequently affect honey quality and sector sustainability [33]. Blockchain-based systems offer a promising solution for tracking organic honey production, ensuring transparency and authenticity while supporting sustainable certification and consumer confidence [21]. Responsible consumption and production patterns, as outlined in SDG 12, are essential to mitigate environmental degradation. Honey, when locally sourced and ethically produced, aligns with these global sustainability targets [34]. Combining DNA metabarcoding with melissopalinological analysis enables a more accurate identification of the honey's botanical origin, thereby strengthening product authenticity control, helping to detect counterfeits, facilitating access to international markets, and increasing consumer confidence [35]. Unsustainable consumption and production are major challenges, contributing to climate change, biodiversity loss, and pollution. Promoting responsible consumption in food systems, such as honey production, is crucial for protecting both livelihoods and the environment for future generations [34]. Unsustainable consumption and production are major challenges, contributing to climate change, biodiversity loss, and pollution. Promoting responsible consumption in food systems, such as honey production, is crucial for protecting both livelihoods and the environment for future generations [35]. In China, honey is increasingly perceived as a healthy and nutritious food, with 74.48% of consumers citing health benefits as their primary motivation for purchase. This highlights the importance of consumer awareness and education in promoting sustainable honey consumption [18]. Despite these contributions, the study has some limitations worth noting. Although the questionnaire reached people from all 51 wilayas, it was shared online, which may have favored younger and more educated respondents. Also, since the data are self-reported, some answers might reflect personal perceptions rather than objective facts. Future studies could include more rural and offline communities, and combine surveys with interviews to better capture the diversity of honey consumption practices across Algeria.

Practical Implications: Based on the findings, several actionable strategies can be proposed to promote sustainable honey consumption in Algerian households. Encourage direct purchases from local beekeepers to strengthen trust and reduce environmental impact. Implement consumer education programs and clear labeling to address misconceptions about crystallization. Highlight honey's health and cosmetic benefits in marketing campaigns targeting younger demographics. Support short supply chains and traceability initiatives to enhance product authenticity and sustainability. Recent studies also highlight honey's health benefits and functional properties [36], the development of innovative honey-based products [37], and the integration of honey into functional food formulations to meet sustainability and health trends [38].

6. Conclusions

This study highlights the cultural and sustainable dimensions of honey consumption among a specific segment of Algerian households. Honey is not only a nutritional product but also a multifunctional substance embedded in traditional practices, with uses in medicine and cosmetics. Consumer behavior is strongly influenced by trust-based sourcing, favoring local and informal channels that support short supply chains and sustainability. To strengthen consumer confidence and reduce misconceptions—such as those related to crystallization—targeted education and clear labeling are essential. Additionally, integrating digital tools such as QR codes for traceability can enhance transparency and authenticity, connecting consumers directly to producers and production practices. These measures, combined with awareness campaigns and support for local beekeepers, can promote responsible consumption and reinforce biodiversity-friendly practices. Future research should expand to rural and offline populations and explore technological innovations, including blockchain and QR-based systems, to build a resilient and transparent honey sector aligned with global sustainability goals.

Supplementary Materials: The following supporting information can be downloaded at: https://www.mdpi.com/article/10.3390/su172310669/s1, File S1: Enquête sur la consommation et l'utilisation traditionnelle du miel en Algérie.

Author Contributions: Conceptualization, R.N. and M.C.S.-C.; methodology, R.N., S.H., Y.S. and A.G.; formal analysis, R.N. and S.H.; data curation, R.N., S.H., A.G., Y.S. and M.S.R.-F.; investigation, R.N.; writing—original draft preparation, R.N., S.H.; writing—review and editing, M.C.S.-C.; supervision, M.C.S.-C., O.E. and M.S.R.-F. All authors have read and agreed to the published version of the manuscript.

Funding: This research received no external funding.

Institutional Review Board Statement: Ethical review and approval were waived for this study by the Institutional Committee due to Spanish national legislation (specifically Ley Orgánica 3/2018 on the protection of personal data and digital rights (BOE link); only data that allow the identification of individuals are considered personal and subject to ethical review. As the survey was fully anonymous and did not collect identifiable information, it was exempt from formal ethics review.

Informed Consent Statement: Informed consent for participation was obtained from all subjects involved in the study.

Data Availability Statement: The data presented in this study are available on request from the corresponding author due to privacy restrictions.

Acknowledgments: The authors sincerely thank all online respondents for their valuable contribution and for generously sharing their experiences and insights, which made this research possible.

Conflicts of Interest: The authors declare that they have no known competing financial interests or personal relationships that could have appeared to have influenced the work reported in this paper.

References

1. Prodanović, R.; Brkić, I.; Soleša, K.; Pelić, D.L.; Pelić, M.; Bursić, V.; Tankosić, J.V. Beekeeping as a tool for sustainable rural development. *J. Agron. Technol. Eng. Manag. JATEM* **2024**, *7*, 1054–1066. [CrossRef]
2. Zanchini, R.; Blanc, S.; Pippinato, L.; Di Vita, G.; Brun, F. Consumers' attitude towards honey consumption for its health benefits: First insights from an econometric approach. *Br. Food J.* **2022**, *124*, 4372–4386. [CrossRef]
3. Bereksi-Reguig, D.; Allali, H.; Taib, N.; Aissaoui, N.; Wlodarczyk-Stasiak, M.; Kowalski, R. Bioactive Compounds, Antioxidant Properties, and Antimicrobial Profiling of a Range of West Algerian Honeys: In Vitro Comparative Screening Prior to Therapeutic Purpose. *Foods* **2024**, *13*, 4120. [CrossRef]
4. Haider, Y.; Adjlane, N.; Haddad, N. Environmental impacts and behavioral adaptations of honeybees in Algeria: A review of *Apis mellifera intermissa* and *Apis mellifera sahariensis* characteristics. *Insects* **2025**, *16*, 617. [CrossRef]
5. Haider, Y.; Adjlane, N.; Martín-Hernandez, R.; Haddad, N. Beekeeping in Algeria: Evaluation of beekeeping practices, trends of management, and challenges. *Afr. J. Food Agric. Nutr. Dev.* **2025**, *25*, 25542–25564. [CrossRef]
6. Di Vita, G.; Pippinato, L.; Zanchini, R.; Blanc, S.; Brun, F. PDO Labeling and Sustainability Perceptions in Mediterranean Honey Markets. *Br. Food J.* **2024**, *126*, 1374–1389. [CrossRef]
7. Fortune Business Insights. *Global Honey Market Size, Share & Industry Analysis, by Type, Application, Packaging, and Regional Forecast, 2024–2032*; Fortune Business Insights: Pune, India, 2025. Available online: https://www.fortunebusinessinsights.com/industry-reports/honey-market-100551 (accessed on 25 November 2025).
8. Maximize Market Research. *Honey Market: Global Industry Analysis by Market Share, Trends, and Forecast (2025–2032)*; Maximize Market Research: Pune, India, 2025. Available online: https://www.maximizemarketresearch.com/market-report/global-honey-market/120330/ (accessed on 25 November 2025).
9. Kleisiari, C.; Kleftodimos, G.; Vlontzos, G. Be(e)ha(i)viour(e): Assessment of honey consumption in Europe. *Br. Food J.* **2023**, *125*, 1374–1389. [CrossRef]
10. Haderbache, L.; Mohammedi, A. Etude sur le comportement de consommation du miel en Algérie: Attentes et préférences. *Rev. Agric.* **2015**, *9*, 19–24.
11. Derrar, S.; Lo Turco, V.; Albergamo, A.; Sgrò, B.; Ayad, M.A.; Litrenta, F.; Saim, M.S.; Potortì, A.G.; Aggad, H.; Rando, R.; et al. Study of Physicochemical Quality and Organic Contamination in Algerian Honey. *Foods* **2024**, *13*, 1413. [CrossRef]
12. Saad, B. Immunomodulatory and Anti-Inflammatory Properties of Honey and Bee Products. *Immuno* **2025**, *5*, 19. [CrossRef]
13. Bendahbia, K.; Nabih, Z.; Abidli, Z.; Soulaymani, A.; Chahbi, A.; Khadmaoui, A. Consumption, preferences and habits of purchasing consumers of honey in Morocco. *J. Hyg. Eng. Des.* **2019**, *28*, 61–65.
14. Vapa-Tankosić, J.; Cvijanović, D.; Tankosić, M.; Vapa-Tankosić, N. Consumers' Willingness to Pay for Organic and Local Honey in Serbia. *Sustainability* **2020**, *12*, 1234. [CrossRef]
15. Mascarello, G.; Pinto, A.; Crovato, S.; Pezzoli, B.T.; Pietropaoli, M.; Bertola, M.; Mutinelli, F.; Formato, G. Consumers' perceptions and behaviors regarding honey purchases and expectations on traceability and sustainability in Italy. *Sustainability* **2024**, *16*, 8846. [CrossRef]
16. Ramos, F.Á.; Mancera, L.P.B.; Bravo, M.B.; Reyes, V.C.; Toledano, B.I.S. Tipología de consumidores de miel con educación universitaria en México. *Rev. Mex. Cienc. Pecu.* **2022**, *13*, 879–893. [CrossRef]
17. Batt, P.J.; Liu, A. Consumer Behaviour Towards Honey Products in Western Australia. *Br. Food J.* **2012**, *114*, 285–297. [CrossRef]
18. Almiani, K.; Mirza, S.B.; Zufferey, C.; Alyammahi, K.M.; Lamghari, F. Fujairah Honey Chain (FHC): A Blockchain Framework for Monitoring Honey Production. *Information* **2025**, *16*, 626. [CrossRef]
19. De, T.; Singh, N.; Ibrahim, K.S.M.K.; Dikkatwar, R.; Chaudhary, M.K. Mindful, Responsible, and Sustainable Consumption: A Hybrid Review of Evolving Research Trends. *Discov. Sustain.* **2025**, *6*, 512. [CrossRef]
20. Mandich, D.; Schaller, A.M. Reinventing Honey Through a Plant-Based Alternative. *Food Business News*, 2 July 2024. Available online: https://www.foodbusinessnews.net/articles/26352-reinventing-honey-through-a-plant-based-alternative (accessed on 25 November 2025).
21. Lukovac, P.; Miletić, A.; Radenković, B. A System for Tracking Organic Honey Production Using Blockchain Technologies. In *Sustainable Business Management and Digital Transformation: Challenges and Opportunities in the Post-COVID Era*; Mihić, M., Jednak, S., Savić, G., Eds.; Springer: Cham, Switzerland, 2022; pp. 239–254. [CrossRef]
22. Vida, V.; Ferenczi, A.F. Trends in honey consumption and purchasing habits in the European Union. *Appl. Stud. Agribus. Commer.* **2023**, *17*, 47–54. [CrossRef]

23. Blanc, S.; Zanchini, R.; Di Vita, G.; Brun, F. The Role of Intrinsic and Extrinsic Characteristics of Honey for Italian Millennial Consumers. *Br. Food J.* **2021**, *123*, 2183–2198. [CrossRef]
24. Ismail, H.B.; Hamzaoui, M.; Jribi, S.; Salem, H.B.; Jmal, S.; Debbabi, H. Assessment of Honey Production System in Tunisia. In *Recent Advances in Environmental Science from the Euro-Mediterranean and Surrounding Regions*, 4th ed.; EMCEI 2022; Springer: Cham, Switzerland, 2024; pp. 527–531. [CrossRef]
25. Herreros, S.; Ali, M. Sustainable Practices in Honey Production. *Int. J. Agric. Nutr.* **2023**, *5*, 54–56. [CrossRef]
26. Bršćić, K.; Šugar, T.; Poljuha, D. An Empirical Examination of Consumer Preferences for Honey in Croatia. *Appl. Econ.* **2017**, *49*, 5877–5889. [CrossRef]
27. Matías, J.; Rodríguez, M.J.; Carrillo-Vico, A.; Casals, J.; Fondevilla, S.; Haros, C.M.; Pedroche, J.; Aparicio, N.; Fernández-García, N.; Aguiló-Aguayo, I.; et al. From 'farm to fork': Exploring the potential of nutrient-rich and stress-resilient emergent crops for sustainable and healthy food in the Mediterranean region in the face of climate change challenges. *Plants* **2024**, *13*, 1914. [CrossRef]
28. Apimondia. Beekeeping contributes to achieve the Sustainable Development Goals. In *Apimondia International Federation of Beekeepers' Associations*; Apimondia: Copenhagen, Denmark, 2021.
29. Hassan, R.; Di Martino, M.; Daher, B. Quantifying Sustainability and Resilience in Food Systems: A Systematic Analysis for Evaluating the Convergence of Current Methodologies and Metrics. *Front. Sustain. Food Syst.* **2025**, *9*, 1479691. [CrossRef]
30. Zeng, M.; Yan, W.Y.; Zeng, Z.J. Analysis of Consumers' Willingness to Pay for Honey in China. *Sustainability* **2023**, *15*, 1500. [CrossRef]
31. Amuko, W.; Kalule, S.W.; Odongo, W. The Relationship between Market Information and Entrepreneurial Orientation: The Case of Smallholder Honey Producers in Northern Uganda. *Agric. Food Econ.* **2023**, *11*, 8. [CrossRef]
32. Febrianto, N.; Akhiroh, P.; Masyithoh, D.; Helmi, M.; Hartono, B. Factors affecting consumers' loyalty and purchase decisions on honey products: An emerging market perspective. *Open Agric.* **2023**, *8*, 20220235. [CrossRef]
33. Rudelli, C.; Bellei, E.; Andreani, G.; Isani, G. An Innovative Multi-Omics Approach Reveals the Interactions Between Honeybees and Their Environment. *Animals* **2025**, *15*, 2660. [CrossRef]
34. Arora, N.K.; Mishra, I. Responsible Consumption and Production: A Roadmap to Sustainable Development. *Environ. Sustain.* **2023**, *6*, 1–6. [CrossRef]
35. Daugaliyeva, S.; Daugaliyeva, A.; Amirova, K.; Yelubayeva, A.; Toktarov, N.; Peletto, S. Identifying Honey Species Composition and Verifying Label Accuracy Using Melissopalynological Analysis and DNA Metabarcoding. *Food Anal. Methods* **2025**, *18*, 697. [CrossRef]
36. Palma-Morales, M.; Huertas, J.R.; Rodríguez-Pérez, C. A Comprehensive Review of the Effect of Honey on Human Health. *Nutrients* **2023**, *15*, 3056. [CrossRef]
37. Arsić, B.; Mrmošanin, J.; Petrović, S.; Kostić, D.; Pavlović, A.; Tošić, S.; Georgijev, A. Creation of Products Made from Honey Based on the Content of Elements Determined by ICP-OES. Environ. *Sci. Pollut. Res.* **2023**, *31*, 40530–40537. [CrossRef] [PubMed]
38. Gulzar, I.; Kaur, S. Development of Honey-Based Functional Foods. *Stud. Sci. Sci.* **2024**, *42*, 747.

sustainability

MDPI

Article

Effect of Silk Fibroin as a Sustainable Solvent on the Extraction of Bixin from Annatto Seeds (*Bixa orellana* L.)

Swanny Ferreira Borges [1,2], Fabricio H. e Holanda [2,3], Kaio C. De Maria [2], Sônia do Socorro do C. Oliveira [2], David E. Q. Jimenez [2], Celisnolia Morais Leite [4], Valtencir Zucolotto [4] and Irlon M. Ferreira [1,2,*]

1 Programa de Pós-Graduação em Inovação Farmacêutica, Departamento de Ciências Biológicas e da Saúde, Curso de Farmácia, Universidade Federal do Amapá, Rod. JK, km 02, Macapá 68902-280, AP, Brazil; swannyborges@gmail.com

2 Laboratório de Biocatálise e Síntese Orgânica Aplicada, Departamento de Ciências Exatas, Curso de Química, Universidade Federal do Amapá, Rod. JK, km 02, Macapá 68902-280, AP, Brazil; holanda_fabricio@yahoo.com.br (F.H.e.H.); kaioquimica21@gmail.com (K.C.D.M.); ssc.oliveira@yahoo.com.br (S.d.S.d.C.O.); derteriom@unifap.br (D.E.Q.J.)

3 Instituto Federal de Ensino Ciência e Tecnologia do Amapá, Rua Nilo Perçanha, Bairro Cajari, Laranjal do Jari 68920-000, AP, Brazil

4 Grupo de Nanomedicina e Nanotoxicologia, Instituto de Física de São Carlos, Universidade de São Paulo, São Carlos 13566-590, SP, Brazil; celisnolia@gmail.com (C.M.L.); zuco@ifsc.usp.br (V.Z.)

* Correspondence: irlon.ferreira@gmail.com; Tel.:+55-96-9147-6445

Abstract

Bixin, an apocarotenoid from *Bixa orellana* seeds, is a valuable natural pigment with industrial and pharmacological applications. Traditional extraction methods rely on organic solvents, but eco-friendly alternatives like silk fibroin solution (SFS) are emerging. This study evaluated SFS for bixin extraction from annatto seeds, optimizing conditions using Box-Behnken Design (BBD). The optimal parameters 1.5% SFS, 60 °C, and 60 min yielded 10.87 mg/mL (liquid extract of annatto seeds, LEAS + SFS) and 150.72 mg/g (solid extract of annatto seeds, SEAS + SFS). Cell viability was assessed in human dermal fibroblasts (HDFn) and RAW 264.7 murine macrophages via MTT assay. After 24 and 72 h, LEAS + SFS, SEAS + SFS, purified bixin (PB), and SFS maintained >70% viability in HDFn cells. Similarly, RAW 264.7 cells showed >70% viability after 24 h, indicating low cytotoxicity. These results highlight the biocompatibility of SFS-extracted bixin, supporting its potential in food, cosmetics, and biomedicine. The study demonstrates that SFS is an effective, sustainable alternative to traditional solvents, offering high extraction efficiency and minimal toxicity. This method aligns with green chemistry principles, providing a promising solution for bixin production.

Keywords: urucum; *Bombyx mori*; solvent eco-friendly; green extraction; MTT assay

1. Introduction

The seeds of *Bixa orellana* (annatto) hold significant economic value as a natural dye source, widely used in the textile, food, cosmetic, and pharmaceutical industries [1]. Furthermore, extracts from *B. orellana* seeds exhibit several pharmacological properties, including antiseptic [2], diuretic [3], hypoglycemic [4], antimicrobial [5,6], anti-inflammatory [7,8], and antioxidant effects [6].

The industrial applications and therapeutic properties of annatto seeds are primarily associated with the carotenoids present in the outer layer of the seeds, particularly an

https://doi.org/10.3390/su17167518

apocarotenoid known as bixin [1,9]. Bixin, [(2*E*,4*E*,6*E*,8*E*,10*E*,12*E*,14*E*,16*Z*,18*E*)-20-methoxy-4,8,13,17-tetramethyl-20-oxoicosa-2,4,6,8,10,12,14,16,18-nonenoic acid)], corresponds to 70–80% of the total pigments extracted from the seeds of *B. orellana* [10,11].

Several solvents and methods are employed to extract pigments from *B. orellana* seeds [1,5–8,10,12–21]. Although some methods improve extraction efficiency and yield, they often require highly toxic solvents, such as acetone, ethanol, ethyl acetate and methanol, that pose risks to human health and the environment or increase production costs [22]. Moreover, certain extraction methods may compromise specific properties of bixin or generate degradation products, as in the case of extraction with hot vegetable oil [12,22]. To overcome these challenges, a sustainable alternative involves replacing synthetic substances with natural compounds, such as silk fibroin, a biopolymer, in the carotenoid extraction process.

Silk is an animal fiber obtained from silkworms, particularly *Bombyx mori*. It is primarily composed of two proteins: fibroin and sericin. Fibroin is the main component of silk, constituting approximately 75% of its structure [23]. Its molecular configuration comprises three subunits: one heavy chain and two light chains [24,25]. This configuration imparts silk fibroin with properties such as biocompatibility, biodegradability, controllable degradation, ease of processability, elasticity, flexibility, and mechanical strength, making it ideal for applications in various sectors, including textiles, food, cosmetics, and biomedicine. The flexible nature of fibroin enables the formation of numerous nanostructures, such as films, fibers, micro- and nanoparticles, and hydrogels [23,24,26,27]. Furthermore, the amphiphilic nature of fibroin, characterized by the presence of hydrophilic and hydrophobic domains in its structure, favors self-organization in aqueous media and allows for versatile interactions with different types of molecules [24,28]. This property contributes to the solubilization of poorly water-soluble compounds, expanding its potential as a matrix for the incorporation and release of bioactive substances [29,30].

Recent studies have demonstrated that silk fibroin solution (SFS) may be used as an alternative emulsifying agent in the formulation of oil/water emulsions containing bioactive agents with larvicidal effects [31]; as controlled-release nanoparticles, obtained from the combination of fatty esters of Amazonian palm oils and SFS [32]; and as a surfactant in the development of polymeric nanoparticles containing SFS and naringenin for in vitro anti-LOX (lipoxygenases) applications [33].

However, there is a notable gap in the literature regarding extracting pigments from annatto seeds using an aqueous protein solution based on silk fibroin as a substitute for organic solvents. To address this gap, we propose optimizing the bixin extraction process using silk fibroin solution (SFS) as an innovative and sustainable alternative. Additionally, we evaluate the viability of HDFn and RAW 264.7 cells exposed to liquid extract of annatto seeds (LEAS + SFS) and solid extract of annatto seeds (SEAS + SFS), aiming to provide insights in human dermal fibroblast into the biocompatibility and potential applications of this method.

2. Materials and Methods

2.1. Reagents and Solvents

Silkworm cocoons were purchased from Bratac (São Paulo, Brazil). Sodium carbonate (99%) was purchased from Cromato Produtos Químicos and $CaCl_2$ (99%) was purchased from Vetec. The solvents *n*-hexane (98.5%), methanol (99.8%) and ethyl acetate (99.5%) were purchased from Synth (São Paulo, Brazil). Chloroform (99.98%) was purchased from Reatec (Neuhausen am Rheinfall, Switzerland) and ethanol (99%) was purchased from Alcohols Commercial LTDA (São Paulo, Brazil). The DMEN culture medium used for cell viability testing was purchased from Vitrocell (Waldkirch, Germany). MTT (3-(4,5-dimethylthiazol-

2-yl)-2,5-diphenyltetrazolium bromide) was purchased from Sigma (São Paulo, Brazil), and DMSO was purchased from Synth (São Paulo, Brazil).

2.2. Plant Material: Collection and Identification

In this study, the seeds of *B. orellana* were of the red phenotype, as described by Oliveira et al., 2022 [6]. The fruits of *B. orellana* were collected in the municipality of Macapá, Amapá, Brazil, in March 2023 (N 00° 15.918′ W 051° 08.141′). The dried plant specimen was stored at the Herbarium Amapaense (HAMAB) at the Institute of Scientific and Technological Research of the State of Amapá (IEPA) under registration number 019143. The biological and botanical nomenclature was described by Cantuária et al., 2022 [34].

2.3. Preparation of Silk Fibroin Solution

The silk fibroin solution (SFS) was prepared based on the method developed by Ferreira et al., 2014 [35] with adaptations. Silkworm cocoons (4.5 g) were chopped and degummed in Na_2CO_3 (2%) (*w*/*v*) at 50 °C for 24 h to remove sericin. The resulting silk fibers were filtered and washed with distilled water (3 × 500 mL) and dried at room temperature for 24 h. After this, the fibers were dissolved in a ternary solution (50 mL) of H_2O: EtOH: $CaCl_2$ (molar ratio 8:2:1) at 50 °C for 24 h. The final solution was dialyzed (cellulose tube with 16 kDa exclusion limit, from Viskase, Brazil) for 3 days at room temperature, with the dialysis water changed every 24 h. The fibroin solution was centrifuged (4000 rpm for 10 min) to remove impurities and larger particles. The SFS concentration was determined in *w*/*w* and adjusted according to experimental needs.

2.4. Experimental Design

The process parameters for the bixin extraction method were determined from the three-level, three-factor Box-Behnken (BBD) experimental design using the Design-Expert® Software statistical package (version 11, Stat-Ease Inc., Minneapolis, MN, USA) [33]. First, the process conditions were defined, and the three input factors or critical process parameters (CPPs) were selected: temperature (40, 50, and 60 °C), extraction time (30, 60, and 90 min), and SFS concentration (0.5, 1.0, and 1.5%). These input factors were designated as x1, x2, and x3, and defined in three levels, i.e., low, medium, and high values, conventionally indicated as −1, 0, and +1, respectively (Table 1). The design included five replicates of the central point and, therefore, consisted of a total of 15 experiments [33]. The measured responses or critical quality attributes (CQAs) were: bixin content in LEAS + SFS (mg/mL) and bixin content in SEAS + SFS (mg/mL).

Table 1. Input factors and their levels applied in the Box-Behnken (BBD) experimental design.

Factor	Variables	Levels		
		−1	0	1
*x*1	Temperature (°C)	40	50	60
*x*2	Time (min)	30	60	90
*x*3	SFS concentration (%)	0.5	1.0	1.5

For each CQA, the influence of input factors and their interactions on the responses could be described through the following nonlinear quadratic model generated by the design as:

$$Y = \beta 0 + \beta 1x1 + \beta 2x2 + \beta 3x3 + \beta 11x12 + \beta 22x22 + \beta 33x32 + \beta 12x1x2 + \beta 13x1x3 + \beta\ 23x2x3 \quad (1)$$

where: Y is the predicted response; b0 is a model constant; b1, b2, and b3 are the linear coefficients; b11, b22, and b33 are the quadratic coefficients; b12, b13, and b23 are the interaction coefficients; and x1, x2, and x3 are independent variables.

2.5. Bixin Extraction Process with Silk Fibroin Solution

The independent variables considered for extraction, defined by the experimental design, are presented in item 2.4, Table 1. Whole seeds of annatto in nature (0.5 g) were subjected to maceration with 5 mL of SFS in different concentrations (0.5, 1.0, and 1.5%), for 30, 60, and 90 min, under magnetic stirring (400 rpm) at temperatures of 40, 50 and 60 °C (Ika MAG HS 7). After maceration, the solution was vacuum filtered using a filter (Whatman paper No. 2, 90 mm, Cytiva, Marlborough, MA, USA). The seeds were separated, and the solid material retained in the filter was stored in amber glass, protected from light, and placed to dry in an oven (35 °C, 24h). After this, this sample was named a solid extract of annatto seeds from SFS (SEAS + SFS). The filtered solution was stored in amber glass, protected from light, and refrigerated (4 °C). This sample was named a liquid extract of annatto seeds from SFS (LEAS + SFS) (Figure 1). Subsequently, the samples were subjected to UV-Vis analysis to quantify the bixin content.

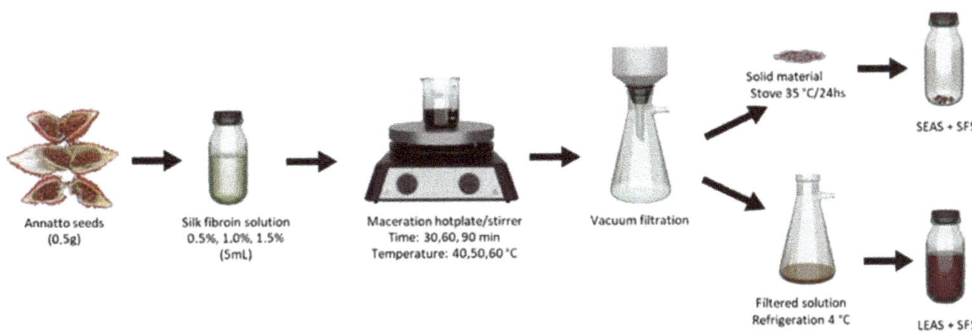

Figure 1. Summary process of bixin extraction with silk fibroin solution.

2.6. Purified Bixin

Purified bixin (PB), used in the cell viability assay (control group), was obtained as described by Oliveira et al., 2022 [6]. Briefly, 25 g of annatto seeds were washed twice with 100 mL of hexane. After discarding the solvent, the seeds were washed twice with 100 mL of methanol, followed by methanol removal. The seeds were then washed twice with ethyl acetate (100 mL). Each washing and extraction step was carried out under magnetic stirring for 15 min, and subsequently subjected to vacuum filtration using a Büchner funnel. Following filtration, the final ethyl acetate extract was dried under reduced pressure using a rotary evaporator. The concentrated extract was then transferred to a container placed in an ice bath. Chloroform (5 mL) was slowly added, followed by the gradual addition of ethanol (20 mL). The solution was then kept at 18 °C for 12 h to allow recrystallization. The resulting crystalline product was further purified by recrystallization in ethanol (50 mL) and filtered again using a Büchner funnel to obtain pure bixin. The purified bixin crystals were stored under protection from heat, moisture, and light. The chemical structure of the purified compound was subsequently verified through Fourier-transform infrared spectroscopy (FTIR), proton nuclear magnetic resonance (^{1}H NMR), and carbon-13 nuclear magnetic resonance (^{13}C NMR) analyses.

2.7. Chemical Characterization

2.7.1. Quantification of Bixin Content by UV-Vis Spectroscopy

The bixin content in each experimental combination (Section 2.4, Table 1, total = 30 samples) was quantified using a spectrophotometer (PerkElmer® Lambda 35 UV-Vis, Vaughan, Canada) equipped with 1 cm quartz cuvettes across a wavelength range of 300 to 600 nm. The standard bixin stock solution, prepared with 0.2 mg/L in ethanol and diluted to different concentrations (1.5, 2.0, 3.0 4.0, 6.0, 8.0, and 10.0 μg/mL), was used to construct the standard curve [y = 0.1216x + 0.0197 (R^2 = 0.991)]. Sample analysis was conducted using stock solutions prepared from LEAS + SFS (0.1 μL of the sample diluted in 9.9 mL of ethanol) and SEAS + SFS (1 mg of the sample diluted in 10 mL of ethanol). Subsequently, 0.5 mL of stock solution (SEAS + SFS and LEAS + SFS) was diluted in 2.5 mL of ethanol for spectrophotometric analysis.

2.7.2. Fourier Transform Infrared (FTIR) Analysis

The best parameter identified by the BBD design (Run 2, Table 2) for bixin extraction was used to prepare the SEAS + SFS and LEAS + SFS samples evaluated in this analysis. A Fourier transform infrared spectrophotometer (Spectrum Two FT; PerkinElmer, Inc., Waltham, MA, USA), with an attenuated total reflection (ATR) sampling accessory, a diamond plate, and a deuterated triglycine sulfate detector was used to record the spectra of SEAS + SFS and LEAS + SFS, as well as SFS and PB. The spectral range was set between 350 and 4000 cm^{-1}, and the resolution was adjusted to 0.5 cm^{-1} [36].

Table 2. Bixin content in each experimental combination of the Box-Behnken design (BBD).

Experiment (Run)	Temperature (°C)	Time (min)	Concentration SFS (%)	Bixin Content (LEAS + SFS) mg/mL	Bixin Content (SEAS + SFS) mg/g
1	40	30	1. 0	6.44	72.48
2	60	60	1.5	10.87	150.72
3	50	30	0.5	2.89	106.68
4	60	30	1.0	3.54	216.36
5	50	60	1.0	4.38	103.32
6	40	90	1.0	5.12	70.56
7	50	60	1.0	3.49	95.52
8	40	60	0.5	2.16	175.44
9	50	90	0.5	4.94	134.52
10	50	60	1.0	6.94	136.56
11	60	90	1.0	5.52	90.6
12	50	90	1.5	9.20	130.56
13	50	30	1.5	6.73	150.24
14	40	60	1.5	6.48	137.4
15	60	60	0.5	2.96	84.72

2.7.3. Analysis of Purified Bixin by ^1H and ^{13}C NMR

The ^1H and ^{13}C NMR spectra of purified bixin were recorded using an Agilent 400/54 Premium Shielded spectrometer (Agilent, Santa Clara, CA, USA) operating at 400 MHz (^1H NMR) and 100 MHz (^{13}C NMR). Deuterated chloroform ($CDCl_3$) was employed as the solvent. Chemical shifts (δ) were expressed in parts per million (ppm) and referenced relative to the internal standard tetramethylsilane (TMS) and the deuterated solvent ($CDCl_3$, δH 7.26; $CDCl_3$, δC 77.16). Spectral data were analyzed using Master New version 9.0.

2.8. Cell Culture

Neonatal human dermal fibroblasts (HDFn cells) and macrophages (RAW 264.7 cells) were cultured in Dulbecco's Modified Eagle's Medium (DMEM, Vitrocell® Embriolife). The medium was supplemented with 10% fetal bovine serum (FBS) (Vitrocell® Embriolife, Brazil). The cultures were maintained in a humidified incubator at 37 °C with 5% CO_2 in the Nanomedicine and Nano-toxicology Laboratory of the Physics Institute of São Carlos, University of São Paulo (São Carlos—SP), for kindly providing the HDFn and RAW 264.7 cell lines.

2.9. Cell Viability Assay

Bixin extracted under the optimal conditions identified by the BBD design (Run 2, Table 2) was utilized for the cell viability assay. The viability of HDFn and RAW 264.7 cells was assessed following treatment with SEAS + SFS, LEAS + SFS, PB, and SFS using the colorimetric 3-[4,5-dimethyl-thiazol-2-yl]-2,5-diphenyltetrazolium bromide (MTT) assay (Sigma-Aldrich, São Paulo, Brazil).

HDFn and RAW 264.7 cells were seeded in 96-well plates at a density of 1×10^4 cells/well and incubated at 37 °C in a 5% CO_2 atmosphere to allow cell adhesion. After 24 h, freshly prepared SEAS + SFS, LEAS + SFS, PB, and SFS samples at varying concentrations (0.016 to 2 μg/L) were added to the cell cultures and incubated for 24 and 72 h. Following the incubation period, the treatments were removed, and 200 μL of MTT solution (0.5 mg/mL in culture medium) was added to each well. The plate was then incubated for an additional 4 h. After this, the supernatant was discarded, and 100 μL of DMSO was added to solubilize the formazan crystals. The optical density of each well was measured at 570 nm using a multi-scanner automatic reader (SpectraMax M3, Molecular Devices, San Jose, CA, USA).

The solvent control consisted of cells treated with 0.1% and 0.5% DMSO, used to solubilize PB and SEAS + SFS, respectively. The negative control consisted of untreated cells maintained in culture medium (100% cell viability), while the positive control consisted of cells treated with 20% DMSO (100% cell death). Results were expressed as a percentage of cell viability relative to the controls, based on absorbance data from three independent experiments performed in triplicate (N = 9 assays per concentration) [37,38].

2.10. Statistical Analysis

The Design-Expert® Software (version 11, Stat-Ease Inc., Minneapolis, MN, USA) statistical package was used for BBD experimental design and data analysis. Analysis of variance (ANOVA) was used to evaluate the extraction efficiency in terms of bixin yield and to determine the significance, influence, and interactions of the independent variables, demonstrating the seed/SFS solution concentration ratio, temperature, and extraction time on bixin yield. All cell viability assays were analyzed in GraphPad Prism® (8.0) and Microsoft™ Excel 2016.

3. Results and Discussion

3.1. Analysis of Bixin Content by UV-Vis Spectroscopy and Optimization of Extraction Process Parameters Using the Box-Behnken Design

Conventionally, bixin extraction from annatto seeds occurs by indirect extraction using organic solvents, such as chloroform, ethanol, acetone and ethyl acetate, which is generally more effective and promotes a purer extraction of the pigment; and by direct extraction using hot vegetable oil (soybean, corn) or dilute alkaline solutions of potassium or sodium hydroxide. Industrially, the most widely used process is extraction with alkaline solution [21,39,40].

Parameters such as temperature, extraction time and seed/solvent ratio are applied in the different extraction methods. Regardless of the technique used, due to the instability of this pigment, its degradation by light is mainly taken into consideration, since bixin is photosensitive, in addition to the temperature and duration of the heating process, as well as oxidation in the presence of certain solvents [12,13].

However, bixin, due to its polarity, requires the use of organic solvents, which are related to human toxicity, environmental pollution, and high production costs, since they require additional separation techniques [7]. Therefore, it is important to develop methods based on "green" technologies for the extraction of bixin, which are efficient, environmentally safe, and economically viable [12,13,41,42].

In this sense, our work proposes the use of silk fibroin solution (SFS), a natural protein of animal origin, as a solvent for the extraction of bixin present in annatto seeds, as an alternative to traditional solvents.

Fibroin is amphiphilic in nature, due to the presence in its molecular structure of hydrophobic domains (heavy, major and nonpolar chain) and hydrophilic domains (light, minor and polar chain) in its molecular structure. The hydrophobic domain, which is crystalline in nature, contains organized and repeated sequences of amino acids (Gly-Ala-Gly-Ala-Ser), which are arranged in a β-sheet conformation. The hydrophilic region, which is amorphous in nature, is composed of amino acids distributed in a disordered manner, with no defined secondary structure [24,28]. Bixin is a predominantly lipid-soluble compound, with a greater affinity for nonpolar solvents, although its structure contains polar functional groups, such as carboxylic acid (polar head) and methyl ester (relatively nonpolar tail), which contribute to a certain degree of polarity [41]. Bixin can occur in *cis* (more unstable, soluble in moderately polar organic solvents) and *trans* (more stable configuration, with greater solubility in oils) forms. Approximately 80% of the bixin present in the seeds is in the cis form, which has low solubility in water due to the presence of the methoxycarbonyl group (–$COOCH_3$) [43]. Furthermore, the presence of a triglyceride layer in the seeds hinders the penetration of solvents into the substrate, compromising extraction efficiency [6,44]. Removal of this lipid fraction favors the access of bixin to solvents, facilitating its extraction [14,44]. Nonpolar solvents are more effective in extracting lipids associated with bixin [6]. It is also observed that solvents of different polarities promote bixin extractions with different yields [12,13,41], which reinforces the notion that bixin has a moderate amphiphilic character, with distinct polarity regions capable of establishing different types of interactions with solvents. Thus, the presence of hydrophobic and hydrophilic domains in fibroin not only favored the removal of the lipid layer from the seeds, but also contributed to a more efficient extraction of bixin, as evidenced in the results presented (Figure 2, Table 2).

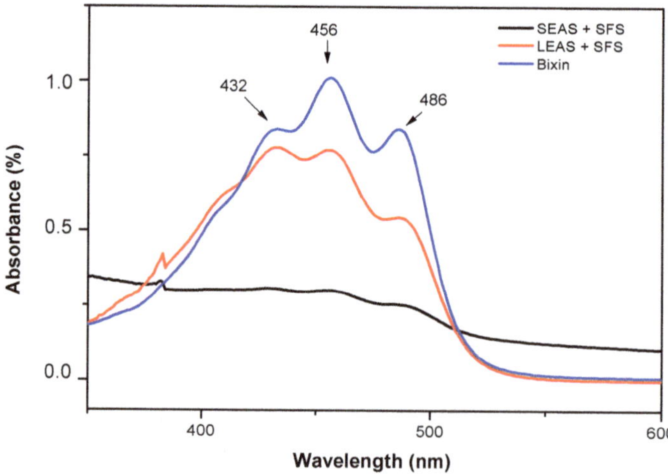

Figure 2. UV-Vis spectrum of samples SEAS + SFS (Run 2), LEAS + SFS (Run 2) and PB.

In addition to using SFS as a solvent to extract bixin, for the extraction method, we applied the Box-Behnken (BBD) experimental design, a statistical optimization of the process, with the aim of investigating the effect of the extraction variables (SFS concentration, temperature and time) on the bixin yield, and also identifying the best conditions for the process. Data analysis is performed based on the response surface methodology and Pareto chart (Figures 3 and 4).

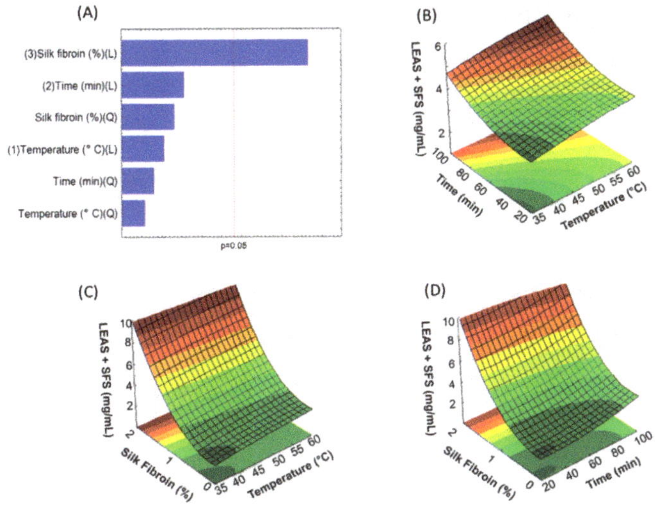

Figure 3. Bixin content response in LEAS + SFS. Pareto chart (**A**) and three-dimensional response surface plots showing the effects of (**B**) time and temperature, (**C**) SFS concentrations and temperature, and (**D**) SFS concentrations and time. The red dotted vertical line of the Pareto chart (subfigure (**A**)) represents the boundary between significant and non-significant effects with a 5% risk of error. The color gradient (subfigures (**B–D**)) indicates the magnitude of the response: green regions indicate lower values, yellow regions intermediate values and orange/red regions the highest values.

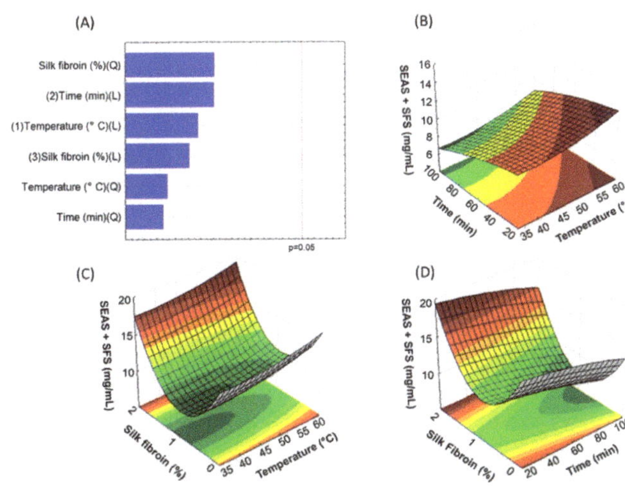

Figure 4. Bixin content response in SEAS + SFS. Pareto chart (**A**) and three-dimensional response surface plots showing the effects of (**B**) time and temperature, (**C**) SFS concentrations and temperature, (**D**) SFS concentrations and time. The red dotted vertical line of the Pareto chart (subfigure (**A**)) represents the boundary between significant and non-significant effects with a 5% risk of error. The color gradient (subfigures (**B–D**)) indicates the magnitude of the response: green regions indicate lower values, yellow regions intermediate values and orange/red regions the highest values.

UV-Vis spectrophotometry is the most widely used method for determining dye concentration in plant extracts [45]. Therefore, the extraction efficiency of SFS on bixin content, in LEAS + SFS and SEAS + SFS, in each experimental combination (item 2.4, Table 1, total = 30 samples), was evaluated using the absorbance spectrophotometry technique in the UV-Vis region in a wavelength range of 300 to 600 nm, and the results are summarized in Table 2.

The conjugated double bond system in bixin constitutes the absorption chromophore above 400 nm (Figure 2). The absorbance spectrum for the standard bixin, solubilized in ethanol, showed peaks at 432, 456 and 486 nm. The SEAS + SFS sample showed an absorbance profile similar to that of the standard bixin (Figure 2), while the LEAS + SFS sample showed lower absorbance values at λ Max (Figure 2), which is in agreement with the results of [41], who reported that bixin has a higher affinity for polar solvents.

From the UV-Vis analysis results, the best parameter identified by the BBD design for bixin extraction was Run 2 (seed/concentration ratio 1.5% SFS at 60 °C for 60 min of magnetic stirring (Table 2), presenting a bixin content of 10.87 mg/mL in LEAS + SFS and 150.72 mg/g in SEAS + SFS (Table 2). This parameter was used to produce the LEAS + SFS and SEAS + SFS samples for infrared analysis and cell viability assay, and its UV-Vis spectrum is also shown in Figure 2.

According to the results, bixin contents in LEAS + SFS and SEAS + SFS ranged from 2.16 mg/mL (Run 8) to 10.87 mg/mL (Run 2) and 70.56 mg/g (Run 6) at 216.36 mg/g (Run 4), respectively (Table 2).

The maximum (10.87 mg/mL) and minimum (2.16 mg/mL) bixin content in LEAS + SFS were observed for the parameter combinations, with a seed/SFS concentration ratio of 1.5% at 60 °C for 60 min of agitation (Run 2) and a seed/SFS concentration ratio of 0.5% at 40 °C for 60 min of agitation (Run 8), respectively (Table 2). In SEAS + SFS, the maximum (216.36 mg/g) and minimum (70.56 mg/g) bixin content was observed for the parameter combinations, with a seeds/SFS concentration ratio of 1.0% at 60 °C for 30 min of agitation (Run 4) and a seed/SFS concentration ratio of 1.0% at 40 °C for 90 min of agitation (Run 6), respectively (Table 2).

The results of SEAS + SFS showed the highest levels of bixin, compared to LEAS + SFS, mainly in Run 4, with a maximum level of 216.36 mg/g. It is suggested that this result is due to a higher bixin content in the aril of *B. orellana* seeds [41]. The aril present on the outer surface of *B. orellana* seeds is rich in carotenoids, of which 80% is represented by the main carotenoid bixin [46].

However, although the yield of LEAS + SFS is lower than that of SEAS + SFS, the results are still comparable, since bixin in LEAS + SFS could be quantified by UV-Vis analysis. This finding indicates that SFS can extract a considerable amount of bixin. Thus, SFS may serve as a viable green alternative to the organic solvent extraction process, albeit with a slightly reduced bixin yield.

To enable factor-response analysis and understand the relationship between the variables in the data set, from the collected results, a Pareto chart and response surface were generated for all variables, to determine the significance of the influence of the factors (SFS concentration, temperature, and time) on the bixin content in LEAS + SFS (Figure 3) and SEAS + SFS (Figure 4).

Figure 3A shows that SFS concentration was the most influential factor on bixin content in the LEAS + SFS sample, with a statistically significant effect ($p < 0.05$).

Regarding SEAS + SFS, none of the factors (SFS concentration, temperature and time) significantly influenced the 95% confidence level for the bixin content response (Figure 4A).

According to the Pareto chart (Figure 3A), SFS was the factor that most significantly influenced the bixin content for the LEAS + SFS sample. Given this, we can conclude that increasing the SFS concentration could increase the extracted bixin levels, since the highest bixin level in LEAS + SFS was observed for the parameter combinations with a seed/SFS concentration ratio of 1.5% (Runs 2, 12, 13 and 14), that is, with SFS at its highest concentration used in this study.

To establish the significance of the adjusted model, analysis of variance (ANOVA) was used (Tables S1 and S2 of Supplementary Materials). A smaller p-value ($p < 0.05$) indicates that an individual factor is significant in the model [13]. In the case of LEAS + SFS, the SFS concentration had a more significant effect on the bixin content, with a p-value < 0.05 (Table S1 of Supplementary Materials). As for SEAS + SFS, none of the factors had a lower p-value ($p < 0.05$), and consequently did not have a significant effect on the bixin content (Table S2 of Supplementary Materials).

The concentration of bixin in *B. orellana* seeds varies according to environmental factors, such as crop variety, soil, climate, cultivation, growth conditions and post-harvest practices. Meanwhile, the extraction method, extraction conditions and parameters, and mainly, the polarity of the solvent used, significantly impact the extraction of bixin, and consequently its final content [6,12,13].

The impact of different organic solvents and their polarities on bixin yield, and the optimization of process parameters such as time, temperature and seed/solvent ratio were investigated in various/different studies.

Jayakumar et al., 2023 [13] showed that extraction with ethyl acetate (medium-nonpolar solvent) and methanol (polar solvent) produced the highest bixin contents, furthermore, bixin content increased with time (10, 20, and 30 min) and temperature (50, 60, and 70 °C) in the extracts in ethyl acetate, methanol and ethanol. Erdawati et al., 2021 [47] also found that ethyl acetate produced high bixin content.

David et al., 2022 [15] observed that increases in temperature and seed/solvent ratio increased bixin yield even in polar solvents, such as ethanol. According to Quiroz et al., 2019 [18], a higher seeds:solvent ratio associated with sufficient contact time promotes an increase in the affinity of the compounds with the solvents, resulting in greater bixin extraction.

Sudha et al., 2023 [12] observed that increasing the extraction time increased the bixin content, but after 30 min of extraction, it started to decrease, due to the thermal degradation effect of bixin pigment under high temperature for a longer time, since rapid increase in temperature facilitates the migration of pigments into the extraction medium [12,46].

In addition to organic solvents, researchers have studied the use of "generally recognized as safe" (GRAS) solvents, such as water, and green solvents, such as PEG and ethyl lactate for bixin extraction. These techniques are being studied with the aim of developing clean extraction technologies with environmental benefits [21].

Handayani et al., 2024 [21] extracted bixin by maceration using distilled water at various pH (4, 7 and 9) and extraction times (5, 7.5 and 10 min). The results showed that the variation in the pH of distilled water and extraction time influences the bixin levels. The highest levels of bixin (61.06%) were extracted in distilled water (pH 7, extraction time 7.5 min). These findings validate the use of distilled water as an alternative solvent to extract annatto pigment.

It was reported that the aqueous extract obtained at 50 °C for 30 min at a concentration ratio of 1:30 (1 g of seeds per 30 mL of water) under magnetic stirring (150 rpm), observed that the bixin content in the extract increased significantly in the extraction time of up to 30 min and remained approximately constant after this period [42]. The maximum bixin content was 5.80 ± 0.32%, which is equivalent to a bixin concentration of 72.21 ± 2.82 mg L^{-1}; therefore, the aqueous extraction showed adequate efficiency, with the advantages of using a safe and environmentally friendly solvent.

In parallel with the use of water as a solvent, compounds such as polyethylene glycols (PEG) have been used as a green solvent for bixin extraction. PEGs have amphiphilic characteristics, which provide an increase in the aqueous solubility of some compounds with low polarity. Another particularity of PEGs is their acceptance in the food area, which has stimulated their use for the extraction of bioactive compounds with applicability in food, becoming an environmentally friendly alternative for bixin extraction [15,48,49].

David et al., 2022 [15] concluded that PEG-400 could produce 40% more dye (2.7 mgBix/gExt) than ethanol in times longer than 50 min, while ethanol achieved the maximum bixin concentration (1.6 mgBix/gExt) in just 34 min. PEG showed slower extraction than ethanol, but with a higher final bixin yield. This result demonstrates that amphiphilic solvents can be a viable alternative for bixin extraction.

Silk fibroin (SF), like PEG, has amphiphilic characteristics and application in food preservation, according to results shown by [50], who developed an edible coating material based on SF for preserving perishable fruits. The results suggested that SF coatings prolonged freshness and firmness, delayed respiration and prevented dehydration of perishable fruits.

Ethyl lactate is a green solvent that in terms of polarity is considered comparable to acetonitrile (polar). In addition, it forms different types of chemical interactions, such as hydrogen bonds and Van der Waals bonds, providing miscibility with polar/hydrophilic and nonpolar/hydrophobic carotenoids [41,51].

Recently, ref. [41] used ethyl lactate to extract bixin from annatto seeds (crushed and whole). The results indicated that the ethyl lactate extracts yielded 14.62% and 16.5% bixin for the whole and crushed seeds, respectively. This finding indicates that ethyl lactate can extract a considerable amount of bixin.

3.2. *Chemical Characterization*

3.2.1. Fourier Transform Infrared (FTIR) Analysis

FTIR analysis identified the spectral profile of SEAS + SFS, LEAS + SFS, PB, and SFS, complementing the data obtained from the UV-Vis analysis. The FTIR spectrum for purified bixin (PB) (Figure 5A) displays characteristic vibration bands of the main functional groups. These include bands at 3176 cm^{-1} (O-H carboxylic acid), at 3033 cm^{-1} (C-H olefinic), at 2981 cm^{-1} (C-H methyl group), at 1716 cm^{-1} (C=O ester group), and 1607 cm^{-1} (C=C conjugated alkenes), consistent with the findings of Bitencourt et al. (2018) [52].

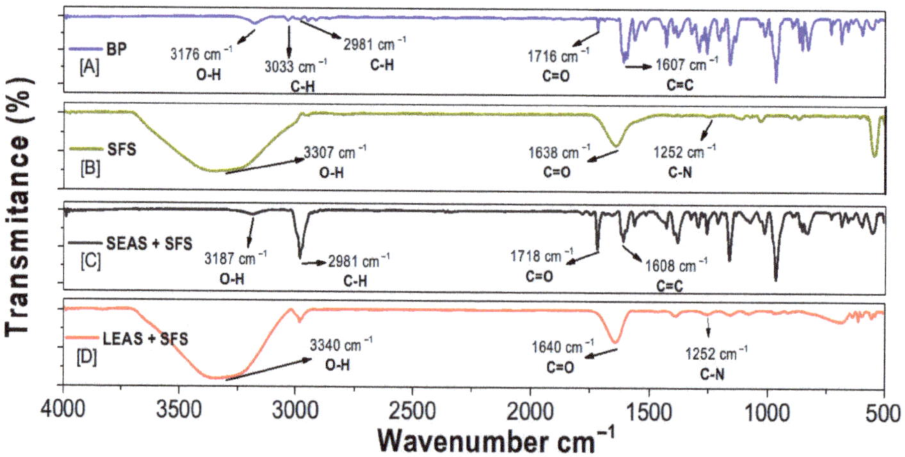

Figure 5. FTIR spectra of purified Bixin (**A**); SFS (**B**); SEAS + SFS (**C**); LEAS + SFS (**D**).

The FTIR spectrum of the silk fibroin solution (SFS) (Figure 5B) exhibited characteristic vibration bands corresponding to the main functional groups in fibroin. These included 3307 cm^{-1} (O-H group), 1638 cm^{-1} (C=O from amide group), and 1252 cm^{-1} (C-N from amide), as reported by Marinho et al. (2023) [32] (Figure 5B).

The SEAS + SFS spectrum (Figure 5C) exhibited vibration bands similar to those in the PB spectrum, such as 3187 cm^{-1} (O-H of the COOH group), 2981 cm^{-1} (CH of the CH3 group), 1718 cm^{-1} (C=O of the ester), and 1608 cm^{-1} of C=C (conjugated alkenes). These bands align with the UV-Vis analysis results, indicating that SEAS + SFS contained the highest bixin levels. On the other hand, the LEAS + SFS spectrum (Figure 5D) displayed only the characteristic vibration bands of fibroin, including 3340 cm^{-1} (O-H group), 1640 cm^{-1} (C=O group), and 1252 cm^{-1} (C-N of the amide group).

3.2.2. Analysis of Purified Bixin by ^{1}H and ^{13}C NMR

Figure 6 shows the results of ^{1}H and ^{13}C NMR analysis to identify signals from PB functional groups and confirm its structure.

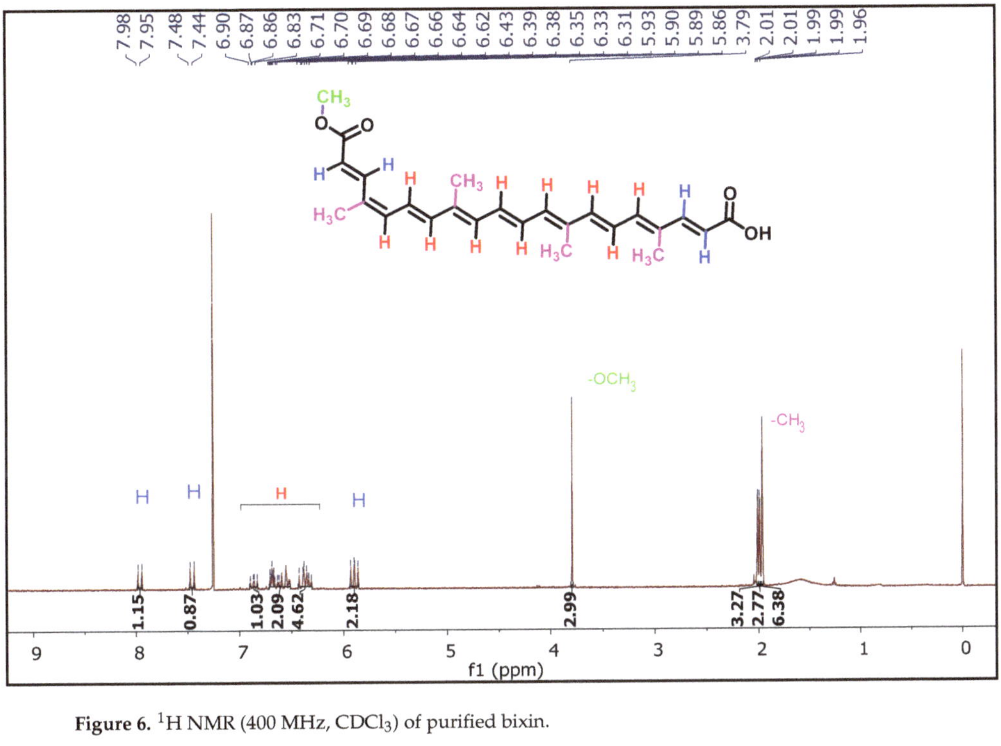

Figure 6. ^{1}H NMR (400 MHz, $CDCl_3$) of purified bixin.

We identified the main signals related to the bixin functional groups by ^{1}H NMR (Figure 6). These include signals from olefinic hydrogens at 7.96 ppm (*J* = 15.4 Hz, 1H); 7.48 ppm (*J* = 15.5 Hz, 1H), and 5.90 ppm (*J* = 15.5, 13.6 Hz, 2H), which correspond to the double bonds adjacent to the carboxylic acid and ester groups, respectively. Signals olefinic hydrogens of the aliphatic chain, with peaks ranging from 6.71–6.30 ppm (multiplets for 10 hydrogens). A singlet at 3.79 ppm corresponds to the three hydrogens of the methoxyl group of the ester group, and the signals from the 12 hydrogens of the CH_3 groups of the aliphatic structure of the molecule that appear in the 2.01–1.96 ppm range. The signal from the hydrogen of the hydroxyl group corresponding to the carboxylic acid does not appear, likely due to isotopic exchange with the deuterated solvent.

^{13}C NMR spectra exhibited carbon signals corresponding to functional groups that support bixin's structural composition (Table 3). The most prominent signals included the -C=O resonances at 170.75 and 167.97 ppm, associated with the carboxylic acid and ester carbonyl groups. Within the 151.0–114.8 ppm range, 17 signals of olefinic carbons appeared. A characteristic signal identified as of the carbon in the $-OCH_3$ group of the ester appeared at 51.58 ppm. Additionally, four signals characteristic of $-CH_3$ carbons appeared between 20.26 and 12.62 ppm (Table 3). So, the analyses of ^{1}H and ^{13}C NMR provided evidence of the main signals from the functional groups in bixin, confirming the structure of the compound, according to the analyses by Patra Soumen et al., 2021 [53] (Table 3).

Table 3. Experimental data from ^{13}C NMR spectroscopy ($CDCl_3$, 100 MHz) for bixin.

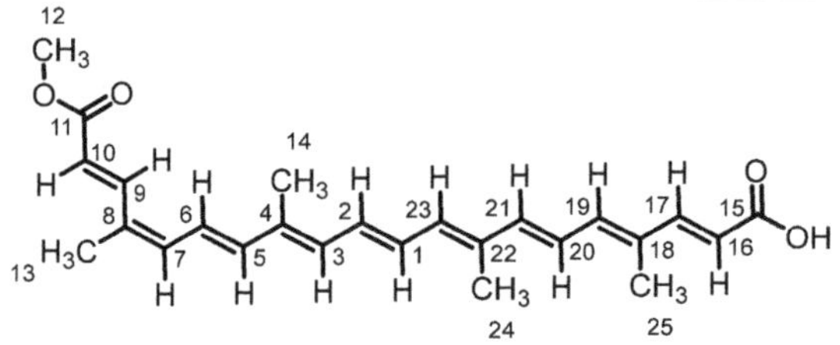

Carbon Number *	δ ^{13}C (ppm)	
	Present Study	**[53]**
1	124.18	130.73
2	130.70	130.73
3	131.42	131.46
4	135.18	135.22
5	137.12	137.14
6	117.52	123.38
7	140.36	140.39
8	133.27	133.57
9	142.34	142.38
10	114.83	117.53
11	167.97	168.01
12	51.58	51.61
13	20.26	20.56
14	12.62	12.63
15	170.75	171.67
16	114.83	115.0
17	151.03	151.08
18	134.18	134.21
19	140.44	140.50
20	123.36	124.21
21	137.91	137.95
22	136.53	136.56
23	131.58	131.60
24	12.99	13.01
25	12.76	12.77

3.3. Cell Viability Assay

The potential pharmaceutical applications of LEAS + SF and SEAS + SFS extracts are contingent upon various factors, including the biocompatibility of these materials. One key parameter for assessing biocompatibility is their impact on cell viability. Therefore, in this study, the viability of HDFn cells and RAW macrophages was evaluated following treatment with these materials using the MTT assay. This method relies on the metabolic activity of viable cells, as their mitochondrial function facilitates the conversion of tetrazolium salt into formazan crystals. The resulting intense purple coloration is directly proportional to cell viability [54,55].

Neonatal human dermal fibroblasts (HDFn cells) and macrophages (RAW 264.7 cells) were selected for the cell viability assay considering the potential biomedical applications of silk fibroin [56–64], annatto seed extract [41,65,66] and bixin [41,67], specifically in the area of tissue repair, with a biological approach to wound healing.

The results demonstrated that exposure of HDFn cells to LEAS + SFS, SEAS + SFS, PB, and SFS for 24 h (acute exposure) or 72 h (long-term effect following acute exposure) (ISO 10993-5, 2009 [68,69]) did not reduce cell viability at any of the tested concentrations compared to the control group ($p < 0.05$), with viability levels remaining within the 70–100% range (Figure 7A). According to the ISO 10993-5 [69] standard, cell viability below 70% indicates cytotoxic potential; therefore, LEAS + SFS, SEAS + SFS, PB, and SFS did not exhibit cytotoxicity at the tested concentrations in HDFn cells. Moreover, the results suggest that LEAS + SFS and SFS promoted HDFn cell proliferation, as cell viability exceeded 100% (Figure 7B).

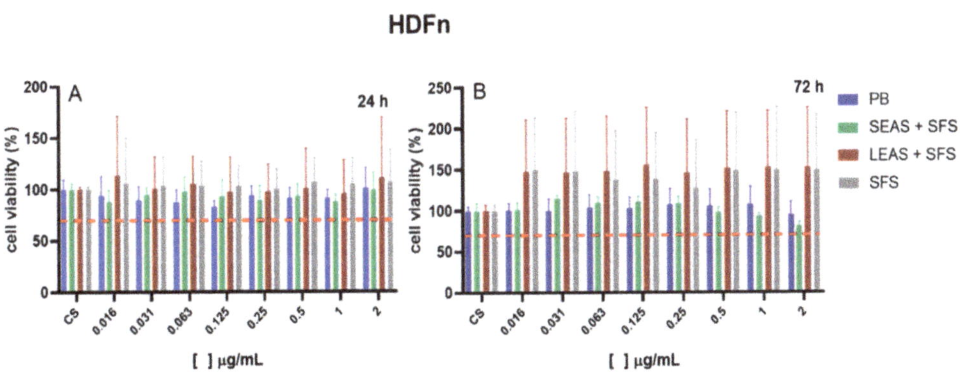

Figure 7. Cytotoxic activity of LEAS + SFS, SEAS + SFS, PB, and SFS at concentrations of 0.016 to 2.0 µg/mL on neonatal human dermal fibroblasts (HDFn cells) at 24 h (**A**) and 72 h (**B**). Data were expressed as a percentage of cell viability. The red dotted horizontal line represents the cutoff point for 70% viability.

For RAW 264.7 cells, exposure to LEAS + SFS, SEAS + SFS, PB, and SFS for 24 and 72 h did not reduce cell viability below 70% at concentrations ranging from 0.016 to 1.0 µg/mL compared to the control group ($p < 0.05$) (Figure 8A,B). However, at a concentration of 2.0 µg/mL PB, and LEAS + SFS exhibited cytotoxic effects on macrophages, with viability decreasing to 69% and 46%, respectively, following prolonged exposure (72 h) (Figure 8B). These findings support previous evidence that bixin can reduce macrophage populations in inflammatory models [70,71].

Fibroblasts and macrophages are cells that play an important role in all stages of the healing process [72] and are widely used to evaluate the cell viability of bioactive compounds [41,59,67,73–76] and in screening the bioactivity of natural products [77–80].

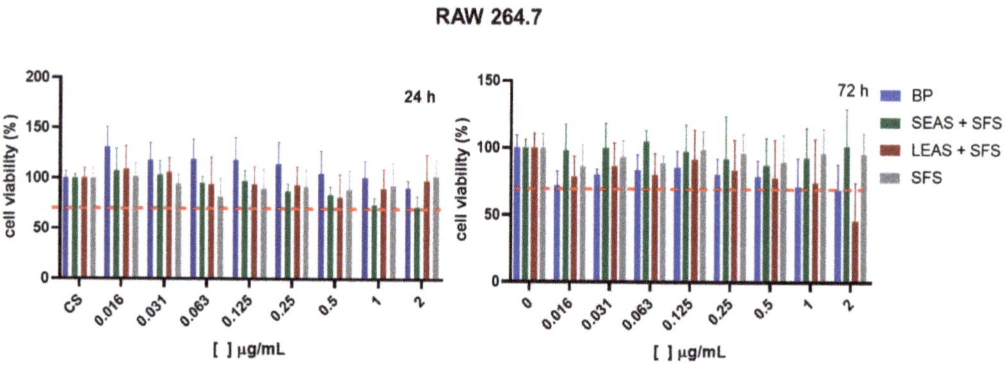

(A)

(B)

Figure 8. Cytotoxic activity of LEAS + SFS, SEAS + SFS, PB and SFS at concentrations of 0.016 to 2.0 µg/mL on macrophages (RAW 264.7 cells) at 24 h (**A**) and 72 h (**B**). The data were expressed as a percentage of cell viability. The red dotted horizontal line represents the cutoff point for 70% viability.

Several bioactive materials and compounds have been investigated for their healing potential, with topical application being preferred in experimental trials due to its direct application to the damaged tissue [81]. Considering that dermal fibroblasts and macrophages represent cell populations abundantly distributed in the epidermal and dermal layers [82], these cell types constitute relevant biological models for evaluating the cutaneous response to topical exposure to bioactive substances. Furthermore, because they are susceptible to irritants, analyzing their viability and functionality can provide important parameters regarding the cytotoxic or immunomodulatory potential of the tested compounds [83].

Furthermore, studies addressing the use of these cell lines to evaluate the cellular viability of these materials are scarce in the literature. The results obtained (non-cytotoxic concentrations) may be used in subsequent studies to evaluate biological activity in vivo.

4. Conclusions

This study demonstrated the technical feasibility and sustainability of using silk fibroin solution (SFS) as a green solvent for the extraction of bixin from annatto seeds (*Bixa orellana* L.). Optimization using the Box-Behnken design identified the optimal extraction conditions, as 1.5% SFS, 60 °C, and 60 min, resulting in bixin concentrations of 10.87 mg/mL (LEAS + SFS) and 150.72 mg/g (SEAS + SFS). These values are comparable to those obtained with conventional organic solvents, without the environmental and toxicological risks associated with these methods.

Chemical characterization confirmed the presence of bixin in the extracts, and cell viability assays showed that SFS and bixin-rich extracts maintained ≥70% viability in HDFn fibroblasts and RAW 264.7 macrophages, indicating low cytotoxicity and good biocompatibility. These findings suggest the potential of extracts obtained with SFS for applications in the food, cosmetics, and biomedical sectors, contributing to clean-label and environmentally responsible production chains.

Limitations of this study include the focus on in vitro analyses with two cell lines and the lack of functional or long-term evaluations. Future work should include in vivo validation of therapeutic properties, assessment of physicochemical stability in formulations, and comparisons with other green solvents to more precisely define the role of SFS in sustainable extraction technologies.

Overall, the use of SFS as a biocompatible and biodegradable solvent is in line with the principles of green chemistry. This approach contributes to the advancement of sustainable extraction processes to obtain high-value-added natural compounds, reinforcing the viability of green solvents.

Supplementary Materials: The following supporting information can be downloaded at: https://www.mdpi.com/article/10.3390/su17167518/s1, Table S1: Analysis of variance (ANOVA) on the effect of different combinations of seed/SFS concentration ratio, temperature and extraction time on bixin content in LEAS + SFS; Table S2: Analysis of variance (ANOVA) on the effect of different combinations of seed/SFS concentration ratio, temperature and extraction time on the bixin content in SEAS + SFS.

Author Contributions: Conceptualization, S.F.B. and I.M.F.; methodology, S.F.B., F.H.e.H., K.C.D.M., S.d.S.d.C.O., D.E.Q.J., C.M.L., V.Z. and I.M.F.; software, F.H.e.H.; formal analysis, S.F.B., F.H.e.H., K.C.D.M., S.d.S.d.C.O., D.E.Q.J., C.M.L., V.Z. and I.M.F.; resources, I.M.F.; data curation, S.F.B., F.H.e.H., D.E.Q.J., C.M.L., V.Z. and I.M.F.; writing—original draft preparation, S.F.B., C.M.L., V.Z. and I.M.F.; writing—review and editing, S.F.B., C.M.L., V.Z. and I.M.F.; supervision, I.M.F.; project administration, I.M.F.; funding acquisition, I.M.F. All authors have read and agreed to the published version of the manuscript.

Funding: This research was funded by the National Council for Scientific and Technological Development (Process No. 444009/2024-8 and 445078/2024-3) and Borges, S.F. received a scholarship funded by the Coordination for the Improvement of Higher Education Personnel—Brazil (CAPES) No. 52001016062P2.

Institutional Review Board Statement: Not applicable.

Informed Consent Statement: Not applicable.

Data Availability Statement: The original contributions presented in this study are included in the article. Further inquiries can be directed to the corresponding author.

Acknowledgments: The authors would like to thank Valtencir Zucolotto, from the Nanomedicine and Nano-toxicology Group of the Physics Institute of São Carlos, University of São Paulo (São Carlos—SP), for kindly providing the HDFn and RAW 264.7 cell lines, as well as for providing the infrastructure necessary to perform the in vitro cytotoxicity assays.

Conflicts of Interest: The authors declare no conflicts of interest. The funders had no role in the design of the study; in the collection, analyses, or interpretation of data; in the writing of the manuscript; or in the decision to publish the results.

Abbreviations

The following abbreviations are used in this manuscript:

PB	Purified bixin
SFS	Silk fibroin solution
BBD	Box-Behnken experimental design
FTIR	Fourier transform infrared
NMR	Nuclear magnetic resonance
MTT	3-(4,5-dimethylthiazol-2-yl)-2,5-diphenyltetrazolium bromide
LEAS + SFS	Liquid extract of annatto seeds from silk fibroin solution
SEAS + SFS	Solid extract of annatto seeds from silk fibroin solution
LOX	Lipoxygenase
HDFn	Human neonatal dermal fibroblasts
RAW 264.7	Murine macrophages
DMEN	Dulbecco's Modified Eagle's Medium
DMSO	Dimethyl sulfoxide or dimethyl sulfoxide
Na_2CO_3	Sodium carbonate
H_2O: EtOH: $CaCl_2$	Water: Ethanol: Calcium chloride

KDa	Kilo Dalton
CO_2	Carbon dioxide
Gly	Glycine
Ala	Alanine
Ser	Serine
MHz	Megahertz
$CDCl_3$	Deuterated chloroform
$CaCl_2$	Calcium chloride

References

1. De Oliveira Júnior, R.G.; Bonnet, A.; Braconnier, E.; Groult, H.; Prunier, G.; Beaugeard, L.; Grougnet, R.; da Silva Almeida, J.R.G.; Ferraz, C.A.A.; Picot, L. Bixin, an Apocarotenoid Isolated from *Bixa orellana* L., Sensitizes Human Melanoma Cells to Dacarbazine-Induced Apoptosis through ROS-Mediated Cytotoxicity. *Food Chem. Toxicol.* **2019**, *125*, 549–561. [CrossRef]
2. Cruz Lima, R.J.; De Deus Moreno, A.J.; Loureiro De Castro, S.F.; Santos Gonçalves, J.D.R.; De Olivera, A.B.; Sasaki, J.M.; Cavalcante Freire, P.D.T. Taninos Hidrolisáveis Em *Bixa orellana* L. *Quim. Nova* **2006**, *29*, 507–509. [CrossRef]
3. Medina-Flores, D.; Ulloa-Urizar, G.; Camere-Colarossi, R.; Caballero-García, S.; Mayta-Tovalino, F.; del Valle-Mendoza, J. Antibacterial Activity of *Bixa orellana* L. (Achiote) against *Streptococcus mutans* and *Streptococcus sanguinis*. *Asian Pac. J. Trop. Biomed.* **2016**, *6*, 400–403. [CrossRef]
4. Keita, H.; dos Santos, C.B.R.; Ramos, M.M.; Padilha, E.C.; Serafim, R.B.; Castro, A.N.; Amado, J.R.R.; da Silva, G.M.; Ferreira, I.M.; Giuliatti, S.; et al. Assessment of the Hypoglycemic Effect of Bixin in Alloxan-Induced Diabetic Rats: In vivo and in silico Studies. *J. Biomol. Struct. Dyn.* **2021**, *39*, 1017–1028. [CrossRef] [PubMed]
5. Nathan, V.K.; Rani, M.E.; Rathinasamy, G.; Narayanan Dhiraviam, K. Antioxidant and Antimicrobial Potential of Natural Colouring Pigment Derived from *Bixa orellana* L. Seed Aril. *Proc. Natl. Acad. Sci. India Sect. B Biol. Sci.* **2019**, *89*, 137–143. [CrossRef]
6. Oliveira, S.D.S.D.C.; Araújo, R.D.C.; da Silva, G.A.; Leitão, J.H.; da Silva Sousa, S.A.B.; Fonseca, L.P.; Carvalho, J.C.T.; Cantuária, P.; Hage-Melim, L.I.D.S.; Ferreira, I.M. *Bixa orellana* L. from Northern Brazil: Morphological Analysis, Phenolic Content, Antioxidant and Antibacterial Activities. *Braz. J. Bot.* **2022**, *45*, 883–896. [CrossRef]
7. Gatsou Djibersou, D.; Rosnay Tietcheu Galani, B.; Dieudonne Djamen Chuisseu, P.; Yanou Njintang, N. Anti-Oxidant and Anti-Inflammatory Potential of Aqueous Extracts of Leaves, Barks and Roots of *Bixa orellana* L. (Bixaceae) on Acetaminophen-Induced Liver Damage in Mice. *Avicenna J. Phytomed.* **2020**, *10*, 428–439.
8. Pacheco, S.D.G.; Gasparin, A.T.; Jesus, C.H.A.; Sotomaior, B.B.; Ventura, A.C.S.S.B.; Redivo, D.D.B.; Cabrini, D.D.A.; Gaspari Dias, J.D.F.; Miguel, M.D.; Miguel, O.G.; et al. Antinociceptive and Anti-Inflammatory Effects of Bixin, a Carotenoid Extracted from the Seeds of *Bixa orellana*. *Planta Med.* **2019**, *85*, 1216–1224. [CrossRef]
9. Rivera-Madrid, R.; Aguilar-Espinosa, M.; Cárdenas-Conejo, Y.; Garza-Caligaris, L.E. Carotenoid Derivates in Achiote (*Bixa orellana*) Seeds: Synthesis and Health Promoting Properties. *Front. Plant Sci.* **2016**, *7*, 1406. [CrossRef]
10. Kapoor, L.; Ramamoorthy, S. Strategies to Meet the Global Demand for Natural Food Colorant Bixin: A Multidisciplinary Approach. *J. Biotechnol.* **2021**, *338*, 40–51. [CrossRef]
11. Tao, S.; Park, S.L.; De La Vega, M.R.; Zhang, D.D.; Wondrak, G.T. Systemic Administration of the Apocarotenoid Bixin Protects Skin against Solar UV-Induced Damage through Activation of NRF2. *Free Radic. Biol. Med.* **2015**, *89*, 690–700. [CrossRef] [PubMed]
12. Sudha, P.; Manoja, V.; Deepa, J.; Jayakumar, J.; Kishore, S.G.; Pandiselvam, R. Optimization of Microwave-Assisted Aqueous Extraction of Pigments from Annatto Seeds Using Box-Behnken Design. *Biomass Convers. Biorefin* **2023**, *14*, 18775–18788. [CrossRef]
13. Jayakumar, J.; Sudha, P.; Rajkumar, P.; Pandiselvam, R.; Gurusamy, K.; Kumaran, K.; Subramanian, P. Comparative Study on the Effect of Solvents on Extraction of Bixin from Annatto Seed (*Bixa orellana* L.) and Optimization of Process Parameters Using Box–Behnken Design. *Biomass Convers. Biorefin.* **2023**, *14*, 19863–19874. [CrossRef]
14. Alcázar-Alay, S.C.; Osorio-Tobón, J.F.; Forster-Carneiro, T.; Meireles, M.A.A. Obtaining Bixin from Semi-Defatted Annatto Seeds by a Mechanical Method and Solvent Extraction: Process Integration and Economic Evaluation. *Food Res. Int.* **2017**, *99*, 393–402. [CrossRef]
15. David, S.L.J.; Julián, G.C.C.; Liliana, V.S.C.; Ayala-Aponte, A.A.; Liliana, S.C. Kinetics and Bixine Extraction Time from Achiote (*Bixa orellana* L.). *J. Food Sci. Technol.* **2022**, *59*, 1239–1246. [CrossRef]
16. Hirko, B.; Getu, A. *Bixa orellana* (Annatto Bixa): A Review on Use, Structure, Extraction Methods and Analysis. *J. Agron. Technol. Eng. Manag.* **2022**, *5*, 687–696.
17. Husa, N.N.; Hamzah, F.; Said, H.M. Characterization and Storage Stability Study of Bixin Extracted from *Bixa orellana* Using Organic Solvent. *IOP Conf. Ser. Mater. Sci. Eng.* **2018**, *358*, 012035. [CrossRef]

18. Quiroz, J.Q.; Torres, A.C.; Ramirez, L.M.; Garcia, M.S.; Gomez, G.C.; Rojas, J. Optimization of the Microwave-Assisted Extraction Process of Bioactive Compounds from Annatto Seeds (*Bixa orellana* L.). *Antioxidants* **2019**, *8*, 37. [CrossRef]
19. Taham, T.; Silva, D.O.; Barrozo, M.A.S. Improvement of Bixin Extraction from Annatto Seeds Using a Screen-Topped Spouted Bed. *Sep. Purif. Technol.* **2016**, *158*, 313–321. [CrossRef]
20. Yolmeh, M.; Habibi Najafi, M.B.; Farhoosh, R. Optimisation of Ultrasound-Assisted Extraction of Natural Pigment from Annatto Seeds by Response Surface Methodology (RSM). *Food Chem.* **2014**, *155*, 319–324. [CrossRef]
21. Handayani, I.; Septiana, A.T.; Sustriawan, B. Propriedades de Pigmentos Naturais e Antioxidantes Do Extrato de Urucum Em Vários PHs de Solventes de Água Destilada e Tempos de Extração. *Food Res.* **2024**, *8*, 489–494. [CrossRef]
22. Bachtler, S.; Bart, H.J. Increase the Yield of Bioactive Compounds from Elder Bark and Annatto Seeds Using Ultrasound and Microwave Assisted Extraction Technologies. *Food Bioprod. Process.* **2021**, *125*, 1–13. [CrossRef]
23. Zheng, H.; Zuo, B. Functional Silk Fibroin Hydrogels: Preparation, Properties and Applications. *J. Mater. Chem. B* **2021**, *9*, 1238–1258. [CrossRef]
24. Kundu, B.; Rajkhowa, R.; Kundu, S.C.; Wang, X. Silk Fibroin Biomaterials for Tissue Regenerations. *Adv. Drug Deliv. Rev.* **2013**, *65*, 457–470. [CrossRef] [PubMed]
25. Partlow, B.P.; Tabatabai, A.P.; Leisk, G.G.; Cebe, P.; Blair, D.L.; Kaplan, D.L. Silk Fibroin Degradation Related to Rheological and Mechanical Properties. *Macromol. Biosci.* **2016**, *16*, 666–675. [CrossRef] [PubMed]
26. Floren, M.; Migliaresi, C.; Motta, A. Processing Techniques and Applications of Silk Hydrogels in Bioengineering. *J. Funct. Biomater.* **2016**, *7*, 26. [CrossRef]
27. Ferreira, I.M.; Yoshioka, S.A.; Comasseto, J.V.; Porto, A.L.M. Immobilization of Amano Lipase from Pseudomonas Fluorescens on Silk Fibroin Spheres: An Alternative Protocol for the Enantioselective Synthesis of Halohydrins. *RSC Adv.* **2017**, *7*, 12650–12658. [CrossRef]
28. Kasoju, N.; Bora, U. Silk Fibroin in Tissue Engineering. *Adv. Healthc. Mater.* **2012**, *1*, 393–412. [CrossRef]
29. Debari, M.K.; King, C.I.; Altgold, T.A.; Abbott, R.D. Silk Fibroin as a Green Material. *ACS Biomater. Sci. Eng.* **2021**, *7*, 3530–3544. [CrossRef]
30. Marinho, V.H.S.; Neves, F.B.; Jimenez, D.E.Q.; Oliveira, F.R.; Santos, A.V.T.L.T.; Ferreira, R.M.A.; Souto, R.N.P.; Carvalho, J.C.T.; Yoshioka, S.A.; Ferreira, I.M. Development of an Environmentally Friendly Formulation of Silk Fibroin Combined with Fatty Acid from *Astrocaryum murumuru* Mart. Effective against *Aedes aegypti* Larvae. *J. Drug Deliv. Sci. Technol.* **2022**, *75*, 103626. [CrossRef]
31. Sarquis, I.R.; Sarquis, R.S.F.R.; Marinho, V.H.S.; Neves, F.B.; Araújo, I.F.; Damasceno, L.F.; Ferreira, R.M.A.; Souto, R.N.P.; Carvalho, J.C.T.; Ferreira, I.M. *Carapa guianensis* Aubl. (Meliaceae) Oil Associated with Silk Fibroin, as Alternative to Traditional Surfactants, and Active against Larvae of the Vector Aedes Aegypti. *Ind. Crops Prod.* **2020**, *157*, 112931. [CrossRef]
32. Marinho, V.H.S.; Holanda, F.H.; Araújo, I.F.; Jimenez, D.E.Q.; Pereira, R.R.; Porto, A.L.M.; Ferreira, A.M.; Carvalho, J.C.T.; Albuquerque de Freitas, A.C.G.; Fernandes, C.P.; et al. Nanoparticles from Silk Fibroin and Amazon Oils: Potential Larvicidal Activity and Oviposition Deterrence against *Aedes aegypti*. *Ind. Crops Prod.* **2023**, *203*, 117133. [CrossRef]
33. Holanda, F.H.; Pereira, R.R.; Marinho, V.H.S.; Jimenez, D.E.Q.; Costa Ferreira, L.M.M.; Ribeiro-Costa, R.M.; de Sousa, F.F.O.; Ferreira, I.M. Development of Nanostructured Formulation from Naringenin and Silk Fibroin and Application for Inhibition of Lipoxygenase (LOX). *RSC Adv.* **2023**, *13*, 23063–23075. [CrossRef]
34. de Castro Cantuária, P.; Medeiros, T.D.S.; Cantuária, M.F.; Soares, A.C.S.; e Silva, B.M.D.S.; Krahl, A.H.; Costa-Campos, C.E.; e Silva, R.B.L. Você Conhece a Nomenclatura Biológica? Aprenda a Forma Correta de Escrever Os Nomes Dos Organismos. *Res. Soc. Dev.* **2022**, *11*, e21711326378. [CrossRef]
35. Maciel Ferreira, I.; Coutinho Rocha, L.; Akinobo Yoshioka, S.; Nitschke, M.; Haroldo Jeller, A.; Pizzuti, L.; Seleghim, M.H.R.; Porto, A.L.M. Chemoselective Reduction of Chalcones by Whole Hyphae of Marine Fungus *Penicillium citrinum* CBMAI 1186, Free and Immobilized on Biopolymers. *Biocatal. Agric. Biotechnol.* **2014**, *3*, 358–364. [CrossRef]
36. de Oliveira Penido, C.A.F.; Pacheco, M.T.T.; Novotny, E.H.; Lednev, I.K.; Silveira, L. Quantification of Cocaine in Ternary Mixtures Using Partial Least Squares Regression Applied to Raman and Fourier Transform Infrared Spectroscopy. *J. Raman Spectrosc.* **2017**, *48*, 1732–1743. [CrossRef]
37. Leite, C.M.; Araujo-Neto, J.H.; Guedes, A.P.M.; Costa, A.R.; Demidoff, F.C.; Netto, C.D.; Castellano, E.E.; Nascimento, O.R.; Batista, A.A. Copper(I)/Triphenylphosphine Complexes Containing Naphthoquinone Ligands as Potential Anticancer Agents. *Inorganics* **2023**, *11*, 367. [CrossRef]
38. Wang, H.; Cheng, H.; Wang, F.; Wei, D.; Wang, X. An Improved 3-(4,5-Dimethylthiazol-2-Yl)-2,5-Diphenyl Tetrazolium Bromide (MTT) Reduction Assay for Evaluating the Viability of Escherichia Coli Cells. *J. Microbiol. Methods* **2010**, *82*, 330–333. [CrossRef] [PubMed]
39. de Toledo, C.D.; Teixeira, D.A.; da Vitória Archanjo, E.; Pereira, F.F.; Siqueira, F.C.; Mininel, F.J.; de Lima, J.S.; da Mota Silveira, K. Revisitação Dos Métodos de Extração de Pigmentos Do Urucum (Review of Urucum Pigment Extraction Methods). *Ciências Exatas e Tecnologia* **2021**, *16*, 24–29. [CrossRef]

40. Taham, T.; Cabral, F.A.; Barrozo, M.A.S. The Journal of Supercritical Fluids Extraction of Bixin from Annatto Seeds Using Combined Technologies. *J. Supercrit. Fluids* **2015**, *100*, 175–183. [CrossRef]
41. Puri, S.; Mandal, S.K.; Jain, H.; Sharma, P.K.; Deepa, P.R. Comparative bioactivity assessment of bixin pigment and associated phytochemicals extracted from annatto seeds using conventional and green solvents. *J. Food Drug Anal.* **2024**, *32*, 168–183. [CrossRef]
42. Miguel, K.B.; Cardoso, V.L.; Reis, M.H.M. Concentration of Pigments and Health-Promoting Bioactive Compounds from Annatto Seeds by Ultrafiltration. *Waste Biomass Valorization* **2024**, *15*, 127–137. [CrossRef]
43. Witono, J.R.; Ramadhany, P.; Santoso, H.; Putri, A. The Potency of Norbixin as an Active Compound of Natural Dye in Textile Industry. *Mater. Today Proc.* **2022**, *63*, S248–S254. [CrossRef]
44. Rodrigues, L.M.; Alcázar-Alay, S.C.; Petenate, A.J.; Meireles, M.A.A. Bixin Extraction from Defatted Annatto Seeds. *Comptes Rendus Chim.* **2014**, *17*, 268–283. [CrossRef]
45. Peters, A.T.; Freeman, H.S. *Physico-Chemical Principles of Color Chemistry*, 1st ed.; Springer: Dordrecht, The Netherlands, 1996; 299p; ISBN 978-0-7514-0210-0.
46. Satyanarayana, A.; Prabhakara Rao, P.G.; Rao, D.G. Chemistry, Processing and Toxicology of Annatto (*Bixa orellana* L.). *J. Food Sci. Technol.* **2003**, *40*, 131–141.
47. Erdawati, E.; Allanas, E.; Wesnina, W. Extraction of Bixin from Annatto Seeds with Microwave. *J. Phys. Conf. Ser.* **2021**, *1869*, 012016. [CrossRef]
48. Jin, X.; Streett, D.A.; Dunlap, C.A.; Lyn, M.E. Application of Hydrophilic–Lipophilic Balance (HLB) Number to Optimize a Compatible Non-Ionic Surfactant for Dried Aerial Conidia of *Beauveria bassiana*. *Biol. Control* **2008**, *46*, 226–233. [CrossRef]
49. Weuts, I.; Kempen, D.; Verreck, G.; Decorte, A.; Heymans, K.; Peeters, J.; Brewster, M.; Mooter, G. Van den Study of the Physicochemical Properties and Stability of Solid Dispersions of Loperamide and PEG6000 Prepared by Spray Drying. *Eur. J. Pharm. Biopharm.* **2005**, *59*, 119–126. [CrossRef]
50. Marelli, B.; Brenckle, M.A.; Kaplan, D.L.; Omenetto, F.G. Silk Fibroin as Edible Coating for Perishable Food Preservation. *Sci. Rep.* **2016**, *6*, 25263. [CrossRef]
51. Kua, Y.L.; Gan, S.; Morris, A.; Ng, H.K. Ethyl Lactate as a Potential Green Solvent to Extract Hydrophilic (Polar) and Lipophilic (Non-Polar) Phytonutrients Simultaneously from Fruit and Vegetable by-Products. *Sustain. Chem. Pharm.* **2016**, *4*, 21–31. [CrossRef]
52. Bitencourt, A.P.R.; Duarte, J.L.; Oliveira, A.E.M.F.M.; Cruz, R.A.S.; Carvalho, J.C.T.; Gomes, A.T.A.; Ferreira, I.M.; Ribeiro-Costa, R.M.; Silva-Júnior, J.O.C.; Fernandes, C.P. Preparation of Aqueous Nanodispersions with Annatto (*Bixa orellana* L.) Extract Using an Organic Solvent-Free and Low Energy Method. *Food Chem.* **2018**, *257*, 196–205. [CrossRef]
53. Patra, S.; Kar, S.; Bag, B.G. Isolation and Biological Activities of Naturally Occurring Apocarotenoid Bixin. *Prayogik Rasayan* **2021**, *5*, 112–119. [CrossRef]
54. Mitra, I.; Mukherjee, S.; Reddy Venkata, P.B.; Dasgupta, S.; Jagadeesh Bose, C.K.; Mukherjee, S.; Linert, W.; Moi, S.C. Benzimidazole Based Pt(II) Complexes with Better Normal Cell Viability than Cisplatin: Synthesis, Substitution Behavior, Cytotoxicity, DNA Binding and DFT Study. *RSC Adv.* **2016**, *6*, 76600–76613. [CrossRef]
55. Stockert, J.C.; Horobin, R.W.; Colombo, L.L.; Blázquez-Castro, A. Tetrazolium Salts and Formazan Products in Cell Biology: Viability Assessment, Fluorescence Imaging, and Labeling Perspectives. *Acta Histochem.* **2018**, *120*, 159–167. [CrossRef]
56. Mazurek, Ł.; Szudzik, M.; Rybka, M.; Konop, M. Silk Fibroin Biomaterials and Their Beneficial Role in Skin Wound Healing. *Biomolecules* **2022**, *12*, 1852. [CrossRef]
57. Chouhan, D.; Mandal, B.B. Silk Biomaterials in Wound Healing and Skin Regeneration Therapeutics: From Bench to bedside. *Acta Biomater.* **2020**, *103*, 24–51. [CrossRef]
58. Guo, P.; Du, P.; Zhao, P.; Chen, X.; Liu, C.; Du, Y.; Li, J.; Tang, X.; Yang, F.; Lv, G. Regulating the Mechanics of Silk Fi Broin Scaffolds Promotes Wound Vascularization. *Biochem. Biophys. Res. Commun.* **2021**, *574*, 78–84. [CrossRef]
59. Hodgkinson, T.; Yuan, X.; Bayat, A. Electrospun Silk Fibroin Fiber Diameter Influences In Vitro Dermal Fibroblast Behavior and Promotes Healing of Ex Vivo Wound Models. *J. Tissue Eng.* **2014**, *5*, 2041731414551661. [CrossRef] [PubMed]
60. Millán-Rivero, J.E.; Martínez, C.M.; Romecín, P.A.; Aznar-cervantes, S.D.; Carpes-Ruiz, M.; Cenis, J.L.; Moraleda, J.M.; Atucha, N.M.; García-bernal, D. Silk Fibroin Scaffolds Seeded with Wharton' s Jelly Mesenchymal Stem Cells Enhance Re-Epithelialization and Reduce Formation of Scar Tissue after Cutaneous Wound Healing. *Stem Cell Res. Ther.* **2019**, *10*, 126. [CrossRef]
61. Woo, H.; Joo, O.; Min, J.; Mi, B.; Jung, H.; Ri, Y.; Chae, M.; Hyeon, S.; Ren, J.; Seok, C.; et al. Wound Healing Effect of Electrospun Silk Fibroin Nanomatrix In burn-model. *Int. J. Biol. Macromol.* **2016**, *85*, 29–39. [CrossRef]
62. Zhang, W.; Chen, L.; Chen, J.; Wang, L.; Gui, X.; Ran, J.; Xu, G.; Zhao, H.; Zeng, M.; Ji, J.; et al. Silk Fibroin Biomaterial Shows Safe and Effective Wound Healing in Animal Models and a Randomized Controlled Clinical Trial. *Adv. Healthc. Mater.* **2017**, *6*, 1700121. [CrossRef]
63. Zhang, J.; Liu, N.; Sun, C.; Wang, Y. Polysaccharides from *Polygonatum Sibiricum* Delar. Ex Redoute Induce an Immune Response in the RAW264.7 Cell Line via an NF-KB/MAPK Pathway. *RSC Adv.* **2019**, *9*, 17988–17994. [CrossRef] [PubMed]

64. Sultan, M.T.; Lee, O.J.; Kim, S.H.; Ju, H.W.; Park, C.H. Silk Fibroin in Wound Healing Process. In *Novel Biomaterials for Regenerative Medicine*; Chun, H.J., Park, K., Kim, C.-H., Khang, G., Eds.; Springer: Singapore, 2018; pp. 115–126, ISBN 978-981-13-0947-2.
65. Capella, S.O.; Tillmann, M.T.; Félix, A.O.C.; Fontoura, E.G.; Fernandes, C.G.; Freitag, R.A.; Santos, M.A.Z.; Félix, S.R.; Nobre, M.O. Potencial Cicatricial Da *Bixa orellana* L. Em Feridas Cutâneas: Estudo Em Modelo Experimental. *Arq. Bras. Med. Vet. Zootec.* **2016**, *68*, 104–112. [CrossRef]
66. Franklin, V.A.; Bach Hi, E.M.; Wadt, N.S.Y.; Bach, E.E. Aqueous Extract from Urucum (*Bixa orellana* L.): Antimicrobial, Antioxidant, and Healing Activity. *Porto Biomed. J.* **2023**, *8*, e183. [CrossRef] [PubMed]
67. Pizoón-Garcia, A.D.; Cassini-vieira, P.; Ribeiro, C.C.; Eduardo, C.; Jensen, D.M.; Barcelos, L.S.; Cortes, M.E.; Sinisterra, R.D. Efficient Cutaneous Wound Healing Using Bixin-Loaded PCL Nanofibers in Diabetic Mice. *J. Biomed. Mat. Res.* **2016**, *105*, 1938–1949. [CrossRef]
68. Nikolaev, A.; Sokolov, N.N.; Kozlov, E.A.; Kutsman, M.E. Isolation and Properties of a Homogenous L Asparaginase Preparation from Pseudomonas Fluorescens AG. *Biokhimiya* **2009**, *40*, 984–989. (In Russian)
69. *ISO 10993-5:2009*; Biological Evaluation of Medical Devices–Part 5: Tests for In Vitro Cytotoxicity. International Organization for Standardization: Geneva, Switzerland, 2009.
70. Figueiredo-Junior, A.T.; Valença, S.S.; Finotelli, P.V.; Anjos, F.d.F.d.; de Brito-Gitirana, L.; Takiya, C.M.; Lanzetti, M. Treatment with Bixin-Loaded Polymeric Nanoparticles Prevents Cigarette Smoke-Induced Acute Lung Inflammation and Oxidative Stress in Mice. *Antioxidants* **2022**, *11*, 1293. [CrossRef]
71. Somacal, S.; Schüler da Silva, L.C.; de Oliveira, J.; Emanuelli, T.; Fabro de Bem, A. Bixin, a New Atheroprotective Carotenoid Candidate, Prevents oxLDL-Induced Cytotoxicity and Mitochondrial Dysfunction in Macrophages: Involvement of the Nrf2 and NF-κB Pathways. *Foods* **2024**, *13*, 2002. [CrossRef]
72. Krzyszczyk, P.; Schloss, R.; Palmer, A.; Berthiaume, F. The Role of Macrophages in Acute and Chronic Wound Healing and Interventions to Promote Pro-Wound Healing Phenotypes. *Front. Physiol.* **2018**, *9*, 419. [CrossRef] [PubMed]
73. Ferreira, L.M.; Sobral, C.S.; Blanes, L.; Ipolito, M.Z.; Horibe, E.K. Proliferation of Fibroblasts Cultured on a Hemi-Cellulose Dressing. *J. Plast. Reconstr. Aesthetic Surg.* **2010**, *63*, 865–869. [CrossRef]
74. Gragnani, A.; Müller, B.R.; Silva, I.D.C.G.D.; Noronha, S.M.R.D.; Ferreira, L.M. Keratinocyte Growth Factor, Tumor Necrosis Factor-Alpha and Interleukin-1 Beta Gene Expression in Cultured Fibroblasts and Keratinocytes from Burned Patients. *Acta Cir. Bras.* **2013**, *28*, 551–558. [CrossRef]
75. Keira, S.M.; Ferreira, L.M.; Gragnani, A.; Duarte, I.D.S.; Santos, I.A.N.D. Experimental Model for Fibroblast Culture. *Acta Cir. Bras.* **2004**, *19*, 11–16. [CrossRef]
76. Campaner, A.; Filho, A.; Morgan, J.; Ferreira, L. Animal Model of Keloids Using Genetically Modified Fibroblasts. *Rev. Bras. Cir. Plást.* **2007**, *22*, 137–142.
77. Ahmad, W.; Jantan, I.; Kumolosasi, E.; Haque, A. Immunomodulatory effects of *Tinospora crispa* Extract and Its Major Compounds on the Immune Functions of RAW 264.7 Macrophages. *Int. Immunopharmacol.* **2018**, *60*, 141–151. [CrossRef]
78. Kang, C.; Kim, J.; Kim, H.; Park, H.M.; Paek, N. Heat—Killed Lactic Acid Bacteria Inhibit Nitric Oxide Production via Inducible Nitric Oxide Synthase and Cyclooxygenase-2 in RAW 264.7 cells. *Probiotics Antimicrob. Proteins* **2021**, *13*, 1530–1538. [CrossRef]
79. Rivera, D.E.; Ocampo, Y.C.; Castro, J.P.; Barrios, L.; Diaz, F.; Franco, L.A. A Screening of Plants Used in Colombian Traditional Medicine Revealed the Anti-Inflammatory Potential of Physalis Angulata Calyces. *Saudi J. Biol. Sci.* **2019**, *26*, 1758–1766. [CrossRef]
80. Trinh, T.A.; Park, J.; Oh, J.H.; Park, J.S.; Lee, D.; Kim, C.E.; Choi, H.-S.; Kim, S.-B.; Hwang, G.S.; Koo, B.A.; et al. Effect of Herbal Formulation on Immune Response Enhancement in RAW 264.7 Macrophages. *Biomolecules* **2020**, *10*, 424. [CrossRef]
81. Eriksson, E.; Griffith, G.L.; Nuutila, K. Topical Drug Delivery in the Treatment of Skin Wounds and Ocular Trauma Using the Platform Wound Device. *Pharmaceutics* **2023**, *15*, 1060. [CrossRef]
82. Hofmann, E.; Schwarz, A.; Fink, J.; Kamolz, L.-P.; Kotzbeck, P. Modelling the Complexity of Human Skin In Vitro. *Biomedicines* **2023**, *11*, 794. [CrossRef]
83. Gupta, R.; Polaka, S.; Rajpoot, K.; Tekade, M.; Sharma, M.C.; Tekade, R.K. Chapter 6—Importance of Toxicity Testing in Drug Discovery and Research. In *Advances in Pharmaceutical Product Development and Research*; Tekade, R.K., Ed.; Academic Press: Cambridge, MA, USA, 2022; Volume 2, pp. 117–144, ISBN 978-0-323-98367-9.

sustainability

MDPI

Article

Impact on Grape Juice Quality and Phenolic Composition of Greek Autochthonous Grapevine Variety Mouhtaro Under Abscisic Acid Biostimulation

Dimitrios-Evangelos Miliordos [1,2,3,*,†], Anastasios Alatzas [2,†], Nikolaos Kontoudakis [4], Marianne Unlubayir [3], Konstantinos Nikolakis [1], Polydefkis Hatzopoulos [2], Arnaud Lanoue [3,*] and Yorgos Kotseridis [1]

1 Laboratory of Oenology and Alcoholic Beverage Drinks, Department of Food Science and Human Nutrition, Agricultural University of Athens, 75 Iera Odos, 11855 Athens, Greece; nikolakiskostas@gmail.com (K.N.); ykotseridis@aua.gr (Y.K.)

2 Molecular Biology Laboratory, Department of Biotechnology, Agricultural University of Athens, 75 Iera Odos, 11855 Athens, Greece; aalatzas@aua.gr (A.A.); phat@aua.gr (P.H.)

3 EA 2106 Biomolécules et Biotechnologie Végétales, UFR des Sciences Pharmaceutiques, Université de Tours, 31 Av. Monge, F37200 Tours, France; marianne.unlubayir@univ-tours.fr

4 Department of Agricultural Biotechnology and Oenology, Democritus University of Thrace, 1st km Drama-Mikrochori, 66100 Drama, Greece; kontoudakis@vo.duth.gr

* Correspondence: dim.miliordos@gmail.com (D.-E.M.); arnaud.lanoue@univ-tours.fr (A.L.)

† These authors contributed equally to the work.

Abstract: Sustainable viticulture practices could be useful tools for ensuring grape and wine quality, especially in the context of climate change. A promising and innovating approach is the use of bioelicitors in order to stimulate productivity and metabolite biosynthesis in an environmentally friendly way. However, the result depends on the variety, the phenological stage, concentration of the biomolecule applied, and climate conditions. The present study examined the impact of the plant hormone abscisic acid on the phenolic compound accumulation in the autochthonous, red-colored Greek grapevine variety Mouhtaro. During 2018 and 2019 vintages berry quality characteristics, and metabolome were evaluated at three stages: véraison, beginning and mid, and harvest. Abscisic acid (ABA) was given at doses of 0.04% w/v and 0.08% w/v during the véraison stage. According to the results, the ABA-treated grape berries were smaller and exhibited lower total soluble solid levels and increased titratable acidity compared to the control. Although no significant differences were observed in amino acids or anthocyanin and stilbene accumulation upon ABA treatment, application of ABA at the higher dose resulted in increased concentrations of phenolic acids, flavan-3-ols, and flavonols. Therefore, the application of ABA could be considered as a promising method for improving the grape quality characteristics of Mouhtaro.

Keywords: grapevine; Mouhtaro; plant hormones; bioelicitors; abscisic acid; phenolic compounds

1. Introduction

Climate change has already induced noticeable changes in viticulture and enology. These impacts include fluctuations in phenological timing, alterations in grape and wine composition, heterogeneous effects on grapevine yield, and decoupling grape maturity from soluble solids and secondary metabolites [1–3]. The predicted increase in average temperature in the coming decades will shift the suitability of wine-growing regions, favoring grapevine cultivation in northern countries but also threatening the established quality characteristic of traditional cultivars in Mediterranean region [4–6]. Given the anticipated negative effects of prolonged summer drought and rising temperatures on grape production and quality, developing and implementing sustainable practices is crucial for the resilience of Mediterranean viticulture.

A promising strategy to address the effects of climate change in viticulture is the application of bioelicitors. In order to promote plant growth and productivity, especially in response to abiotic challenges like heat, salinity, and drought, this approach uses biomolecules from several sources, including proteins, oligo-polysaccharides, plant hormones, peptides, and lipids [7–9]. Bioelicitors trigger diverse plant responses, including the regulation of specialized metabolism and antioxidant defenses, by regulating the expression of related genes [10–15]. The application of these compounds at the appropriate plant growth stage and the optimal concentration can enhance crop yield and quality characteristics under stress conditions [16].

Abscisic acid is a key plant hormone involved in various developmental processes, including fruit ripening and drought response [17–19]. ABA treatments on grapevine improve berry quality features and enhance the biosynthesis of tannins, flavonoids, anthocyanins, and stilbenes [17,20–22]. Moreover, ABA treatment was found to improve soluble sugar and phenolic compound accumulation under stress conditions [23,24].

Although research on bioelicitors is extensive and continually expanding [25,26], our understanding of their optimal application, crop-specific effects, and interactions with environmental conditions remains incomplete. This study seeks to assess the impact of ABA application on grape berry secondary metabolism of the autochthonous, red-colored variety Mouhtaro in the challenging conditions of a Greek vineyard. Only the Muses Valley in Askri, Central Greece, is home to the grapevine variety "Mouhtaro", which yields few concentrated grapes. The berry is small to medium in size and is found in a medium-sized bunch. Additionally, grapevines are rigorous and distinguished by their late ripening and late bud break. There are currently no available scientific data about DNA genotyping. A two-vintage comprehensive trial was conducted and berry quality traits combined with metabolomic data were assessed throughout the ripening period. The observed alterations in the phenolic composition of grape berries subsequent to ABA treatment can potentially enhance our understanding and contribute to the development of more sustainable viticulture practices, ultimately aimed at ensuring improvement in grape production quality across diverse agricultural settings. This research holds significant implications for viticulture, as it not only addresses existing gaps in knowledge but also proposes innovative approaches that could lead to improved sustainability and quality in grape cultivation. Furthermore, the insights gained from this study may serve as a valuable reference for future research endeavors aimed at optimizing the utilization of bioelicitors in various horticultural applications. Thus, through this investigation, we aspire to contribute to the broader discourse regarding sustainable agricultural practices and the complex interactions among plant physiology and environmental factors.

2. Materials and Methods

2.1. Experimental Design

Experiment was carried out in productive vineyard in Muses Valley, near the town of Thiva, in Central Greece. Vineyard is located at GPS 38°19′30.9″ N and 23°05′37.7″ E, at an altitude of 450 m. The vineyard was planted in 2007; the training system is double cordon and planted on R110 rootstocks with a planting density of 2.5 m between and 1.2 in rows. All experimental vines were pruned uniquely; each cordon has three spurs. Without irrigation, the experimental plot's vineyard management was consistent and followed the regionally advised agricultural techniques. Three treatments were compared in the trial, resulting from a combination of two levels of ABA and the control. More specifically: the untreated vines (control), and the vines sprayed with 0.04% *w/v* (low dose) and 0.08% *w/v* (high dosage) abscisic acid (s-abscisic acid 10.4% *w/v*, Protone SL, Hellafarm, Peania, Greece). These doses and the timing were chosen on the basis of previous studies conducted on other red grapevine varieties [20–23] as well as according to the suppliers' instruction. The grape zone (all bunches of the experimental vines) was sprayed with ABA during véraison (81–85, based on the BBCH scale) [27], then again three and six days following the initial application. The different treatments did not sample buffer portions, which had more than three grapevine plants per row. In three completely randomized blocks, each treatment was given in triplicate, with 10 vines in a row for each treatment [28].

2.2. Meteorological Data

The meteorological data concerning the experimental period of both vintages (i.e., from July to September) were acquired from the Automatic Network of the National Observatory of Athens [29].

2.3. Grape Sampling and Physicochemical Must Analysis

The sampling dates were performed as shown in Table S1 (three distinct maturity levels: at véraison, immediately prior to the 1st treatment application, at middle véraison, and at the optimum grape maturity stage), and grapes were harvested on 30 August 2018 and on 3 September 2019, respectively. A weekly sample approach was used to track the ripening process and determine the optimum grape level for harvest. Fifty berries were randomly selected from each experimental treatment at each sample point, and the fresh weight of the berries was measured on an analytical balance. The sampled berries were collected on both sides of each of the ten plants, in both direct sunshine and shade. Prior to their chemical analysis, grape samples were transported on dry ice and were carefully stored at −80 °C. Weekly measurements were made to track the level of grape maturity. The Compendium of International Methods of Wine and Must Analysis's official procedures were followed to evaluate the pH, titratable acidity (g L^{-1} tartaric acid), and total soluble solids content (°Brix) [30].

2.4. UPLC–MS-Based Metabolic Profiling

Using liquid nitrogen, the frozen (−80 °C) grape berries were ground into powder and utilized for metabolic profiling using modified techniques. [15,31]. Briefly, 50 mg of grounded dry berries was extracted using in a methanol/water mixture (80/20; *v/v*). Following sonication, the samples were extracted for 15 h at 4 °C. UPLC–MS analyses were performed using an ACQUITY™ electrospray ionization (ESI) source that is managed by Masslynx 4.1 software (Waters, Milford, MA, USA), which is connected to an Ultra Performance Liquid Chromatography system via a Xevo TQD mass spectrometer. As stated in Miliordos et al. [28], the peak annotation was carried out using retention times, m/z values, and UV spectra, as well as by comparison with pure standards, own purified substances, or data from the literature. Data collection was carried out with selected ion monitoring (SIM). Absolute quantifications were conducted using pure standards and using a five-point calibration curve (0–20 ppm).

2.5. Statistical Analysis

All of the values are presented as the mean standard deviation. The statistical analysis was carried out with GraphPad Prism (GraphPad Software, version 8.0.1). One-way ANOVA with Tukey's test or an unpaired t-test were used to assess the results' significance. Additionally, SIMCA P+ version 15 (Umetrics AB, Umeå, Sweden) was used to conduct a multivariate statistical data analysis (MVA) of the samples.

3. Results

3.1. Meteorological Conditions

The research took place in a Mouhtaro single vineyard located in a narrow valley at 450 m altitude in Central Greece, roughly 100 km northwest of the city of Athens. Muses Valley has a Mediterranean climate with mild, wet winters and dry summers. Considering that Mouhtaro is an early-harvested cultivar, the period of ripening (from véraison to harvest) is limited to July and August. In the study presented, the grapes were harvested on 30 August and 3 September of 2018 and 2019, respectively. Using meteorological data from the neighboring town of Askri, (38°18′51.1″ N 23°6′42.8″ E), monthly maximum temperatures were higher during August in 2019 vintage (39.5 °C) compared to 2018 (35 °C) (Figure S1). In comparison, the total precipitation amount in July and August was higher in 2018 (66 mm) compared to 2019 (35 mm) (Figure S1). Specifically, the precipitation during the ripening period of 2019 was observed two weeks prior to véraison, while most of the rainfall of 2018 was recorded the week after véraison and the days prior to harvest (Figure 1).

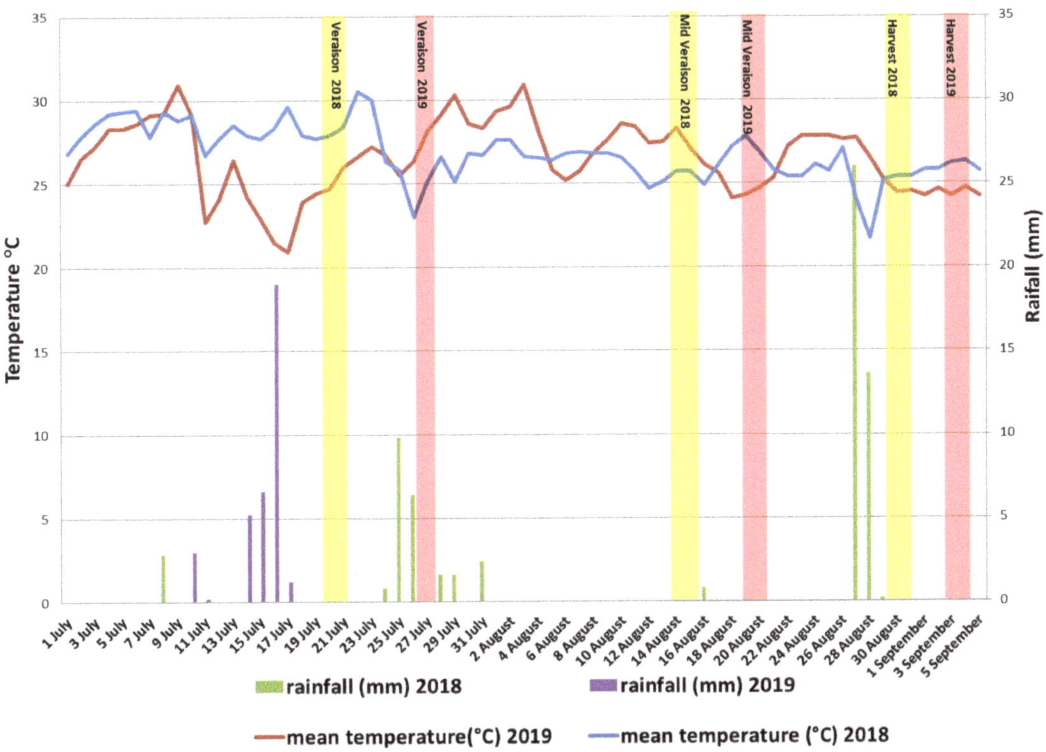

Figure 1. Meteorological data from July 1st to September 5th in Muses Valley during 2018 and 2019 vintages. Purple and green bars indicate the daily amount of rainfall, while the red and blue lines on the plot show the evolution of the daily mean temperature. The yellow and pink bars show the three sampling points (i.e., véraison, middle véraison, and harvest) of 2018 and 2019, respectively.

3.2. Grape Weight and Must Conventional Analysis

Berry size was constantly increased during maturation in both control and treated plants. The ABA treatment resulted in significantly decreased berry size only at harvest stage of both vintages, while no difference was observed at the two previous stages

(Table 1). The differences between the high and low dose of applied ABA were negligible. Surprisingly, compared to 2018, berry size in both control and ABA-treated vines grew considerably at all sample dates during ripening and at the harvest stage in 2019 (Table 1). The increased berry size observed in 2019 samples could be the result of the amount of rainfall recorded prior to véraison (Figure 1). During this period, grape berries accumulate a substantial amount of water, leading to an increase in berry weight, which may account for the differences observed between the two vintages

Table 1. Physicochemical characteristics of Mouhtaro grapes at three phenological stages (i.e., véraison, middle véraison, and harvest). Data represent the mean ± std. deviation (n = 3). According to the t-test at the 5% probability level, different letters in the same column and phenological stage indicate significant differences.

Stage	Treatment	Berry Weight (mg/berry)	Total Soluble Solids (°Brix)	pH	Total Acidity (g/L of Tartaric Acid)
			2018		
Véraison	Control	1.14 ± 0.15 a	14.33 ± 0.16 a	2.96 ± 0.05 a	15.32 ± 1.32 a
	ABA Low	1.13 ± 0.09 a	14 ± 0.07 a	2.97 ± 0.09 a	15.67 ± 1.12 a
	ABA High	1.17 ± 0.10 a	14.16 ± 0.22 a	2.90 ± 0.10 a	15 ± 0.98 a
Middle Véraison	Control	1.76 ± 0.18 a	19.70 ± 1.62 a	3.61 ± 0.22 ab	11.1 ± 1.08 a
	ABA Low	1.73 ± 0.11 a	18.33 ± 0.85 b	3.33 ± 0.16 b	12.8 ± 0.91 a
	ABA High	1.74 ± 0.08 a	16.83 ± 1.15 c	3.71 ± 0.21 b	12.5 ± 1.20 a
Harvest	Control	1.98 ± 0.04 a	21.90 ± 0.77 a	3.71 ± 0.12 b	6.9 ± 0.21 b
	ABA Low	1.90 ± 0.10 ab	19.79 ± 1.01 b	3.69 ± 0.17 b	7.80 ± 0.14 a
	ABA High	1.89 ± 0.03 b	17.23 ± 1.06 c	3.90 ± 0.11 a	7.5 ± 0.25 a
			2019		
Véraison	Control	1.27 ± 0.08 a	10.00 ± 0.20 a	2.42 ± 0.01 a	12.35 ± 0.48 a
	ABA Low	1.37 ± 0.09 a	10.40 ± 0.17 a	2.43 ± 0.03 a	13.47 ± 0.31 a
	ABA High	1.33 ± 0.10 a	9.83 ± 0.66 a	2.42 ± 0.03 a	13.27 ± 0.44 a
Middle Véraison	Control	1.91 ± 0.34 a	19.6 ± 0.50 a	3.50 ± 0.10 a	8.98 ± 0.20 a
	ABA Low	1.82 ± 0.06 a	19.13 ± 0.85 a	3.60 ± 0.06 a	8.99 ± 0.35 a
	ABA High	1.81 ± 0.26 a	18.13 ± 1.05 a	3.43 ± 0.17 a	9.95 ± 0.79 a
Harvest	Control	2.24 ± 0.05 a	23.36 ± 0.28 a	3.31 ± 0.03 ab	6.25 ± 0.08 c
	ABA Low	2.19 ± 0.01 ab	22.82 ± 0.65 ab	3.34 ± 0.06 a	6.88 ± 0.07 a
	ABA High	2.15 ± 0.05 b	22.95 ± 0.05 b	3.24 ± 0.01 b	6.69 ± 0.08 b

The composition of the grape must, which is primarily determined by the pH, titratable acidity (TA, stated in tartaric acid g/L), and total soluble solids (TSS, expressed as °Brix), is a significant determinant in berry quality. Throughout their development, grape berries from both vintages showed a steady rise in total soluble solids. At the harvest stage of both vintages, the TSS content in ABA-treated plants was significantly lower than that of the controls. At the earlier sample points, no changes were seen (Table 1). Additionally, the 2019 vintage had a greater TSS content throughout maturity than the 2018 vintage (Table 1), suggesting that the weather circumstances were different.

Titratable acidity values were gradually decreased during the ripening period, while the pH content was increased in all treatments. Only at the harvest stages of both vintages were there statistically significant variations in titratable acidity and pH between ABA-treated berries and control samples; no differences were observed at the two earlier stages. (Table 1). In particular, as compared to controls, TA values were noticeably greater for both administered ABA dosages. However, only grapes treated with the higher dose of ABA showed noticeably different pH values, and the impact varied by vintage (i.e., higher and lower pH values in 2018 and 2019, respectively, compared to control and ABA medium dose) (Table 1). In contrast to the TSS profile of the two vintages, the 2018 samples had greater TA and pH values than the 2019 samples (Table 1).

Taken together, the results of berry size measurements and the conventional must analysis indicate that ABA application resulted in smaller grape berries, with lower TSS content and pH and higher TA. It is worth mentioning that the remarkable impact of the weather conditions on berry size and composition was also evident in the two vintages.

3.3. UPLC_MS Analysis of Grape Metabolites Univariate Statistics

At véraison, middle véraison, and harvest, grape samples were harvested from ABA-treated and untreated grapevines, and UPLC-MS analysis were carried out. UPLC-MS revealed 42 compounds in berry samples (Table S2), including one organic compound (citric acid), one stilbene (*E*-piceid), nine flavonols, eight flavan-3-ols, five anthocyanins diOH, eight anthocyanins triOH, six amino acids, and four phenolic acids.

The application of ABA on grape berries had no effect on the amino acid concentration at harvest in 2018 and throughout ripening in 2019. Further, amino acid levels found to be similar at harvest stage of both vintages (Figure 2A–C). On the contrary, the effect of ABA treatment was evident on phenolic acids content. Both doses of ABA in 2018 and the higher dose in 2019 resulted in increased phenolic acids level at véraison and harvest stages, compared to the controls. Worth mentioning, phenolic acid content was higher at the harvest stage of 2018 compared to the next vintage (Figure 2D–F).

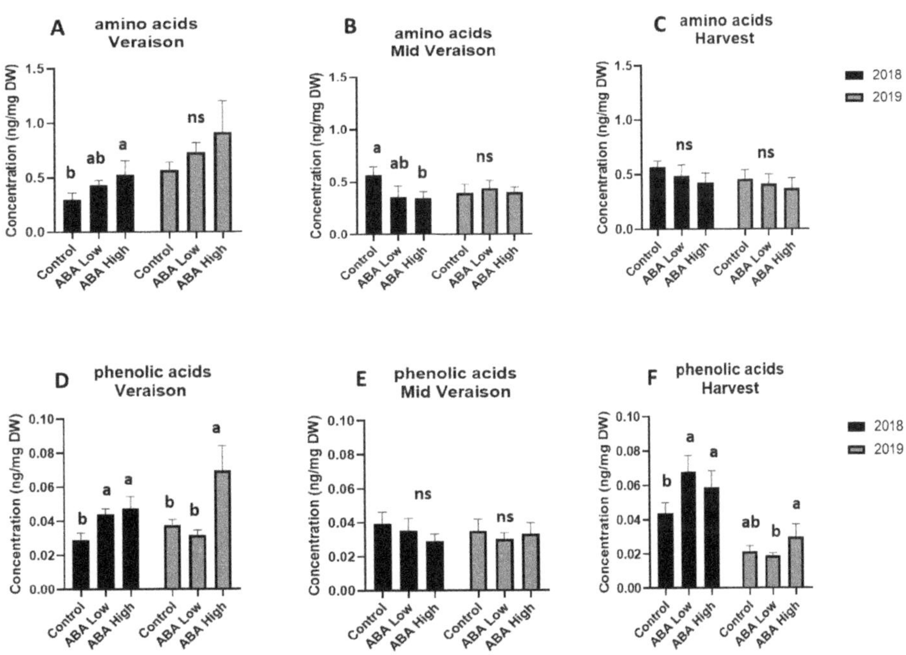

Figure 2. Total quantity of amino acids (**upper panel**) and phenolic acids (**lower panel**) in grape berries at véraison (**A**,**D**), middle véraison (**B**,**E**), and at harvest (**C**,**F**) stage in 2018 (black bars) and 2019 (gray bars) in control and ABA-treated vines. Statistically significant differences between mean values (n = 6) are indicated with different letters (one way ANOVA, p-value < 0.05). Error bars represent the standard deviation.

Anthocyanins are responsible for giving grape berries their red color. According to our metabolomic analysis, there were no significant differences in anthocyanin di-OH and tri-OH levels between control and ABA-treated berries at harvest stages of both vintages (Figure 3). Similarly, no significant difference was observed in anthocyanin content at harvest stages of 2018 and 2019 vintage (Figure 3).

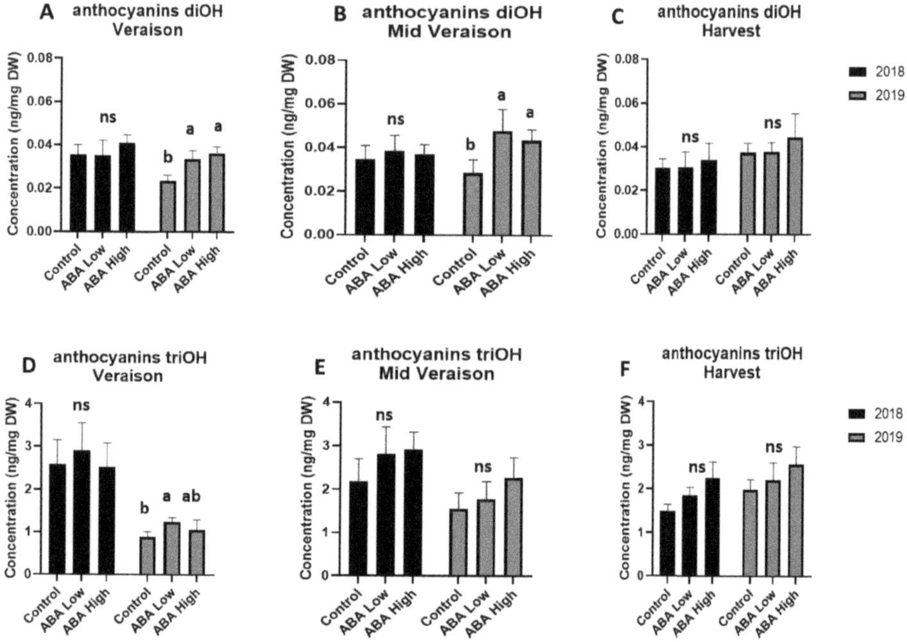

Figure 3. Total concentrations of anthocyanins diOH (**upper panel**) and anthocyanin triOH (**lower panel**) in grape berries at véraison (**A**,**D**), middle véraison (**B**,**E**), and at harvest (**C**,**F**) stage in 2018 (black bars) and 2019 (gray bars) in control and ABA-treated vines. Statistically significant differences between mean values (n = 6) are indicated with different letters (one-way ANOVA, p-value < 0.05). Error bars represent the standard deviation.

The UPLC-MS analysis also revealed that ABA treatment altered the content of flavan-3-ols and flavonols during ripening. The application of ABA did not affect flavan-3-ol levels at the véraison and middle véraison stages in 2018 but resulted in a significant increase at harvest (Figure 4A–C). The same trend was also observed during the 2019 vintage with the higher dose ABA-treated berries recording higher flavan-3-ol concentrations than the control and the lower dose-treated berries at the véraison and harvest stages (Figure 4A–C). On the other hand, the application of ABA had diverse effects on total flavonol levels in the two vintages of the trial. During 2018 vintage, the ABA-treated grapes exhibited higher level of flavonols at the two first stages while no difference to the controls was observed at harvest (Figure 4D–F). On the contrary, ABA treatment increased the flavonols level at harvest stage of 2019 (Figure 4D–F). Noteworthy, flavonol content was higher in both control and ABA-treated grapes at harvest stage of 2019 compared to 2018 (Figure 4D–F).

A compound belonging to the stilbenes class, *E*-piceid, was also detected by UPLC-MS. The application of both a low and high dose of ABA resulted in higher levels of *E*-piceid compared to the control at middle véraison stage of both vintages (Figure 5). However, no statistically significant differences were observed between control and ABA-treated vines at harvest stage (Figure 5). It is worth mentioning that *E*-piceid content was higher at the harvest stage of 2019 compared to the 2018 (Figure 5).

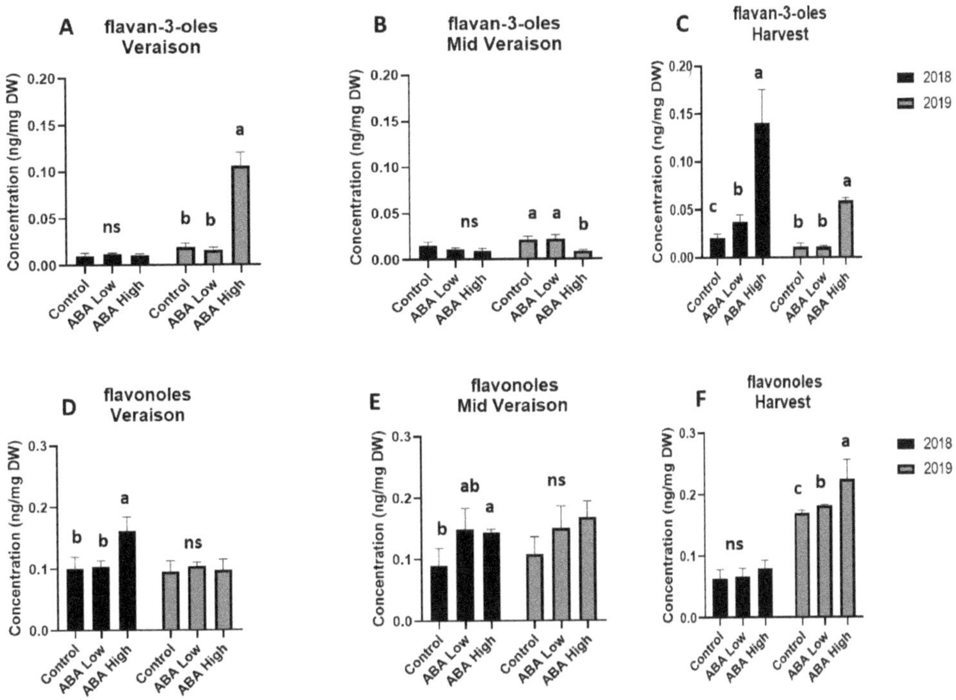

Figure 4. Total concentrations of flavan-3-ols (**upper panel**) and flavonols (**lower panel**) in grape berries at véraison (**A**,**D**), middle véraison (**B**,**E**), and at harvest (**C**,**F**) stage in 2018 (black bars) and 2019 (gray bars) in control and ABA-treated vines. Statistically significant differences between mean values (n = 6) are indicated with different letters (one-way ANOVA, p-value < 0.05). Error bars represent the standard deviation.

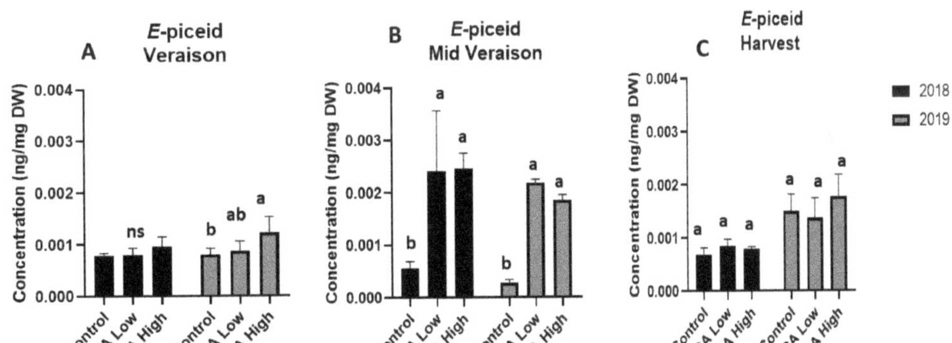

Figure 5. Total concentrations of E-piceid in grape berries at véraison (**A**), middle véraison (**B**), and at harvest (**C**) stage in 2018 (black bars) and 2019 (gray bars) in control and ABA-treated vines. Statistically significant differences between mean values (n = 6) are indicated with different letters (one-way ANOVA, p-value < 0.05). Error bars represent the standard deviation.

Taken together, the metabolomic analysis showed that ABA treatment resulted in increased concentrations of phenolic acids and flavan-3-ols at harvest stage, regardless of the vintage. The flavonol levels were increased upon ABA treatment only the second vintage of the trial, while no significant effect was observed on amino acid, anthocyanin, and stilbene concentrations. Additionally, the flavonols may benefit from the lower daily temperatures that were recorded throughout the 2019 ripening season. High temperatures are known to reduce the formation of phenolic compounds, and it has been proposed that some secondary metabolites, such as kaempferol and flavonols in general, may serve as markers of warming-related declines in fruit quality. Under mild climatic circumstances, exogenously applied biostimulants can have a positive impact on grape composition.

3.4. Multivariate Statistics

In order to gain an overall view of the results and to examine the variability among the control and ABA-treated samples, different subgroups of metabolic data were independently analyzed and PCA plots on grape berries from the véraison, middle véraison (Figure S1), and harvest (Figure 6) stages from 2018 and 2019 vintages were produced. The vintage effect was evident at both phenological phases with a distinct separation along the PC1 axis, but the PCA score plots at véraison and middle véraison did not provide any distinction between the control and ABA-treated grape samples (Figure S1). The samples were discriminated along PC2, indicating the impact of the greater dose of ABA treatment on berry metabolism, in addition to the vintage effect (i.e., the separation along the PC1 axis) (Figure 6A).

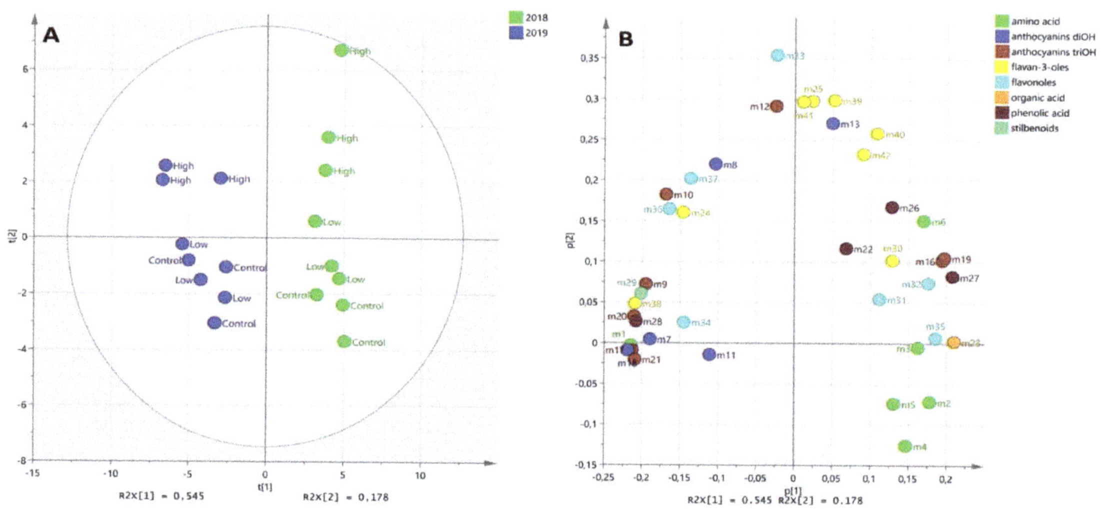

Figure 6. Unsupervised classification using PCA on metabolomic data from control and ABA-treated grape berries at harvest stage in 2018 and 2019. Samples in the score plot (**A**) were colored according to the vintage, and variables in the loading plot (**B**) were colored according to the metabolic class. Numbers indicate the ID of metabolites, as follows: L-proline (m1); L-leucine (m2); L-isoleucine (m3); L-phenylalanine (m4;) L-tyrosine (m5); L-tryptophan (m6); cyanidin-3-*O*-glucoside (m7); peonidin-3-*O*-glucoside (m8); delphinidin-3-*O*-glucoside (m9); petunidin-3-*O*-glucoside (m10); cyanidin-3-*O*-(6-*O*-acetyl)-glucoside (m11); malvidin-3-*O*-glucoside (m12); peonidin-3-*O*-(6-acetyl-glucoside) (m13); dimethyl quercetin hexoside (m15); petunidin-3-O-(6-*O*-acetyl)-glucoside (m16); malvidin-3-*O*-(6-*O*-acetyl)-glucoside (m17); peonidin-3-*O*-(6-p-coumaroyl-glucoside) (m18); petunidin-3-*O*-(6-p-coumaroyl)-glucoside (m19); malvidin-3-*O*-(6-p-coumaroyl)-glucoside (m20); malvidin-3,5-*O*-diglucoside (m21); gallic acid (m22); citric acid (m23); catechin (m24); epicatechin (m25); coutaric acid (m26); caftaric acid (m27); fertaric acid (m28); *E*-piceid (m29); catechin gallate (m30); kaempferol-3-*O*-glucoside (m31); quercetin-3-*O*-glucoside (m32); quercetin-*O*-gluronide m33); quercetin-3-*O*-glucuronide (m34); myricetin hexoside 1 (m35); myricetin glucoside (m36); quercetin (m37); procyanidinB1 (m38); procyanidinB2 (m39); procyanidinB3 (m40); procyanidin B4 (m41); procyanidin gallate (m42).

The PCA score plot of the grape berries at harvest stage of the 2018 and 2019 vintages explained 72.8% of the variance. The metabolites that caused this separation were also shown in the loading plot (Figure 6B). The metabolites were mostly grouped according to their structural class, especially phenolic acids, flavonols, and flavan-3-ols (Figure 6B). The PC2 positive axis projection of flavan-3-ols, flavonols, and phenolic acids demonstrated that these substances were in charge of differentiating between samples treated with greater doses of ABA. This analysis confirmed that the higher dose treatment with ABA increased the concentrations of some phenolic compounds in the treated grapes at harvest stage, independently of the meteorological conditions during both vintages.

The amino acid and anthocyanin di-OH accumulation was correlated with the control and in lower dose ABA-treated berries, while flavan-3-ols were correlated with the berries treated with the higher dose of ABA (Figure 6B). The levels of specific flavonols (i.e., quercetin-*O*-glucuronide, myricetin glucoside, and quercetin), flavan-3-ols (i.e., procyanidins B2, B3, and B4, and procyanidin gallate) and anthocyanins (i.e., petunidin-3-*O*-glucoside and malvidin-3-*O*-glucoside) were significantly affected by the higher dose ABA treatment (Figure 6B).

4. Discussion

Central Greece's Muses Valley is defined by extinguishing climatic and topographical characteristics that have fostered grapevine cultivation since antiquity. Nearly 90% of the area vineyards are Mouhtaro, an autochthonous red winemaking variety. It is an early/mid-harvested red variety, and the wine produced is characterized by middle to high color intensity and low astringency, while regarding the aroma is characterized by caramel, strawberry, and vegetal notes and forest fruit aromas [32].

There was a discernible vintage effect on the physicochemical properties of the grape berries at harvest as a result of the two years varying climatic circumstances, which affected the maturation process. For example, compared to the previous vintage, the 2019 vintage's berries were larger because to the higher rainfall before véraison. Additionally, both control and ABA-treated grapes were characterized by higher TSS levels and decreased TA and pH values compared to 2018 vintage.

The results of berry size measurements and the conventional must analysis showed that ABA application affected the physiochemical characteristics of grape berries. The ABA-treated berries' weight at harvest stage was lower, with lower TSS content and higher TA compared to the controls. These observations imply a delay in maturation upon the treatment. Although plant hormone application was found to have limited effect on berry sugar content [33,34], similar results to our study were obtained upon application of another bioelicitor, benzothiadiazole (BTH), on Mouhtaro and ABA on the white-colored Savvatiano grapes in trials conducted in the same vineyard [18,35].

Phenolic compounds represent a class of intensively studied bioactive molecules. They are related with the organoleptic characteristics of wines, like color, astringency, and bitterness. Moreover, they possess numerous health benefits and for this reason are used in the pharmaceutical and food industry [36–38]. The metabolomics analysis showed that ABA treatment affected the accumulation of phenolic compounds. More specifically, the ABA-treated grapes exhibited increased concentrations of phenolic acids and flavan-3-ols at harvest stage, regardless of the vintage, while the flavonols level was increased upon ABA treatment only for the second vintage of the trial. On the other hand, no significant differences to the controls were observed in amino acid, anthocyanin, and stilbene concentrations. Remarkably, BTH application on Mouhtaro grapes also had no effect on anthocyanins but, on the contrary, stilbenes level was increased [35], as well as upon ABA application on Savvatiano [28].

Earlier research has demonstrated that ABA application increased the concentration of phenolic compounds in grape berries, leading to improved attributes [21–23,39–43]. However, the diverse effects observed in various studies suggest that the timing, the concentration of ABA application, and the environmental conditions are critical factors in optimizing phenolic compounds accumulation in grape berries [12,44,45]. The application of ABA on Savvatiano grapes in a previous trial showed that another crucial parameter is the cultivar. Studies have shown that ABA treatment can enhance the content of anthocyanins, flavonols, and stilbenes in various grape varieties. For instance, in Malbec grapes, ABA increased low molecular weight polyphenols and stilbenes like trans-resveratrol and piceid [22]. Similarly, in Yan 73 and Cabernet Sauvignon, ABA treatment enhanced anthocyanins and non-anthocyanin phenolics, with varying effects depending on the variety (Luan et al., 2014) (Xi et al., 2013) [46,47]. For instance, contrary to ABA-treated grapes of Mouhtaro, which exhibited increased levels of flavan-3-ols and flavonols in the 2019 vintage compared to the controls, their concentrations were decreased or unaffected in Savvatiano. On the other hand, *E*-piceid was increased in the white variety upon ABA application whereas no effect was observed in Mouhtaro [28]. ABA treatment has been consistently shown to increase anthocyanin content in grape berries. For instance, studies on the Savvatiano and Kyoho white grape varieties demonstrated that ABA upregulates genes involved in anthocyanin biosynthesis, such as UDP-glucose:flavonoid 3-O-glucosyltransferase (UFGT) and glutathione S-transferase 4 (GST4), leading to higher anthocyanin accumulation [28,48,49]. Specifically, ABA treatment was found to enhance the production of petunidin- and malvidin-type anthocyanins, which are associated with deeper berry color [49].

The principal component analyses of the metabolomics data confirmed that both the vintage and the ABA treatment had a strong impact on grape berry phenolic composition. The PCA score plots at véraison and middle véraison showed that the first discrimination among the samples was due to the vintage. Although the vintage effect was also evident at harvest stage, an additional discrimination between controls/ABA lower dose and higher dose ABA samples indicated the impact of the treatment. Further, a more detailed analysis showed that the treatment with the higher dose of ABA increased the concentrations of specific phenolic compounds in the treated grapes at harvest stage, independently of the weather conditions during the two vintages.

The combination of a variety's genetics and environmental conditions, including soil, terrain, and climate, determines its distinctive grape and wine quality traits. Given that grapevines have historically been grown in the Mediterranean region, the anticipated global warming scenario puts existing cultivation techniques to the test. As a result, sustainable agronomic practices may be helpful in reducing the adverse consequences of climate change while maintaining the high standards of the historically grown cultivars. Utilizing plant hormones and bioelicitors in viticulture provides a sustainable way to reduce the need for pesticides and fertilizers while improving the qualitative characteristics of grape berries in an eco-friendly way.

5. Conclusions

Applications of biostimulants are advantageous and successful viticultural techniques for improving grape and wine quality, particularly in view of the difficult climate change scenario. However, it is crucial to ascertain the best time and focus for their use. While ABA treatment reduced size and TSS in our two-vintage study, it also enhanced levels of phenolic chemicals, including flavonols, phenolic acids, and flavan-3-ols. As a result, using ABA may be regarded as a viable agronomic approach to improving the quality of grape berries. Further comprehensive studies, incorporating a wider range of indigenous grapevine varieties and local climate conditions, are needed to clarify grapevine reactions to various biostimulants and their unique impacts on each cultivar's metabolic profiles requires taking into account a greater variety of indigenous grapevine varieties and local climate circumstances.

Supplementary Materials: The following supporting information can be downloaded at: https://www.mdpi.com/article/10.3390/su17104385/su17104385/s1, Table S1: ABA applications and sampling dates during 2018 and 2019 vintages; Table S2: Metabolites identified by UPLC-MS in grape berry samples; Figure S1: The monthly climate conditions during the 2018 and 2019 vintages; Figure S2: Unsupervised classification using PCA on metabolomic data from control and ABA-treated grape berries at véraison and middle véraison stages in 2018 and 2019.

Author Contributions: Conceptualization, D.-E.M.; methodology, D.-E.M. and N.K.; software, D.-E.M.; validation, D.-E.M., A.A., N.K., K.N., P.H., A.L. and Y.K.; formal analysis, D.-E.M. and A.A.; investigation, D.-E.M. and A.A.; resources, D.-E.M. and A.A.; data curation, M.U. and D.-E.M.; writing—original draft preparation, D.-E.M. and A.A.; writing—review and editing, D.-E.M., A.A., N.K, K.N., P.H., A.L. and Y.K.; visualization, D.-E.M. and A.A.; supervision, D.-E.M.; project administration, D.-E.M.; funding acquisition, D.-E.M., A.L. and Y.K. All authors have read and agreed to the published version of the manuscript.

Funding: The Project is Co Funded by Measure 16 Cooperation: Rural Development Program 2014–2020, Sub-measure 16.1–16.2 "Establishment and Functioning of Business Groups of the European Innovation Partnership for Agricultural Productivity and Sustainability" (project code: M16ΣΥΝ2-00292). This work was supported by the French Embassy in AthensGreece with the program "Programme de bourses pour séjour scientifique de haut niveau (SSHN) en France 2020–2021". The authors wish to thank C-Valo for the grant to LOCASARM project funded by FEDER and Région Centre-Val de Loire.

Data Availability Statement: The data presented in this study are available on request from the corresponding authors (pending privacy and ethical considerations).

Acknowledgments: The authors would like to thank the winemaker Nikos Zacharias of the winery Muses Estate for providing the Mouhtaro single vineyard in Muses Valley.

Conflicts of Interest: The authors declare no conflicts of interest.

References

1. Cabre, F.; Mario, N.; Nuñez, M. Impacts of climate change on viticulture in Argentina. *Reg. Environ. Change* **2020**, *20*, 12. [CrossRef]
2. Droulia, F.; Charalampopoulos, I. Future climate change impacts on European viticulture: A review on recent scientific advances. *Atmosphere* **2021**, *12*, 495. [CrossRef]
3. Jones, G.V.; Edwards, E.J.; Bonada, M.; Sadras, V.O.; Krstic, M.; Herderich, M. Climate change and its consequences for viticulture. In *Managing Wine Quality*, 2nd ed.; Woodhead Publishing: Cambridge, UK, 2022; pp. 727–778. [CrossRef]
4. Hannah, L.; Roehrdanz, P.R.; Ikegami, M.; Shepard, A.V.; Shaw, M.R.; Tabor, G.; Zhi, L.; Marquet, P.A.; Hijmans, R.J. Climate change, wine, and conservation. *Proc. Natl. Acad. Sci. USA* **2013**, *110*, 6907–6912. [CrossRef] [PubMed]
5. Drappier, J.; Thibon, C.; Rabot, A.; Geny-Denis, L. Relationship between wine composition and temperature: Impact on Bordeaux wine typicity in the context of global warming. *Crit. Rev. Food Sci. Nutr.* **2017**, *59*, 14–30. [CrossRef]
6. Santos, J.A.; Fraga, H.; Malheiro, A.C.; Moutinho-Pereira, J.; Dinis, L.-T.; Correia, C.; Moriondo, M.; Leolini, L.; Dibari, C.; Costafreda-Aumedes, S.; et al. A review of the potential climate change impacts and adaptation options for European viticulture. *Appl. Sci.* **2020**, *10*, 3092. [CrossRef]
7. Ratnakumar, P.; Khan, M.L.R.; Minhas, P.S.; Farooq, M.; Sultana, R.; Per, T.S.; Deokate, P.P.; Khan, N.A.; Rane, J. Can plant bio-regulators minimize crop productivity losses caused by drought, heat and salinity stress? An integrated review. *J. Appl. Bot. Food Qual.* **2016**, *89*, 113–125. [CrossRef]
8. Bernardo, S.; Dinis, L.-T.; Machado, N.; Moutinho-Pereira, J. Grapevine abiotic stress assessment and search for sustainable adaptation strategies in Mediterranean-like climates. A review. *Agron. Sustain. Dev.* **2018**, *38*, 66. [CrossRef]

9. Small, C.C.; Degenhardt, D. Plant growth regulators for enhancing revegetation success in reclamation: A review. *Ecol. Eng.* **2018**, *118*, 43–51. [CrossRef]
10. Dufour, M.C.; Lambert, C.; Bouscauta, J.; Merillon, J.M.; Corio-Costet, M.F. Benzothiadiazole-primed defence responses and enhanced differential expression of defence genes in *Vitis vinifera* infected with biotrophic pathogens *Erysiphe necator* and *Plasmopara viticola*. *Plant Pathol.* **2013**, *62*, 370–382. [CrossRef]
11. Gil-Muñoz, R.; Bautista-Ortín, A.B.; Ruiz-García, Y.; Fernández-Fernández, J.I.; Gómez-Plaza, E. Improving phenolic and chromatic characteristics of Monastrell, Merlot and Syrah wines by using methyl jasmonate and benzothiadiazole. *J. Int. Sci. Vigne Vin* **2017**, *51*, 17–27. [CrossRef]
12. Koyama, R.; Roberto, S.R.; de Souza, R.T.; Borges, W.F.S.; Anderson, M.; Waterhouse, A.L.; Cantu, D.; Fidelibus, M.W.; Blanco-Ulate, B. Exogenous Abscisic Acid Promotes Anthocyanin Biosynthesis and Increased Expression of Flavonoid Synthesis Genes in *Vitis vinifera* X *Vitis labrusca* Table Grapes in a Subtropical Region. *Front. Plant Sci.* **2018**, *9*, 323. [CrossRef] [PubMed]
13. Singh, R.K.; Soares, B.; Goufo, P.; Castro, I.; Cosme, F.; Pinto-Sintra, A.L.; Inês, A.; Oliveira, A.A.; Falco, V. Chitosan Upregulates the Genes of the ROS Pathway and Enhances the Antioxidant Potential of Grape (*Vitis vinifera* L. 'Touriga Franca' and 'Tinto Cão') Tissues. *Antioxidants* **2019**, *8*, 525. [CrossRef] [PubMed]
14. Singh, R.K.; Martins, V.; Soares, B.; Castro, I.; Falco, V. Chitosan Application in Vineyards (*Vitis vinifera* L. cv. Tinto Cão) Induces Accumulation of Anthocyanins and Other Phenolics in Berries, Mediated by Modifications in the Transcription of Secondary Metabolism Genes. *Int. J. Mol. Sci.* **2020**, *21*, 306. [CrossRef] [PubMed]
15. Martins, V.; Unlubayir, M.; Teixeira, A.; Gerós, H.; Lanoue, A. Calcium and methyl jasmonate cross-talk in the secondary metabolism of grape cells. *Plant Physiol. Biochem.* **2021**, *165*, 228–238. [CrossRef]
16. Sabir, A.; Kucukbasmaci, A.; Taytak, M.; Bilgin, O.F.; Jawshle, A.I.M.; Mohammed, O.J.M.; Gayretli, Y. Sustainable viticulture practices on the face of climate change. *Agric. Res. Technol.* **2018**, *17*, 133–137. [CrossRef]
17. Koyama, L.; Sadamatsu, K.; Goto-Yamamoto, N. Abscisic acid stimulated ripening and gene expression in berry skins of the Cabernet Sauvignon grape. *Funct. Integr. Genom.* **2010**, *10*, 367–381. [CrossRef]
18. Ferrandino, A.; Lovisolo, C. Abiotic stress effects on grapevine (*Vitis vinifera* L.): Focus on abscisic acid-mediated consequences on secondary metabolism and berry quality. *Environ. Exp. Bot.* **2014**, *103*, 138–147. [CrossRef]
19. Muhammad Aslam, M.; Waseem, M.; Jakada, B.H.; Okal, E.J.; Lei, Z.; Saqib, H.S.A.; Yuan, W.; Xu, W.; Zhang, Q. Mechanisms of Abscisic Acid-Mediated Drought Stress Responses in Plants. *Int. J. Mol. Sci.* **2022**, *23*, 1084. [CrossRef]
20. Peppi, M.C.; Walker, M.A.; Fidelibus, M.W. Application of abscisic acid rapidly upregulated UFGT gene expression and improved color of grape berries. *Vitis J. Grapevine Res.* **2008**, *47*, 11–14.
21. Villalobos-González, L.; Peña-Neira, A.; Ibáñez, F.; Pastenes, C. Long-term effects of abscisic acid (ABA) on the grape berry phenylpropanoid pathway: Gene expression and metabolite content. *Plant Physiol. Biochem.* **2016**, *105*, 213–223. [CrossRef]
22. Alonso, R.; Berli, F.J.; Fontana, A.; Piccoli, P.; Bottini, R. Abscisic acid's role in the modulation of compounds that contribute to wine quality. *Plants* **2021**, *10*, 938. [CrossRef] [PubMed]
23. Neto, F.J.D.; Junior, A.P.; Borges, C.V.; Cunha, S.R.; Callili, D.; Lima, G.P.P.; Roberto, S.R.; Leonel, S.; Tecchio, M.A. The exogenous application of abscisic acid induce accumulation of anthocyanins and phenolic compounds of the 'Rubi' grape. *Am. J. Plant Sci.* **2017**, *8*, 2422–2432. [CrossRef]
24. Karimi, R.; Ebrahimi, M.; Amerian, M. Abscisic acid mitigates NaCl toxicity in grapevine by influencing phytochemical compounds and mineral nutrients in leaves. *Sci. Hortic.* **2021**, *288*, 110366. [CrossRef]
25. Gutiérrez-Gamboa, G.; Romanazzi, G.; Garde-Cerdán, T.; Pérez-Álvarez, E.P. A review of the use of biostimulants in the vineyard for improved grape and wine quality: Effects on prevention of grapevine diseases. *J. Sci. Food Agric.* **2019**, *99*, 1001–1009. [CrossRef]
26. Monteiro, E.; Concalves, B.; Cortez, I.; Castro, I. The Role of biostimulants as alleviators of biotic and abiotic stresses in grapevine: A review. *Plants* **2022**, *11*, 396. [CrossRef] [PubMed]
27. Lorenz, D.H.; Eichhorn, K.W.; Bleiholder, H.; Klose, R.; Meier, U.; Weber, E. Growth Stages of the Grapevine: Phenological growth stages of the grapevine (*Vitis vinifera* L. ssp. *vinifera*)—Codes and descriptions according to the extended BBCH scale. *Aust. J. Grape Wine Res.* **1995**, *1*, 100–103. [CrossRef]
28. Miliordos, D.E.; Alatzas, A.; Kontoudakis, N.; Kouki, A.; Unlubayir, M.; Gémin, M.-P.; Tako, A.; Hatzopoulos, P.; Lanoue, A.; Kotseridis, Y. Abscisic Acid and Chitosan Modulate Polyphenol Metabolism and Berry Qualities in the Domestic White-Colored Cultivar Savvatiano. *Plants* **2022**, *11*, 1648. [CrossRef]
29. Lagouvardos, K.; Kotroni, V.; Bezes, A.; Koletsis, I.; Kopania, T.; Lykoudis, S.; Mazarakis, N.; Papagiannaki, K.; Vougioukas, S. The automatic weather stations NOANN network of the National Observatory of Athens: Operation and database. *Geosci. Data J.* **2017**, *4*, 4–16. [CrossRef]
30. OIV. *Compendium of International Methods of Analysis of Wines and Musts, Methods, OIVMA–AS313–01; OIV–MA–AS2–10*; International Organisation of Vine and Wine: Paris, France, 2018; Volume 2. Available online: https://www.oiv.int/public/medias/3731/oiv-ma-as313-01.pdf (accessed on 31 March 2025).

31. Billet, K.; Delanoue, G.; Arnault, I.; Besseau, S.; Oudin, A.; Courdavault, V.; Marchand, P.A.; Giglioli-Guivarc'h, N.; Guérin, L.; LaNoue, A. Vineyard evaluation of stilbenoid-rich grape cane extracts against downy mildew: A large-scale study. *Pest Manag. Sci.* **2018**, *75*, 1252–1257. [CrossRef]
32. Miliordos, D.-E.; Tsiknia, M.; Kontoudakis, N.; Zaharias, N.; Kotseridis, Y. A holistic approach to using biostimulants on the red grapevine variety, Mouhtaro—from grape to wine: Sourced from the research article: "Impact of Application of Abscisic Acid, Benzothiadiazole and Chitosan on Berry Quality Characteristics and Plant Associated Microbial Communities of Vitis vinifera L var. Mouhtaro Plants." (Sustainability, 2021). Original language of the article: English. *IVES Tech. Rev. Vine Wine* **2022**. [CrossRef]
33. Jeong, S.; Goto-Yamamoto, N.; Kobayashi, S.; Esaka, M. Effects of plant hormones and shading on the accumulation of anthocyanins and the expression of anthocyanin biosynthetic genes in grape berry skins. *Plant Sci.* **2004**, *167*, 247–252. [CrossRef]
34. Cocco, M.; Mercenaro, L.; Lo Cascio, M.; Nieddu, G. Effects of Vine Water Status and Exogenous Abscisic Acid on Berry Composition of Three Red Wine Grapes Grown under Mediterranean Climate. *Horticulturae* **2020**, *6*, 12. [CrossRef]
35. Miliordos, D.E.; Alatzas, A.; Kontoudakis, N.; Unlubayir, M.; Hatzopoulos, P.; Lanoue, A.; Kotseridis, Y. Benzothiadiazole Affects Grape Polyphenol Metabolism and Wine Quality in Two Greek Cultivars: Effects during Ripening Period over Two Years. *Plants* **2023**, *12*, 1179. [CrossRef] [PubMed]
36. Górniak, I.; Bartoszewski, R.; Króliczewski, J. Comprehensive review of antimicrobial activities of plant flavonoids. *Phytochem. Rev.* **2019**, *18*, 241–272. [CrossRef]
37. Malinowska, M.; Billet, K.; Drouet, S.; Munsch, T.; Unlubayir, M.; Tungmunnithum, D.; Giglioli-Guivarch, N.; Hano, C.; Lanoue, A. Grape cane extracts as multifunctional rejuvenating cosmetic ingredient: Evaluation of sirtuin activity, tyrosinase inhibition and bioavailability potential. *Molecules* **2020**, *25*, 2203. [CrossRef]
38. Dias, M.C.; Pinto, D.C.; Silva, A.M. Plant flavonoids: Chemical characteristics and biological activity. *Molecules* **2021**, *26*, 5377. [CrossRef]
39. Ruiz-García, Y.; Gil-Muñoz, R.; López-Roca, J.M.; Martínez-Cutillas, A.; Romero-Cascales, I.; Gómez-Plaza, E. Increasing the Phenolic Compound Content of Grapes by Preharvest Application of Abcisic Acid and a Combination of Methyl Jasmonate and Benzothiadiazole. *J. Agric. Food Chem.* **2013**, *61*, 3978–3983. [CrossRef]
40. Sun, Y.; Liu, Q.; Xi, B.; Dai, H. Study on the regulation of anthocyanin biosynthesis by exogenous abscisic acid in grapevine. *Sci. Hortic.* **2019**, *250*, 294–301. [CrossRef]
41. Alenazi, M.M.; Shafiq, M.; Alobeed, R.S.; Alsdon, A.A.; Abbasi, N.A.; Ali, I.; Mubushar, M.; Javed, I. Application of abscisic acid at véraison improves red pigmentation and accumulation of dietary antioxidants in red table grapes cv. Red Globe at harvest. *Sci. Hortic.* **2019**, *257*, 108672. [CrossRef]
42. He, L.; Ren, Z.-Y.; Wang, Y.; Fu, Y.-Q.; Li, Y.; Meng, N.; Pan, Q.-H. Variation of Growth-to-Ripening Time Interval Induced by Abscisic Acid and Synthetic Auxin Affecting Transcriptome and Flavor Compounds in Cabernet Sauvignon Grape Berry. *Plants* **2020**, *9*, 630. [CrossRef]
43. Liu, B.; Zhang, Y.; Wang, S.; Wang, W.; Xu, X.; Wu, J.; Fang, Y.; Ju, Y. Effects of strigolactone and abscisic acid on the quality and antioxidant activity of grapes (*Vitis vinifera* L.) and wines. *Food Chem. X* **2022**, *16*, 100496. [CrossRef] [PubMed]
44. Malovini, E.; Arancibia, C.; Durán, M.; Fontana, A.; de Rosas, M.I.; Deis, L.; Gargantini, R.; Bottini, R.; Cavagnaro, B.; Martínez, L. Abscisic acid and methyl jasmonic acid module anthocyanins and trans-resveratrol accumulation in berry skin of five red Vitis vinifera cultivars in two contrasting viticultural regions of mendoza-Argentina. *Rev. Fac. Cienc. Agrar.* **2019**, *51*, 451–460.
45. Paladines-Quezada, D.F.; Moreno-Olivares, J.D.; Fernández-Fernández, J.I.; Bleda-Sánchez, J.A.; Martínez-Moreno, A.; Gil-Muñoz, R. Elicitors and Pre-Fermentative Cold Maceration: Effects on Polyphenol Concentration in Monastrell Grapes and Wines. *Biomolecules* **2019**, *9*, 671. [CrossRef] [PubMed]
46. Luan, L.Y.; Zhang, Z.W.; Xi, Z.M.; Huo, S.S.; Ma, L.N. Comparing the effects of exogenous abscisic acid on the phenolic composition of Yan 73 and Cabernet Sauvignon (*Vitis vinifera* L.) wines. *Eur. Food Res. Technol.* **2014**, *239*, 203–213. [CrossRef]
47. Xi, Z.M.; Meng, J.F.; Huo, S.S.; Luan, L.Y.; Ma, L.N.; Zhang, Z.W. Exogenously applied abscisic acid to Yan73 (*V. vinifera*) grapes enhances phenolic content and antioxidant capacity of its wine. *Int. J. Food Sci. Nutr.* **2013**, *64*, 444–451. [CrossRef]
48. Guo, S.; Zhang, M.; Feng, M.; Liu, G.; Torregrosa, L.; Tao, X.; Xu, T. miR156b-targeted VvSBP8/13 functions downstream of the abscisic acid signal to regulate anthocyanins biosynthesis in grapevine fruit under drought. *Hortic. Res.* **2024**, *11*, uhad293. [CrossRef]
49. Katayama-Ikegami, A.; Sakamoto, T.; Shibuya, K.; Katayama, T.; Gao-Takai, M. Effects of abscisic acid treatment on berry coloration and expression of flavonoid biosynthesis genes in grape. *Am. J. Plant Sci.* **2016**, *7*, 1325. [CrossRef]

sustainability

MDPI

Review

Extraction Methods, Encapsulation Techniques, and Health Benefits of Astaxanthin

Ioannis Panagiotakopoulos and Constantina Nasopoulou *

Laboratory of Food Chemistry and of Technology and Quality of Animal Origin Food, Department of Food Science and Nutrition, School of Environment, University of Aegean, Metropolitan Ioakeim 2, 81400 Lemnos, Greece; panagiotakopoulos.ioannes@gmail.com
* Correspondence: knasopoulou@aegean.gr; Tel.: +30-2254083124

Abstract: Astaxanthin, a red carotenoid pigment found in marine species like microalgae, shrimp, and salmon, is a powerful bioactive molecule with several health effects. Astaxanthin, despite its potential, is highly vulnerable to degradation from external elements, including light, oxygen, and temperature, requiring meticulous extraction and stabilization methods. Astaxanthin can be extracted using solvent extraction, ultrasound-assisted extraction (UAE), microwave-assisted extraction (MAE), supercritical fluid extraction (SFE), and enzymatic extraction. Additionally, encapsulation methods that improve the stability and bioavailability of astaxanthin are examined, highlighting their efficacy in maintaining the chemical in unfavorable conditions. This review discusses the extensive range of astaxanthin's medicinal capabilities, encompassing its antioxidant, anticancer, antidiabetic, neuroprotective, and skin-protective activities. This research seeks to emphasize the significance of astaxanthin as a functional bioactive component with substantial potential in nutraceutical and pharmaceutical applications by describing the extraction and encapsulation techniques and their health-promoting attributes.

Keywords: astaxanthin; xanthophyll; carotenoids; marine bioactive; extraction methods; encapsulation; health benefits; marine by-products

1. Introduction

Astaxanthin (Figure 1), a red carotenoid pigment, can be found in microalgae, yeast, salmon, trout, krill, shrimps, and crayfish. Chemically known as 3,3′-dihydroxy-β,β-carotene-4,4′-dione, the substance is a part of the xanthophyll class of carotenoids. Astaxanthin has 40 carbon atoms and is ring-shaped at both ends due to a number of conjugated double bonds, often known as polyene complexes. Since they have a longer conjugated double-bond structure than other isoprenoids, carotenoids are less stable than other compounds; thus, care must be taken to prevent the formation of artifacts and the degradation of the pigment. Carotenoids are highly vulnerable to the damaging effects of light, temperature, acids, and oxygen. Enzymatic degradation can also happen during the extraction of biological materials. Some of the characteristics of astaxanthin, including its capacity to be esterified, more polar nature, and high antioxidant capacity, are explained by the presence of hydroxyl (OH) and carbonyl (C=O) in each ionone ring [1].

Marine-derived astaxanthin holds significant potential as a sustainable bioactive compound, particularly in the context of its extraction and utilization. The use of marine by-products as primary sources for astaxanthin aligns with global sustainability goals [2] by promoting the responsible use of marine resources and reducing the ecological impact of traditional harvesting practices. A crucial aspect of sustainability in astaxanthin production is the efficient utilization of by-products. In the marine and aquaculture industries, large amounts of by-products are often discarded as waste, leading to environmental pollution and resource inefficiency. By incorporating these by-products into astaxanthin production, the industry can reduce waste and improve resource recovery [3]. For instance, marine by-products such as shells of crustaceans and residuals from algae can serve as sources for extracting valuable bioactive compounds, including astaxanthin [4]. This valorization of by-products not only minimizes waste but also contributes to a circular economy, where materials are continuously reused rather than discarded, supporting more sustainable production and consumption practices [5]. In particular, shrimp by-products offer a promising avenue for sustainable astaxanthin extraction. Shrimp shells and heads, which are often discarded after processing, are rich in carotenoids, including astaxanthin. Instead of contributing to marine waste or being used solely for low-value purposes like animal feed, these by-products can be processed and refined to extract astaxanthin efficiently. Utilizing shrimp by-products reduces the need for raw material sourcing from primary marine organisms [6], thereby lowering the pressure on marine ecosystems and contributing to more sustainable seafood processing practices.

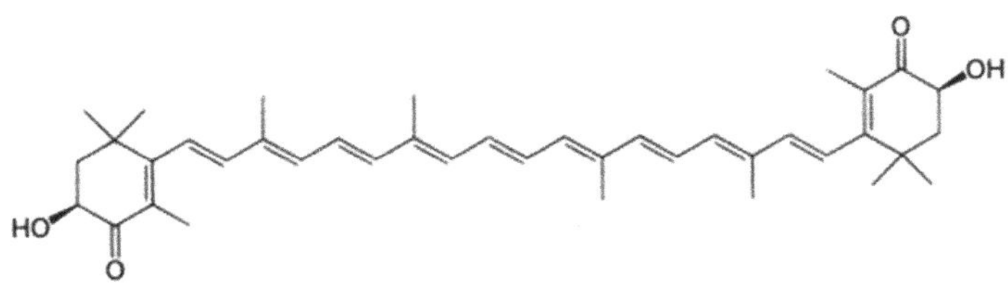

Figure 1. Chemical structure of astaxanthin.

This powerful carotenoid has garnered significant attention for its extensive health benefits and diverse applications in the food, pharmaceutical, and nutraceutical industries. Its extraction has advanced beyond traditional solvent and vegetable oil methods [7] to include innovative, eco-friendly techniques such as ultrasound-assisted extraction (UAE), microwave-assisted extraction (MAE), supercritical fluid extraction (SFE), enzymatic extraction, high-pressure extraction, and microbial fermentation. These methods enhance yield, purity, and sustainability while preserving astaxanthin's bioactive properties [8,9].

Encapsulation is crucial for stabilizing astaxanthin, protecting it from environmental degradation, and improving bioavailability. This involves coating the active compound with biocompatible materials to ensure safety and functionality in various applications. Techniques such as spray drying, freeze drying, coacervation, and liposome formation enable controlled release and compatibility with functional foods and pharmaceuticals [10–12].

Astaxanthin's health-promoting properties include exceptional antioxidant activity, anti-inflammatory effects, neuroprotection, and cardiovascular health benefits. It has also shown anticancer properties, making it a versatile compound for preventive and therapeutic use [13,14]. The convergence of advanced extraction, encapsulation technologies, and evidence of health benefits positions astaxanthin as a critical bioactive compound in promoting overall well-being.

By focusing on marine sources of astaxanthin, valorizing by-products (such as shrimp waste), and discussing green extraction and encapsulation techniques, this review contributes to the broader goal of developing sustainable, eco-friendly methods for producing valuable bioactive compounds. These efforts support sustainable marine resource management while advancing the understanding of how marine biotechnology can play a vital role in both the environmental and human health sectors.

2. Astaxanthin Extraction Methods

Astaxanthin can be extracted either by conventional methods such as oil and organic solvent extraction or by alternative methods like ultrasound-assisted extraction (UAE), microwave-assisted extraction (MAE), supercritical fluid extraction (SFE), enzymatic extraction, high-pressure extraction (HPE), and microbial fermentation. According to the existing literature, a combination of methods, such as oil extraction and ultrasound-assisted extraction, can also be performed.

2.1. Oil Extraction Method

Pu et al. [15] have reported that shrimp byproducts heated for 60 min at 60 °C with stirring contained 6.23 mg of astaxanthin per 100 g of FOA (flaxseed oil astaxanthin) oil. Shrimp waste was extracted by using flaxseed oil. Handayani et al. [16] used palm oil to extract astaxanthin from dried shrimp waste at three different temperatures (50, 60, and 70 °C). The astaxanthin concentration was evaluated every 15 min until a consistent concentration was reached. Depending on the outcomes, the astaxanthin concentration in palm oil was stable at 30–70 °C; however, heat treatment at 80 and 90 °C reduced the astaxanthin content by 10% and 14%, respectively. The effects of different vegetable oils (sunflower, groundnut, gingelly, mustard, soybean, coconut, and rice) and extraction conditions, such as oil-to-waste ratio, time, and temperature, on the carotenoid extraction from shrimp by-product indicated an oil-to-waste ratio of 2:1 v/w and a temperature of 70 °C for 150 min. According to Sachindra and Mahendrakar [7], refined sunflower oil has the greatest carotenoid extraction rate (26.3 μg/g waste). Pu and Sathivel [17] also examined the extraction of astaxanthin from crawfish by-products using flaxseed oil. After heating at 30 °C, there was barely any oxidation of the lipids in the flaxseed oil, both with and without astaxanthin. However, at higher temperatures (40–60 °C for 4 h), the rate of lipid oxidation with astaxanthin was lower than that of flaxseed oil without astaxanthin. An equal ratio of flaxseed oil to waste was used to extract about 30.2 μg of astaxanthin from crawfish waste at 60 °C for 60 min. Astaxanthin also extracted with soybean oil and the shrimp waste sample was heated at 70 °C for 2 h. The pigmented oil of the waste showed an astaxanthin content of 27.48 μg/g [18]. Similarly, El-Bialy and El-Khalek [19] mixed shrimp wastes with a variety of green solvents (coconut oil, corn oil, flaxseed oil, sesame oil, sunflower oil, and wheat germ oil) in a 4:1 (w/v) ratio. The mixture was heated in a shaker water bath for 60 min at 60 °C. The results demonstrate the potential of three vegetable oils to recover astaxanthin up to 5.60, 4.89, and 4.69 μg/g. These oils were corn oil, flaxseed oil, and sesame oil, respectively.

Oil extraction is notable for utilizing edible oils, making it food-grade and simplifying the process without complex equipment. However, it offers lower efficiency compared to other techniques and may result in the co-extraction of unwanted lipophilic compounds. Sachindra and Mahendrakar [7] explored this method, highlighting its simplicity but noting its lower yields compared to solvent-based methods.

2.2. Organic Solvent Extraction

Organic solvent extraction is the most extensively used technique for recovering carotenoids and other bioactive components. Solvent extraction is widely used due to its high efficiency, especially with polar solvents like acetone. Its advantages include being well understood and effective, but it poses potential health and environmental hazards from solvent toxicity and risks of residual solvents in the final product. Dong et al. [9] emphasized the importance of careful solvent selection to balance efficiency and safety. Traditional organic solvent extractions have been carried out under many conditions and solvents. Sharayei et al. [20] examined, among several organic solvents, petroleum ether, n-hexane, ethanol, acetone, and a ternary mixture of petroleum ether, acetone, and water with ratios of 15:75:10, 50:45:5, and 15:50:35. With a consistent sample-to-solvent ratio, extraction was performed in each of the solvents for varying lengths of time (2, 4, and 6 h) at boiling point. The extraction with the highest yield (48.47 μg/g) between the solvents was achieved by the petroleum ether/acetone/water 15:75:10 mixture in 6 h. Organic solvent mixture combinations and condition modification were also reported by Sachindra et al. [21]. The method uses a 25 mL combination of n-hexane and isopropyl alcohol (IPA). To separate the phases and eliminate IPA from the n-hexane phase, the obtained extracts were repeatedly rinsed with an equal volume (75 mL) of a 0.1% saline solution before being dried. A mixture of IPA and hexane produced a higher yield (43.9 μg/g) of astaxanthin than pure acetone (40.6 μg/g) and isopropanol (40.8 μg/g) extraction. In another study, Dalei and Sahoo [22] reported that extraction of astaxanthin from crustacean shell waste was investigated by using different organic solvents. The acetonic extracts produced the maximum carotenoid yield of 48.64 μg/g compared to hexane, methanol, ethanol, petroleum ether, and chloroform, which yielded 36.28 μg/g, 30.47 μg/g, 28.62 μg/g, 11.9 μg/g, and 2.14 μg/g, respectively. Moreover, Dave et al. [23] mentioned that a solvent combining of hexane and isopropanol provided the highest amount of astaxanthin (73.56 g/g, wet weight basis) from crustaceans, while methanol recovered the lowest quantity of astaxanthin (3.50 g/g, wet weight basis). The same organic solvent mixture (isopropanol: hexane (50:50 (*v*/*v*)) was used by Takeungwongtrakul et al. [24], who reported that the greatest carotenoid content of 336.40 mg/kg was extracted from the hepatopancreas of pacific white shrimps (*Litopenaeus vannamei*). On the contrary, Sindhu and Sherief [25] found that acetone extraction afforded the greatest astaxanthin yield of 87.14 μg/g from red shrimp (*Aristeus alcocki*) shell materials. Armenta-Lopez et al. [26] examined shrimp pre-fermented residue for its effectiveness in extracting pigment from three organic solvent systems (chloroform: methanol: water (1:2:4), petroleum ether: acetone: water (15:75:10), and ethanol: water (40:60)). When petroleum ether, acetone, and water were combined, the finding showed that the greatest value (15:75:10) was obtained, followed by chloroform, methanol, and water (1:2:4). In another study, Radzali et al. [27] described that using acetone–methanol (70:30 vol%) recovered 86.52 μg/g dry waste of astaxanthin from shrimp by-product.

2.3. *Ultrasound-Assisted Extraction*

Ultrasound-assisted extraction (UAE) is one of the most researched and efficient developing technologies for recovering natural pigments from by-products. This method involves using sound waves with specific properties, such as frequency, amplitude, and wavelength, to modify the physicochemical characteristics of the propagation medium. Cavitation is a fundamental phenomenon in the application of ultrasound (Figure 2 [28]). It refers to the formation, growth, and implosive collapse of microbubbles or cavities within a liquid medium when exposed to high-intensity ultrasonic waves. This process happens due to the medium's rapid pressure changes brought on by the propagation of ultrasound waves, particularly during the rarefaction phase, when the liquid's dissolved gases can bubble up due to the negative pressure. These bubbles expand and subsequently collapse when subjected to the compression phase of the wave. The implosive collapse of cavitation bubbles generates intense forces, including high temperatures, pressure spikes, and shock waves. This mechanical energy can disrupt cellular structures or enhance chemical reactions [28]. Ultrasound-assisted extraction (UAE) enhances efficiency by disrupting cell walls and reducing extraction time and solvent use. However, it requires specialized equipment and may cause localized heating, leading to degradation of heat-sensitive compounds. Gong and Bassi [29] reviewed UAE's effectiveness in improving yields while cautioning against potential degradation. In a recent study conducted by Panagiotakopoulos et al. [30], the potential of ultrasound-assisted extraction (UAE) for extracting astaxanthin from shrimp by-products was investigated using three different vegetable oils: olive oil, sunflower oil, and flaxseed oil. The optimal conditions for the process were determined to be a by-product-to-vegetable oil ratio of 1:60, an extraction time of 210 min, a 60% amplitude of the extraction process, and the use of olive oil as the extracting medium. Under these conditions, a yield of 235 g of astaxanthin was obtained per gram of by-products. Astaxanthin (50.78 μg/g) was extracted from green tiger (*Penaeus semisulcatus*) shrimp shell under ultrasound-assisted extraction [20]. In another study, shrimp byproducts were extracted under a frequency of 20 kHz and power of 200 W. The recovered yield of astaxanthin was 75 μg/g [31]. Prayitno et al. [32] reported that the optimal extraction time of rebon shrimp (cincalok) for obtaining the highest astaxanthin yield was 3 min at 30% amplitude. Using olive, sesame, grape seeds, coconut, and virgin coconut oil, the astaxanthin levels achieved after 3 min of extraction were 32.54, 53.46, 26.57, 46.34, and 100.62 μg/g of dry cincalok, respectively. Mario et al. [33] examined *H. pluvialis* samples using ultrasound-assisted extraction in different solvent systems. The extraction operated at a 25 kHz frequency, 450 and 648 Watts, and a temperature of 50 °C for 20 min. The maximum yield was obtained at 648 W (42.45 mg/g). In some cases, ultrasound is used for cells disruption. Gogate and Nadar [34], used acid and ultrasound pretreatment followed by solvent extraction. By destroying cells with 3 M lactic acid and 15 min of sonication at 80 W, a maximum of 93% yield was reached. A similar study was conducted by Haque et al. [35], and the most efficient extraction method was ultrasonication with sodium hydroxide pretreatment, followed by methanol extraction. In comparison with ultrasonication and solvent extraction alone, the recovery of astaxanthin increased by 65–213% when it was combined with ultrasonication and chemical pretreatment of the cells (*Haematococcus pluvialis*). Gao et al. [36] recovered astaxanthin from shrimp waste (*Penaeus vannamei*) by ultrasonic-assisted extraction using ionic liquid-in-water microemulsions. Four different times (30, 60, 90, and 120 min) and power levels (30, 50, 70, and 90 W) of ultrasonic-assisted extraction were used. The optimum conditions for extracting astaxanthin from shrimp waste were reported to be an ultrasonic power of 50 W and an extraction time of 60 min, and the extraction efficiency was reached at 284.48 µg/g. Zhao et al. [37] recovered astaxanthin from *Haematococcus pluvialis* with operational conditions at 100 W, 40 °C for 60 min. The astaxanthin concentration was 8.56 mg/100 mg. Finally, Wu et al. [38] used the ultrasonic-assisted extraction method for the extraction of astaxanthin from *Xanthophyllomyces dendrorhous* and the recovered yield was 1472.85 µg/g.

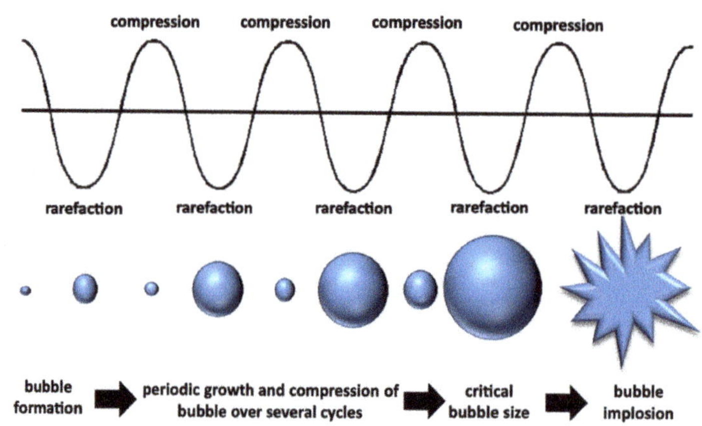

Figure 2. Cavitation principle.

2.4. *Microwave-Assisted Extraction*

Microwave-assisted extraction (MAE) is an innovative and affordable technology that combines microwaves and the conventional solvent method. Microwaves are used to heat the solvents for the extraction of carotenoids in a brief period while reducing the amount of solvent used [39]. Microwave-assisted extraction (MAE) offers a rapid process with reduced solvent consumption and efficient heating for better cell disruption. Despite these advantages, there is a risk of thermal degradation of astaxanthin, and the method is not easily scalable for industrial applications [40]. Dewati et al. [41] examined astaxanthin microwave-assisted extraction from *Haematococcus pluvialis* using four different solvents (acetone, methanol, ethanol, and dichloromethane). *Haematococcus pluvialis* was pretreated with HCl for cell disruption. The microwave extraction conditions were 800 W of power and a frequency of 2450 MHz. Acetone was identified to be the most effective solvent for obtaining the maximum recovery rate (100%) followed by 62.80, 49.40, and 48.27% recovery in ethanol, dichloromethane, and methanol. Similarly, Zhao et al. [42] extracted astaxanthin from *Haematococcus pluvialis* using ethanol and ethyl acetate in a 2:1 (v/v) ratio. The optimized conditions for microwave extraction were found at 141 W power and an extraction time of 83 s. About 594 µg/g of astaxanthin were recovered below these parameters.

In another study, between four extraction methods, MAE was the most efficient, with 74% astaxanthin recovery from microalgae *Haematococcus pluvialis*. The study results indicated that acetone provided the best astaxanthin recovery at 75 °C in a short time [8]. Moreover, Zhao et al. [37] used extracted *Haematococcus pluvialis* powder at 40 °C for 40 min. MAE showed the extraction efficiency of astaxanthin at 36.88%. Additionally, Ahmad et al. [43] reported that microwave-assisted extraction using ethanol 90% was found to be the most efficient technique compared to ultrasound-assisted extraction and hot soaking. The xanthophylls gained from this method reached 13.411 mg/g. A yeast that is well known for its astaxanthin content is the *Phaffia rhodozyma*. Zhu et al. [44] presented a microwave extraction optimization to recover astaxanthin from *Phaffia rhodozyma*. Microwaves were initially used for cell disruption followed by extraction with 3 mL of dimethyl sulfoxide and 12.6 mL of anhydrous alcohol. The most efficient temperature and extraction time were 50 °C and 15 min, respectively, while the microwave frequency was 416.5 MHz. The astaxanthin yield obtained was 21.56% higher than the original yield. Apart from microalgae and yeasts, microwave-assisted extraction has been used for astaxanthin recovery from shrimp shells. Nanda et al. [45] examined the combination of MAE with NADES solvents. The extraction was optimized when the microwave power was 180 W and the extraction time 5 min, with an astaxanthin yield of 7466 ppm. According to Ahmad et al. [43], microwave-assisted extraction of xanthophylls from microalga *Chlorella luteoviridis* appeared to be more effective than hot soaking and ultrasound-assisted extraction with 4.154 mg/g using 90% ethanol.

2.5. Supercritical Fluid Extraction

Supercritical fluid extraction (SFE) is an environmentally friendly technique to recover pigments. For the extraction of bioactive compounds, this procedure includes GRAS solvents (generally recognized as safe). It improves the amount of time it takes to extract and is the most important method for heat-sensitive materials like carotenoids. Supercritical fluid extraction (SFE) uses non-toxic CO_2, yielding solvent-free extracts with high selectivity and efficiency. Its downsides include the need for precise pressure and temperature control [46]. Carbon dioxide is cheap, chemically inert, nonflammable, easy to obtain in high purity, and reusable. Sanzo et al. [47] examined different temperatures, extraction time, pressure, and CO_2 flow rate for the microalgae *Haematococcus pluvialis*. The findings demonstrate that at 50 °C, 120 min, 550 bars, and a flow rate of 3.62 g/min the most astaxanthin that could be recovered was 98.6%. Accordingly, Molino et al. [48] recovered astaxanthin from *Haematococcus pluvialis*, and the findings demonstrated that 65 °C and 550 bar provided the maximum astaxanthin capacity of 18.5 mg/g dry weight (92%). Radzali et al. [27,49] conducted research to optimize the extraction parameters for Asian tiger shrimp (Penaeus monodon) waste and found that using ethanol as a co-solvent at 60 °C and 20 MPa yielded the highest recovery of astaxanthin, both in its complex form (comprising both free and esterified astaxanthin) and in its free form, with 58.03 μg/g and 12.25 μg/g, respectively. In subsequent research, Radzali et al. [49] reported that 21.5 MPa, 56.88 °C, and 1.89 mL/min obtained 58.50 μg/g of astaxanthin yield. On the other side, Ali-Nehari et al. [50] reported that 25 MPa and 45 °C proved to be the best conditions to isolate astaxanthin from krill (*Euphausia superba*), and the astaxanthin yield was 8.62 mg/100 g. The supercritical CO_2 extraction of astaxanthin from Brazilian red-spotted shrimp (*Farfantepenaeus paulensis*) was enhanced by Sanchez-Camargo et al. [51]. According to this research, extreme heat led to a decrease in the quantity of astaxanthin, whereas increased pressure had only a small impact. At 43 °C and 37 MPa, the maximum yields of 20 μg astaxanthin/g (dry weight basis), or a 37% recovery of the whole pigment, were obtained. In order to extract astaxanthin over a variety of temperatures, pressures, and moisture contents, crawfish byproducts were treated with SC-CO_2. The average amount of astaxanthin extracted was 157.1 mg/kg [52]. In another study, Cheng et al. [53] performed an extraction experiment, and the astaxanthin was recovered with a 92% efficiency, utilizing SC-CO_2 and 20% (*v*/*v*) ethanol at 55 °C for 15 min under low pressure (8 MPa). Sanchez-Camargo et al. [54] also reported that the astaxanthin extraction yields increased significantly as the amount of ethanol in the ethanol/SC-CO_2 mixture was increased. The ethanol levels ranged from 5 to 15%. When an ethanol proportion of 15% (m/m) was utilized, the greatest astaxanthin concentration in the extract was obtained with 34.8 µg astaxanthin/g of dry residue. In other cases, different methods have been combined for higher performance. Nunes et al. [55] pretreated brown crab (*Cancer pagurus*) waste with microwaves with ethanol as solvent at 140 °C and 300 W for 90 s, followed by supercritical fluid extraction with optimal conditions at 50 MPa, 40 °C, and 13 wt % ethanol content in the supercritical fluid mixture. The yield recovered within 30 min of the extraction reached at 4.44 µg astaxanthin/g waste.

2.6. Enzymatic Extraction

Another eco-friendly method that is increasingly being investigated for the use of extracted value-added products in nutraceuticals is enzymatic extraction, which uses less energy. This extraction method, when conducted under mild conditions, preserves astaxanthin's bioactivity. However, it is costly due to the enzymes required and involves longer extraction times. Researchers [56] emphasized the eco-friendliness of enzymatic extraction while noting the need for cost-effective enzyme solutions. Astaxanthin can be extracted enzymatically by applying lipases and proteases from different sources. Enzymes can be used at different stages of the process, producing a variety of products and byproducts because they are sensitive to temperature, acidity, and other environmental factors. Enzymes facilitate the extraction of astaxanthin in the carotenoprotein form, which is a complex of carotenoid and lipoprotein, resulting in the simultaneous provision of carotenoids and protein. Klomklao et al. [57] studied the trypsin from bluefish (*Pomatomus saltatrix*) and the impact of the enzyme on recovering carotenoproteins from the shells of black tiger shrimp (*Penaeus monodon*). When using pure trypsin, they discovered that the yield of astaxanthin was 87.91 mg/g. By adding 25 mg of cod trypsin to the extracting solvent containing 0.5 N of ethylene diamine tetraacetic acid (EDTA), 64% of the astaxanthin from shrimp waste was extracted within 24 h. Moreover, 49% of the astaxanthin was obtained when 25 g of bovine trypsin were utilized. De Holanda and Netto [58] conducted a comparative study for recovering astaxanthin from shrimp waste (*Xiphopenaeus kroyeri*) using the enzymatic hydrolysis method. The compared enzymes were alcalase and pancreatin, and the findings showed that pancreatin was less effective than alcalase, which increased astaxanthin retrieval from 4.7 to 5.7 mg/100 g of dry waste. Similarly, Babu et al. [59] evaluated three different enzymes (trypsin, papain, and pepsin) for their extractive efficiency in shrimp waste of four different species of shrimp. The researchers noted that trypsin recovered the most carotenoids, although pepsin and papain were also highly effective. The enzymatic technique is also used as an efficient pre-treatment. Zhao et al. [60] described that astaxanthin separation yield could be improved by using enzymes. In comparison to pectinases, the effectiveness of cellulase-aided extraction was assessed. The findings demonstrated that the pectinase-assisted extraction yield (75.30%) was considerably higher than the cellulase yield (67.15%). Jafari et al. [61] recovered pigments from shrimp wastes by combining enzymatic and alkaline treatment. The outcomes showed that the combination of trypsin–alkaline extraction was more effective than trypsin alone. In another study, Wang et al. [62] extracted astaxanthin from Arctic sweet shrimp shells using eight different enzymes (neutral protease, alkaline protease, papain, amylase, lipase, esterase, and pectinase). The neutral protease between them yielded the best results. When neutral protease was used to extract astaxanthin from shrimp shells, it produced 128.30 µg/g waste.

2.7. High-Pressure Extraction

High-pressure extraction is efficient for cell disruption, leading to higher yields in shorter times. Nevertheless, it consumes significant energy and risks degrading sensitive compounds. Khan et al. [63] noted its efficiency but highlighted challenges related to energy consumption. High-pressure extraction (HPE) methods have been shown to significantly enhance astaxanthin recovery from shrimp waste and other biological matrices. Li et al. [64]

utilized high-pressure processing (HPP) on Penaeus vannamei shrimp waste, achieving a yield of 67.8% at optimal conditions (400 MPa, 50 °C, for 10 min), with notable improvement in antioxidant activity. Irna et al. [65] compared HPE with chemical extraction across six shrimp species, reporting that HPE yielded astaxanthin amounts up to 85% higher than chemical methods, with the highest extraction efficiency found in carapaces of Penaeus monodon. Torres-Haro et al. [66] conducted a comparative study using non-conventional high-pressure techniques for Xanthophyllomyces dendrorhous, optimizing conditions at 400 MPa and 60 °C, resulting in a 72% recovery of astaxanthin. Similarly, Irna et al. [67] applied response surface methodology to optimize high-pressure extraction, identifying 238.54 MPa as optimal and achieving an astaxanthin yield of 80.94 μg/g of shrimp waste.

2.8. Microbial Fermentation

Microbial fermentation extraction is a sustainable extraction method that can achieve high yields through metabolic engineering. Its challenges include complex optimization processes and high initial setup costs. Zhang et al. [68] reviewed this method, discussing its potential and the current hurdles to its widespread adoption. Microbial fermentation has emerged as an efficient method for extracting astaxanthin, utilizing diverse microorganisms to convert waste substrates into high-value products. Jafari et al. [69] used lactic acid bacteria for the fermentation of shrimp waste, optimizing temperature, pH, and substrate concentration, resulting in a yield of 95.34 μg/g of shrimp waste astaxanthin esters. Harith et al. [70] investigated the yeast Xanthophyllomyces dendrorhous, identifying optimal conditions of pH 5.5 and elevated agitation, which produced a yield of 3.6 mg/L astaxanthin. Hamdi et al. [71] conducted a comparison of microbial and chemical methods, revealing that fermentation utilizing Saccharomyces cerevisiae and Lactobacillus acidophilus achieved yields similar to those of chemical extraction, while also resulting in reduced environmental impacts.

Astaxanthin extraction methods from various sources are presented in Table 1.

Table 1. Astaxanthin extraction methods.

Astaxanthin Source	Extraction Method	References
Shrimp waste	Oil extraction	[7,15,16,18,19]
Crawfish byproducts	Oil extraction	[17]
Shrimp waste	Organic solvent extraction	[20–23,25–27]
Hepatopancreas of Pacific white shrimp	Organic solvent extraction	[24]
Shrimp byproducts	Ultrasound-assisted extraction	[30,31,36]
Fermented rebon shrimp	Ultrasound-assisted extraction	[32]
Haematococcus Pluvialis	Ultrasound-assisted extraction	[33,35,37]
Phaffia rhodozyma	Ultrasound-assisted extraction	[34]
Xanthophyllomyces dendrorhous	Ultrasound-assisted extraction	[38]
Haematococcus Pluvialis	Microwave-assisted extraction	[37,41,42]
Chlorella luteoviridis	Microwave-assisted extraction	[43]
Phaffia Rhodozyma	Microwave-assisted extraction	[44]
Shrimp shell	Microwave-assisted extraction	[45]
Haematococcus Pluvialis	Supercritical fluid extraction	[47,48,53]
Shrimp waste	Supercritical fluid extraction	[27,49,51,54]
Krill (*Euphausia superba*)	Supercritical fluid extraction	[50]
Crawfish byproducts	Supercritical fluid extraction	[52]
Crab waste	Supercritical fluid extraction	[55]
Shrimp waste	Enzymatic extraction	[57–59,61,62]
Haematococcus Pluvialis	Enzymatic extraction	[60]
Shrimp waste	High-pressure extraction	[64,65,67]
X. dendrorhous	High-pressure extraction	[66]
Shrimp waste	Microbial fermentation	[68,70]
X. dendrorhous	Microbial fermentation	[69]
Crab waste	Microbial fermentation	[71]

2.9. Comparison of Extraction Methods

Solvent extraction is highly efficient and scalable but has medium purity and significant environmental drawbacks due to solvent toxicity and residue risks. Ultrasound-assisted extraction (UAE) enhances efficiency and purity through cell wall disruption and reduces solvent use, but it requires specialized equipment and carries a risk of compound degradation. Microwave-assisted extraction (MAE) is rapid and efficient, but it has medium purity and limited scalability, with potential thermal damage to astaxanthin. Supercritical fluid extraction (SFE) uses non-toxic CO_2, achieving very high purity and efficiency while being environmentally friendly, though it has high costs and moderate scalability. Enzymatic extraction operates under mild conditions, preserving astaxanthin's bioactivity with minimal environmental impact, but it is slower, costlier, and less scalable [72,73]. Microbial fermentation offers very high purity and sustainability but is time-intensive, expensive, and still being developed for large-scale production. Finally, supercritical fluid extraction (SFE) and microbial fermentation are the most environmentally sustainable methods, offering the highest purity [74]. For applications requiring cost efficiency, solvent extraction remains the most economical but comes with significant environmental trade-offs. UAE and solvent extraction are more suitable for large-scale operations, offering better scalability and time efficiency. The choice of method depends on the specific application and the need to balance cost, purity, environmental impact, and scalability.

The quality of extracted astaxanthin is highly affected by the extraction method, as various procedures affect the compound's purity, bioactivity, and stability [75]. Supercritical fluid extraction (SFE) continuously produces superior-quality astaxanthin by functioning under gentle circumstances, hence preventing thermal or chemical degradation. Enzymatic extraction retains the bioactivity of astaxanthin, yielding high-purity extracts with low contaminants. Conversely, solvent extraction, although effective, frequently leaves behind residual solvents and contaminants that diminish quality. UAE and MAE can yield high-quality astaxanthin if operational parameters are carefully controlled, but they risk degradation under high-energy conditions [76].

3. Astaxanthin Encapsulation Method

Encapsulation is the process of covering or trapping a substance inside another material to keep it from coming into contact with the exterior environment. The encapsulated material, which might be a liquid, solid, or gas, is known as the core, active substance, or internal phase, whereas the encapsulating agent is known as the wall material, membrane, coating, or shell [77]. In the food industry, the encapsulation technique is utilized to create liquid and solid substances that serve as efficient barriers over external factors like oxygen, light, and free radicals [78]. Encapsulation methods, which enclose sensitive ingredients in a wall material, can improve bioactive molecules [79]. Particles produced by different methods vary in size from microscale to nanoscale and are categorized accordingly [77]. Encapsulating materials can also be utilized to improve the preservation of bioactive substances. The major purposes of the encapsulation technology are to protect the core materials from external environmental conditions, to prevent compound reactivity, to protect the compounds from degradation, to mask undesirable flavors of the core materials, to control the release of core materials, and finally, to provide better storability by preventing degradative reactions like dehydration and oxidation. In this section of the review, the different encapsulation methods of astaxanthin will be discussed.

3.1. Coacervation

Coacervation is the procedure of balancing a polymer-rich phase (coacervate) with another liquid phase. Coacervation is the process of separating the liquid phase of a coating material from a complex solution with diverse polymers and encasing the liquid phase around suspended core particles in a uniform layer [80]. Simple coacervation is mostly about a single biopolymer system, while complex coacervation is mostly about at least two biopolymer systems. Electrostatic interactions between cationic biopolymers (like gelatin and chitosan) and anionic biopolymers (like pectin, alginate, and arabic gum) cause complex coacervation [81,82]. Complex coacervation, in more detail, is a phase separation process that occurs when a colloidal liquid system divides into a colloid-rich and a colloid-poor phase. The first one is called "coacervate", and the second is "equilibrium". This procedure is based on the fact that two oppositely charged polymers interact electrostatically, which is mostly caused by a change in pH and leads to complexation and then phase separation [83].

Gomez-Estaca et al. [84] examined the complex coacervation technique of encapsulating astaxanthin from shrimp byproducts using gelatin. Astaxanthin's polymorphic microcapsules had an average size of 32.7 μm and >59.9% encapsulation efficiency. A study of accelerated stability (43 days at 80% relative humidity and 36 °C) revealed that there was no lipid oxidation by TBARS (thiobarbituric acid reactive substances) throughout the storage period and that the encapsulation effectively slowed astaxanthin degradation as compared to non-encapsulated lipid extract. Taksima et al. [85] conducted another study with encapsulated astaxanthin from shrimp waste by complex coacervation into alginate–chitosan beads using an ultrasonic atomizer. Encapsulated astaxanthin with 1.2% (*w*/*v*) alginate and 1.0% (*w*/*v*) chitosan demonstrated up to 90% encapsulation efficiency and >50% DPPH scavenging activity. Furthermore, when utilized as a functional component in yogurt, the stability of the encapsulated astaxanthin could be significantly increased. This showed that the use of alginate–chitosan beads provided adequate astaxanthin protection as well as a longer shelf life. Zhou et al. [86] observed that encapsulation by complex coacervation managed to reduce the astaxanthin loss during storage in comparison to free oleoresin. The pH value affected the structure of the microcapsules; those held at pH 4.0 were more stable than those at pH 3.0 and 7.0. Gomez-Estaca et al. [84] examined the storage stability of astaxanthin-rich microcapsules using a gelatin–gum arabic complex. The encapsulation efficiency was measured at 93.5%. This technique improved the complex's stability and covered up its potentially unpleasant tastes and smells.

3.2. Drying Methods

Spray-drying microencapsulation is the most often used method in the food industry because it is simple and converts liquids to solids, allowing for easy integration and dispersion in food products when only small amounts need to be incorporated [87]. Spray drying also is one of the oldest and most used procedures for drying or microencapsulating food goods and bioactive substances, mostly because of its quick and affordable operation. Additionally, it offers advantages common to other encapsulating techniques, such as transforming hydrophobic substances into water-dispersible powders and improving the stability of bioactives [88]. Shen and Quek [89] used the spray-drying method to examine a mixture of milk proteins and soluble corn fiber to encapsulate astaxanthin. The spray-dried emulsion had high physical stability (95%), according to the results. Furthermore, Bustos-Garza et al. [87] studied astaxanthin encapsulation using different wall materials. The greatest encapsulation yields (61.2–70.1% (*w*/*w*) dry weight) were achieved with whey protein, either by itself or in combination with gum arabic, among the wall materials. However, the microcapsules of astaxanthin with 100% WP exhibited the most increased temperature stability. Astaxanthin from *Haematococcus pluvialis* was encapsulated using maltodextrin and gelatin as a wall coating. The results revealed that the highest encapsulation efficiency was 71.76%, while the astaxanthin encapsulation yield was 38.02% [60]. Similarly, Montero et al. [90] utilized various wall materials to encapsulate a lipid extract from shrimp waste using spray drying. Even though lipid oxidation and astaxanthin loss were partially induced by heat treatment, no additional astaxanthin loss was seen after chilled storage (110 days), and lipid oxidation was minor, indicating the durability of the produced components. In another study, shrimp extract was encapsulated and added to cookies. Even after 12 days of storage in the light, there were no changes in the amount of EPA, DHA, and astaxanthin in the cookies. The efficacy of spray-dried shrimp lipid extract as a technical element for aqueous food was assessed by Gómez-Guillén et al. [91], and the results showed that the color, astaxanthin concentration, and fatty acid composition of the encapsulated lipid extract were extremely stable.

Freeze drying, also known as lyophilization or cryodesiccation, is a widely known method applied for heat-sensitive bioactive substances and living cells. The technique relies on the subsequent drying of aqueous samples by water sublimation under low pressure (<ca. 5 mbar) after they have been frozen at extremely low temperatures (−80 to −40 °C) [92]. In comparison to other drying techniques, the main drawbacks are high energy consumption, lengthy operation time, and expensive production cost [93]. Freeze drying offers significant protection for carotenoids from oxidation and isomerization that can happen with conventional dehydration techniques utilizing hot air streams. In contrast to heat processing, freeze drying has a much lower influence on carotenoid degradation and encapsulation effectiveness because of the low temperature and pressure involved, and it does not cause water-phase reactions or oxidation. This is also confirmed by Ahmed et al. [94], who ascertained that freeze-drying in *Haematococcus pluvialis* extract produced a higher yield of astaxanthin due to the lack of heat treatment, while spray-drying resulted in a decrease in the astaxanthin amount. Finally, Marin et al. [95] evaluated the outcome of integrating an astaxanthin-containing shrimp lipid extract into a surimi-based product after freeze drying. After freeze drying, the particle sizes of astaxanthin capsules increased from 199 nm to 283 nm. The use of the freeze-dried liposomes reduced the gel's strength and managed to maintain the gels' stability during long-term freezing storage.

3.3. Liposomes

Liposomes are vesicular and colloidal delivery systems made up of at least one bilayer amphiphilic lipid membrane and a hydrophilic core. These structures have many benefits, such as the ability to encapsulate components that are hydrophilic, hydrophobic, or amphiphilic, and permit the sustained release of bioactive substances at certain temperatures, i.e., above the phospholipids' melting point (between 180 and 200 °C). Another advantage is combining liposome formation with drying methods, which can be a cost-effective and sustainable alternative for encapsulation and the capacity to prolong the shelf life of products. The bioactive substance is trapped during microencapsulation either in the inner aqueous phase or within the membrane, with carriers ranging in size from 30 nm to a few millimeters [96–100].

Pan et al. [101] studied astaxanthin-loaded liposomes that were made with soybean phosphatidylcholine and thin-film ultrasound. The outcome showed a high encapsulation efficiency of 97.68%, strong antioxidant activity, and good storage stability at low temperatures. Moreover, the high encapsulation efficiency of astaxanthin in liposomes is thought to be directly correlated with its good physicochemical features. In another study, Pan, Wang, and Gu [102] produced n reduced-particle-size nanoliposomes, which showed improved permeation and targeting characteristics. In this study, astaxanthin-loaded liposomes were made with soybean phosphatidylcholine and a film-dispersion ultrasonic technique. Nanoliposomes enabled greater encapsulation efficiency (97.49%) and a particle size of 80 nm on average compared to previous reports. Astaxanthin-loaded liposomes were 17 times easier to dissolve than pure astaxanthin, and they dispersed well in water without precipitation or insoluble particles. To examine the release of compounds, a pure astaxanthin solution and nanoliposomes were used in an in vitro experiment. After 24 h, the release from nanoliposomes was much slower (28.74%), than from the pure solution (95.27%), demonstrating that nanoliposomes have the potential for continuous release. In another study, water-dispersible liposomes with astaxanthin were made, and the ability of the liposomes to scavenge the hydroxyl radical was studied. A significant amount of astaxanthin was encapsulated due to the liposomal structure [103]. Astaxanthin and vitamin E were encapsulated in liposomes by Kamezaki et al. [104]. When astaxanthin and vitamin E were co-administered in this system, the antioxidant activity rose considerably. Finally, the above results were also confirmed by another study [105].

Astaxanthin encapsulation methods are presented in Table 2.

Table 2. Astaxanthin encapsulation methods.

Astaxanthin Sources	Encapsulation Method	References
Shrimp lipid extract	Coacervation	[84]
Shrimp waste	Coacervation	[85]
Haematococcus Pluvialis extract	Coacervation	[86]
Haematococcus Pluvialis	Drying method	[60]
Haematococcus Pluvialis cyst cells	Drying method	[87]
Astaxanthin standard	Drying method	[89]
Shrimp waste lipid extract	Drying method	[90]
Shrimps	Drying method	[91]
Astaxanthin standard	Liposomes	[101]

3.4. Comparison of Encapsulation Techniques

Astaxanthin requires effective encapsulation techniques to enhance its stability, bioavailability, and controlled release. Among the various techniques, coacervation, drying methods, and liposome encapsulation offer distinct advantages and limitations [106]. Coacervation, a phase-separation method, is especially efficient at encapsulating hydrophobic substances such as astaxanthin. The method facilitates high encapsulation efficiency and secures the core material from environmental deterioration, but the process is often sensitive to pH and temperature variations, potentially affecting scalability and uniformity [106]. Drying techniques, including spray drying and freeze drying, are extensively utilized for their efficiency and economic viability. These techniques yield dry, stable powders with prolonged shelf life; nevertheless, they may induce heat stress (in spray drying) or structural damage (in freeze drying), potentially diminishing astaxanthin's bioactivity [107]. Liposome encapsulation utilizes phospholipid bilayers to create biocompatible vesicles, improving the bioavailability and prolonged release of astaxanthin. Liposomes offer superior protection against oxidation but can be expensive to manufacture and susceptible to instability over time [108]. In terms of effectiveness, liposomes typically provide enhanced bioavailability, coacervation is effective at maintaining antioxidants under regulated environmental conditions, and drying techniques offer practical and scalable solutions for industrial use. The selection of method consequently hinges on the particular application criteria, including stability, cost, and distribution efficiency.

4. Astaxanthin Health Benefits

Astaxanthin, a naturally occurring carotenoid pigment, has emerged as a potent asset in the endeavor to enhance holistic health. This vibrant compound, found in microorganisms, seafood, and select plants, offers a spectrum of health benefits that have garnered considerable attention. Primarily, it is noteworthy to emphasize the exceptional antioxidant qualities exhibited by astaxanthin. In terms of its capacity to counteract detrimental free radicals, it surpasses numerous other antioxidants. This attribute confers notable benefits in promoting skin health, mitigating the manifestations of aging, and safeguarding the skin against the deleterious impacts of ultraviolet radiation. Moreover, astaxanthin is recognized for its anti-inflammatory properties, which can help alleviate joint discomfort and promote musculoskeletal health.

Furthermore, astaxanthin has exhibited potential in increasing cardiovascular performance and alleviating oxidative stress, hence promoting heart health, in addition to its physical benefits. Additionally, it demonstrates the capacity to improve cognitive function and sustain brain health. The inclusion of astaxanthin in one's wellness routine is supported by its diverse range of health benefits, which arise from its notable antioxidant and anti-inflammatory characteristics. This compound offers a comprehensive strategy for preserving and improving overall health.

4.1. Antioxidant Activity

Antioxidants are compounds that play a vital role in preventing oxidation caused by free radicals and reactive oxygen species (ROS) which are highly reactive molecules produced during normal aerobic metabolism in organisms. Excessive amounts of these oxidative molecules can result in protein and lipid oxidation, as well as DNA damage, which are associated with various disorders. Both endogenous and exogenous antioxidants, such as carotenoids, can help prevent this damage by inhibiting the formation of these oxidative molecules. Carotenoids possess a polyene chain characterized by the presence of a long, conjugated system, which enables them to quench singlet oxygen and scavenge radicals, effectively terminating the chain reactions. The beneficial effects of carotenoids on biological systems may be attributed to their antioxidant properties, which stem from their interactions with cell membranes [109]. Astaxanthin is extensively utilized in aquaculture feeds, the food industry, pharmaceutical applications, cosmetic sectors, and medical research endeavors [110].

The antioxidant properties of astaxanthin against various free radicals, reactive oxygen species (ROS), and reactive nitrogen species (RNS) have been observed in in vitro studies using liposomes as a model of a cell membrane. It is worth mentioning that astaxanthin demonstrated superior efficacy in the removal of peroxyl radicals ($RO_2\bullet$) compared to α-tocopherol and other carotenoids, such as β-carotene and lycopene [111]. In addition, astaxanthin demonstrated a higher efficacy in neutralizing hydroxyl radicals (HO•), peroxyl radicals ($RO_2\bullet$), and hypochlorous acid (HOCl) compared to other carotenoids, such as zeaxanthin, fucoxanthin, and canthaxanthin. According to Rodrigues et al. [112], β-carotene was identified as the most effective compound in scavenging peroxynitrite anions (ONOO−). However, astaxanthin exhibited a greater capacity in scavenging this reactive nitrogen species (RNS) compared to α-tocopherol or lycopene. The incorporation of astaxanthin into liposomes that contain polyunsaturated fatty acids resulted in a showing of potent antioxidant properties. This was achieved through the inhibition of lipid hydroperoxide (LOOH) formation and the preservation of membrane structure integrity. In contrast, McNulty et al. [113] found that β-carotene and lycopene, both of which exhibit pro-oxidant properties, caused disruption to the membrane bilayer. The enhanced efficacy of astaxanthin in countering lipid peroxidation can be attributed to its capacity to scavenge radicals not only along its conjugated polyene chain but also within its polar terminal ring structures. This characteristic grants astaxanthin antioxidant properties both within the membrane and on its surface, which are achieved through intermolecular and intramolecular hydrogen bonding [114]. In addition, these polar functional groups engage in interactions with hydrophilic cofactors, such as vitamin C. These cofactors have the ability to accept the radical cations produced and thereby restore the electron transfer capability of astaxanthin that has undergone degradation [115]. The fluorescence anisotropy study conducted by Liang et al. [116] demonstrated that the inclusion of astaxanthin in the system led to an increase in membrane fluidity. This effect was attributed to bimolecular radical reactions, which resulted in reduced diffusion and enhanced antioxidant efficiency.

Astaxanthin has also been studied using in vivo models where the results confirmed the high antioxidant capacity. Oxidative damage caused by reactive oxygen species (ROS) in rat cells can be effectively reduced by astaxanthin. In addition, it resulted in a reduction in the creation of reactive oxygen species within the mitochondria [117]. Several sources, such as *H. pluvialis* and *Botryococcus braunii*, exhibited significant antioxidant capacity. In comparison to *H. Pluvialis*, *Botryococcus braunii* demonstrated superior bioavailability and enhanced antioxidant properties through the augmentation of enzymes such as catalase, peroxidase, lipid peroxidation, and superoxide dismutase [118,119]. Another research demonstrated similar outcomes where consumption of astaxanthin led to increased concentrations of antioxidant enzymes, including catalase and superoxide dismutase, within the mouse brain. The researchers observed that the administration of astaxanthin increased the activity of the aforementioned enzymes, leading to a subsequent elevation in the levels of glutathione within the brain [120]. It has been stated that the compound also exhibited the ability to inhibit the cytotoxicity and oxidative stress induced by 1-methyl-4-phenylpyridinium ion (MPP+) in cultured PC12 rat pheochromocytoma cells. This was accomplished by upregulating nuclear factor erythroid 2-related factor 2 (Nrf2), a transcription factor that regulates the expression of several genes involved in endogenous antioxidant defense and xenobiotic metabolism and suppressing the production of reactive oxygen species (ROS) [121]. Additionally, the compound enhanced the expression of heme oxygenase-1 (HO-1) at both mRNA and protein levels, while suppressing the expression of NAD(P)H oxidase 2 (NOX2) at the mRNA and protein levels [99]. These findings suggest that the compound possesses potential therapeutic properties in mitigating oxidative stress and cytotoxicity. In this study, cultured primary rat hepatocytes were exposed to 2,3,7,8,-tetrachlorodibenzo-p-dioxin (TCDD), a substance that is both highly toxic and persistent, classified as an organic pollutant. The effects of the carotenoid on the reduced total antioxidant capacity (TAC) ratios and the level of 8-hydroxy-deoxyguanosine (8-OHdG), which serves as an indicator of oxidative DNA damage, were investigated. The results demonstrated that astaxanthin exhibited a dose-dependent increase in the TAC ratios and a decrease in the level of 8-OHdG [122].

4.2. Anti-Inflammatory Activity

Inflammation is a multi-step immune response that serves as a defense mechanism or reaction to bodily injuries, aiming to initiate the tissue repair process. Although it is a necessary response, an excessive or unregulated inflammatory reaction can cause harm to the host, potentially leading to cellular and tissue damage [123,124]. The connection between chronic inflammation and the emergence of various pathologies, including cancer, cardiovascular disease, and atherosclerosis, is widely recognized [125]. Additionally, it has been proposed that inflammation not only plays a significant role in the progression of cardiovascular disease (CVD) but also has far-reaching implications for the onset of other CVD-related conditions, including hypertension, hypercholesterolemia, and obesity [126–128]. Furthermore, it has been shown that astaxanthin's ability to alleviate gastric inflammation caused by bacterial infections has been observed to impact the intestinal microbiota, leading to reduced inflammation and oxidative stress in both local and systemic contexts in mice [110]. Choi et al. [129] found that astaxanthin can prevent the formation of pro-inflammatory regulators in BV-2 microglial cells that have been stimulated by lipopolysaccharides (LPSs). This is achieved by suppressing the initiation and breakdown of iNOS and COX-2 proteins. The study conducted by Park et al. [130] demonstrated that the administration of astaxanthin led to a reduction in the expression of COX-2, iNOS, and ICAM-1 protein in rats with diabetes induced by streptozotocin (STZ). This reduction in protein expression resulted in a decrease in inflammation. Another researcher provided evidence that astaxanthin effectively inhibited inflammation exposure to UV light by reducing the expression of iNOS and COX-2 proteins and mRNAs [131]. Astaxanthin can block the expression or production of cytokines and inflammatory mediators, as well as hinder the activity of inducible nitric oxide synthase and cyclooxygenase-2. These effects have potential implications for various diseases, including brain inflammatory disease, atherosclerosis, and inflammatory bowel disease, among others. Furthermore, it was observed that astaxanthin exhibited a protective effect on redox-sensitive lymphocytes, potentially attributable to its anti-inflammatory properties [132]. Research conducted by Macedo et al. [133] showed that astaxanthin displayed a significant decrease in the synthesis of pro-inflammatory cytokines, specifically tumor necrosis factor-a and interleukin-6, in neutrophils activated by lipopolysaccharides. The outcomes of the study also demonstrated that astaxanthin enhanced the ability of neutrophils to absorb and destroy microorganisms, while simultaneously reducing the production of harmful reactive oxygen species such as superoxide anions and hydrogen peroxide. Studies conducted on BALB/cA mice infected with *Helicobacter pylori* and administered astaxanthin orally have shown a reduction in the inflammation score of their gastric mucosa [134]. The possible anti-inflammatory properties of astaxanthin could possibly contribute to its efficacy in the prevention or therapy of asthma. A study conducted by Haines et al. [135] showed that asthmatic animals that were administered astaxanthin, Ginkgo biloba extract, and vitamin C either individually or in combination exhibited a notable reduction in the number of inflammatory cells in the bronchoalveolar lavage fluid. The effectiveness of this treatment was found to be comparable to, or even superior to, that of ibuprofen, a commonly used nonsteroidal anti-inflammatory drug. In a clinical study conducted by Park et al. [136], the potential immune-enhancing, antioxidative, and anti-inflammatory effects of astaxanthin in young, healthy adult females were investigated. The findings demonstrated that astaxanthin supplementation was capable of decreasing biomarkers of DNA oxidative damage and inflammation and enhancing immune response. Specifically, supplementation with astaxanthin extracted from *H. pluvialis* at a dose of 2 mg/day for eight weeks resulted in a reduction in plasma concentration of C-reactive protein, a protein marker of inflammatory status. Additional evidence was presented by another researcher, demonstrating the efficacy of astaxanthin in inhibiting inflammation caused by excessive physical activity [137].

4.3. Cardiovascular Disease Prevention

Cardiovascular diseases (CVDs), which encompass a range of illnesses affecting the heart and blood vessels, such as cerebrovascular disease, coronary heart disease, peripheral artery disease, rheumatic heart disease, congenital heart disease, and heart failure, are major health concerns [138]. Reactive oxygen species (ROS) play a significant role in the pathophysiology of numerous cardiovascular disorders. One notable example is the involvement of oxidative modification of low-density lipoprotein (LDL) in the pathogenesis of atherosclerosis. Reactive oxygen species (ROS) are additionally accountable for the pathophysiological mechanisms underlying cardiac hypertrophy, ischemia/reperfusion injury, ventricular remodeling, myocardial infarction, and cardiomyopathy [139]. Astaxanthin demonstrates a unique ability to protect the heart by reducing the harmful effects of homocysteine on the heart, which causes mitochondrial dysfunction and oxidative damage [140]. The protective potential of disodium disuccinate astaxanthin (DDA) against myocardial damage was evaluated using an animal model of myocardial ischemia–reperfusion. Following a four-day pre-treatment regimen with DDA in Sprague–Dawley rats and rabbits, the size of myocardial infarctions was found to be reduced in both rats and rabbits. The pre-treatment dosages administered were 25, 50, and 75 mg/kg of body weight [141,142]. Moreover, the presence of astaxanthin was observed in the myocardium tissue of rats following pre-treatment with DDA at doses of 150 and 500 mg/kg/day for a period of seven days [143]. The link between dyslipidemia and oxidative stress in the development of atherosclerosis is widely recognized. Yang et al. [121] found that the consumption of astaxanthin derived from *H. pluvialis* resulted in a reduction in plasma levels of total cholesterol (TC) and triglycerides (TGs), while also enhancing the endogenous antioxidant defense system in apo$E^{-/-}$ mice. According to a study conducted by Monroy-Ruiz et al. [144], administering an astaxanthin-rich diet to hypertensive rats resulted in a reduction in blood pressure and an enhancement of cardiovascular parameters, without requiring any additional intervention. The presence of astaxanthin was detected in the plasma, heart, liver, and platelets of mice that were fed an astaxanthin derivative at a dose of 500 mg/kg/day for a period of 14 days. In contrast to the control group of mice, the experimental group exhibited notable enhancements in basal arterial blood flow and substantial prolongation in the occurrence of occlusive thrombus subsequent to vascular endothelial injury [145]. Nakao et al. [146] evaluated the potential of dietary astaxanthin in reducing oxidative stress and improving cardiac function in mice. The findings indicated that the administration of a diet containing 0.08% astaxanthin resulted in elevated levels of heart mitochondrial membrane potential and the contractility index compared to the control group. Another study investigated the impact of the antioxidant astaxanthin on hypercholesterolemic rabbits, focusing on paraoxonase and thioredoxin reductase activities, oxidative stress parameters, and lipid profiles. The hypercholesterolemic diet induced unfavorable changes in lipids and oxidative stress markers, while astaxanthin supplementation, particularly at

100 and 500 mg/100 g, mitigated protein oxidation and preserved thioredoxin reductase and paraoxonase activities. The findings suggest that astaxanthin may have a protective role in cardiovascular diseases by restoring specific enzymatic activities related to oxidative stress [147].

4.4. Anti-Cancer Activity

The production of superoxide, hydroxyl radical, hydrogen peroxide, singlet oxygen, and peroxyl radicals is frequently related to aerobic metabolism. These molecules are generated during photochemical reactions and the peroxidation of lipids. These processes have been associated with the pathogenesis of age-related diseases, including cancer, as well as the occurrence of oxidative damage to proteins, DNA, and lipids [148]. The growth of invasive cancer can potentially be suppressed by employing naturally occurring substances or pharmaceutical agents. These substances can either prevent the initiation of carcinogenesis or halt or reverse the advancement of tumors [149]. Astaxanthin has demonstrated a superior and efficient antitumor effect compared to other carotenoid antioxidants, such as β-carotene and canthaxanthin [150]. Its potent immunomodulatory, antioxidant, and anti-inflammatory properties may contribute to its potential in the prevention of cancer [136]. Furthermore, several in vitro and in vivo tests have provided evidence that astaxanthin possesses the ability to mitigate tumorigenesis. This is achieved through the suppression of cell proliferation, arrest of the cell cycle, and stimulation of cell apoptosis [151]. Feeding mice with astaxanthin has been shown to effectively suppress the expression of inflammatory cytokines, specifically tumor necrosis factor (TNF)-α and interleukin (IL)-1β. In addition, it inhibits the proliferation and induces apoptosis of colonic adenocarcinomas [152]. According to a study conducted by Palozza et al. [153], an extract rich in astaxanthin, derived from *H. pluvialis*, has been found to inhibit the growth of HCT-116 colon cancer cells by disrupting cell cycle progression and promoting apoptosis. In their study, Rao et al. [154] examined the efficacy of astaxanthin mono-(AXME) and diesters (AXDE) in combating skin cancer induced by UV-7.2 dimethylbenz(a)anthracene (DMBA) in rats. The researchers observed that at a dosage of 200 μg/kg body weight, both AXDE and AXME demonstrated significant reductions in tumor incidences caused by UV-DMBA, with AXDE achieving a reduction of up to 96% and AXME achieving a reduction of up to 88%. The effects of astaxanthin on oral cancer induced by 4-nitroso quinoline-1-oxide were investigated by Nagendraprabhu et al. [155]. In a study involving F344 male mice, the administration of 100 mg/kg of AST for a period of 32 weeks resulted in a significantly lower incidence of tumors in the AST-consuming group compared to the 4-nitroso quinoline-1-oxidation group, with no oral tumors observed in the former. Moreover, research exploring the potential anti-cancer properties of astaxanthin has revealed the feasibility of combining antioxidants and chemotherapeutic drugs in the field of oncology. Particularly, findings have demonstrated that when astaxanthin is combined with carbendazim, an anticancer agent, it can have a more significant impact on inhibiting the proliferation of MCF-7 breast cancer cells compared to carbendazim utilized alone. Notably, astaxanthin was found to mitigate the increase in reactive oxygen species (ROS) levels that can occur during carbendazim therapy [156]. Astaxanthin was shown to inhibit the growth of H22 mice hepatoma cells in a dose- and time-dependent manner by inducing apoptosis through the suppression of the JAK/STAT3 signaling pathway. This was achieved by both hindering the growth of H22 cells and promoting cell death, as well as causing cell cycle arrest in the G2 phase, both in vitro and in vivo in mice [157]. By employing silico molecular-docking methods, Suganya et al. [158] demonstrated that astaxanthin may exhibit a more prominent impact on hepatocellular carcinoma, the most prevalent form of liver cancer, than sorafenib, which is a conventional chemotherapy medication.

4.5. Neuroprotective Activity

The connection between oxidative damage and increased neuroinflammation plays a crucial role in the progression of late-onset severe neuronal loss in neurodegenerative disorders. Therefore, the possible neuroprotective effects of natural compounds, such as astaxanthin, have attracted considerable attention as a complementary treatment and preventive measure for these diseases [159]. The most commonly observed neurodegenerative disorders include Alzheimer's disease and Parkinson's disease [160,161]. Parkinson's disease (PD) is recognized as a gradually advancing, neurodegenerative disorder affecting movement. It is distinguished by the degeneration of dopaminergic neurons in the nigrostriatal pathway, specifically in the substantia nigra [99,162]. Alzheimer's disease is a progressive neurodegenerative disorder that primarily affects the brain, leading to memory loss and cognitive decline. Alzheimer's disease (AD) is a neurodegenerative condition associated with aging, characterized by the accumulation of beta-amyloid peptide plaques and intracellular neurofibrillary tangles, as well as neuronal loss within the brain [163]. Central nervous system disorders result in the activation of microglial cells, the resident macrophages of the brain, which release immune mediators and pro-inflammatory cytokines [164]. A study conducted by Grimming et al. [165] on a mouse model indicated that astaxanthin possesses neuroprotective properties in the central nervous system against neurodegeneration caused by 1-methyl-4-phenyl-1,2,3,6-tetrahydropyridine (MPTP), which results in the death of dopaminergic cells. In a separate investigation, Grimming and associates [166] demonstrated that astaxanthin had the capability to mitigate the activation of microglia in the cerebral tissue of mice. Rat neuronal cells known as PC12 are commonly utilized as an artificial model for studying neurodegeneration, particularly Alzheimer's disease (AD). In this study, these cells were found to be protected from neurotoxicity when treated with 30 μM of beta-amyloid peptide and 0.1 μM of astaxanthin [167]. Liu et al. [162] found that in the SH-SY5Y human neuroblastoma cells, pretreatment with astaxanthin diminished the toxicity resulting from exposure to docosahexaenoic acid hydroperoxide (DHA-OOH) or 6-hydroxydopamine (6-OHDA), both of which are neurotoxins that generate reactive oxygen species (ROS). Furthermore, it exerted a substantial inhibitory effect on apoptosis, intracellular reactive oxygen species (ROS) production, and mitochondrial abnormalities observed in the cells subjected to this treatment. In their study, Kim et al. [168] provided evidence that the presence of astaxanthin, acting as an extracellular factor, boosted the effectiveness of stem cells by increasing the rate of cell division in neural stem cells, and by enhancing their ability to differentiate into osteoblasts and adipocytes.

Astaxanthin health benefits are presented in Table 3.

Table 3. Astaxanthin health benefits.

Biological Activities	Experimental Model	References
Antioxidant activity	Liposomes	[111]
Antioxidant activity	Mice	[117]
Antioxidant activity	Rat	[119]
Anti-inflammatory activity	Mice	[110]
Anti-inflammatory activity	Cell culture	[129]
Anti-inflammatory activity	Rat	[130]
Anti-inflammatory activity	Clinical study	[137]
Cardiovascular disease	Mice	[121]
Cardiovascular disease	Cell culture/mice	[140]
Cardiovascular disease	Rabbits	[141]
Cardiovascular disease	Rats	[142]
Anticancer activity	Rats	[118]
Anticancer activity	Mice	[152]
Anticancer activity	Cell culture	[153]
Anticancer activity	In silico	[158]
Neuroprotective activity	Mice	[165]
Neuroprotective activity	Cell culture	[167]

4.6. Safety of Astaxanthin

Astaxanthin is widely regarded as safe [169,170]. However, specific studies have highlighted potential side effects under certain conditions. A comprehensive safety assessment conducted by Niu et al. [171] examined its acute toxicity, genotoxicity, and distribution in addition to repeat-dose toxicity studies in gestational mice. The study found that astaxanthin exhibited no acute toxic effects at high single-dose exposures, with a median lethal dose (LD50) exceeding practical consumption levels. Genotoxicity tests, including bacterial reverse mutation and micronucleus assays, revealed no mutagenic potential, supporting the compound's genetic safety profile. However, the study's findings from repeated-dose toxicity tests highlighted some important considerations. At elevated doses, astaxanthin resulted in mild gastrointestinal disturbances, likely due to its lipid-soluble nature and potential impact on digestive processes. Furthermore, a minor but statistically significant reduction in body weight gain was observed in high-dose groups during gestation, indicating a possible dose-dependent effect on maternal metabolic processes. Although no teratogenic effects were noted, the study emphasized caution when using high concentrations during pregnancy due to potential impacts on nutrient metabolism.

5. Conclusions and Future Perspectives

Astaxanthin, a potent red carotenoid pigment, is highlighted by its unique bioactive properties, such as its antioxidant, anticancer, and neuroprotective properties, which have been demonstrated in a variety of therapeutic applications. Its importance as a functional component for nutraceutical and pharmaceutical use is underscored by its natural occurrence in marine species and its potent health-promoting properties. Nevertheless, the instability of astaxanthin, which is susceptible to environmental factors such as light, oxygen, and temperature, requires the development of innovative methods for its efficient extraction, stability, and bioavailability improvement. The exploration of advanced extraction methods like ultrasound-assisted extraction (UAE), microwave-assisted extraction (MAE), supercritical fluid extraction (SFE), high-pressure extraction (HPE), and enzymatic extraction underscores the progress in obtaining astaxanthin while preserving its integrity and minimizing degradation. Furthermore, encapsulation techniques have shown considerable promise in stabilizing astaxanthin and enhancing its bioavailability, making it more effective for therapeutic use. These advancements underline the need for multidisciplinary approaches to maximize the potential of astaxanthin in various applications. Future research on astaxanthin should prioritize optimizing extraction techniques to achieve higher yields and purity while minimizing energy consumption and environmental impact. Exploring hybrid methods that combine existing technologies may enhance efficiency and sustainability. Advanced encapsulation technologies, such as nanoencapsulation and liposomal formulations, hold great promise for improving the stability, controlled release, and targeted delivery of astaxanthin, making it more effective for therapeutic applications. Large-scale clinical trials are crucial to validating the safety and efficacy of astaxanthin in humans, facilitating its transition from preclinical research to mainstream medical applications. Innovations in formulation, such as incorporating astaxanthin into functional foods, dietary supplements, and topical applications, will broaden its accessibility and utility. Additionally, exploring synergistic effects with other bioactive compounds could unlock novel therapeutic potentials. By focusing on these areas, future efforts can fully harness astaxanthin's potential as a cornerstone of nutraceutical and pharmaceutical advancements, improving health outcomes and driving innovation in the field.

Author Contributions: Conceptualization, I.P. and C.N.; methodology, C.N.; validation, C.N.; investigation, I.P.; writing—original draft preparation, I.P.; writing—review and editing, C.N.; supervision, C.N. All authors have read and agreed to the published version of the manuscript.

Funding: This research received no external funding.

Data Availability Statement: Data are contained within the review.

Conflicts of Interest: The authors declare no conflict of interest.

References

1. Johnson, E.A.; An, G.-H. Astaxanthin from Microbial Sources. *Crit. Rev. Biotechnol.* **1991**, *11*, 297–326. [CrossRef]
2. Ali, S.M.; Appolloni, A.; Cavallaro, F.; D'Adamo, I.; Di Vaio, A.; Ferella, F.; Gastaldi, M.; Ikram, M.; Kumar, N.M.; Martin, M.A.; et al. Development Goals towards Sustainability. *Sustainability* **2023**, *15*, 9443. [CrossRef]
3. Ling Wen Xia, F.; Supri, S.; Djamaludin, H.; Nurdiani, R.; Leong Seng, L.; Wee Yin, K.; Rovina, K. Turning Waste into Value: Extraction and Effective Valorization Strategies of Seafood by-Products. *Waste Manag. Bull.* **2024**, *2*, 84–100. [CrossRef]
4. Senadheera, T.R.L.; Hossain, A.; Shahidi, F. Marine Bioactives and Their Application in the Food Industry: A Review. *Appl. Sci.* **2023**, *13*, 12088. [CrossRef]
5. Cooney, R.; de Sousa, D.B.; Fernández-Ríos, A.; Mellett, S.; Rowan, N.; Morse, A.P.; Hayes, M.; Laso, J.; Regueiro, L.; Wan, A.H.; et al. A Circular Economy Framework for Seafood Waste Valorisation to Meet Challenges and Opportunities for Intensive Production and Sustainability. *J. Clean. Prod.* **2023**, *392*, 136283. [CrossRef]
6. Rossi, N.; Grosso, C.; Delerue-Matos, C. Shrimp Waste Upcycling: Unveiling the Potential of Polysaccharides, Proteins, Carotenoids, and Fatty Acids with Emphasis on Extraction Techniques and Bioactive Properties. *Mar. Drugs* **2024**, *22*, 153. [CrossRef]
7. Sachindra, N.M.; Mahendrakar, N.S. Process Optimization for Extraction of Carotenoids from Shrimp Waste with Vegetable Oils. *Bioresour. Technol.* **2005**, *96*, 1195–1200. [CrossRef]
8. Ruen-ngam, D.; Shotipruk, A.; Pavasant, P. Comparison of Extraction Methods for Recovery of Astaxanthin from *Haematococcus pluvialis*. *Sep. Sci. Technol.* **2010**, *46*, 64–70. [CrossRef]
9. Dong, S.; Huang, Y.; Zhang, R.; Wang, S.; Liu, Y. Four Different Methods Comparison for Extraction of Astaxanthin from Green Alga *Haematococcus pluvialis*. *Sci. World J.* **2014**, *2014*, 694305. [CrossRef]
10. Yang, L.; Li, F.; Cao, X.; Qiao, X.; Xue, C.; Xu, J. Stability and Bioavailability of Protein Matrix-encapsulated Astaxanthin Ester Microcapsules. *J. Sci. Food Agric.* **2022**, *102*, 2144–2152. [CrossRef]
11. Martínez-Álvarez, Ó.; Calvo, M.M.; Gómez-Estaca, J. Recent Advances in Astaxanthin Micro/Nanoencapsulation to Improve Its Stability and Functionality as a Food Ingredient. *Mar. Drugs* **2020**, *18*, 406. [CrossRef]
12. Niizawa, I.; Espinaco, B.Y.; Zorrilla, S.E.; Sihufe, G.A. Natural Astaxanthin Encapsulation: Use of Response Surface Methodology for the Design of Alginate Beads. *Int. J. Biol. Macromol.* **2019**, *121*, 601–608. [CrossRef]
13. Liu, X.; Xie, J.; Zhou, L.; Zhang, J.; Chen, Z.; Xiao, J.; Cao, Y.; Xiao, H. Recent Advances in Health Benefits and Bioavailability of Dietary Astaxanthin and Its Isomers. *Food Chem.* **2023**, *404*, 134605. [CrossRef]
14. Cao, Y.; Yang, L.; Qiao, X.; Xue, C.; Xu, J. Dietary Astaxanthin: An Excellent Carotenoid with Multiple Health Benefits. *Crit. Rev. Food Sci. Nutr.* **2023**, *63*, 3019–3045. [CrossRef]
15. Pu, J.; Bechtel, P.J.; Sathivel, S. Extraction of Shrimp Astaxanthin with Flaxseed Oil: Effects on Lipid Oxidation and Astaxanthin Degradation Rates. *Biosyst. Eng.* **2010**, *107*, 364–371. [CrossRef]
16. Handayani, A.D.; Sutrisno; Indraswati, N.; Ismadji, S. Extraction of Astaxanthin from Giant Tiger (*Panaeus monodon*) Shrimp Waste Using Palm Oil: Studies of Extraction Kinetics and Thermodynamic. *Bioresour. Technol.* **2008**, *99*, 4414–4419. [CrossRef]
17. Pu, J.; Sathivel, S. Kinetics of Lipid Oxidation and Degradation of Flaxseed Oil Containing Crawfish (*Procambarus clarkii*) Astaxanthin. *J. Am. Oil Chem. Soc.* **2010**, *88*, 595–601. [CrossRef]
18. E Silva, D.; Damasceno, K.; Ribeiro, P.; Alcântra, M.; Cordeiro, A.; Passos, T.; de Sousa, F., Jr.; de Assis, C. Chemical Characteristics and Antioxidant Activity of Astaxanthin Extracted from Shrimp Residues Using Soybean Oil. *J. Braz. Chem. Soc.* **2021**, *32*, 1277–1285. [CrossRef]
19. El-Bialy, H.A.A.; El-Khalek, H.H.A. A Comparative Study on Astaxanthin Recovery from Shrimp Wastes Using Lactic Fermentation and Green Solvents: An Applied Model on Minced Tilapia. *J. Radiat. Res. Appl. Sci.* **2020**, *13*, 594–605. [CrossRef]
20. Sharayei, P.; Azarpazhooh, E.; Zomorodi, S.; Einafshar, S.; Ramaswamy, H.S. Optimization of Ultrasonic-Assisted Extraction of Astaxanthin from Green Tiger (*Penaeus semisulcatus*) Shrimp Shell. *Ultrason. Sonochem.* **2021**, *76*, 105666. [CrossRef]
21. Sachindra, N.M.; Bhaskar, N.; Mahendrakar, N.S. Recovery of Carotenoids from Shrimp Waste in Organic Solvents. *Waste Manag.* **2006**, *26*, 1092–1098. [CrossRef] [PubMed]
22. Sahoo, D. Extraction and Characterization of Astaxanthin from the Crustacea Shell Waste from Shrimp Processing Industries. *Int. J. Pharm. Sci. Res.* **2015**, *6*, 2532–2537.
23. Dave, D.; Liu, Y.; Pohling, J.; Trenholm, S.; Murphy, W. Astaxanthin Recovery from Atlantic Shrimp (*Pandalus borealis*) Processing Materials. *Bioresour. Technol. Rep.* **2020**, *11*, 100535. [CrossRef]
24. Takeungwongtrakul, S.; Benjakul, S.; Santoso, J.; Trilaksani, W.; Nurilmala, M. Extraction and Stability of Carotenoid-Containing Lipids from Hepatopancreas of Pacific White Shrimp (*Litopenaeus vannamei*). *J. Food Process Preserv.* **2013**, *39*, 10–18. [CrossRef]
25. Sindhu, S.; Sherief, P.M. Extraction, Characterization, Antioxidant and Anti-Inflammatory Properties of Carotenoids from the Shell Waste of Arabian Red Shrimp Aristeus Alcocki, Ramadan 1938. *Open Conf. Proc. J.* **2011**, *2*, 95–103. [CrossRef]
26. Armenta-Lopez, R.; Guerrero, I.L.; Huerta, S. Astaxanthin Extraction from Shrimp Waste by Lactic Fermentation and Enzymatic Hydrolysis of the Carotenoprotein Complex. *J. Food Sci.* **2002**, *67*, 1002–1006. [CrossRef]
27. Radzali, S.A.; Baharin, B.S.; Othman, R.; Markom, M.; Rahman, R.A. Co-Solvent Selection for Supercritical Fluid Extraction of Astaxanthin and Other Carotenoids from *Penaeus monodon* Waste. *J. Oleo Sci.* **2014**, *63*, 769–777. [CrossRef]

28. Izadifar, Z.; Babyn, P.; Chapman, D. Ultrasound Cavitation/Microbubble Detection and Medical Applications. *J. Med. Biol. Eng.* **2018**, *39*, 259–276. [CrossRef]
29. Gong, M.; Bassi, A. Carotenoids from Microalgae: A Review of Recent Developments. *Biotechnol. Adv.* **2016**, *34*, 1396–1412. [CrossRef]
30. Panagiotakopoulos, I.; Karantonis, H.C.; Kartelias, I.G.; Nasopoulou, C. Ultrasonic-Assisted Extraction of Astaxanthin from Shrimp By-Products Using Vegetable Oils. *Mar. Drugs* **2023**, *21*, 467. [CrossRef]
31. Zhang, H.; Tang, B.; Row, K.H. A Green Deep Eutectic Solvent-Based Ultrasound-Assisted Method to Extract Astaxanthin from Shrimp Byproducts. *Anal. Lett.* **2014**, *47*, 742–749. [CrossRef]
32. Prayitno, D.I.; Dewi, E.N.; Pringgenies, D.; Brotosudarmo, T.H.P. Green Ultrasound-Assisted Extraction of Astaxanthin from Fermented Rebon Shrimp (Cincalok) Using Vegetable Oils as Solvents. *OCL* **2022**, *29*, 15. [CrossRef]
33. Mario, C.; Maria, C.V.; Sofia, P.; Marina, S.; Magdalini, K. Optimization of Mild Extraction Methods for the Efficient Recovery of Astaxanthin, a Strong Food Antioxidant Carotenoid from Microalgae. *Chem. Eng. Trans.* **2021**, *87*, 151–156. [CrossRef]
34. Gogate, P.R.; Nadar, S.G. Ultrasound-Assisted Intensification of Extraction of Astaxanthin from *Phaffia rhodozyma*. *Indian Chem. Eng.* **2015**, *57*, 240–255. [CrossRef]
35. Haque, F.; Dutta, A.; Thimmanagari, M.; Chiang, Y.W. Intensified Green Production of Astaxanthin from *Haematococcus pluvialis*. *Food Bioprod. Process.* **2016**, *99*, 1–11. [CrossRef]
36. Gao, J.; You, J.; Kang, J.; Nie, F.; Ji, H.; Liu, S. Recovery of Astaxanthin from Shrimp (*Penaeus vannamei*) Waste by Ultrasonic-Assisted Extraction Using Ionic Liquid-in-Water Microemulsions. *Food Chem.* **2020**, *325*, 126850. [CrossRef]
37. Zhao, X.; Zhang, X.; Fu, L.; Zhu, H.; Zhang, B. Effect of Extraction and Drying Methods on Antioxidant Activity of Astaxanthin from *Haematococcus pluvialis*. *Food Bioprod. Process.* **2016**, *99*, 197–203. [CrossRef]
38. Wu, W.; Yu, X. Optimization of Ultrasound-Assisted Extraction Procedure to Determine Astaxanthin in *Xanthophyllomyces dendrorhous* by Box-Behnken Designn. *Adv. J. Food Sci. Technol.* **2013**, *5*, 1536–1542. [CrossRef]
39. Singh, A.; Ahmad, S.; Ahmad, A. Green Extraction Methods and Environmental Applications of Carotenoids—A Review. *RSC Adv.* **2015**, *5*, 62358–62393. [CrossRef]
40. Zhou, X.; Ding, W.; Jin, W. Microwave-Assisted Extraction of Lipids, Carotenoids, and Other Compounds from Marine Resources. In *Innovative and Emerging Technologies in the Bio-Marine Food Sector*; Elsevier: Amsterdam, The Netherlands, 2022; pp. 375–394.
41. Dewati, P.R.; Rochmadi, R.; Rohman, A.; Yuliestyan, A.; Budiman, A. Equilibrium Modeling of Astaxanthin Extraction from *Haematococcus pluvialis*. *Indones. J. Chem.* **2021**, *21*, 554. [CrossRef]
42. Zhao, L.; Chen, G.; Zhao, G.; Hu, X. Optimization of Microwave-Assisted Extraction of Astaxanthin from *Haematococcus pluvialis* by Response Surface Methodology and Antioxidant Activities of the Extracts. *Sep. Sci. Technol.* **2009**, *44*, 243–262. [CrossRef]
43. Ahmad, N.; Mounsef, J.R.; Lteif, R. A Simple and Fast Experimental Protocol for the Extraction of Xanthophylls from Microalga *Chlorella luteoviridis*. *Prep. Biochem. Biotechnol.* **2021**, *51*, 1071–1075. [CrossRef] [PubMed]
44. Zhu, C.; Han, W.; Chen, Z.; Han, Z. Statistical Optimization of Microwave-Assisted Astaxanthin Extraction from Phaffia Rhodozym. In Proceedings of the 2010 3rd International Conference on Biomedical Engineering and Informatics, Yantai, China, 16–18 October 2010; IEEE: New York, NY, USA, 2010; pp. 2104–2109.
45. Nanda, E.V.; Erdawati; Pratiwi, Y.; Putri, E.R. Characteristic and Photostability of Astaxanthin Extract from Shrimp Shells by Microwave Assisted Extraction Using Nades Solvent. *J. Phys. Conf. Ser.* **2022**, *2309*, 12036. [CrossRef]
46. Vafaei, N.; Rempel, C.B.; Scanlon, M.G.; Jones, P.J.H.; Eskin, M.N.A. Application of Supercritical Fluid Extraction (SFE) of Tocopherols and Carotenoids (*Hydrophobic antioxidants*) Compared to Non-SFE Methods. *AppliedChem* **2022**, *2*, 68–92. [CrossRef]
47. Sanzo, G.; Mehariya, S.; Martino, M.; Larocca, V.; Casella, P.; Chianese, S.; Musmarra, D.; Balducchi, R.; Molino, A. Supercritical Carbon Dioxide Extraction of Astaxanthin, Lutein, and Fatty Acids from *Haematococcus pluvialis* Microalgae. *Mar. Drugs* **2018**, *16*, 334. [CrossRef]
48. Molino, A.; Mehariya, S.; Iovine, A.; Larocca, V.; Di Sanzo, G.; Martino, M.; Casella, P.; Chianese, S.; Musmarra, D. Extraction of Astaxanthin and Lutein from Microalga *Haematococcus pluvialis* in the Red Phase Using CO_2 Supercritical Fluid Extraction Technology with Ethanol as Co-Solvent. *Mar. Drugs* **2018**, *16*, 432. [CrossRef]
49. Radzali, S.A.; Baharin, B.S.; Rahman, R.A. Optimisation of Supercritical Fluid Extraction of Astaxanthin from *Penaeus monodon* Waste Using Ethanol-Modified Carbon Dioxide. *J. Eng. Sci. Technol.* **2016**, *11*, 722–736.
50. Ali-Nehari, A.; Kim, S.-B.; Lee, Y.-B.; Lee, H.; Chun, B.-S. Characterization of Oil Including Astaxanthin Extracted from Krill (*Euphausia superba*) Using Supercritical Carbon Dioxide and Organic Solvent as Comparative Method. *Korean J. Chem. Eng.* **2011**, *29*, 329–336. [CrossRef]
51. Sánchez-Camargo, A.P.; Martinez-Correa, H.A.; Paviani, L.C.; Cabral, F.A. Supercritical CO_2 Extraction of Lipids and Astaxanthin from Brazilian Redspotted Shrimp Waste (*Farfantepenaeus paulensis*). *J. Supercrit. Fluids* **2011**, *56*, 164–173. [CrossRef]
52. Charest, D.J.; Balaban, M.O.; Marshall, M.R.; Cornell, J.A. Astaxanthin Extraction from Crawfish Shells by Supercritical CO_2 with Ethanol as Cosolvent. *J. Aquat. Food Prod. Technol.* **2001**, *10*, 81–96. [CrossRef]
53. Cheng, X.; Qi, Z.; Burdyny, T.; Kong, T.; Sinton, D. Low Pressure Supercritical CO_2 Extraction of Astaxanthin from *Haematococcus pluvialis* Demonstrated on a Microfluidic Chip. *Bioresour. Technol.* **2018**, *250*, 481–485. [CrossRef] [PubMed]
54. Sánchez-Camargo, A.P.; Meireles, M.Â.A.; Ferreira, A.L.K.; Saito, E.; Cabral, F.A. Extraction of -3 Fatty Acids and Astaxanthin from Brazilian Redspotted Shrimp Waste Using Supercritical CO_2+ethanol Mixtures. *J. Supercrit. Fluids* **2012**, *61*, 71–77. [CrossRef]

55. Nunes, A.N.; Roda, A.; Gouveia, L.F.; Fernández, N.; Bronze, M.R.; Matias, A.A. Astaxanthin Extraction from Marine Crustacean Waste Streams: An Integrate Approach between Microwaves and Supercritical Fluids. *ACS Sustain. Chem. Eng.* **2021**, *9*, 3050–3059. [CrossRef]
56. Das, S.; Nadar, S.S.; Rathod, V.K. Integrated Strategies for Enzyme Assisted Extraction of Bioactive Molecules: A Review. *Int. J. Biol. Macromol.* **2021**, *191*, 899–917. [CrossRef] [PubMed]
57. Klomklao, S.; Benjakul, S.; Visessanguan, W.; Kishimura, H.; Simpson, B.K. Extraction of Carotenoprotein from Black Tiger Shrimp Shells with the Aid of Bluefish Trypsin. *J. Food Biochem.* **2009**, *33*, 201–217. [CrossRef]
58. De Holanda, H.D.; Netto, F.M. Recovery of Components from Shrimp (*Xiphopenaeus kroyeri*) Processing Waste by Enzymatic Hydrolysis. *J. Food Sci.* **2006**, *71*, C298–C303. [CrossRef]
59. Babu, C.M.; Chakrabarti, R.; Sambasivarao, K.R.S. Enzymatic Isolation of Carotenoid-Protein Complex from Shrimp Head Waste and Its Use as a Source of Carotenoids. *LWT Food Sci. Technol.* **2008**, *41*, 227–235. [CrossRef]
60. Zhao, X.; Zhang, X.; Liu, H.; Zhu, H.; Zhu, Y. Enzyme-Assisted Extraction of Astaxanthin from *Haematococcus pluvialis* and Its Stability and Antioxidant Activity. *Food Sci. Biotechnol.* **2019**, *28*, 1637–1647. [CrossRef]
61. Jafari, A.M.; Gharibi, S.; Farjadmand, F.; Sadighara, P. Extraction of Shrimp Waste Pigments by Enzymatic and Alkaline Treatment: Evaluation by Inhibition of Lipid Peroxidation. *J. Mater. Cycles Waste Manag.* **2012**, *14*, 411–413. [CrossRef]
62. Wang, L.; Hu, J.; Lv, W.; Lu, W.; Pei, D.; Lv, Y.; Wang, W.; Zhang, M.; Ding, R.; Lv, M. Optimized Extraction of Astaxanthin from Shrimp Shells Treated by Biological Enzyme and Its Separation and Purification Using Macroporous Resin. *Food Chem.* **2021**, *363*, 130369. [CrossRef]
63. Khan, S.A.; Aslam, R.; Makroo, H.A. High Pressure Extraction and Its Application in the Extraction of Bio-active Compounds: A Review. *J. Food Process Eng.* **2019**, *42*, e12896. [CrossRef]
64. Li, J.; Sun, W.; Ramaswamy, H.S.; Yu, Y.; Zhu, S.; Wang, J.; Li, H. High Pressure Extraction of Astaxanthin from Shrimp Waste (*Penaeus vannamei* Boone): Effect on Yield and Antioxidant Activity. *J. Food Process Eng.* **2017**, *40*, e12353. [CrossRef]
65. Irna, C.; Jaswir, I.; Othman, R.; Jimat, D.N. Comparison Between High-Pressure Processing and Chemical Extraction: Astaxanthin Yield from Six Species of Shrimp Carapace. *J. Diet. Suppl.* **2018**, *15*, 805–813. [CrossRef] [PubMed]
66. Torres-Haro, A.; Arellano-Plaza, M.; Mateos-Díaz, J.C.; Espinosa-Andrews, H.; Castillo-Herrera, G.A. Non-conventional High-pressure Extraction Process: A Comparative Study for Astaxanthin Recovery from *Xanthophyllomyces dendrorhous*. *Int. J. Food Sci. Technol.* **2022**, *57*, 1040–1049. [CrossRef]
67. Irna, C.; Jaswir, I.; Othman, R.; Jimat, D.N. Optimization of High-pressure Processing in Extraction of Astaxanthin from *Penaeus monodon* Carapace Using Response Surface Methodology. *J. Food Process Eng.* **2018**, *41*, e12880. [CrossRef]
68. Zhang, C.; Chen, X.; Too, H.-P. Microbial Astaxanthin Biosynthesis: Recent Achievements, Challenges, and Commercialization Outlook. *Appl. Microbiol. Biotechnol.* **2020**, *104*, 5725–5737. [CrossRef]
69. Jafari, R.; Homaei, A.; Ahmadi, A.-R.; Kamrani, E. Optimization and Identification of Astaxanthin Esters from Shrimp Waste Using Microbial Fermentation Method. *Biomass Convers. Biorefinery* **2024**, *14*, 22893–22908. [CrossRef]
70. Harith, Z.T.; Charalampopoulos, D.; Chatzifragkou, A. Optimised Production and Extraction of Astaxanthin from the Yeast *Xanthophyllomyces dendrorhous*. *Microorganisms* **2020**, *8*, 430. [CrossRef]
71. Hamdi, S.A.H.; Ghonaim, G.M.; El Sayed, R.R.; Rodríguez-Couto, S.; Abd El-Ghany, M.N. Bioprocess of Astaxanthin Extraction from Shrimp Waste via the Common Microorganisms Saccharomyces Cerevisiae and Lactobacillus Acidophilus in Comparison to the Chemical Method. *Biomass Convers. Biorefinery* **2024**, *14*, 8333–8339. [CrossRef]
72. Cruz-Casas, D.E.; Aguilar, C.N.; Ascacio-Valdés, J.A.; Rodríguez-Herrera, R.; Chávez-González, M.L.; Flores-Gallegos, A.C. Enzymatic Hydrolysis and Microbial Fermentation: The Most Favorable Biotechnological Methods for the Release of Bioactive Peptides. *Food Chem. Mol. Sci.* **2021**, *3*, 100047. [CrossRef]
73. Cannavacciuolo, C.; Pagliari, S.; Celano, R.; Campone, L.; Rastrelli, L. Critical Analysis of Green Extraction Techniques Used for Botanicals: Trends, Priorities, and Optimization Strategies—A Review. *TrAC Trends Anal. Chem.* **2024**, *173*, 117627. [CrossRef]
74. Fraguela-Meissimilly, H.; Bastías-Monte, J.M.; Vergara, C.; Ortiz-Viedma, J.; Lemus-Mondaca, R.; Flores, M.; Toledo-Merma, P.; Alcázar-Alay, S.; Gallón-Bedoya, M. New Trends in Supercritical Fluid Technology and Pressurized Liquids for the Extraction and Recovery of Bioactive Compounds from Agro-Industrial and Marine Food Waste. *Molecules* **2023**, *28*, 4421. [CrossRef] [PubMed]
75. Cuellar-Bermudez, S.P.; Aguilar-Hernandez, I.; Cardenas-Chavez, D.L.; Ornelas-Soto, N.; Romero-Ogawa, M.A.; Parra-Saldivar, R. Extraction and Purification of High-value Metabolites from Microalgae: Essential Lipids, Astaxanthin and Phycobiliproteins. *Microb. Biotechnol.* **2015**, *8*, 190–209. [CrossRef] [PubMed]
76. Chemat, F.; Rombaut, N.; Sicaire, A.-G.; Meullemiestre, A.; Fabiano-Tixier, A.-S.; Abert-Vian, M. Ultrasound Assisted Extraction of Food and Natural Products. Mechanisms, Techniques, Combinations, Protocols and Applications. A Review. *Ultrason. Sonochem.* **2017**, *34*, 540–560. [CrossRef]
77. Tolve, R.; Galgano, F.; Caruso, M.C.; Tchuenbou-Magaia, F.L.; Condelli, N.; Favati, F.; Zhang, Z. Encapsulation of Health-Promoting Ingredients: Applications in Foodstuffs. *Int. J. Food Sci. Nutr.* **2016**, *67*, 888–918. [CrossRef]
78. Desai, K.G.H.; Park, H.J. Encapsulation of Vitamin C in Tripolyphosphate Cross-Linked Chitosan Microspheres by Spray Drying. *J. Microencapsul.* **2005**, *22*, 179–192. [CrossRef]
79. SAENZ, C.; TAPIA, S.; CHAVEZ, J.; ROBERT, P. Microencapsulation by Spray Drying of Bioactive Compounds from Cactus Pear (Opuntia Ficus-Indica). *Food Chem.* **2009**, *114*, 616–622. [CrossRef]
80. Wilson, N.; Shah, N.P. Microencapsulation of Vitamins 1. *ASEAN Food J.* **2007**, *14*, 1.

81. De Kruif, C.G.; Weinbreck, F.; de Vries, R. Complex Coacervation of Proteins and Anionic Polysaccharides. *Curr. Opin. Colloid Interface Sci.* **2004**, *9*, 340–349. [CrossRef]
82. Ducel, V.; Richard, J.; Saulnier, P.; Popineau, Y.; Boury, F. Evidence and Characterization of Complex Coacervates Containing Plant Proteins: Application to the Microencapsulation of Oil Droplets. *Colloids Surf. A Physicochem. Eng. Asp.* **2004**, *232*, 239–247. [CrossRef]
83. Timilsena, Y.P.; Akanbi, T.O.; Khalid, N.; Adhikari, B.; Barrow, C.J. Complex Coacervation: Principles, Mechanisms and Applications in Microencapsulation. *Int. J. Biol. Macromol.* **2019**, *121*, 1276–1286. [CrossRef] [PubMed]
84. Gomez-Estaca, J.; Comunian, T.A.; Montero, P.; Favaro-Trindade, C.S. Physico-Chemical Properties, Stability, and Potential Food Applications of Shrimp Lipid Extract Encapsulated by Complex Coacervation. *Food Bioprocess Technol.* **2018**, *11*, 1596–1604. [CrossRef]
85. Taksima, T.; Limpawattana, M.; Klaypradit, W. Astaxanthin Encapsulated in Beads Using Ultrasonic Atomizer and Application in Yogurt as Evaluated by Consumer Sensory Profile. *LWT Food Sci. Technol.* **2015**, *62*, 431–437. [CrossRef]
86. Zhou, Q.; Yang, L.; Xu, J.; Qiao, X.; Li, Z.; Wang, Y.; Xue, C. Evaluation of the Physicochemical Stability and Digestibility of Microencapsulated Esterified Astaxanthins Using in Vitro and in Vivo Models. *Food Chem.* **2018**, *260*, 73–81. [CrossRef] [PubMed]
87. Bustos-Garza, C.; Yáñez-Fernández, J.; Barragán-Huerta, B.E. Thermal and PH Stability of Spray-Dried Encapsulated Astaxanthin Oleoresin from *Haematococcus pluvialis* Using Several Encapsulation Wall Materials. *Food Res. Int.* **2013**, *54*, 641–649. [CrossRef]
88. Bakry, A.M.; Abbas, S.; Ali, B.; Majeed, H.; Abouelwafa, M.Y.; Mousa, A.; Liang, L. Microencapsulation of Oils: A Comprehensive Review of Benefits, Techniques, and Applications. *Compr. Rev. Food Sci. Food Saf.* **2015**, *15*, 143–182. [CrossRef]
89. Shen, Q.; Quek, S.Y. Microencapsulation of Astaxanthin with Blends of Milk Protein and Fiber by Spray Drying. *J. Food Eng.* **2014**, *123*, 165–171. [CrossRef]
90. Montero, P.; Calvo, M.M.; Gómez-Guillén, M.C.; Gómez-Estaca, J. Microcapsules Containing Astaxanthin from Shrimp Waste as Potential Food Coloring and Functional Ingredient: Characterization, Stability, and Bioaccessibility. *LWT* **2016**, *70*, 229–236. [CrossRef]
91. Gómez-Guillén, M.C.; Montero, P.; López-Caballero, M.E.; Baccan, G.C.; Gómez-Estaca, J. Bioactive and Technological Functionality of a Lipid Extract from Shrimp (*L. Vannamei*) Cephalothorax. *LWT* **2018**, *89*, 704–711. [CrossRef]
92. Soukoulis, C.; Bohn, T. A Comprehensive Overview on the Micro- and Nano-Technological Encapsulation Advances for Enhancing the Chemical Stability and Bioavailability of Carotenoids. *Crit. Rev. Food Sci. Nutr.* **2017**, *58*, 1–36. [CrossRef]
93. Desobry, S.A.; Netto, F.M.; Labuza, T.P. Comparison of Spray-Drying, Drum-Drying and Freeze-Drying for -Carotene Encapsulation and Preservation. *J. Food Sci.* **1997**, *62*, 1158–1162. [CrossRef]
94. Ahmed, F.; Li, Y.; Fanning, K.; Netzel, M.; Schenk, P.M. Effect of Drying, Storage Temperature and Air Exposure on Astaxanthin Stability from *Haematococcus pluvialis*. *Food Res. Int.* **2015**, *74*, 231–236. [CrossRef] [PubMed]
95. Marin, D.; Alemán, A.; Montero, P.; Gómez-Guillén, M.C. Encapsulation of Food Waste Compounds in Soy Phosphatidylcholine Liposomes: Effect of Freeze-Drying, Storage Stability and Functional Aptitude. *J. Food Eng.* **2018**, *223*, 132–143. [CrossRef]
96. Tan, C.; Zhang, Y.; Abbas, S.; Feng, B.; Zhang, X.; Xia, S. Modulation of the Carotenoid Bioaccessibility through Liposomal Encapsulation. *Colloids Surf. B Biointerfaces* **2014**, *123*, 692–700. [CrossRef]
97. Costa, R.; Santos, L. Delivery Systems for Cosmetics—From Manufacturing to the Skin of Natural Antioxidants. *Powder Technol.* **2017**, *322*, 402–416. [CrossRef]
98. Alves, G.P.; Santana, M.H.A. Phospholipid Dry Powders Produced by Spray Drying Processing: Structural, Thermodynamic and Physical Properties. *Powder Technol.* **2004**, *145*, 139–148. [CrossRef]
99. Ye, Q.; Huang, B.; Zhang, X.; Zhu, Y.; Chen, X. Astaxanthin Protects against MPP+-Induced Oxidative Stress in PC12 Cells via the HO-1/NOX2 Axis. *BMC Neurosci.* **2012**, *13*, 156. [CrossRef]
100. Moraes, M.; Carvalho, J.M.P.; Silva, C.R.; Cho, S.; Sola, M.R.; Pinho, S.C. Liposomes Encapsulating Beta-Carotene Produced by the Proliposomes Method: Characterisation and Shelf Life of Powders and Phospholipid Vesicles. *Int. J. Food Sci. Technol.* **2012**, *48*, 274–282. [CrossRef]
101. Pan, L.; Zhang, S.; Gu, K.; Zhang, N. Preparation of Astaxanthin-Loaded Liposomes: Characterization, Storage Stability and Antioxidant Activity. *CyTA—J. Food* **2018**, *16*, 607–618. [CrossRef]
102. Pan, L.; Wang, H.; Gu, K. Nanoliposomes as Vehicles for Astaxanthin: Characterization, In Vitro Release Evaluation and Structure. *Molecules* **2018**, *23*, 2822. [CrossRef]
103. Hama, S.; Uenishi, S.; Yamada, A.; Ohgita, T.; Tsuchiya, H.; Yamashita, E.; Kogure, K. Scavenging of Hydroxyl Radicals in Aqueous Solution by Astaxanthin Encapsulated in Liposomes. *Biol. Pharm. Bull.* **2012**, *35*, 2238–2242. [CrossRef] [PubMed]
104. Kamezaki, C.; Nakashima, A.; Yamada, A.; Uenishi, S.; Ishibashi, H.; Shibuya, N.; Hama, S.; Hosoi, S.; Yamashita, E.; Kogure, K. Synergistic Antioxidative Effect of Astaxanthin and Tocotrienol by Co-Encapsulated in Liposomes. *J. Clin. Biochem. Nutr.* **2016**, *59*, 100–106. [CrossRef] [PubMed]
105. KOGURE, K. Novel Antioxidative Activity of Astaxanthin and Its Synergistic Effect with Vitamin E. *J. Nutr. Sci. Vitaminol.* **2019**, *65*, S109–S112. [CrossRef]
106. Wang, B.; Akanbi, T.O.; Agyei, D.; Holland, B.J.; Barrow, C.J. Coacervation Technique as an Encapsulation and Delivery Tool for Hydrophobic Biofunctional Compounds. In *Role of Materials Science in Food Bioengineering*; Elsevier: Amsterdam, The Netherlands, 2018; pp. 235–261.

107. Akbarbaglu, Z.; Peighambardoust, S.H.; Sarabandi, K.; Jafari, S.M. Spray Drying Encapsulation of Bioactive Compounds within Protein-Based Carriers; Different Options and Applications. *Food Chem.* **2021**, *359*, 129965. [CrossRef]
108. Amiri, H.; Shabanpour, B.; Pourashouri, P.; Kashiri, M. Encapsulation of Marine Bioactive Compounds Using Liposome Technique: Evaluation of Physicochemical Properties and Oxidative Stability during Storage. *Food Struct.* **2023**, *35*, 100308. [CrossRef]
109. Ngo, D.-H.; Wijesekara, I.; Vo, T.-S.; Van Ta, Q.; Kim, S.-K. Marine Food-Derived Functional Ingredients as Potential Antioxidants in the Food Industry: An Overview. *Food Res. Int.* **2011**, *44*, 523–529. [CrossRef]
110. Bhuvaneswari, S.; Arunkumar, E.; Viswanathan, P.; Anuradha, C.V. Astaxanthin Restricts Weight Gain, Promotes Insulin Sensitivity and Curtails Fatty Liver Disease in Mice Fed a Obesity-Promoting Diet. *Process Biochem.* **2010**, *45*, 1406–1414. [CrossRef]
111. Naguib, Y.M.A. Antioxidant Activities of Astaxanthin and Related Carotenoids. *J. Agric. Food Chem.* **2000**, *48*, 1150–1154. [CrossRef]
112. Rodrigues, E.; Mariutti, L.R.B.; Mercadante, A.Z. Scavenging Capacity of Marine Carotenoids against Reactive Oxygen and Nitrogen Species in a Membrane-Mimicking System. *Mar. Drugs* **2012**, *10*, 1784–1798. [CrossRef]
113. McNulty, H.; Jacob, R.F.; Mason, R.P. Biologic Activity of Carotenoids Related to Distinct Membrane Physicochemical Interactions. *Am. J. Cardiol.* **2008**, *101*, S20–S29. [CrossRef]
114. Goto, S.; Kogure, K.; Abe, K.; Kimata, Y.; Kitahama, K.; Yamashita, E.; Terada, H. Efficient Radical Trapping at the Surface and inside the Phospholipid Membrane Is Responsible for Highly Potent Antiperoxidative Activity of the Carotenoid Astaxanthin. *Biochim. Biophys. Acta BBA Biomembr.* **2001**, *1512*, 251–258. [CrossRef] [PubMed]
115. Pashkow, F.J.; Watumull, D.G.; Campbell, C.L. Astaxanthin: A Novel Potential Treatment for Oxidative Stress and Inflammation in Cardiovascular Disease. *Am. J. Cardiol.* **2008**, *101*, S58–S68. [CrossRef] [PubMed]
116. Liang, J.; Tian, Y.-X.; Yang, F.; Zhang, J.-P.; Skibsted, L.H. Antioxidant Synergism between Carotenoids in Membranes. Astaxanthin as a Radical Transfer Bridge. *Food Chem.* **2009**, *115*, 1437–1442. [CrossRef]
117. Nakajima, Y.; Inokuchi, Y.; Shimazawa, M.; Otsubo, K.; Ishibashi, T.; Hara, H. Astaxanthin, a Dietary Carotenoid, Protects Retinal Cells against Oxidative Stress in-Vitro and in Mice in-Vivo. *J. Pharm. Pharmacol.* **2008**, *60*, 1365–1374. [CrossRef] [PubMed]
118. Rao, A.R.; Sindhuja, H.N.; Dharmesh, S.M.; Sankar, K.U.; Sarada, R.; Ravishankar, G.A. Effective Inhibition of Skin Cancer, Tyrosinase, and Antioxidative Properties by Astaxanthin and Astaxanthin Esters from the Green Alga *Haematococcus pluvialis*. *J. Agric. Food Chem.* **2013**, *61*, 3842–3851. [CrossRef]
119. Ranga Rao, A.; Raghunath Reddy, R.L.; Baskaran, V.; Sarada, R.; Ravishankar, G.A. Characterization of Microalgal Carotenoids by Mass Spectrometry and Their Bioavailability and Antioxidant Properties Elucidated in Rat Model. *J. Agric. Food Chem.* **2010**, *58*, 8553–8559. [CrossRef]
120. Raza, S.H.A.; Naqvi, S.R.Z.; Abdelnour, S.A.; Schreurs, N.; Mohammedsaleh, Z.M.; Khan, I.; Shater, A.F.; Abd El-Hack, M.E.; Khafaga, A.F.; Quan, G.; et al. Beneficial Effects and Health Benefits of Astaxanthin Molecules on Animal Production: A Review. *Res. Vet. Sci.* **2021**, *138*, 69–78. [CrossRef]
121. Yang, Y.; Seo, J.M.; Nguyen, A.; Pham, T.X.; Park, H.J.; Park, Y.; Kim, B.; Bruno, R.S.; Lee, J. Astaxanthin-Rich Extract from the Green Alga *Haematococcus pluvialis* Lowers Plasma Lipid Concentrations and Enhances Antioxidant Defense in Apolipoprotein E Knockout Mice. *J. Nutr.* **2011**, *141*, 1611–1617. [CrossRef]
122. Turkez, H.; Geyikoglu, F.; Yousef, M.I.; Togar, B.; Gürbüz, H.; Celik, K.; Akbaba, G.B.; Polat, Z. Hepatoprotective Potential of Astaxanthin against 2,3,7,8-Tetrachlorodibenzo-p-Dioxin in Cultured Rat Hepatocytes. *Toxicol. Ind. Health* **2012**, *30*, 101–112. [CrossRef]
123. Turrin, N.P.; Rivest, S. Molecular and Cellular Immune Mediators of Neuroprotection. *Mol. Neurobiol.* **2006**, *34*, 221–242. [CrossRef]
124. Brown, G.C.; Neher, J.J. Inflammatory Neurodegeneration and Mechanisms of Microglial Killing of Neurons. *Mol. Neurobiol.* **2010**, *41*, 242–247. [CrossRef] [PubMed]
125. Speranza, L.; Pesce, M.; Patruno, A.; Franceschelli, S.; de Lutiis, M.A.; Grilli, A.; Felaco, M. Astaxanthin Treatment Reduced Oxidative Induced Pro-Inflammatory Cytokines Secretion in U937: SHP-1 as a Novel Biological Target. *Mar. Drugs* **2012**, *10*, 890–899. [CrossRef] [PubMed]
126. Solak, Y.; Afsar, B.; Vaziri, N.D.; Aslan, G.; Yalcin, C.E.; Covic, A.; Kanbay, M. Hypertension as an Autoimmune and Inflammatory Disease. *Hypertens. Res.* **2016**, *39*, 567–573. [CrossRef] [PubMed]
127. Guarner, V.; Rubio-Ruiz, M.E. Low-Grade Systemic Inflammation Connects Aging, Metabolic Syndrome and Cardiovascular Disease. In *Aging and Health—A Systems Biology Perspective*; S. Karger AG: Basel, Switzerland, 2014; pp. 99–106.
128. Tall, A.R.; Yvan-Charvet, L. Cholesterol, Inflammation and Innate Immunity. *Nat. Rev. Immunol.* **2015**, *15*, 104–116. [CrossRef] [PubMed]
129. Choi, S.-K.; Park, Y.-S.; Choi, D.-K.; Chang, H.-I. Effects of Astaxanthin on the Production of NO and the Expression of COX-2 and INOS in LPS-Stimulated BV2 Microglial Cells. *J. Microbiol. Biotechnol.* **2008**, *18*, 1990–1996. [CrossRef]
130. Park, C.H.; Xu, F.H.; Roh, S.-S.; Song, Y.O.; Uebaba, K.; Noh, J.S.; Yokozawa, T. Astaxanthin and Corni Fructus Protect Against Diabetes-Induced Oxidative Stress, Inflammation, and Advanced Glycation End Product in Livers of Streptozotocin-Induced Diabetic Rats. *J. Med. Food* **2015**, *18*, 337–344. [CrossRef]
131. Yoshihisa, Y.; Rehman, M.U.; Shimizu, T. Astaxanthin, a Xanthophyll Carotenoid, Inhibits Ultraviolet-induced Apoptosis in Keratinocytes. *Exp. Dermatol.* **2014**, *23*, 178–183. [CrossRef]

132. Bolin, A.P.; Macedo, R.C.; Marin, D.P.; Barros, M.P.; Otton, R. Astaxanthin Prevents in Vitro Auto-Oxidative Injury in Human Lymphocytes. *Cell Biol. Toxicol.* **2010**, *26*, 457–467. [CrossRef]
133. Macedo, R.C.; Bolin, A.P.; Marin, D.P.; Otton, R. Astaxanthin Addition Improves Human Neutrophils Function: In Vitro Study. *Eur. J. Nutr.* **2010**, *49*, 447–457. [CrossRef]
134. Wang, X.; Willén, R.; Wadström, T. Astaxanthin-Rich Algal Meal and Vitamin C Inhibit Helicobacter Pylori Infection in BALB/cA Mice. *Antimicrob. Agents Chemother.* **2000**, *44*, 2452–2457. [CrossRef]
135. Haines, D.D.; Varga, B.; Bak, I.; Juhasz, B.; Mahmoud, F.F.; Kalantari, H.; Gesztelyi, R.; Lekli, I.; Czompa, A.; Tosaki, A. Summative Interaction between Astaxanthin, Ginkgo Biloba Extract (EGb761) and Vitamin C in Suppression of Respiratory Inflammation: A Comparison with Ibuprofen. *Phytother. Res.* **2010**, *25*, 128–136. [CrossRef] [PubMed]
136. Park, J.S.; Chyun, J.H.; Kim, Y.K.; Line, L.L.; Chew, B.P. Astaxanthin Decreased Oxidative Stress and Inflammation and Enhanced Immune Response in Humans. *Nutr. Metab.* **2010**, *7*, 18. [CrossRef] [PubMed]
137. Baralic, I.; Andjelkovic, M.; Djordjevic, B.; Dikic, N.; Radivojevic, N.; Suzin-Zivkovic, V.; Radojevic-Skodric, S.; Pejic, S. Effect of Astaxanthin Supplementation on Salivary IgA, Oxidative Stress, and Inflammation in Young Soccer Players. *Evid. Based Complement. Altern. Med.* **2015**, *2015*, 783761. [CrossRef] [PubMed]
138. Laslett, L.J.; Alagona, P.; Clark, B.A.; Drozda, J.P.; Saldivar, F.; Wilson, S.R.; Poe, C.; Hart, M. The Worldwide Environment of Cardiovascular Disease: Prevalence, Diagnosis, Therapy, and Policy Issues. *J. Am. Coll. Cardiol.* **2012**, *60*, S1–S49. [CrossRef] [PubMed]
139. Giordano, F.J. Oxygen, Oxidative Stress, Hypoxia, and Heart Failure. *J. Clin. Investig.* **2005**, *115*, 500–508. [CrossRef]
140. Fan, C.; Sun, J.; Fu, X.; Hou, Y.; Li, Y.; Yang, M.; Fu, X.; Sun, B. Astaxanthin Attenuates Homocysteine-Induced Cardiotoxicity in Vitro and in Vivo by Inhibiting Mitochondrial Dysfunction and Oxidative Damage. *Front. Physiol.* **2017**, *8*, 1041. [CrossRef]
141. Lauver, D.A.; Lockwood, S.F.; Lucchesi, B.R. Disodium Disuccinate Astaxanthin (Cardax) Attenuates Complement Activation and Reduces Myocardial Injury Following Ischemia/Reperfusion. *J. Pharmacol. Exp. Ther.* **2005**, *314*, 686–692. [CrossRef]
142. Gross, G.J.; Lockwood, S.F. Acute and Chronic Administration of Disodium Disuccinate Astaxanthin (CardaxTM) Produces Marked Cardioprotection in Dog Hearts. *Mol. Cell. Biochem.* **2005**, *272*, 221–227. [CrossRef]
143. Gross, G.J.; Hazen, S.L.; Lockwood, S.F. Seven Day Oral Supplementation with Cardax TM (Disodium Disuccinate Astaxanthin) Provides Significant Cardioprotection and Reduces Oxidative Stress in Rats. *Mol. Cell. Biochem.* **2006**, *283*, 23–30. [CrossRef]
144. Monroy-Ruiz, J.; Sevilla, M.-Á.; Carrón, R.; Montero, M.-J. Astaxanthin-Enriched-Diet Reduces Blood Pressure and Improves Cardiovascular Parameters in Spontaneously Hypertensive Rats. *Pharmacol. Res.* **2011**, *63*, 44–50. [CrossRef]
145. Khan, S.K.; Malinski, T.; Mason, R.P.; Kubant, R.; Jacob, R.F.; Fujioka, K.; Denstaedt, S.J.; King, T.J.; Jackson, H.L.; Hieber, A.D.; et al. Novel Astaxanthin Prodrug (CDX-085) Attenuates Thrombosis in a Mouse Model. *Thromb. Res.* **2010**, *126*, 299–305. [CrossRef] [PubMed]
146. Nakao, R.; Nelson, O.L.; Park, J.S.; Mathison, B.D.; Thompson, P.A.; Chew, B.P. Effect of Astaxanthin Supplementation on Inflammation and Cardiac Function in BALB/c Mice. *Anticancer. Res.* **2010**, *30*, 2171–2175. [PubMed]
147. Augusti, P.R.; Quatrin, A.; Somacal, S.; Conterato, G.M.M.; Sobieski, R.; Ruviaro, A.R.; Maurer, L.H.; Duarte, M.M.F.; Roehrs, M.; Emanuelli, T. Astaxanthin Prevents Changes in the Activities of Thioredoxin Reductase and Paraoxonase in Hypercholesterolemic Rabbits. *J. Clin. Biochem. Nutr.* **2012**, *51*, 42–49. [CrossRef] [PubMed]
148. Ryu, S.K.; King, T.J.; Fujioka, K.; Pattison, J.; Pashkow, F.J.; Tsimikas, S. Effect of an Oral Astaxanthin Prodrug (CDX-085) on Lipoprotein Levels and Progression of Atherosclerosis in $LDLR^{-/-}$ and $ApoE^{-/-}$ Mice. *Atherosclerosis* **2012**, *222*, 99–105. [CrossRef]
149. Jyonouchi, H.; Sun, S.; Iijima, K.; Gross, M.D. Antitumor Activity of Astaxanthin and Its Mode of Action. *Nutr. Cancer* **2000**, *36*, 59–65. [CrossRef]
150. Nishino, H.; Murakoshi, M.; Ii, T.; Takemura, M.; Kuchide, M.; Kanazawa, M.; Mou, X.Y.; Wada, S.; Masuda, M.; Ohsaka, Y.; et al. Carotenoids in Cancer Chemoprevention. *Cancer Metastasis Rev.* **2002**, *21*, 257–264. [CrossRef]
151. Faraone, I.; Sinisgalli, C.; Ostuni, A.; Armentano, M.F.; Carmosino, M.; Milella, L.; Russo, D.; Labanca, F.; Khan, H. Astaxanthin Anticancer Effects Are Mediated through Multiple Molecular Mechanisms: A Systematic Review. *Pharmacol. Res.* **2020**, *155*, 104689. [CrossRef]
152. Yasui, Y.; Hosokawa, M.; Mikami, N.; Miyashita, K.; Tanaka, T. Dietary Astaxanthin Inhibits Colitis and Colitis-Associated Colon Carcinogenesis in Mice via Modulation of the Inflammatory Cytokines. *Chem. Biol. Interact.* **2011**, *193*, 79–87. [CrossRef]
153. Palozza, P.; Torelli, C.; Boninsegna, A.; Simone, R.; Catalano, A.; Mele, M.C.; Picci, N. Growth-Inhibitory Effects of the Astaxanthin-Rich Alga *Haematococcus pluvialis* in Human Colon Cancer Cells. *Cancer Lett.* **2009**, *283*, 108–117. [CrossRef]
154. Ranga Rao, A.; Baskaran, V.; Sarada, R.; Ravishankar, G.A. In Vivo Bioavailability and Antioxidant Activity of Carotenoids from Microalgal Biomass—A Repeated Dose Study. *Food Res. Int.* **2013**, *54*, 711–717. [CrossRef]
155. Nagendraprabhu, P.; Sudhandiran, G. Astaxanthin Inhibits Tumor Invasion by Decreasing Extracellular Matrix Production and Induces Apoptosis in Experimental Rat Colon Carcinogenesis by Modulating the Expressions of ERK-2, NFkB and COX-2. *Investig. New Drugs* **2009**, *29*, 207–224. [CrossRef] [PubMed]
156. Atalay, P.B.; Kuku, G.; Tuna, B.G. Effects of Carbendazim and Astaxanthin Co-Treatment on the Proliferation of MCF-7 Breast Cancer Cells. *In Vitro Cell. Dev. Biol. Anim.* **2018**, *55*, 113–119. [CrossRef] [PubMed]
157. Shao, Y.; Ni, Y.; Yang, J.; Lin, X.; Li, J.; Zhang, L. Astaxanthin Inhibits Proliferation and Induces Apoptosis and Cell Cycle Arrest of Mice H22 Hepatoma Cells. *Med. Sci. Monit.* **2016**, *22*, 2152–2160. [CrossRef] [PubMed]

158. Suganya, V.; Anuradha, V. In Silico Molecular Docking of Astaxanthin and Sorafenib with Different Apoptotic Proteins Involved in Hepatocellular Carcinoma. *Biocatal. Agric. Biotechnol.* **2019**, *19*, 101076. [CrossRef]
159. Galasso, C.; Orefice, I.; Pellone, P.; Cirino, P.; Miele, R.; Ianora, A.; Brunet, C.; Sansone, C. On the Neuroprotective Role of Astaxanthin: New Perspectives? *Mar. Drugs* **2018**, *16*, 247. [CrossRef]
160. Barnham, K.J.; Masters, C.L.; Bush, A.I. Neurodegenerative Diseases and Oxidative Stress. *Nat. Rev. Drug Discov.* **2004**, *3*, 205–214. [CrossRef]
161. Hardy, J.; Selkoe, D.J. The Amyloid Hypothesis of Alzheimer's Disease: Progress and Problems on the Road to Therapeutics. *Science (1979)* **2002**, *297*, 353–356. [CrossRef]
162. Liu, X.; Shibata, T.; Hisaka, S.; Osawa, T. Astaxanthin Inhibits Reactive Oxygen Species-Mediated Cellular Toxicity in Dopaminergic SH-SY5Y Cells via Mitochondria-Targeted Protective Mechanism. *Brain Res.* **2009**, *1254*, 18–27. [CrossRef]
163. Wang, H.-Q.; Sun, X.-B.; Xu, Y.-X.; Zhao, H.; Zhu, Q.-Y.; Zhu, C.-Q. Astaxanthin Upregulates Heme Oxygenase-1 Expression through ERK1/2 Pathway and Its Protective Effect against Beta-Amyloid-Induced Cytotoxicity in SH-SY5Y Cells. *Brain Res.* **2010**, *1360*, 159–167. [CrossRef]
164. Barros, M.; Poppe, S.; Bondan, E. Neuroprotective Properties of the Marine Carotenoid Astaxanthin and Omega-3 Fatty Acids, and Perspectives for the Natural Combination of Both in Krill Oil. *Nutrients* **2014**, *6*, 1293–1317. [CrossRef]
165. Grimmig, B.; Daly, L.; Hudson, C.; Nash, K.R.; Bickford, P.C. Astaxanthin Attenuates Neurotoxicity in a Mouse Model of Parkinson's Disease. *Funct. Foods Health Dis.* **2017**, *7*, 562. [CrossRef]
166. Grimmig, B.; Kim, S.-H.; Nash, K.; Bickford, P.C.; Douglas Shytle, R. Neuroprotective Mechanisms of Astaxanthin: A Potential Therapeutic Role in Preserving Cognitive Function in Age and Neurodegeneration. *Geroscience* **2017**, *39*, 19–32. [CrossRef] [PubMed]
167. Chang, C.-H.; Chen, C.-Y.; Chiou, J.-Y.; Peng, R.Y.; Peng, C.-H. Astaxanthine Secured Apoptotic Death of PC12 Cells Induced by β-Amyloid Peptide 25–35: Its Molecular Action Targets. *J. Med. Food* **2010**, *13*, 548–556. [CrossRef] [PubMed]
168. Kim, J.H.; Nam, S.-W.; Kim, B.W.; Kim, W.-J.; Choi, Y.H. Astaxanthin Improves the Proliferative Capacity as Well as the Osteogenic and Adipogenic Differentiation Potential in Neural Stem Cells. *Food Chem. Toxicol.* **2010**, *48*, 1741–1745. [CrossRef]
169. Satoh, T. Astaxanthin. In *Nutraceuticals*; Elsevier: Amsterdam, The Netherlands, 2016; pp. 531–539.
170. Stewart, J.S.; Lignell, Å.; Pettersson, A.; Elfving, E.; Soni, M.G. Safety Assessment of Astaxanthin-Rich Microalgae Biomass: Acute and Subchronic Toxicity Studies in Rats. *Food Chem. Toxicol.* **2008**, *46*, 3030–3036. [CrossRef]
171. Niu, T.; Zhou, J.; Wang, F.; Xuan, R.; Chen, J.; Wu, W.; Chen, H. Safety Assessment of Astaxanthin from *Haematococcus pluvialis*: Acute Toxicity, Genotoxicity, Distribution and Repeat-Dose Toxicity Studies in Gestation Mice. *Regul. Toxicol. Pharmacol.* **2020**, *115*, 104695. [CrossRef]

MDPI AG
Grosspeteranlage 5
4052 Basel
Switzerland
Tel.: +41 61 683 77 34

Sustainability Editorial Office
E-mail: sustainability@mdpi.com
www.mdpi.com/journal/sustainability

www.ingramcontent.com/pod-product-compliance
Lightning Source LLC
Chambersburg PA
CBHW061455210926
51850CB00008B/1727